AMERICAN ART MUSEUM

ARCHITECTURE

DOCUMENTS AND DESIGN

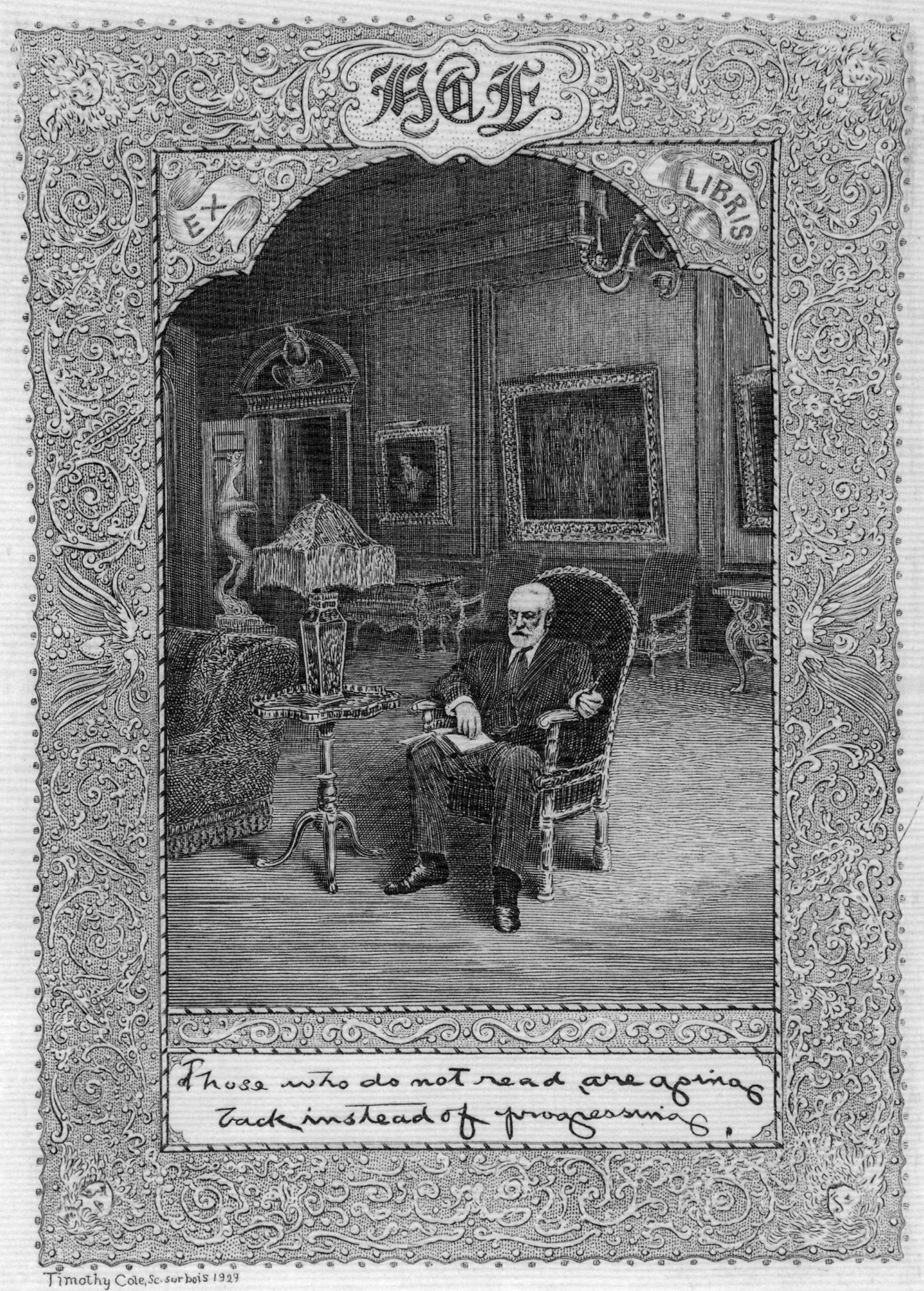

Frontispiece:
Bookplate of Henry Clay Frick. *Courtesy of the Frick Collection/ Frick Art Reference Library Archives.*

AMERICAN ART MUSEUM ARCHITECTURE
DOCUMENTS AND DESIGN

ERIC M. WOLF

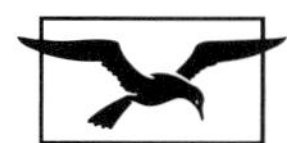

W. W. Norton and Company, Inc.

New York   London

For Patricia J. Barnett and Carol K. Rusk,

dear friends and inspirational mentors

Copyright © 2010 by Eric M. Wolf

For information about permission to reproduce selections from this book, write to
Permissions, W. W. Norton & Company, Inc., 500 Fifth Avenue, New York, NY 10110

For information about special discounts for bulk purchases, please contact W. W. Norton
Special Sales at specialsales@wwnorton.com or 800-233-4830

Manufacturing by Friesens
Book design by Abigail Sturges
Production manager: Leeann Graham

Library of Congress Cataloging-in-Publication Data

Wolf, Eric Michael.
  American art museum architecture : documents and design / Eric M.
Wolf. -- 1st ed.
      p. cm.
  Includes bibliographical references and index.
  ISBN 978-0-393-73280-1 (hardcover)
  1. Art museum architecture--United States. 2. Architectural
design--United States. 3. Museum techniques--United States. I. Title.
  NA6696.U6W64 2010
  727'.70973--dc22
                              2009022681

ISBN: 978-0-393-73280-1

W. W. Norton & Company, Inc., 500 Fifth Avenue, New York, N.Y. 10110
                       www.wwnorton.com
W. W. Norton & Company Ltd., Castle House, 75/76 Wells Street, London W1T 3QT

1 2 3 4 5 6 7 8 9 0

CONTENTS

ACKNOWLEDGMENTS

This book is largely the result of the good fortune of being in the right place at the right time. Inge Heckel, since retired as president of the New York School of Interior Design, invited me to curate an exhibition in 2007 at the school's gallery. Kristen Holt-Browning, associate managing editor at Norton Professional Books, attended my opening lecture and invited me to write a book. I elected not to write on the subject of that exhibition, but Ms. Holt-Browning was gracious enough to allow me to submit a proposal on the subject of art museum design—a subject in which I have been interested for a very long time. This book is the fruit of that proposal.

At the Frick Collection and Frick Art Reference Library Archives, I would like to thank archivists Sally Brazil, Susan Chore, and Julie Ludwig for their invaluable and expert assistance with the papers from the Institutional Archives of the Frick Collection and the Archives of the Helen Clay Frick Foundation. I am ever grateful to Patricia J. Barnett, Andrew Mellon Chief Librarian of the Frick Art Reference Library (since retired) for her hospitality and support above and beyond professional courtesy. I am also in great debt to Anne L. Poulet, director of the Frick Collection, for taking the time to allow me to interview her personally about her unique vision for the future of the Frick Collection.

At the Menil Collection, I am deeply indebted to Geraldine Aramanda. Not only did she extend amazing help with archival research and provide me with a complete "behind-the-scenes" tour of the facilities, she also let me tap into her knowledge of and acquaintance with, both professional and personal, the de Menil family itself, as she has worked with the family members and their collection since the 1960s. Many thanks are also due to Lisa Barkley, assistant archivist at the Menil Collection. These two very efficient professionals made sure that I left after my three-day visit to Houston with copies of all the documents I wanted in my hands. I am most grateful to Josef Helfenstein, the director, for granting me an interview to discuss his vision for the future of the Menil Collection.

Working in the library and archives of the Whitney Museum of American Art was made both successful and pleasurable by the generosity of Carol K. Rusk, Benjamin and Irma Weiss Librarian, who, in spite of her extremely demanding schedule and small staff, never failed to make me feel not only welcome but even a high priority. Kristen Leipert, archivist at the Whitney, was extremely helpful and knowledgeable in navigating the archives and providing me with scans of important documents within days of my requests. Thanks are also due to Anita Duquette for her help in obtaining period images and identifying their contents.

Research at the Georgia O'Keeffe Museum library and archives, housed in the lovely research center, was made most enjoyable by the skill and generosity of Eumie

Imm-Stroukoff, librarian and assistant director of the research center. On short notice she was able to equip me with a full set of gallery literature from all of the exhibitions mounted at the museum! She clearly and concisely laid out the rather complicated personal and corporate history of all the personalities and entities that worked together and merged to form what are now the Georgia O'Keeffe Museum and its collections. I would also like to thank Barbara Buhler Lynes, Ph.D., chief curator and director of the research center, for allowing me to interview her regarding the philosophies and future visions of the museum and research center.

The staff of the library and archives of the Museum of Modern Art was most gracious and helpful, even anticipating my needs by pulling related documents I did not know to request. In the archives Michelle Harvey, MacKenzie Bennett, and Miriam Gianni were particularly helpful. Milan Hughston and Jenny Tobias in the library also warrant thanks for their assistance.

At the Art Institute of Chicago I am indebted to Bart H. Ryckbosch and Deborah Webb for providing me with terrific assistance and information on a very tight schedule. Working archival visits around participation in the Renaissance Society of American conference was difficult, and they were most accommodating.

For secondary research the staff of the Watson Library at the Metropolitan Museum of Art was essential. Many thanks are due to library director Ken Soehner for introducing weekend hours there! Also at the Metropolitan Museum thanks are due to Andy Gessner of the image library for helping me acquire images of the Whitney Wing of the Met that never was.

Any sincere acknowledgment of where my thoughts on art museums come from would be incomplete without mentioning many friends and colleagues. First, I must thank my parents, David and Ruth Wolf, for taking me to art museums as a child and encouraging my interests in art and architecture. Without early visits to the Getty, Los Angeles County Museum of Art, Norton Simon Museum, and the California Palace of the Legion of Honor, I would never have become interested in this topic in the first place. Since I will never know where many thoughts here presented first germinated, I would like to thank all of the people with whom I have discussed these issues over the years. These people include (but are not limited to) Randy Bird, Meg Black, Peter Brandt, Mark Bresnan, Sharon Chickanzeff, Sherman Clarke, Mary Daniels, Henry Fernandez, Nara Garber, V. Heidi Hass, Florent Heintz, Deborah Kempe, Harriet and Irwin Kurlander, Britta Le Va, Barbara Lowenthal, Chris Livanos, Mary Lynch, John Maier, Edgar Munhall, Christina Peter, Maggie Portis, Christopher D. H. Row, Chris Spinelli, Sam Van Essen-Fishman, Dan Wiley, Cathrine Wolcott, Ben Wolf, Miriam Wolf, Louisa Wood Ruby, and Henri Zerner.

Most importantly, I must thank my wife Amy Kurlander for all of her help, support, and encouragement with this project. I know she often wanted to talk about other topics than museums, but her knowledge on the subject is encyclopedic. The sacrifice of weekend and vacation time together for the writing of this book had as profound an effect on her life as it did on mine. I am very grateful for her understanding.

INTRODUCTION

From entering the dramatic rotunda and walking up the corkscrew ramp of the Solomon R. Guggenheim Museum, to riding the tram up the hill to the J. Paul Getty Museum, to passing from one clean white cube gallery to the next at the Menil Collection, to crossing through beautiful flower gardens to enter the galleries in the former home of railroad baron Henry Huntington at the Huntington Library, Art Collections and Botanical Gardens, one quickly comprehends the importance of architecture and design in the experience of visiting a museum. Each of these very different experiences was deliberately worked out through the joint efforts of museum directors, trustees, and the architects and designers they hired. These design elements are all intended to be experienced and enjoyed by the general public.

Behind the scenes art must be stored and conserved; curators research and write up exhibitions, acquire works of art, negotiate loans. Museum directors and trustees entertain potential donors, ponder new directions in contemporary art that must be represented in the collection, and perhaps even consider adding a new wing to house these new works. Museum registrars, librarians, archivists, preparators, conservators, and guards are in constant movement to ensure that exhibitions go up on time, catalogs are well researched, and loans are shipped out and received on time in a safe and secure environment. Architects and designers engage in designing spaces for all of these necessary functions the public never sees.

This book investigates what goes into museum design. Looking at the history of art museums in America, with particular emphasis on six case studies, all aspects of museum architecture are explored, from the aesthetic to the functional, the dramatic to the mundane. From large public entrances and atria to the archives housed in a basement closet, a properly functioning museum must contain a myriad of different spaces and functions. The particular needs of a given institution are closely linked to the specific collections it houses and the types of programming it offers; over time even these considerations might change at any given institution. So, like museums themselves, museum architecture is always evolving.

ORGANIZATION AND SCOPE OF THIS BOOK

Although much has been written on large new museum building projects, and a great deal of attention has been given to the aesthetic decisions made in their design, relatively few pages have been dedicated to a broad analysis of the relationship between design, function, and mission in the building type of the museum. This is indeed a very wide topic, as museums come in all different shapes and sizes, collecting everything from dinosaur bones to stage coaches to fine and decorative arts. In order to give this study some coherency and depth, the investigation here is limited to art museums. Doubtless, equally interesting analyses could be written on science museums, history museums, or related types of institutions such as zoos, botanical gardens, or aquaria. Further, great undertakings in art museum design have occurred throughout the world; however, for reasons of expediency and, again, coherency, the close analysis in this book is limited to art museums in the United States. Developments and trends in the rest of the world, particularly Europe, are considered only insofar as they relate to the history of the building type and directly affect museum design in America.

By limiting the study to art museums, certain elements and problems can be discussed that are common to all art museums; further, those problems and elements that are unique to certain subgroups of art museums can be contextualized and highlighted. Functional requirements for the exhibition, storage, conservation, and research of works of art, and different approaches to the realization of these requirements emerge from this investigation. Differences in emphases and missions of various institutions lead to different weightings of these many functions, and at times even lead to additions of other functions (e.g., facilities for lectures, film series, children's programming). In other cases, some of these "fundamental" requirements might not be addressed by a given institution (e.g., conservation might be outsourced to another institution).

Many of these different emphases in individual institutions, both in their original venues and in all of their subsequent moves, expansions, and renovations, are not, however, chiefly the result of decisions made by designers in close consultation with a principal client (though there are exceptions). Rather, these decisions are more often based in a long and complex dialogue between architects, designers, and clients (usually building committees from governing boards of trustees) and, often most importantly, are influenced by the institutional history of the museum in question. What is this institutional history, and how can it influence, and at times even overrule, clients and architects? It is everything, binding and nonbinding, that went into the formation of the museum, both as a corporate entity and as a collection. Many museums are founded in wills and do not become public institutions until the death of the person principally responsible for their foundation. Such wills often contain requirements for what can and cannot be done. Similar constraints are found in deeds of trust written by living donors who sign control of their collections to a board of trustees. Articles of incorporation, constitutions, and bylaws all contain guidelines that can limit the freedom of both clients and designers.

Although not as binding as the documents mentioned above, other types of documents and material can also lead clients and designers in various directions. Mission statements, though not usually carved in stone, provide a concise summary of where an institution positions itself at a given time. Of course, these statements are periodically rewritten and are also useful in documenting how institutions change course and redefine themselves and their goals and agendas. A close look at such statements and their changes over time is also useful in understanding the trends of the field of art museums generally, as well as specific institutional histories. While many institutions are founded with very narrow and sometimes unique mission statements and goals, over time, with changing attitudes of society at large, those missions may expand to encompass broader foci and more general goals. The original intents may have been specific to a moment in the history of art and culture, and may no longer be seen as having relevance or being fiscally tenable in the present without major revision.

Of course, the most important historical influence on the design of an art museum is the institution's collection of art. Not only are the size and scale of galleries directly affected by what will be displayed therein, but the size and scale of all ancillary functions and spaces are also dependent on collections. Loading docks, corridors, and doorways all must be scaled to allow for the entrance and movement of the largest work that might be exhibited. Questions of natural versus artificial light as well as heating, ventilation, and air conditioning must be resolved in terms of the best interests of the works of art as well as the comfort of the museum visitor. Should an institution design and build to best accommodate the collection they have now, or should they proceed with an eye to where they want to move the collection through future acquisitions? If an institution collects, and intends to go on collecting, contemporary art, how can they plan for exhibiting art that has not been made? How can a client or designer anticipate future trends in art history?

A museum must also be designed to provide for all of its ancillary, nonexhibition-related functions. These functions range from those that serve primarily the museum staff, to amenities for visitors (which often provide revenue for the museum) and the necessary provision of spaces for ephemeral activities (such as fund-raising events, corporate events used to generate revenue, lectures, concerts, etc.). Museum staff must have office space, art storage space (often with specific heating, ventilation, and air-conditioning requirements), a loading dock, a conservation laboratory, a research or reference library, and institutional archives—all spaces the public will most likely never see, but all necessary for the smooth running of the institution. In addition to galleries, the public generally expects most museums to have certain amenities such as bookstores and gift shops (sometimes separate, sometimes together in one store), bars, cafes or restaurants, theaters that can be used for films and lectures, numerous spacious and deluxe restrooms, and full compliance with the Americans with Disabilities Act. Many of these amenities also serve to raise revenue for institutions, occasionally becoming destinations in themselves. More and more, museums require that designers create spaces that can serve multiple purposes—spaces that can work as public venues during regular museum hours and be transformed into party locations for museum fundraisers and openings and even rented as venues for outside corporate events.

Such events are an important source of revenue for museums at present. Well-designed spaces of this variety can also serve well as locations for a museum's educational and other public programming.

This book examines the origins, history, and development of the building type of the museum discussed in this introduction. To understand the contemporary state of the museum in America, it is necessary to understand the formation and evolution of the institutional type as well as the buildings that housed it from ancient times through the nineteenth century in Europe—for, like so many American public institutions, the basis of the art museum in European history and traditions, as well as departures from these, are seminal. This introduction also surveys the American art museum and its development from the first efforts in the nineteenth century to the present.

The bulk of this study, however, provides in-depth case studies of some very important art museums in the United States. These studies focus on institutions representative of various different types of art museums, some very specialized, others broad in their collecting scopes. Each study traces the specific institution from its origins and foundation to the present, even looking forward to future plans for further expansion and new goals and changes in mission. Whenever possible, interviews with sitting museum directors were conducted to provide their current visions for the future. In addition to analysis of the design history of each museum, a close investigation of institutional documents is conducted to elucidate the original (and often changing) institutional goals that underlie the design decisions that inform the actual buildings that house the collections and programming. To understand this often complex history, all historic venues inhabited by each institution are discussed, not merely those where each museum is currently housed. Each case study begins with an "at-a-glance" summary of the particular museum, containing basic information such as location, date of construction of each major project, architect, collecting scope, major units, public programs, and visitor amenities offered. An appendix contains comparative qualitative and quantitative information derived from all of the case studies. The case studies also address projects that were envisioned, designed, and intended, but for various reasons, never executed.

Following the case studies, two thematic chapters are offered that bring together the general challenges arising from the analysis offered in the case studies. These chapters address the problems of designing for contemporary art and how the physical design of a museum affects how museumgoers interact with the works exhibited within the museum's walls. In addition, these chapters briefly discuss the solutions of other institutions to the same problems addressed in greater depth in the case studies. Lastly, some large and important supporting documents are provided in an appendix.

It is hoped that this study of design and its relation to institutional history will fill a void in the general understanding of both the history of the building type and the institutional type of the American art museum. Such an enhanced understanding of this relationship should be helpful to museum professionals; museum designers; students; anyone interested in the history of art, collecting, or museology; as well as to museumgoers and people with a general interest in architecture, design, art history, and the cultural history of the United States. Looking at museum design as part of the general program of a museum rather than as merely an aesthetic end in itself can perhaps help us to understand why some museum buildings age better than others, and why architecture sometimes dominates one's experience of a museum visit, whereas at other times, one cannot even remember what the building looked or felt like, only what one saw exhibited. These two diametrically opposed reactions are the result of decisions made between clients and architects and revolve around collections and how they are installed and exhibited.

THE SELECTION OF CASE STUDIES

Perhaps the most difficult decision in undertaking this project was selecting which museums would be included in (and therefore which would have to be excluded from) the in-depth case studies. This decision was made in a way that was, at the same time, completely scientific and completely arbitrary. It was completely scientific in that each was selected as an example of a different type of institution, to present a broad cross-section of American art museums. No two institutions are too similar in mission, size, constituency, history, or collecting scope. This requirement leads to the arbitrary aspect of the decision-making process: if two or more institutions are similar, which one should be selected? To limit the arbitrariness, this determination was made following a number of criteria. First and foremost was the availability of archival material and the relative ease of access to it. Although virtually all museums have institutional archives, some have devoted much more effort to ensuring the processing, organization, and scholarly access to them than others. Some museums provide access to archives through their libraries or relatively open archives, whereas others house such information in business offices and legal departments. Autonomous archives and archives controlled by museum libraries tend to be more open to outside researchers.

Another concern was the task of selecting case studies that would offer very different aesthetic solutions to similar problems. When limiting a field as broad as this one to a relatively small number of case studies, it is important to avoid redundancy. Museums founded in different eras and in different regions of the country, for example, were favored for inclusion, as were museums of different sizes and collecting scopes. Further, certain institutions naturally complement each other in such a study, as they were sometimes conceived from the beginning as a reaction to another museum, either by continuing or challenging decisions and practices of that institution.

Here is a brief overview of the institutions selected for case studies, and a short explanation of the reasoning behind their inclusion:

- *The Frick Collection.* The Frick Collection was chosen to represent a museum built around the collection and home of its founder. It is the archetypal collection of a baron of turn-of-the-century industry. Although it went through two major expansion projects (the first in 1935, the second in 1977), it preserves the look and feel of a Beaux-Arts mansion, and most visitors assume that both the building and the collection it houses are original. Its collections are those one would expect to find in the possession of a collector of the very first ranks of Henry Clay Frick's time: the very finest European Old Master paintings, the best American art of the nineteenth century, and superb bronzes, furniture, and decorative arts. The Frick is also home to the Frick Art Reference Library, one of the very few quality art research libraries open to the general public. The Frick is perhaps the finest example of a museum that has stayed true to its founder's intent and original mission.

- *The Menil Collection.* Like the Frick, the Menil Collection is based on the private collection of giants of industry; however, John and Dominique de Menil represent the industry of the twentieth century, and their collection encompasses everything that Frick did not collect: twentieth-century modern art, ancient art, African art, Byzantine art, and art of Oceania and the Americas. The museum and its surrounding campus were built to house the collection as a series of galleries, with lighting and movable walls to present it in as flexible a way as possible. Although largely built on a domestic scale, the works are presented in an environment that in no way evokes a private residence. Further, the collecting scope of the Menil Collection preserves a philosophy originally investigated but never adopted by the Museum of Modern Art in the 1930s; it therefore serves as a permanent monument to an important moment in the history of art and museology.

- *The Whitney Museum of American Art.* Any study of American art museums would be lax without addressing the foremost museum dedicated solely to American art. Though an heiress to the Vanderbilt fortune, Gertrude Vanderbilt Whitney was not a captain of industry; rather, she was a practicing sculptor and patron of contemporary artists. The Whitney has changed venues twice since her death, but it continues to host the Whitney Biennial—the first, and still one of the most important, exhibitions of contemporary American art. This unique commitment to American art allowed the Whitney to acquire a unique collection that, at various times, was nearly merged with such important institutions as the Metropolitan Museum of Art and the Museum of Modern Art. Further, the Whitney is important for its various buildings as well as for those it planned but was unable to execute for various reasons.

- *The Georgia O'Keeffe Museum.* The Georgia O'Keeffe Museum is one of the few important museums in the United States dedicated to the work of a single artist. In addition to housing the largest collection of O'Keeffe's work in the world, the museum runs the Georgia O'Keeffe Museum Research Center and owns and preserves the two New Mexico houses where O'Keeffe lived and maintained her studio. The Georgia O'Keeffe Museum illustrates the challenges that come with designing an institution around the aesthetics and sensibilities of one individual and her work without degenerating into caricature and kitsch.

• *The Museum of Modern Art.* Arguably the most important cultural institution of the twentieth century, the Museum of Modern Art did more to win the acceptance of modern art by the general public than any other museum. Although today few would argue with the placement of industrial design objects, photography, and motion pictures in a museum dedicated to the fine arts, when the Modern first began doing so in the 1930s, there was much controversy indeed. Perhaps no museum has ever done more in its first fifty years to influence popular tastes than the Museum of Modern Art. The very success of this institution in its early years set the bar at a level so high that it has long struggled with how to stay on the leading edge of modern and contemporary art and its exhibition. The successive building campaigns of this museum reflect the history of modern and contemporary arts and the spatial needs of works in ever-fluctuating scales and media. The Modern has always been a leader in adopting new strategies for the acquisition and display of modern and contemporary art that are later adopted by scores of other institutions. Programming and amenities that originate at the Museum of Modern Art are usually emulated at institutions across America and the world.

• *The Art Institute of Chicago.* The Art Institute of Chicago is one of the great encyclopedic museums of the United States. What sets it apart from other similar museums is its history. Founded as the gallery of an art school and housed in a main building that was originally built as a congress hall for a world's fair, the Art Institute of Chicago has continued to expand over the decades. Although each new wing is connected to the central building, each also has its own personality and aesthetic. As a visitor moves from one gallery to the next, he or she also moves from one period of museum design to the next, making the Art Institute both a broad and deep collection of art and itself a three-dimensional document illustrating the history of museum design in the United States.

Perhaps two institutions are conspicuous in their absence. Many would argue, and with a very strong case. that the two greatest art museums in the country are the Metropolitan Museum of Art and the National Gallery of Art. Both of these are general in nature, both are housed in Beaux-Arts buildings with post-war twentieth-century additions, and therefore both are rather similar in aesthetic and collecting scope to the Art Institute of Chicago. Further, an excellent study of the architectural history of the Metropolitan Museum of Art was recently published, and thus analysis here would be largely redundant.[1] The National Gallery, run by the federal government as part of the Smithsonian Institution, has a history and corporate structure so complex as to require too much ancillary research and explanation. Because both institutions are similar in scope and aesthetic to the simpler and, frankly, more interesting institutional history of the Art Institute of Chicago, I chose the latter to represent the long-established American encyclopedic museum.

Finally, it is important to note the personal nature of the selection of case studies in this book. Any author addressing a subject this vast will have his or her own preferences and prejudices. I have tried to select institutions that are not only representative of various subcategories of American art museums, but that are extremely positive and successful projects. It is hoped that these case studies represent not only good architecture and design, fascinating histories, and interesting connections and points of contrast, but also show how architecture and design can work hand in hand with great collections and strong missions to produce long-lasting institutions. Failed designs can also enhance our understanding of how museums exist in time, and how aesthetics and museology are, in themselves, always in flux. As contemporary art changes—and as our understanding of the art of the past changes as well— the institutions and buildings that house this art also sometimes must change. Further, our experience of both art and the host museums changes in response to our own sensibilities, values, and tastes. A museum building itself is thus a time-sensitive institutional document.

HISTORY OF THE EUROPEAN MUSEUM AS BUILDING TYPE FROM ANTIQUITY TO NINETEENTH CENTURY

The history of the museum as an institution has a vast and complex literature of its own; only some of the highlights of this history are presented here to provide the necessary background for this study.

The word *museum* is derived from the ancient Greek word meaning the "place of the Muses" (the deities of poetry, literature, music, dance, astronomy, philosophy, and all intellectual pursuits) or a place connected to the arts inspired by them.[2] The most well-known of such ancient museums was located in Alexandria, Egypt and was associated with, but separate from, the famous Library of Alexandria. This museum was chiefly a center for scholarship and symposia rather than an institution dedicated to the collection, conservation, and exhibition of objects like its modern namesakes. However, it is natural that such a name would eventually be used to identify cultural institutions that advance and preserve the work inspired by the deities of the creative and intellectual arts.

Although not called museums, the world of classical antiquity did have buildings that housed various precious artifacts for public exhibition. Often times, spoils from the wars of the Roman world were brought back to Rome and displayed in newly dedicated temples. The Templum Pacis, or Temple of Peace, built by Emperor Vespasian following the sack of Jerusalem, is an important example. Here were displayed the artifacts brought back from the Temple of Solomon, including the famous seven-branched menorah and perhaps the Ark of the Covenant. The ancient Jewish historian Josephus, writing in the first century C.E., describes the Templum Pacis thus:

After these triumphs were over, and after the affairs of the Romans were settled on the surest foundations, Vespasian resolved to build a temple to Peace, which was finished in so short a time, and in so glorious a manner, as was beyond all human expectation and opinion: for he having now by Providence a vast quantity of wealth, besides what he had formerly gained in his other exploits, he had this temple adorned with pictures and statues; for in this temple were collected and deposited all such rarities as men aforetime used to wander all over the habitable world to see, when they had a desire to see one of them after another; he also laid up therein those golden vessels and instruments that were taken out of the Jewish temple, as ensigns of his glory. But still he gave order that they should lay up their law, and the purple veils of the holy place in the royal palace itself, and keep them there. [3]

The Templum Pacis contained gardens and was surrounded by colonnades forming a sort of forum. It would have been open to citizens and used as a public meeting place as well as for religious functions. This notion of a building whose chief purpose was to display the great aesthetic objects of a vast empire can be seen as the blueprint for such relatively modern institutions as the British Museum in London, established in the nineteenth century and still one of the great public collections of the Old World. It also highlights the continuing debate concerning the proper home of cultural patrimonies (e.g., should the Elgin Marbles remain in London, or should they be returned to Greece?).

While the Templum Pacis was particularly grand in both scale and quality of the items it contained, it was by no means unique in the Roman world. Temples, fora, basilicas, and other public buildings often contained collections of public and religious art as well as objects brought back as war spoils. Unlike the Greek museums, most of these Roman sites were not fundamentally educational or cultural institutions. Rather the objects on display were the property of the Roman state or the gifts of the emperors and were placed as adornments to the city or monuments to important citizens, leaders, generals, gods, or victories.

The fall of the Roman Empire, however, brought an end to the practice of public collecting for quite some time. Certainly artifacts were collected throughout the Middle Ages, the Renaissance, and the Enlightenment; however, this primarily resulted in private collection, ranging from the small cabinets of curiosities of German or Italian noblemen, to the picture galleries in the country houses of the English aristocracy, to the vast royal collections of the monarchs of France or Britain. As early as the Renaissance in Italy, however, we do see the beginning of more modern collecting practices, with particular collectors forming specific and unique collections. Whereas some collectors were indeed generalists and might collect virtually any type of object that was out of the ordinary, others began to concentrate on a very narrow range of objects.

Indeed many of these form the nuclei of the great collections that are even now on display in public institutions in Europe (e.g., the Galleria Nazionale delle

Marche, housed in the splendid Ducal Palace of Urbino, Italy; the core of this now-public collection was the private collection of Duke Federico da Montefeltro, which he begun to assemble in the fifteenth century and which was continued by his heirs). Many of the great royal collections of Europe are intact and now open to the general public. Most of these collections became public museums in the nineteenth century, through nonviolent means. However, the first great public museum in the modern sense of the world was the Louvre in Paris—and it became a public collection as part of the French Revolution. The Louvre was the Royal Palace of the Bourbon monarchy in Paris (their principal abode was at Versailles, a short distance from the capital); the collection housed within it at the time of the revolution was the royal collection. Of course, the royal art was merely the beginning of the Louvre's collection; as first General, then Consul, then Emperor Napoleon Bonaparte led his seemingly ever-victorious army around Europe, he continually sent back to Paris works of art that would enter the Louvre.

The importance of the Louvre and the French Revolution cannot be underestimated in a discussion of the emergence of the modern art museum. The notion of an artistic patrimony, belonging to the people of a nation, is clearly derived from the opening of the Louvre to the public. This model was followed throughout Europe in the nineteenth century, with virtually every major European country opening its great royal collections to the public. Indeed, to this day the great European museums are owned and operated by the state: the museums of France, the National Gallery and British Museum in the United Kingdom, the State Hermitage Museum in Russia, the Vatican Museums in Vatican City, and so on. The fact that the architectural form of the Louvre was that of a royal palace was significant in establishing the form of the great public collections. It is not surprising that an institution such as the Hermitage in St. Petersburg was kept in the building where it was first assembled: in part of the Tsar's Winter Palace. What may be surprising is the fact that this building and collection were opened to the public by Tsar Nicholas I in 1852, not following the Bolshevik Revolution. Museum buildings that were not repurposed royal palaces often took forms similar to such buildings, for example, the British Museum or the National Gallery in London.

THE AMERICAN ART MUSEUM FROM
THE NINETEENTH CENTURY TO THE PRESENT

As the modern art museum became ubiquitous in the capitals of Europe in the nineteenth century, it is not surprising that the United States, which was simultaneously becoming an important world power, would want to place itself on equal cultural footing by establishing art museums within its boundaries. American culture differed greatly from European culture in the nineteenth century, however. The United States, as the world's first great democracy, had no great royal collection to open to the public; furthermore the frontier spirit of American capitalism discouraged major state patronage for the arts (the United States would not create its own National Gallery, in Washington, D.C., until 1937, the building not opening until 1941). So the means of establishing art museums had to come from other sources. It was really only after the Civil War that the great American art museums came into being: the institution that would become the Art Institute of Chicago, the Chicago Academy of Design, was founded in 1866; the Metropolitan Museum of Art in New York City was founded in 1870.

Lacking a royal collection or state patronage, American museums were, and largely remain, the domain of private capital and the philanthropy of the very wealthy. Of the six case studies presented in this book, only the Art Institute of Chicago does not spring principally from the wealth of one donor or family with a fortune made from industry. The Art Institute's precursor was incorporated by a group of artists as an art school with a gallery. The remaining five institutions investigated here all came from the private wealth of major industrial barons: the Frick Collection coming from Henry Clay Frick's coke and coal fortune; the Menil Collection coming from the Schlumberger oil prospecting company's wealth; the Whitney coming from the Vanderbilt fortune inherited by the museum's founder, Gertrude Vanderbilt Whitney; the Georgia O'Keeffe Museum being founded by Anne Marion, heiress of the Burnett Oil Company of Fort Worth, Texas; and the Museum of Modern Art's endowment coming largely from the Rockefeller family's wealth, derived from the Standard Oil Company. Not surprisingly, the nineteenth-century fortunes were acquired from railroads (Whitney) and coal, the fuel of that time (Frick), whereas twentieth-century wealth was derived from the oil industry (Menil, O'Keeffe, Museum of Modern Art). The financing of the case studies is indeed representative of the great museums of the country, other examples being the J. Paul Getty Museum in Los Angeles (oil) and the Huntington Library, Art Collections and Botanical Gardens in San Marino, California (railroads). The great industrial cities of the American Midwest (e.g., Cleveland, Detroit) all have their own terrific museums, financed largely by their local industries. Doubtless he or she who solves the current problem of finding the alternative energy sources that will fuel the twenty-first century will likely build this century's great museum and art collection.

The architectural form of American museums in the nineteenth and early twentieth centuries largely followed the lead of their European models. The classical Beaux-Arts architecture of museums such as the Art Institute of Chicago and the Metropolitan Museum of Art, with their grand staircases, great halls, and temple fronts, recalls buildings such as the Louvre and the British Museum. Indeed a museum as "young" as the West Building of the National Gallery of Art in Washington, D.C. (opened in 1941) is still an example of such architecture. However, it is in America where this form began to be challenged irrevocably. The Museum of Modern Art's first purpose-built venue, which opened in 1939, was the first major modernist public building in New York City. The Solomon R. Guggenheim Museum, also in New York City, perhaps marks the definitive break with tradition regarding museum architecture. Frank Lloyd Wright's radical design made the museum building itself an object of aesthetic value, not merely a venue for the display of such objects. Of course, a building of such architectural ambition creates an entirely new set of problems because it ceases to be a neutral vessel for the work exhibited within and can generate a tension with that work. This problem is investigated further in Chapter 7.

As art itself changes, the building types that house it must also change. The revolutionary art movements of the twentieth century have changed not only what art looks likes, but the very media that museums collect. Where a nineteenth- or early-twentieth-century art museum only needed to be concerned with the exhibition, storage, and conservation of painting and sculpture, art museums of the later twentieth and twenty-first centuries must accommodate art in all media, from installations to film and video to traditional media, on a truly colossal scale. Many older institutions have been forced to expand merely to properly house the types of art that did not exist when their original venues were constructed. The current emphasis in the art world of collecting contemporary art rather than just the Old Masters further complicates museum design, as it is difficult to design a space looking toward the future in a world as dynamic as that of contemporary art practices. Chapter 8 considers this particular problem in greater depth.

The early twenty-first century is an exciting time for art museums and their buildings. Of the six case studies presented in this book, one, the Art Institute of Chicago, opened its modern wing in May 2009; another, the Whitney Museum of American Art is embarking on a large new venue. The difficult economic times we now face in many ways parallel the Great Depression; although this is disturbing, such times are often fertile periods for contemporary art and the institutions that collect it. The Museum of Modern Art, perhaps the greatest art museum of the twentieth century, arose in the Depression. Following the excesses of the 1980s and 1990s, artists, museum boards, directors, and architects all must look carefully at their priorities and decisions. Our times lack the unified artistic vision of America's gilded age or the moment of high modernism between the World Wars. That very lack of unity makes this an exciting era, as much is in flux and it is difficult to predict the direction contemporary art and architecture might take. It is my sincere hope that this close examination of six of the nation's premier art museums, their histories and buildings, as well as the exploration of the common themes and problems facing the museum world, will be of some use to the museum professionals, boards, architects, students, and public who are not only interested in the history of the American art museum, but who are also invested in the future of this most important enterprise.

CHAPTER 1

THE FRICK COLLECTION

"The collection is recognized as one of the world's great treasuries of art. It was asssembled by Mr. Frick not only as an art lover himself but for use as part of his home and practically every piece of it fitted into his conception of that home. It was his desire, too, that that conception be carried out in bequeathing the Collection to the public."

— Excerpt from Press Packet Cover Letter
  December 11,1935, The Frick Collection Central Files, 1935
  The Frick Collection/Frick Art Reference Library Archives
  The Frick Collection

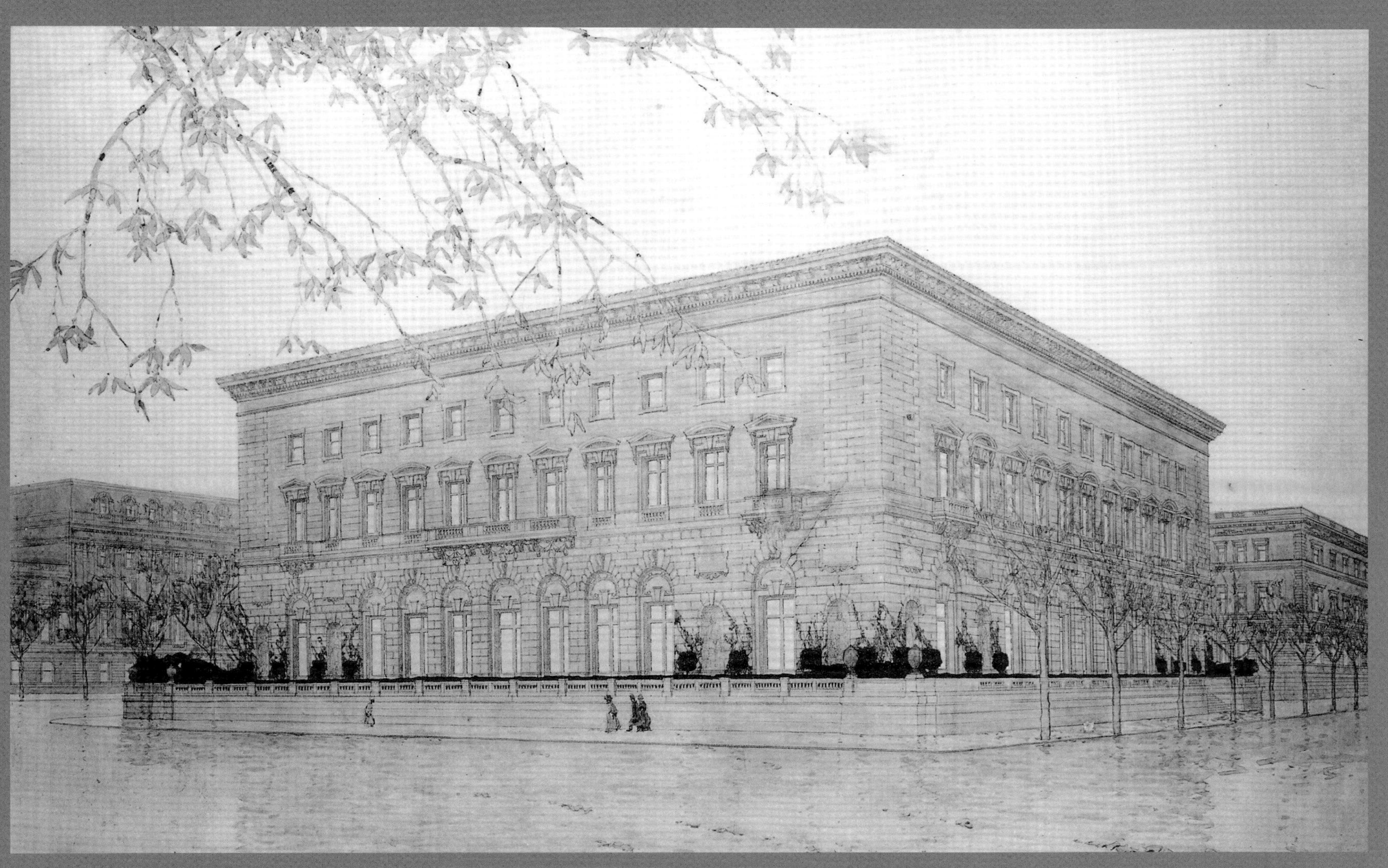

1.1. Perspective rendering of early proposal for the Frick Residence on Fifth Avenue, Thomas Hastings, c. 1912. Courtesy of the Frick Collection/Frick Art Reference Library Archives.

THE FRICK COLLECTION AT A GLANCE

Corporate name:	The Frick Collection
Address:	1 East 70th Street, New York, New York 10021
House completion date:	1914
Architect of house:	Thomas Hastings (Carrère & Hastings)
Opening as a museum:	1935
Architect of conversion:	John Russell Pope
Major addition:	1977
Architect of addition:	John Barrington Bayley
Collecting scope:	European and American fine and decorative arts, Chinese Porcelains
Major units:	Frick Collection, Frick Art Reference Library, Center for the History of Collecting in America
Public programs:	Concert series, Frick symposium, lecture series
Amenities:	Bookshop

HENRY CLAY FRICK
AND HIS HOUSE ON FIFTH AVENUE

Pittsburgh coked-coal and steel magnate Henry Clay Frick was born on December 19, 1849 and died in New York on December 2, 1919. Mr. Frick was already collecting works of art as early as the 1870s and purchased his first oil painting in 1881.[1] In 1906, he had begun to acquire the land on the block of Fifth Avenue between East 70th and East 71st Streets on Manhattan's luxurious Upper East Side. Although there is no documented proof that he already intended the house that he would construct on this site to become a museum following his death or that of his wife, the scope and planning of this house, from the very earliest stages, suggest that this was indeed on his mind. It is clear from his will, dated June 24, 1915, that this was his intention around the time he first occupied the house:

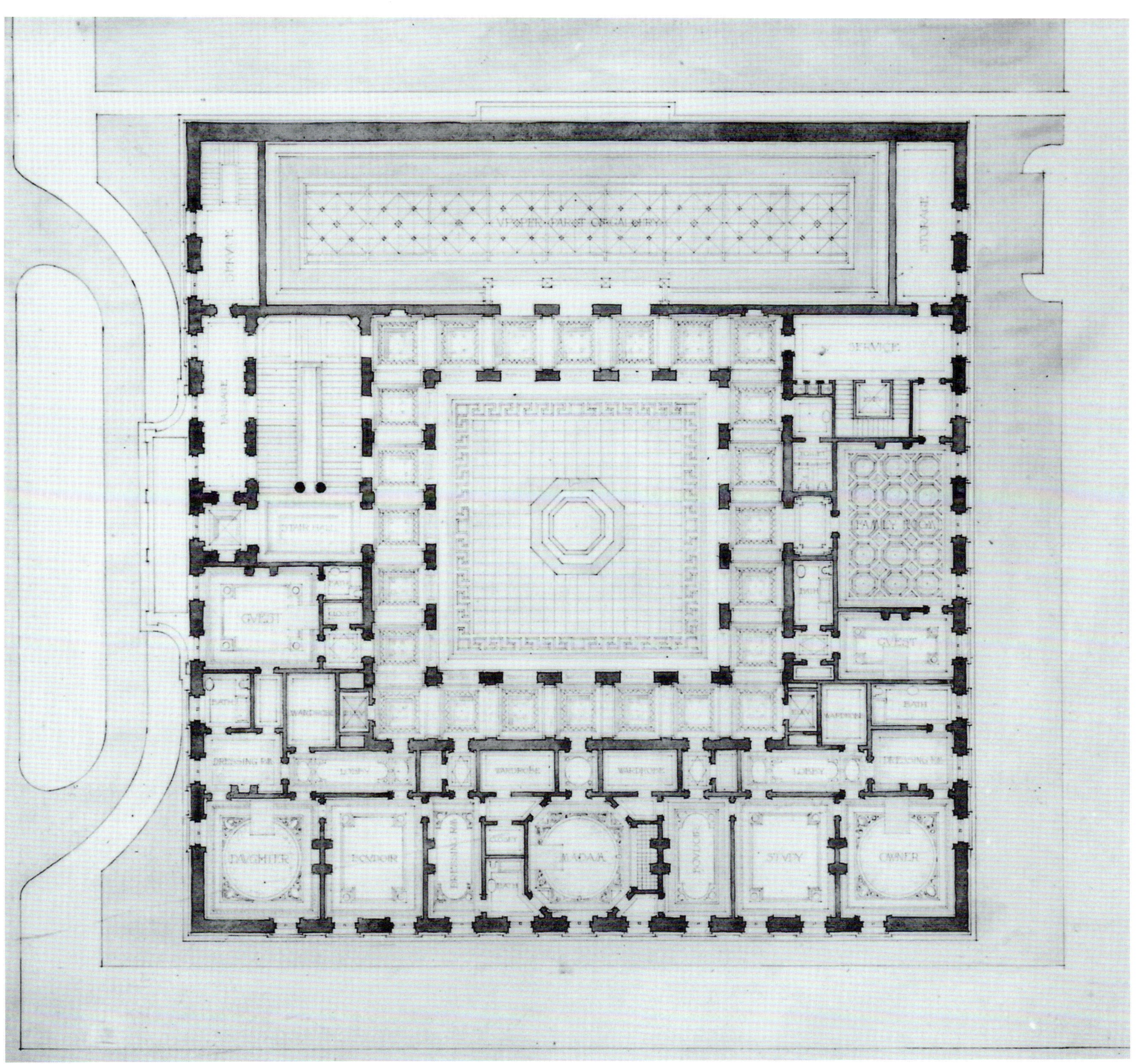

I give, devise and bequeath my dwelling house situate on the easterly side of Fifth Avenue, in the Borough of Manhattan, City of New York, together with all the land upon which the same is erected or which is appurtenant thereto, being all the land now owned by me in the block bounded by Fifth Avenue, Seventieth Street, Madison Avenue and Seventy-first Street, and also all other land, if any, situate in said block, which I may hereafter acquire and which I shall own at the time of my death, and all the tenements, hereditaments and appurtenances thereunto belonging or in any wise appertaining, unto my wife, Adelaide H. C. Frick, To have and To hold the same unto her, my said wife, so long only as she shall occupy the same as one of her residences; and upon the death of my said wife, or if prior thereto my said wife shall cease to occupy said premises as a residence, or shall at any time in writing notify the trustees hereinafter in this article of my will named, or the corporation hereinafter directed to be formed, of her election to discontinue the use of said premises as a residence, then upon the happening of whichever of said events shall first occur, I give, devise and bequeath all the said dwelling house, lands and property, with the appurtenances, unto the corporation hereinafter in this article directed be formed. (Article IV, Section 1)[2]

In 1912 Henry Clay Frick hired Thomas Hastings (of the firm Carrère & Hastings) to be the architect of his Fifth Avenue residence, which would later be transformed into a museum exhibiting his already superlative and growing collection of masterpieces of European and American painting. Carrère & Hastings were among the premiere Beaux-Arts architects of New York and had recently completed the New York Public Library on Fifth Avenue at Forty-Second Street. Soon after he was hired, Hastings submitted plans and elevations of a first scheme to Mr. Frick (see figs. 1.1 and 1.2). This early project would have little in common with what was eventually built, but it is very revealing in allowing a clear distinction to be made between the Beaux-Arts architecture typical of the times and the personal tastes of Mr. Frick. These drawings clearly reveal a typically symmetrical building much more in keeping with the mansions being built by the very wealthy barons of capitalism and industry of the time.

By April 1912 the general plan of the house was agreed upon, and excavation of the site and construction began that year. The final plan was much less monumental and looked away from the then-orthodox Italian revivalism and much more toward a French aesthetic. The plan was no longer a symmetrical square, but rather an el-shaped plan, with a large garden bounded by Fifth Avenue to the west and 70th Street to the south. The long arm of the el was to the east of the garden, and the north of the garden was enclosed by an asymmetrical gallery wing with a covered portico, all of which survives intact in the current state of the Frick Collection (see figs. 1.3–1.5).

The house was entered through an arched carriageway on East 70th Street at the east end of the building (fig. 1.6). This arch has since been moved and

1.3. View of the Frick Residence from Fifth Avenue, 1914. Courtesy of the Frick Collection/Frick Art Reference Library Archives.

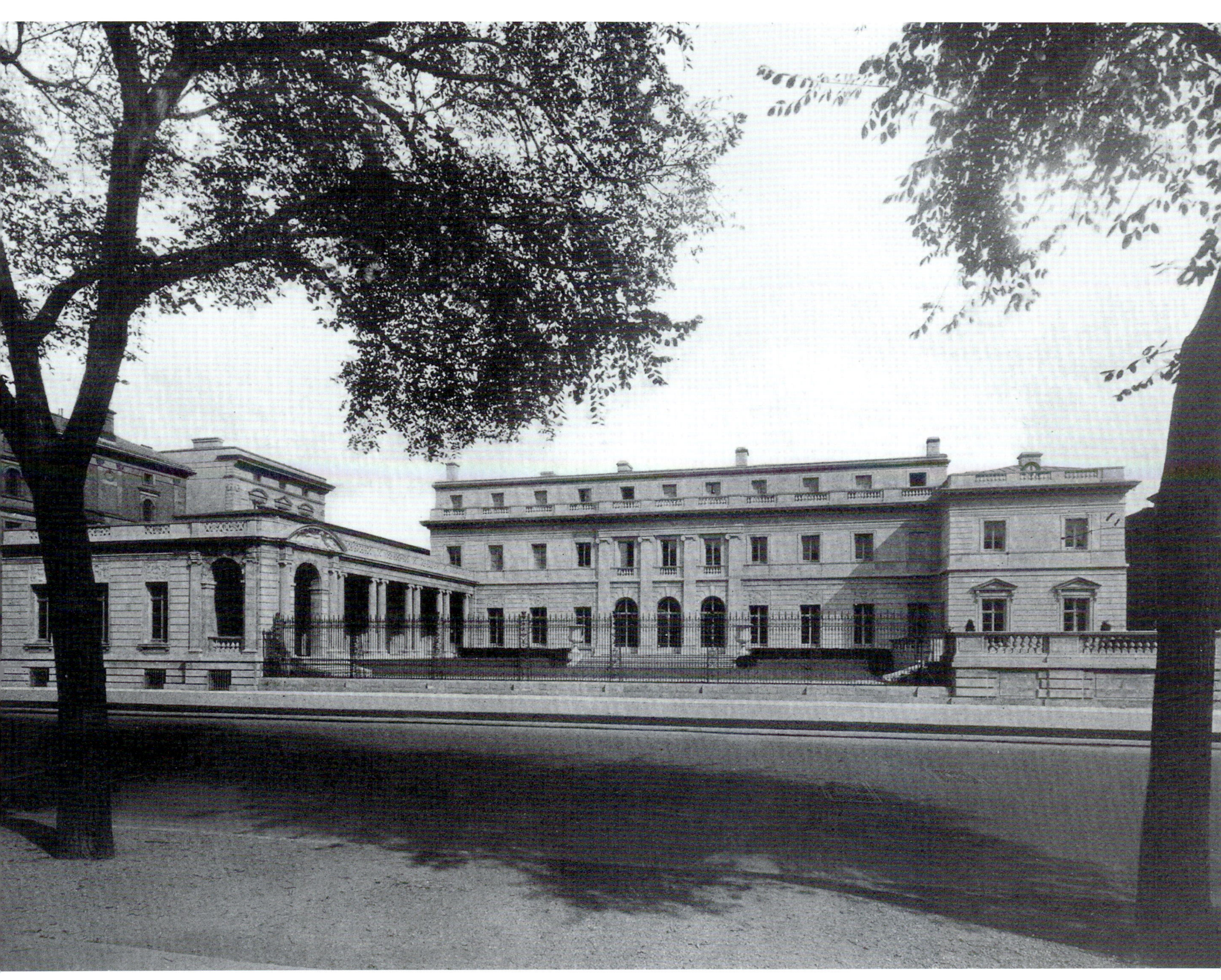

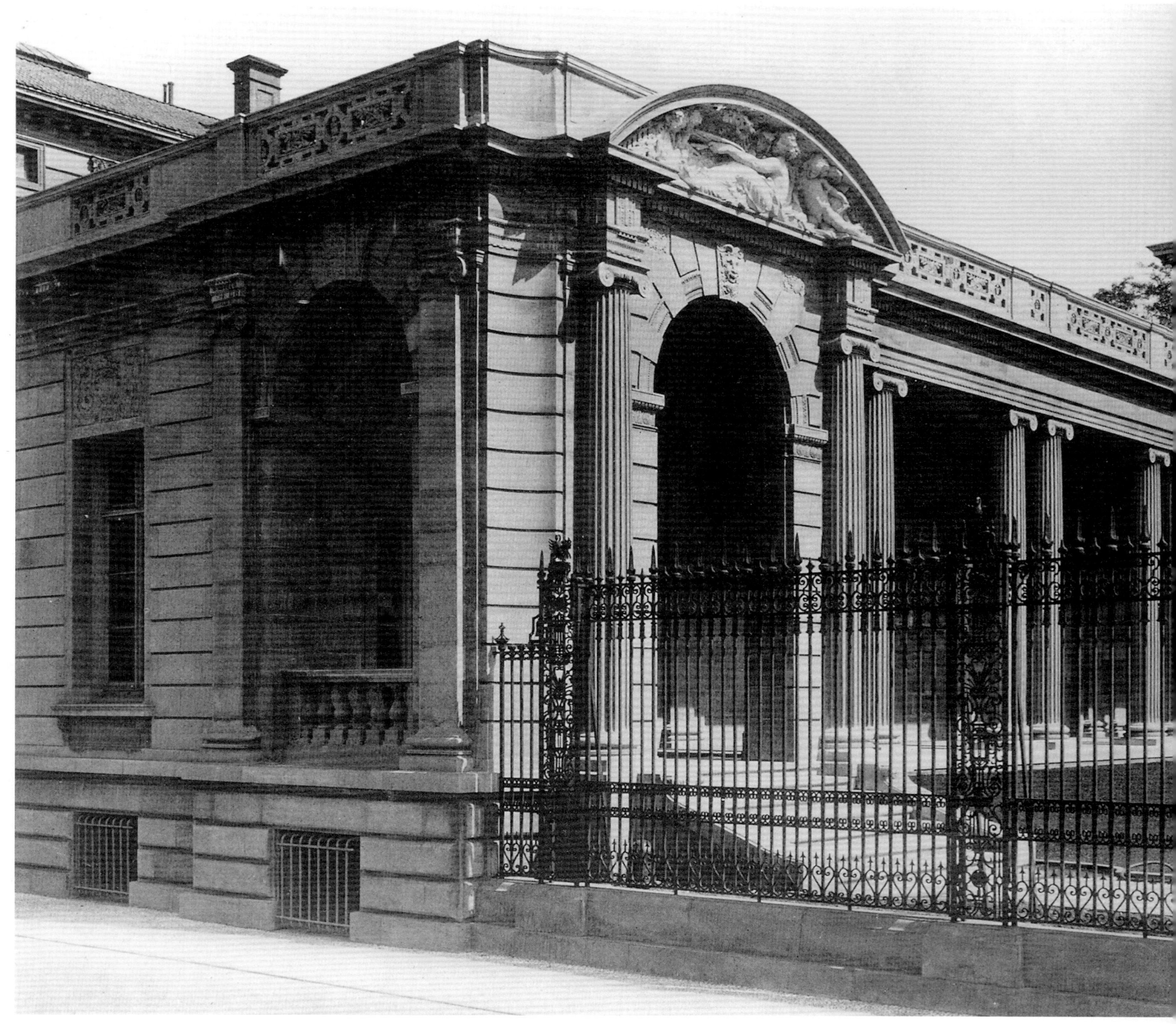

1.4. Gallery wing and portico, from
Fifth Avenue, 1914. Courtesy of the Frick
Collection/Frick Art Reference Library Archives.

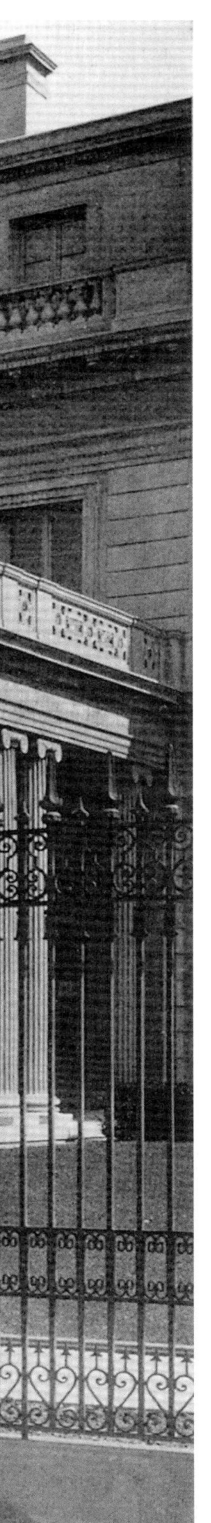

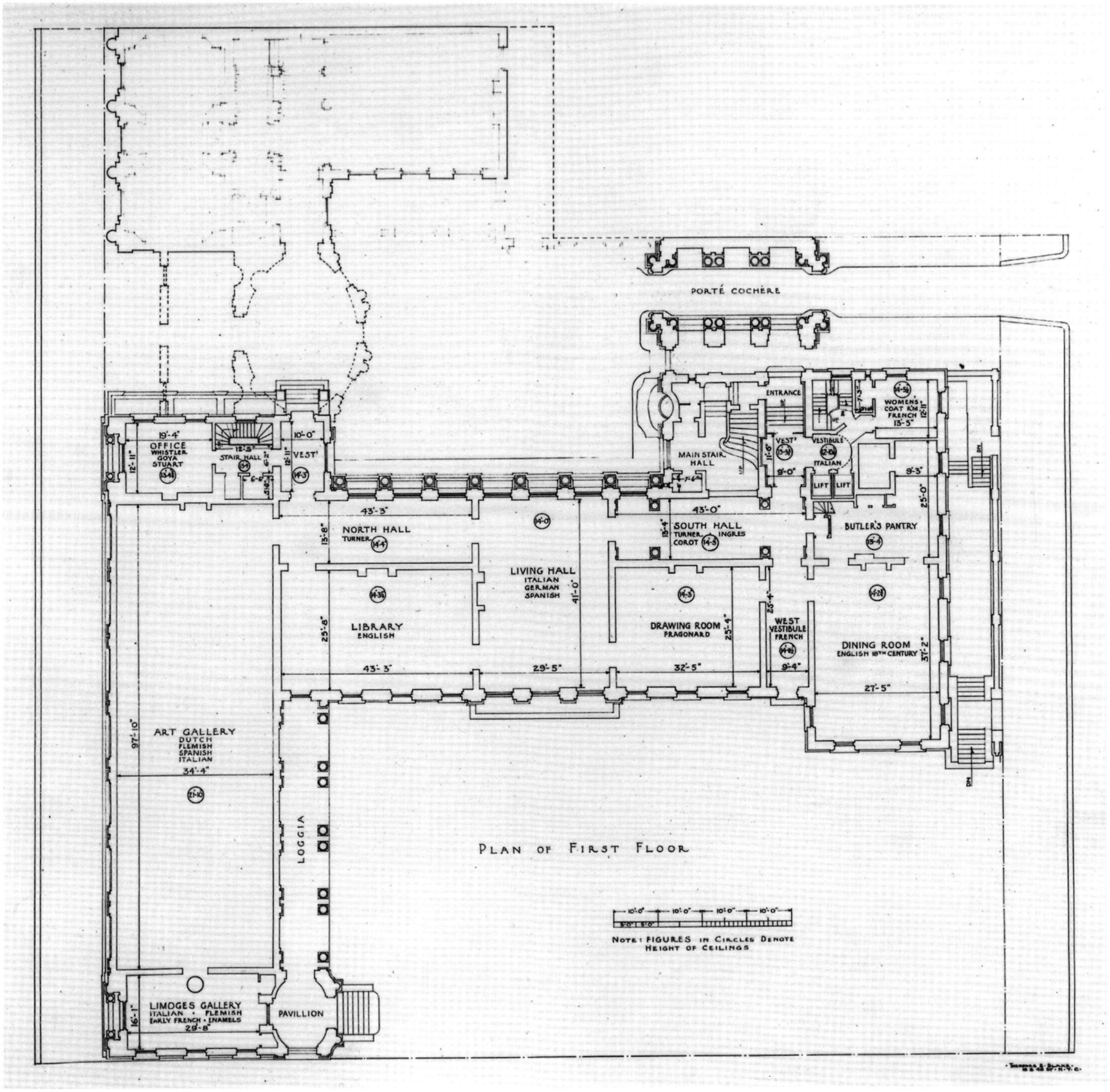

1.5. Frick Residence, plan of first floor showing outline of proposed sculpture gallery, pre-1935 renovation. *Courtesy of the Frick Collection/Frick Art Reference Library Archives.*

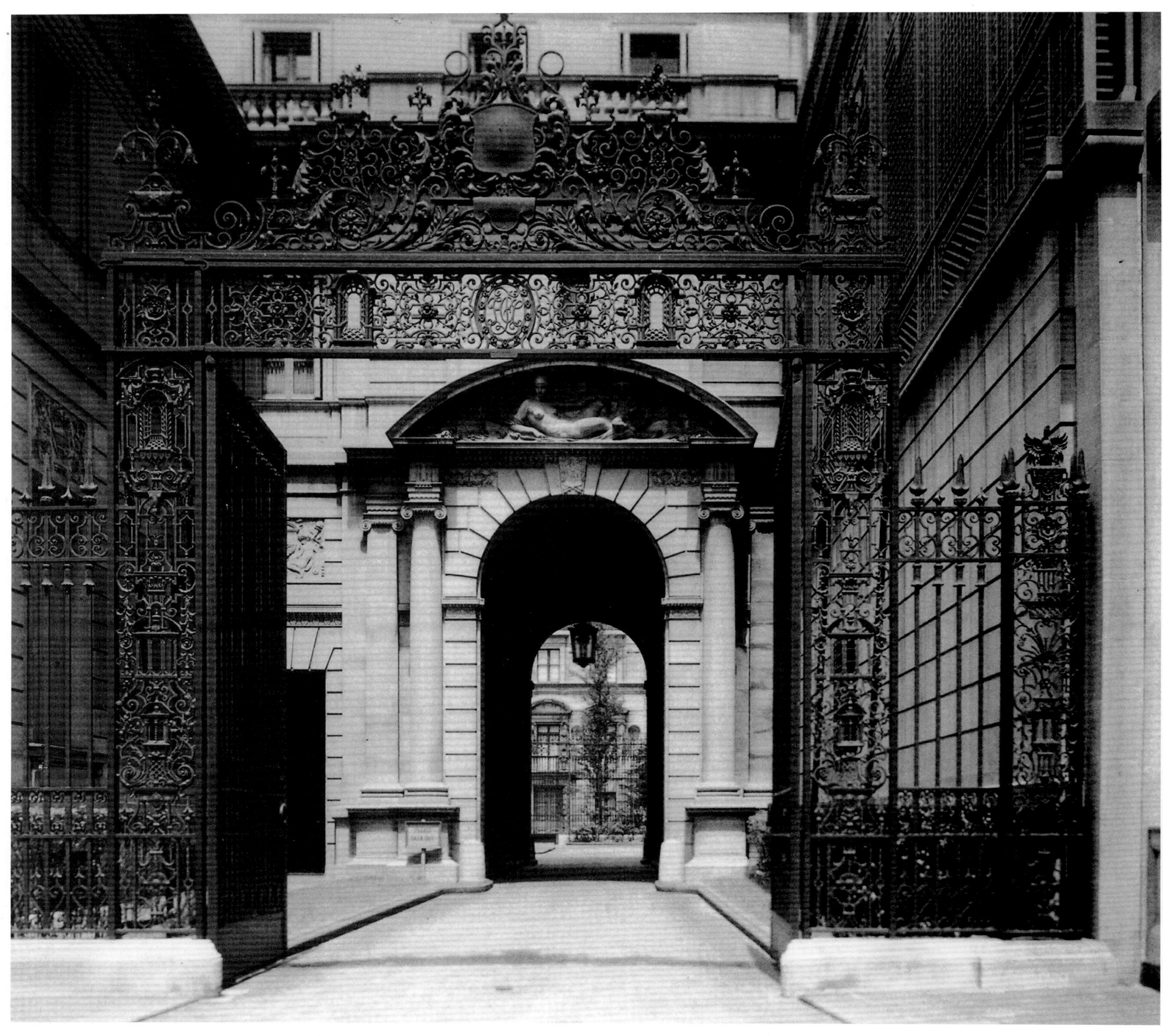

1.6 Carriageway arch and driveway, East 70th Street, 1927. *Courtesy of the Frick Collection/Frick Art Reference Library Archives.*

1.7 Courtyard of the Frick Residence, 1927, before construction of John Russell Pope's Garden Court. *Courtesy of the Frick Collection/Frick Art Reference Library Archives.*

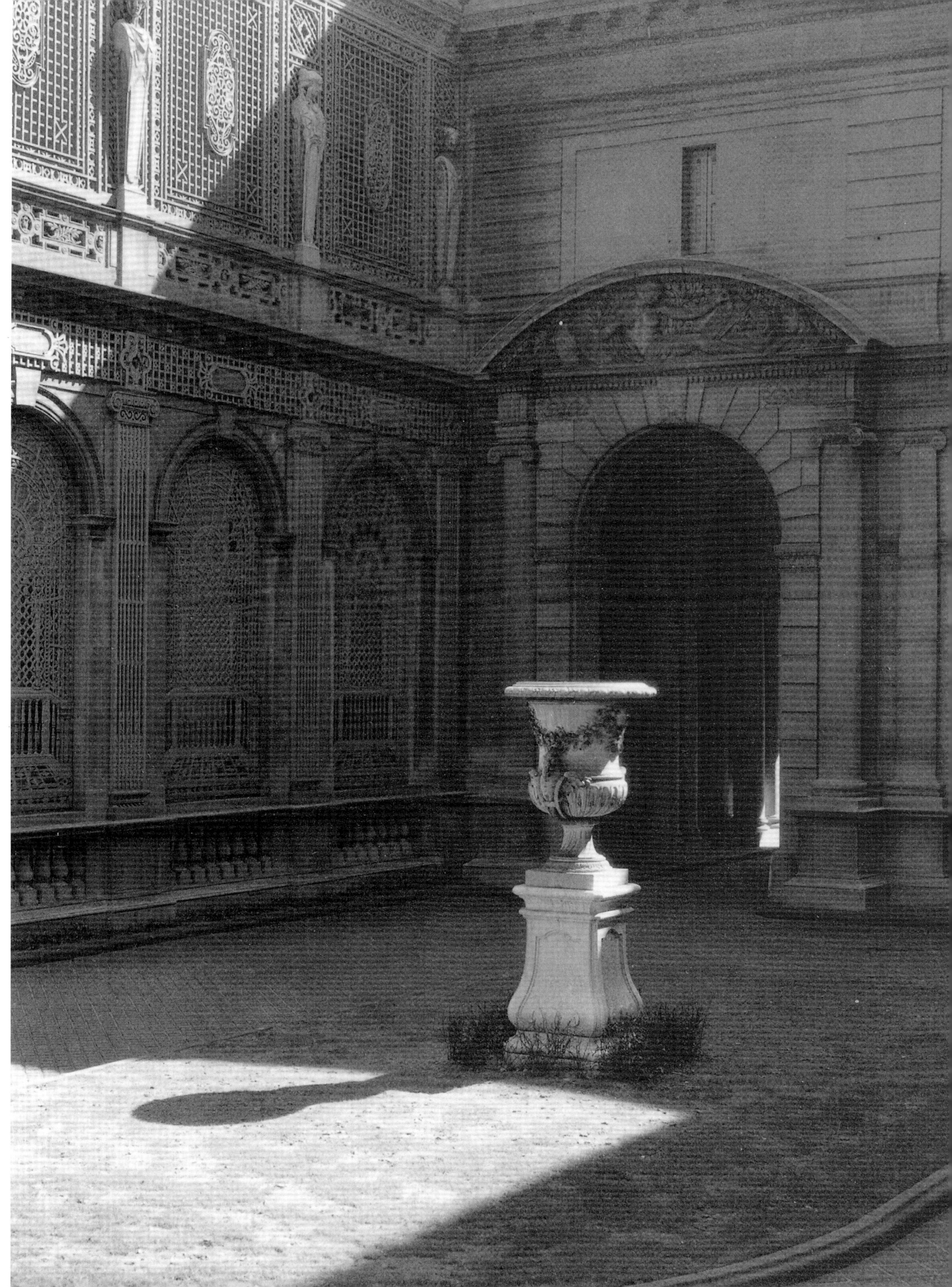

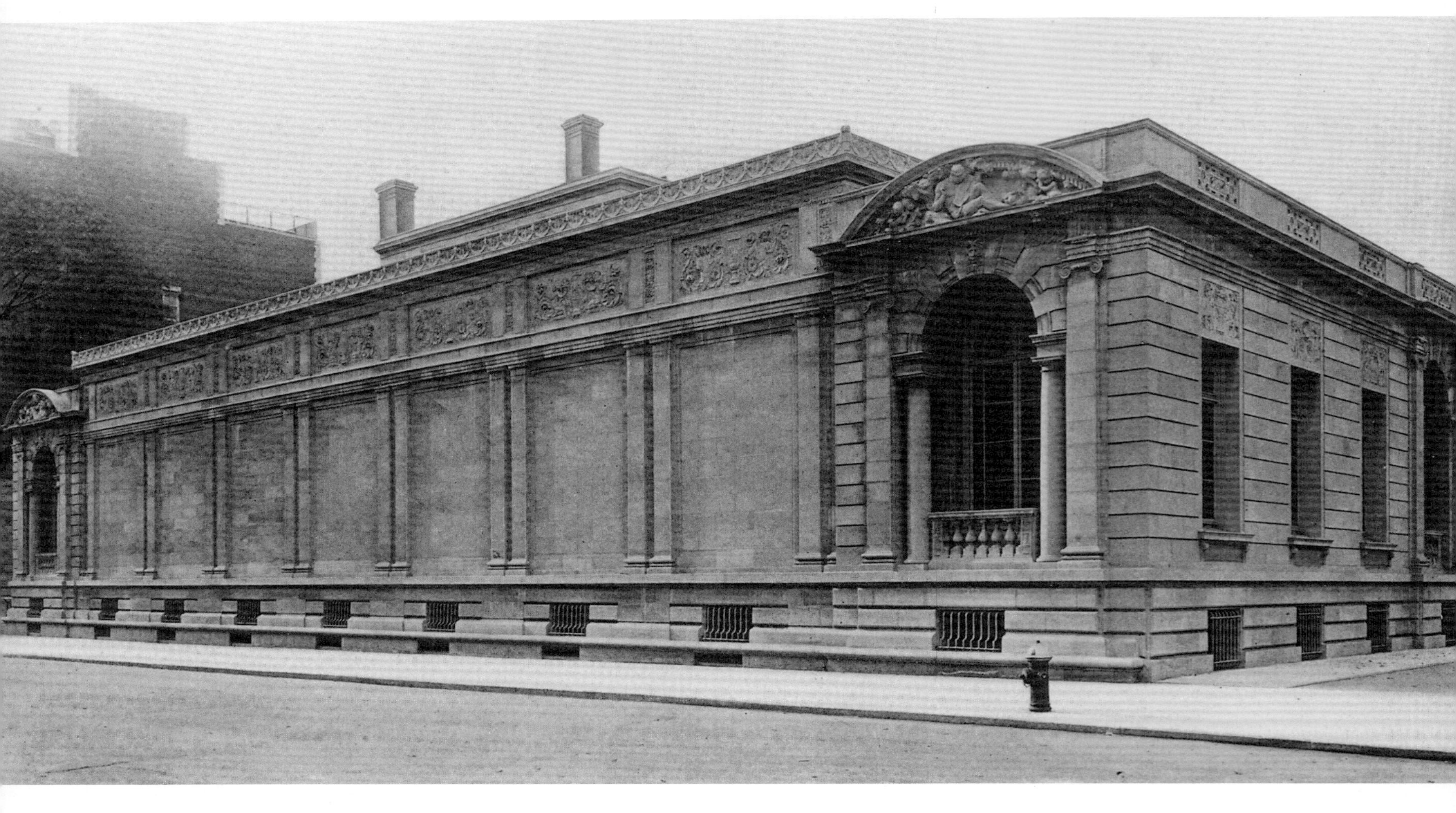

enclosed and now serves as the public entrance to the Frick Collection (discussed below). In the original scheme, however, the house was entered via a door on the wall of the west side of the carriageway, facing east, under the arch. The arched passage led to an open courtyard with an ornamental wall to the east, screening the courtyard from the buildings to the east of Mr. Frick's property (fig. 1.7). The 71st Street elevation of the house was a series of blind bays separated by coupled pilasters and bounded by open arches under richly carved pediments on the east and west ends (fig. 1.8). Behind this wall was the Picture Gallery (now the West Gallery of the Frick Collection). In the basement below this was contained Mr. Frick's two-lane bowling alley (fig. 1.9).

In 1913 Sir Charles Carrick Allom, of the firm of White, Allom & Co., was hired to begin the interior decoration of the ground floor rooms; these were the formal reception spaces of the house. Later, in 1914, the famous decorator Elsie de Wolfe was brought on to decorate the upper rooms, which were reserved for more private, family use. Allom decorated all of the ground floor, with the exception of the Ladies' Reception Room (now the Boucher Room). De Wolfe

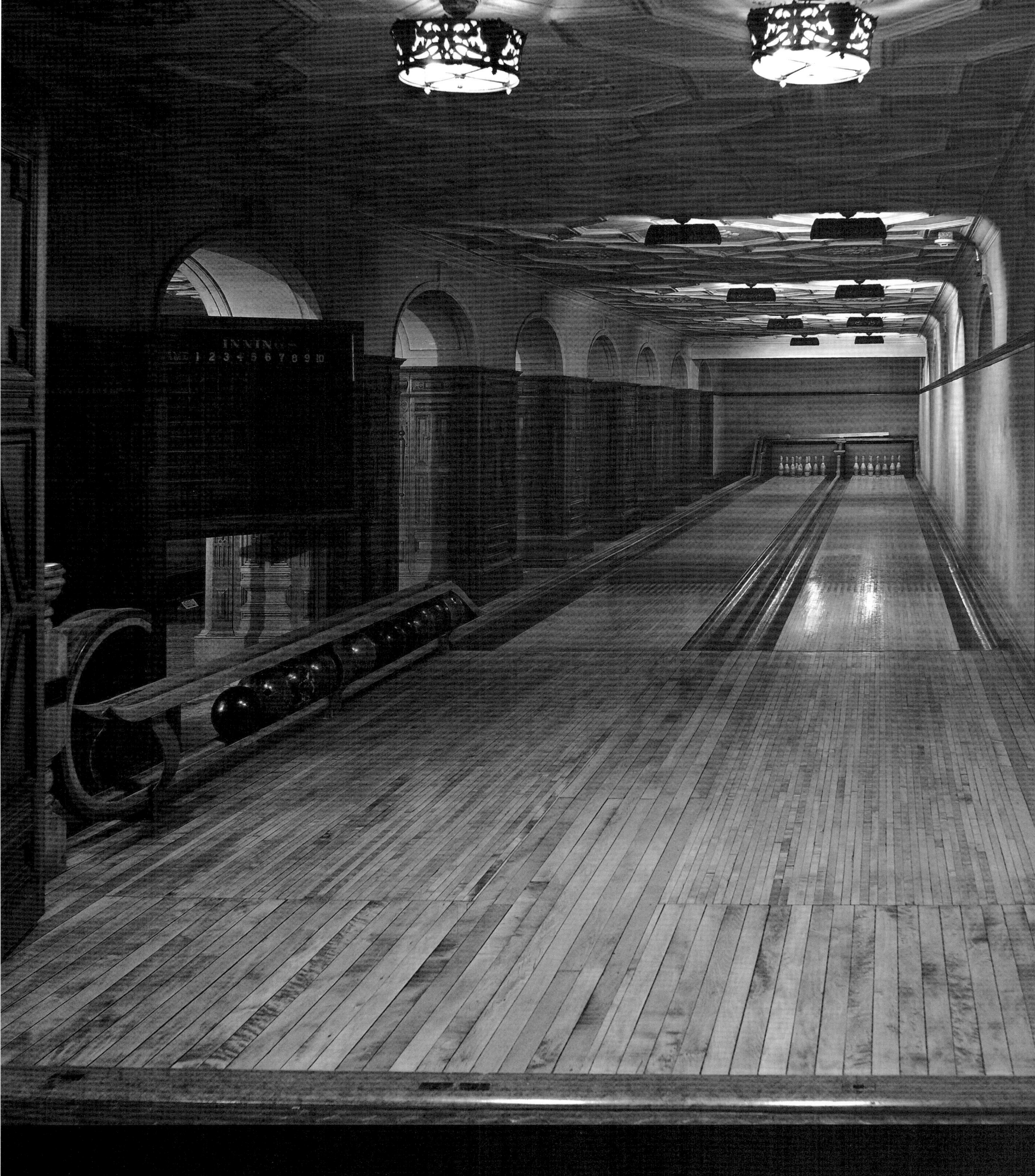

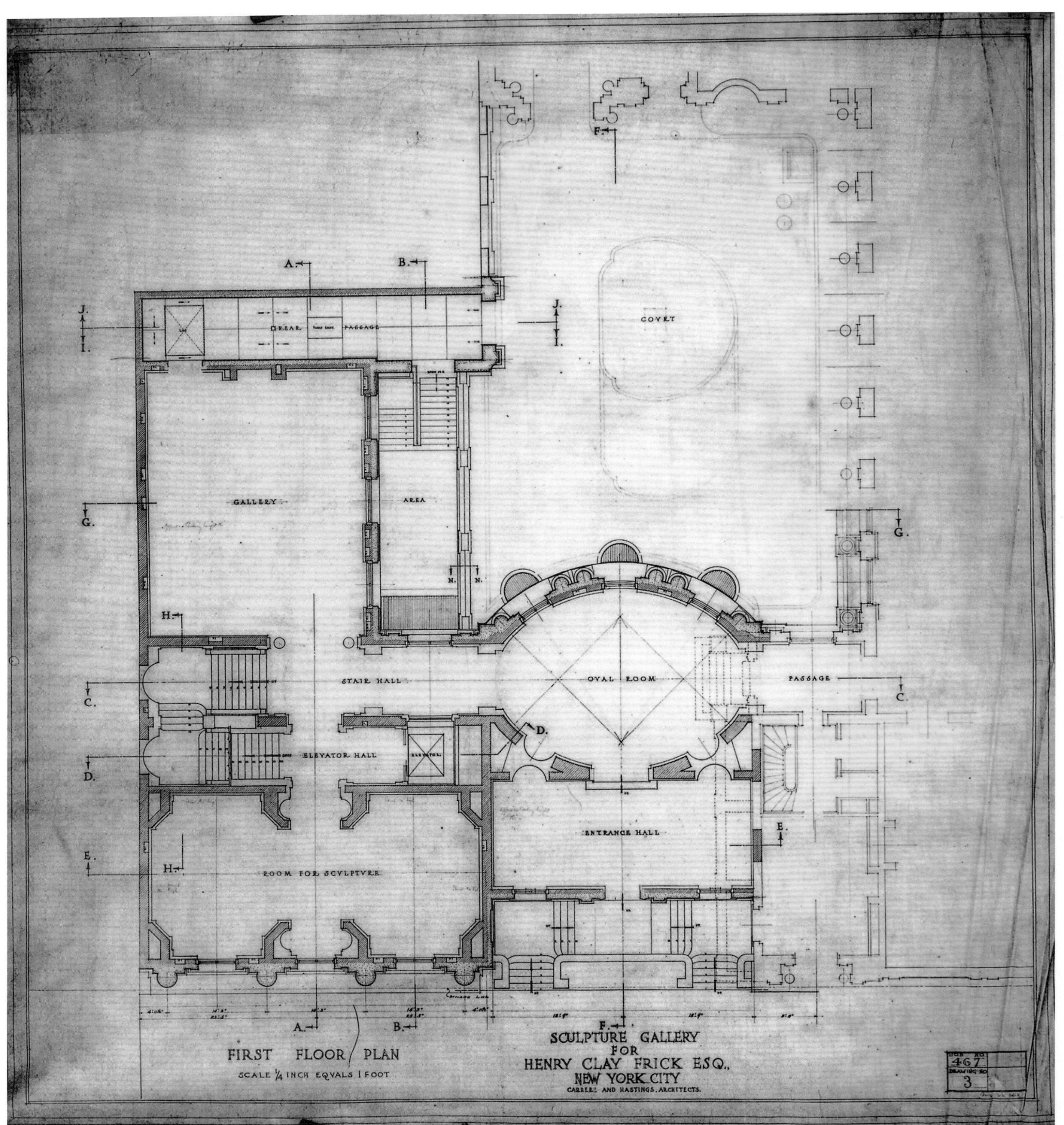
GREAT PASSAGE
COVET
GALLERY
AREA
STAIR HALL
OVAL ROOM
PASSAGE
ELEVATOR HALL
ELEVATOR
ENTRANCE HALL
ROOM FOR SCULPTURE
FIRST FLOOR PLAN
SCALE 1/4 INCH EQUALS 1 FOOT
SCULPTURE GALLERY
FOR
HENRY CLAY FRICK ESQ.,
NEW YORK CITY
CARRERE AND HASTINGS, ARCHITECTS.
467
DRAWING NO
3

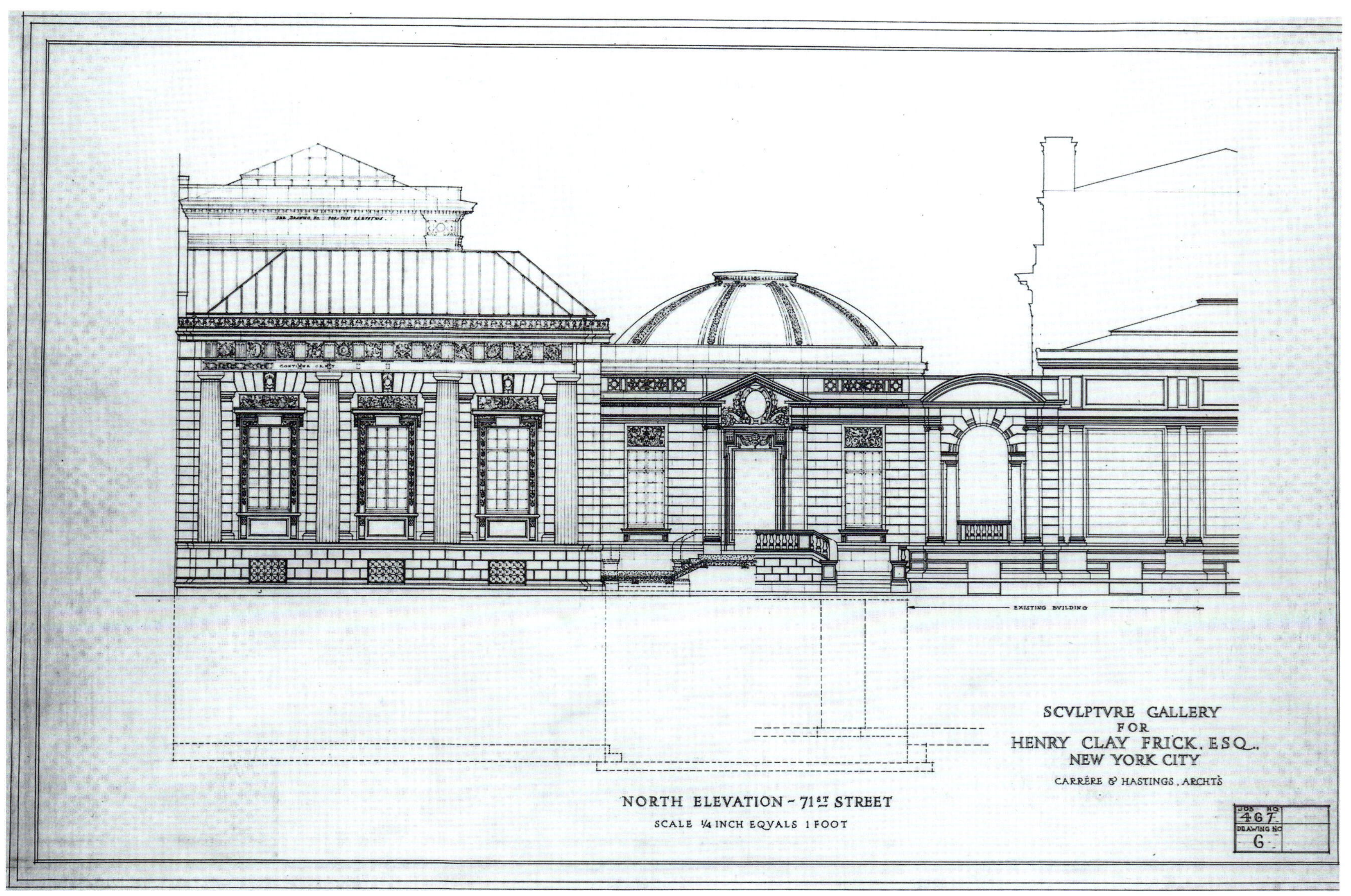

decorated the rooms on the second and third floors, except for the Breakfast Room (now the deputy director's office) and Mr. Frick's sitting room (now the chief curator's office), which were decorated by Allom. At this point, Mr. Frick was primarily a collector of fine art and had not yet begun to emphasize the decorative arts and furniture that later commanded a great deal of his attention. The Frick family took up residence in November 1914—though the interior decoration was still unfinished, the house was habitable and in use. In September of that year, Mr. Frick was already consulting Thomas Hastings regarding possible expansion. He had acquired the adjoining property on East 71st Street and was considering the addition of a Sculpture Gallery (figs. 1.10 and 1.11). Although this plan was not executed, the façade was built, on the same site, as the façade of the first purpose-built home for the Frick Art Reference Library.

FACING PAGE

1.10. Plan of proposed Sculpture Gallery on East 71st Street, Thomas Hastings, 1916. *Courtesy of the Frick Collection/ Frick Art Reference Library Archives.*

ABOVE

1.11. Façade of proposed Sculpture Gallery on East 71st Street, Thomas Hastings, 1916. *Courtesy of the Frick Collection/Frick Art Reference Library Archives.*

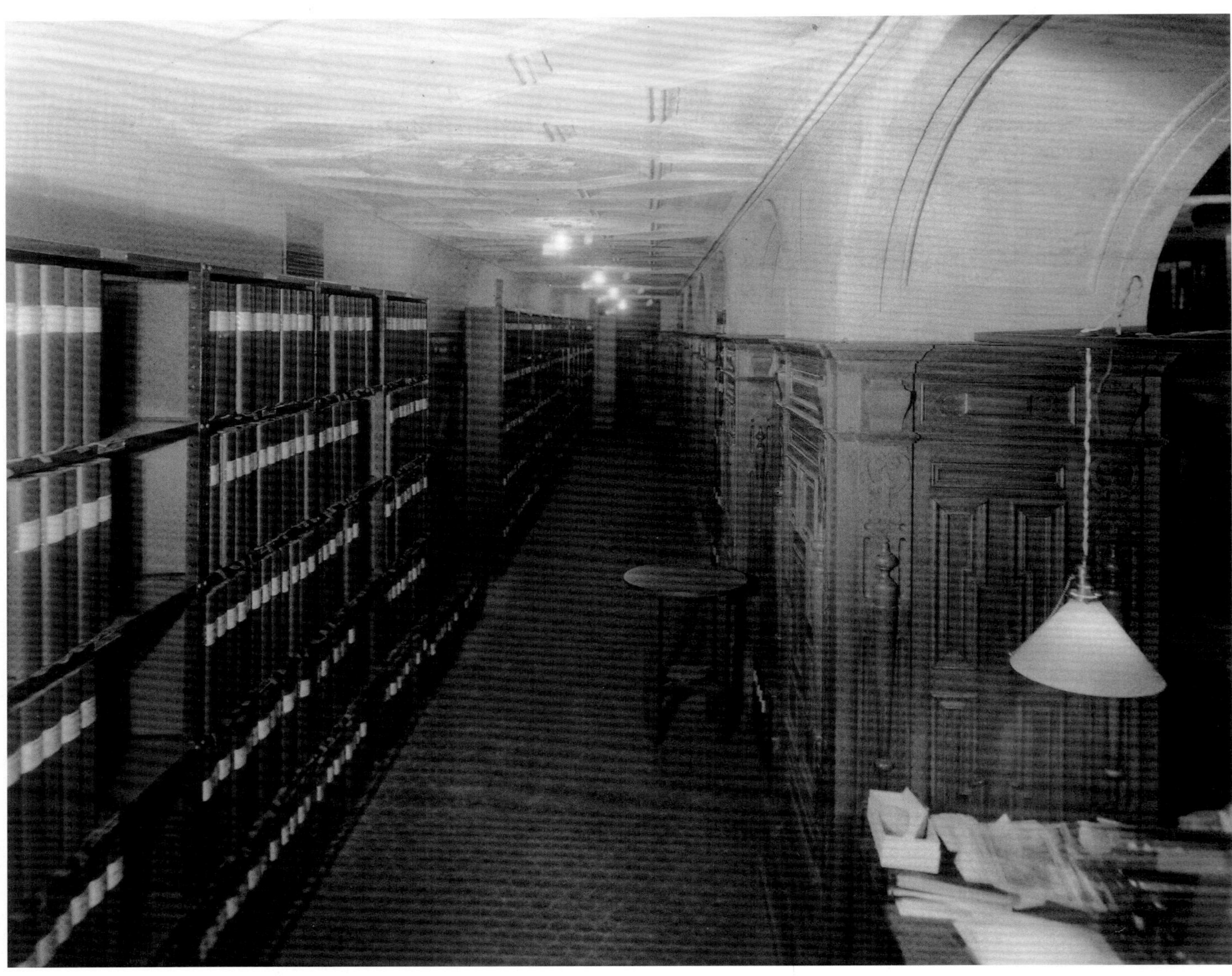

1.12. Interior of bowling alley, converted to photoarchive stacks, 1923. Courtesy of the Frick Collection/Frick Art Reference Library Archives.

FROM PRIVATE RESIDENCE TO PUBLIC COLLECTION

Though Mr. Frick died on December 2, 1919, his will (quoted above) stated that his wife could continue to inhabit the residence until her passing or until she no longer desired to live there. Nonetheless, another section of the will, immediately upon the death of Henry Clay Frick, formed a corporation, named trustees, and established the parameters of the museum that would eventually be housed within the Fifth Avenue residence. The will addresses the contents of the newly formed "Frick Collection":

> All the books, pictures, paintings, engravings, porcelains, enamels, bronzes, statuary, rugs, tapestries, carpets, curtains, antique or artistic furniture and furnishings, bric-a-brac and other works of art which at the time of my death

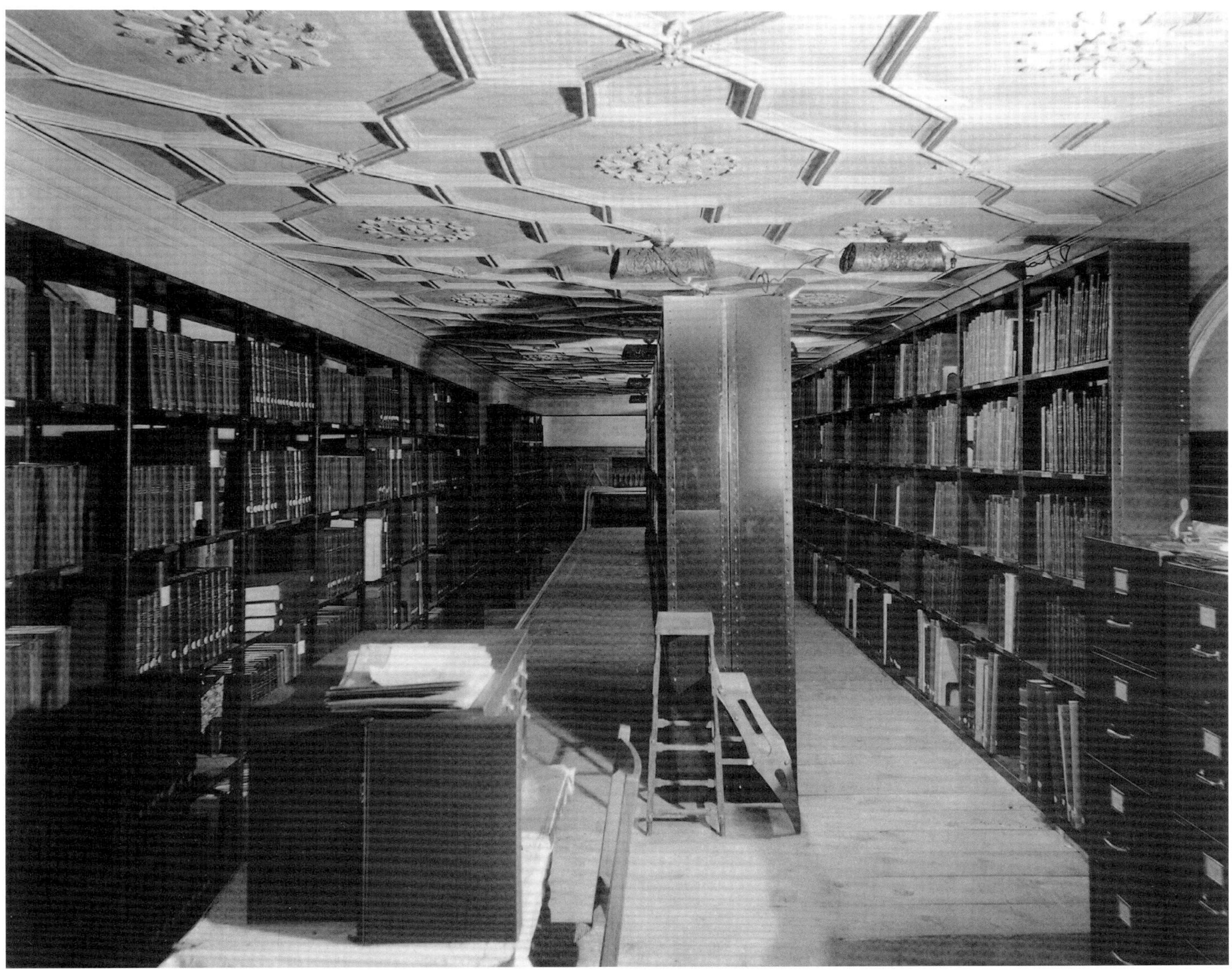

1.13. Interior of bowling alley, showing library book stacks, 1923. Courtesy of the Frick Collection/Frick Art Reference Library Archives.

shall be contained in or usually kept by me in my dwelling house aforesaid, together with all other articles of personal property which at the time of my death shall form a part of the furnishing and equipment of my said dwelling house, including the organ therein installed, I give and bequeath unto my wife, Adelaide H. C. Frick, my daughter, Helen C. Frick, my son, Childs Frick, George F. Baker, Junior, J. Horace Harding, Walker D. Hines, Lewis Cass Ledyard, John D. Rockefeller, Junior, and Horace Havemeyer, and the survivors and survivor of them and their successors, In Trust; to hold, maintain and preserve the same in the house aforesaid until the incorporation of the institution aforesaid, and upon said incorporation to assign, transfer and deliver, and I hereby give and bequeath the same, unto the said corporation to be known as "The Frick Collection." (Article IV, Section 3)

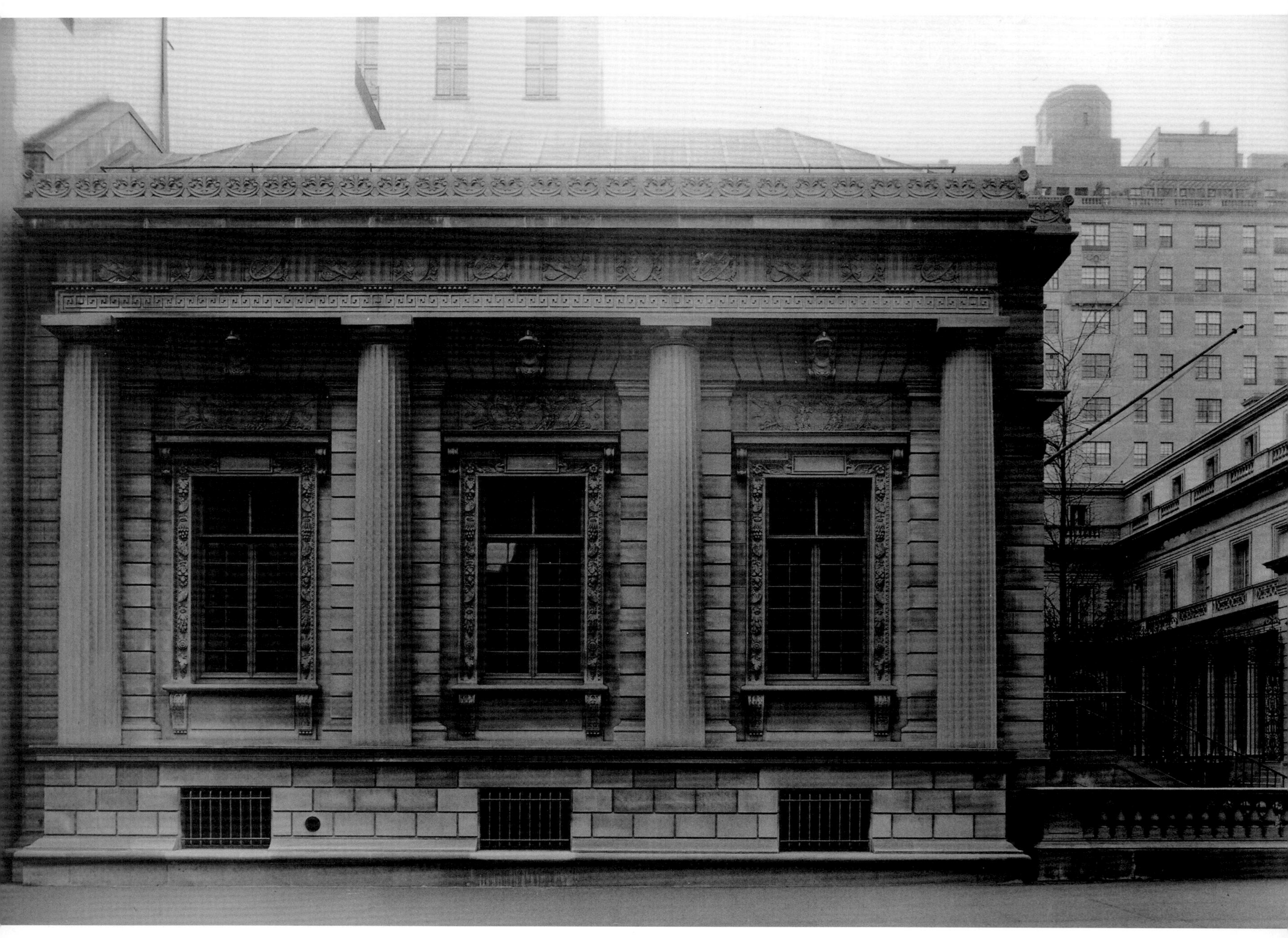

1.14. Seventy-first Street façade of
original Frick Art Reference Library,
c.1924–1932. Courtesy of the Frick
Collection/Frick Art Reference Library Archives.

Henry Clay Frick further used his estate to provide for the liberal endowment
of his new corporation and art gallery:

I give and bequeath unto my wife, Adelaide H. C. Frick, my daughter, Helen
C. Frick, my son, Childs Frick, George F. Baker, Junior, J. Horace Harding,
Walker D. Hines, Lewis Cass Ledyard, John D. Rockefeller, Junior, and Horace
Havemeyer, and the survivors and survivor of them, and their successors, the
sum of Fifteen Million Dollars, In Trust, [. . . .] I hereby give and bequeath, all

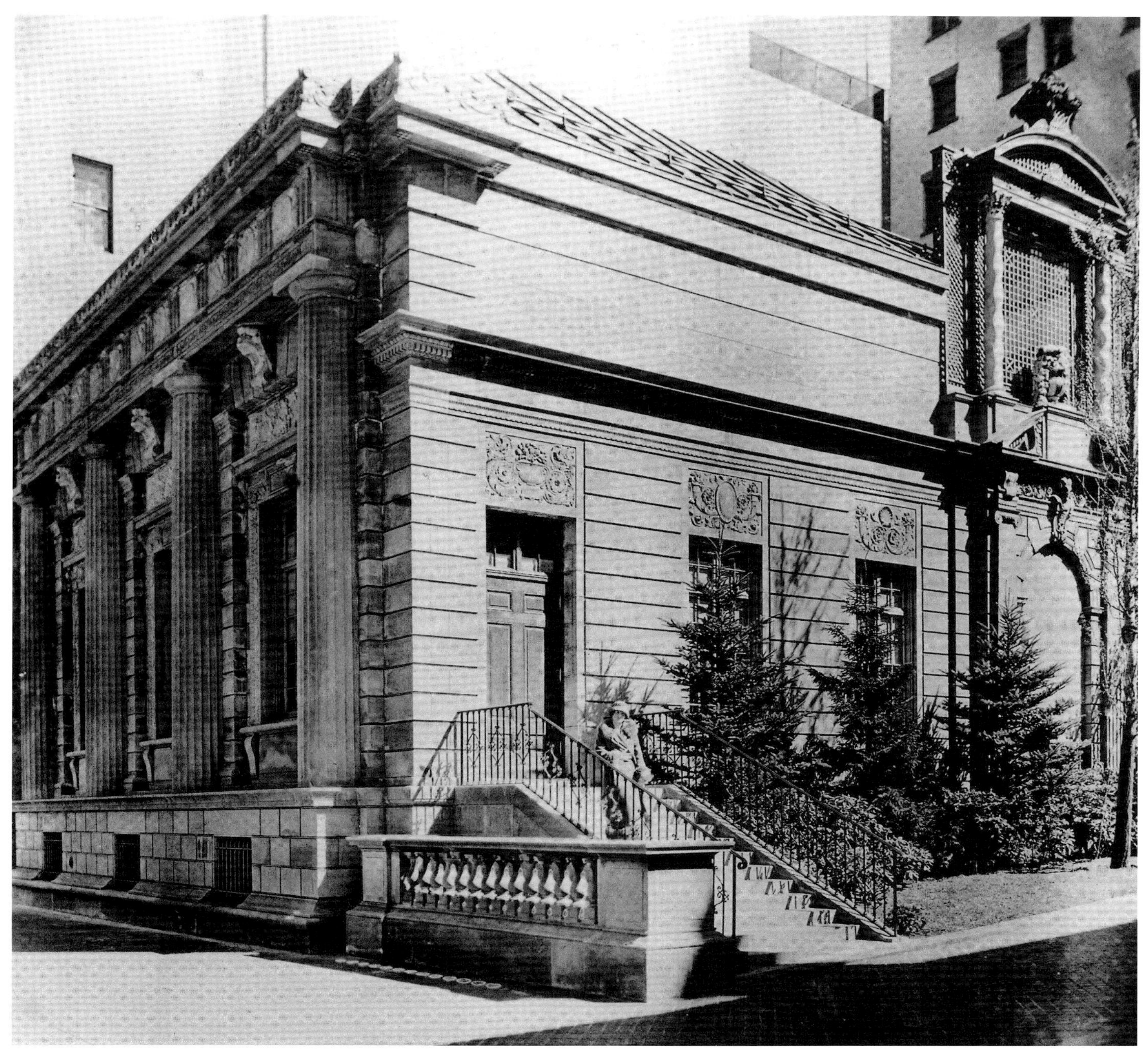

1.15. Entrance, from carriageway, to original Frick Art Reference Library, c. 1924–1932. Courtesy of the Frick Collection/Frick Art Reference Library Archives.

of the said trust fund unto the said corporation hereinbefore directed to be formed and to be known as "The Frick Collection," the same to constitute and form a permanent endowment fund to be used for the maintenance, care, protection and support of said gallery of art and the personal property therein contained, and the making of any alterations, improvements, additions or betterments in or to said premises, and any surplus of such income to be expended from time to time as the directors, trustees or managers of said corporation may determine in the purchase of other suitable works of art to form part of such gallery of art, and any other corporate purposes of said corporation. (Article IV, Section 4)

As prescribed by the will, the entity known as "The Frick Collection" was duly incorporated, the Act of Incorporation being passed by the New York State Assembly on April 15, 1920, the State Senate on April 16, 1920, and signed into law by the governor on April 27, 1920.[3]

As allowed under the will, however, Henry Clay Frick's widow, Mrs. Adelaide Frick, and daughter, Helen Clay Frick, continued to live in the residence, delaying the implementation of the will's provisions to turn the house and collection into a public art gallery. Nonetheless, the trustees, led by Board President Childs Frick and Secretary Helen Clay Frick, began to advance the programs of what would become the Frick Collection. Even while her father was still alive, Helen Clay Frick had begun assembling an art history reference library to help with the study and cataloging of the collection. Although she did compile early catalogs of her father's collection, she did not begin acquiring books for her library until after his death. This early effort became the seed from which the Frick Art Reference Library, still a major unit of the Frick Collection, would spring.[4] Traveling in England in 1920, Ms. Frick was exposed to the Witt Photoarchive (now housed at the Courtauld Institute in London). Returning to New York, she decided to use this as a model for creating a comprehensive art photoarchive on a similar scale in the United States. There was, however, little space in the Frick residence to house this growing library and photoarchive; spaces that were no longer used on a regular basis, such as the late Henry Clay's bowling alley and billiards room (in the basement below the Picture Gallery), were filled with shelves and became the stacks of this proto-Frick Art Reference Library (figs. 1.12 and 1.13).

By late 1922 the trustees of the corporation decided that a proper home for this library and photoarchive should be constructed. Thomas Hastings was brought back and the land that was previously considered for the addition of a sculpture gallery was selected for the construction of a one-floor structure across the carriageway from the street façade of the picture galley on East 71st Street. The 71st Street façade of the new library building (fig. 1.14) would be a resurrection of the eastern pavilion of Hastings's abandoned sculpture gallery of 1916. The new library was entered through a narrow doorway on the east side of the still open carriageway, running clear through the block from East 70th Street to East 71st Street (fig. 1.15). Behind the 71st Street façade was the reading room (fig. 1.16), complete with fresco on the east wall, which was later moved to the reading room of the current Frick Art Reference Library. South of the reading room were the book stacks, photoarchive, librarian's office, and service areas. The Frick Art Reference Library was opened to the public in June 1924.

Mrs. Adelaide Frick passed away in October 1931, setting all the provisions in the will regarding the conversion of the residence on Fifth Avenue into a public art gallery into action. The Board of Trustees immediately appointed art

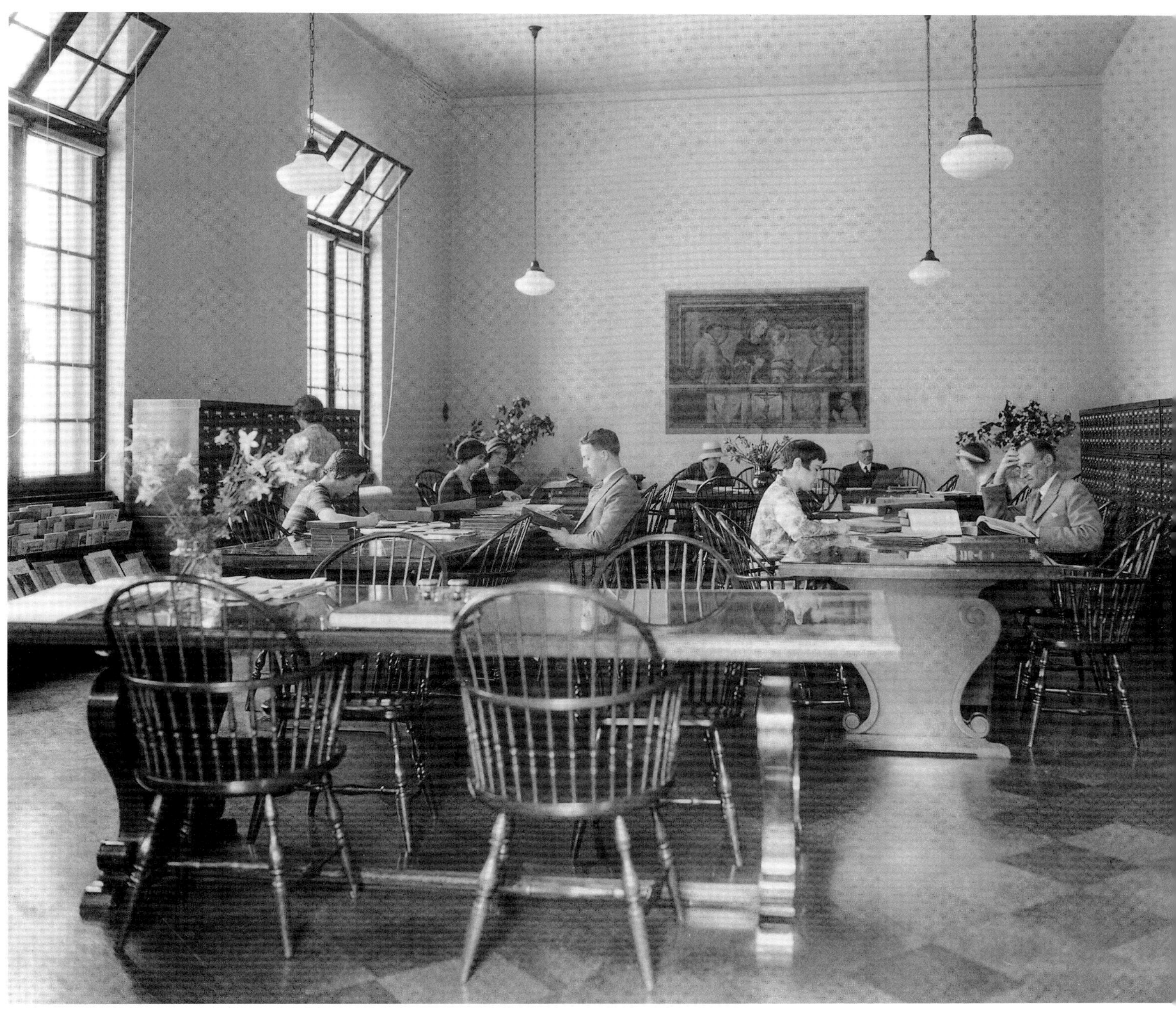

1.16. Interior of the reading room of the original Frick Art Reference Library, c. 1924–1932. Courtesy of the Frick Collection/Frick Art Reference Library Archives.

historian Frederick Mortimer Clapp as advisor to The Frick Collection, and he was made organizing director between March, 1932 and January 4, 1933 (there is a discrepancy in the record); he was charged with planning and executing the conversion of the house into a museum, pursuant to Mr. Frick's will. The architect of this project would not be Thomas Hastings, as he had died in 1929. Mr. Clapp wasted no time in beginning to execute his new charge. Between his assumption of the position in 1931 and The Frick Collection's opening in 1935, Clapp generated a steady flow of documents outlining the transformation and expansion of Mr. Frick's

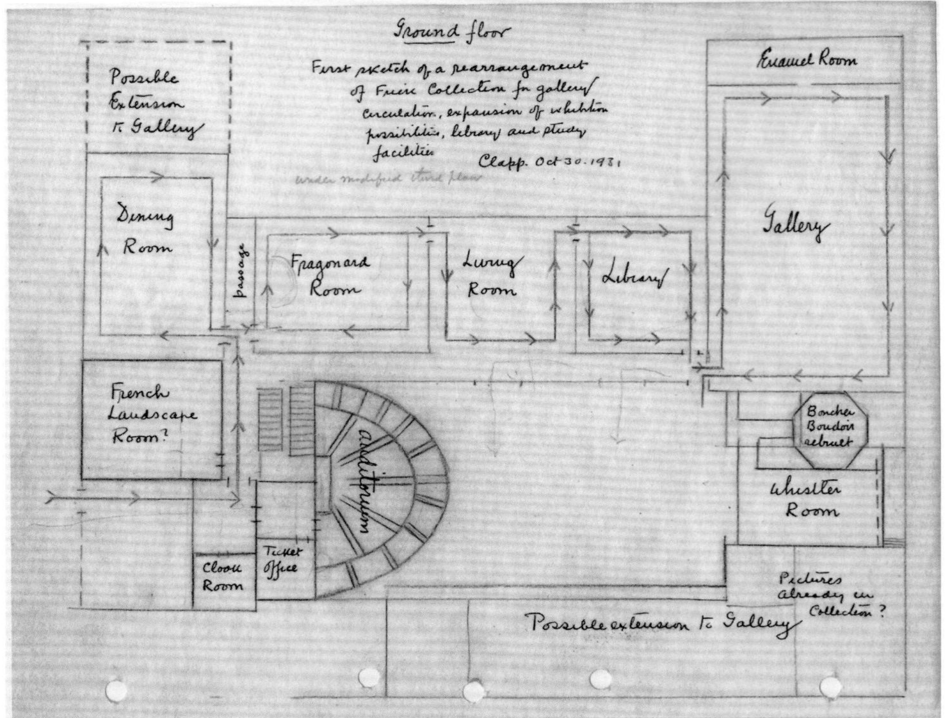

1.17. Frederick Mortimer Clapp's sketch for possible first floor layout of the Frick Collection, 1931. Clapp Notebooks, Courtesy of the Frick Collection/Frick Art Reference Library Archives.

house into the museum we know today.[5] In a document from January 28, 1932, Clapp had already reached many important decisions that would remain intact to the present:

Partially agreed upon:

1. Confine public view to ground floor
2. Construction of connecting gallery on 71st Street
3. Public entrance via 70th Street and connecting gallery through
   a. Open court
   b. Corridor
   c. Closed court
4. Closed system of circulation for public (no new door in library)
5. Large lecture room on second floor
6. Washed ventilation for the whole
7. Enlargement of Art Reference Building with entrance on 71st Street
8. Connecting corridor only on second floor[6]

Of these points, the only major digressions from what would eventually be executed are the placement of the "large lecture room" on the second floor (it is today's "music room" and is on the ground floor) and the "connecting corridor only on second floor" (the buildings are connected on both basement and first floors

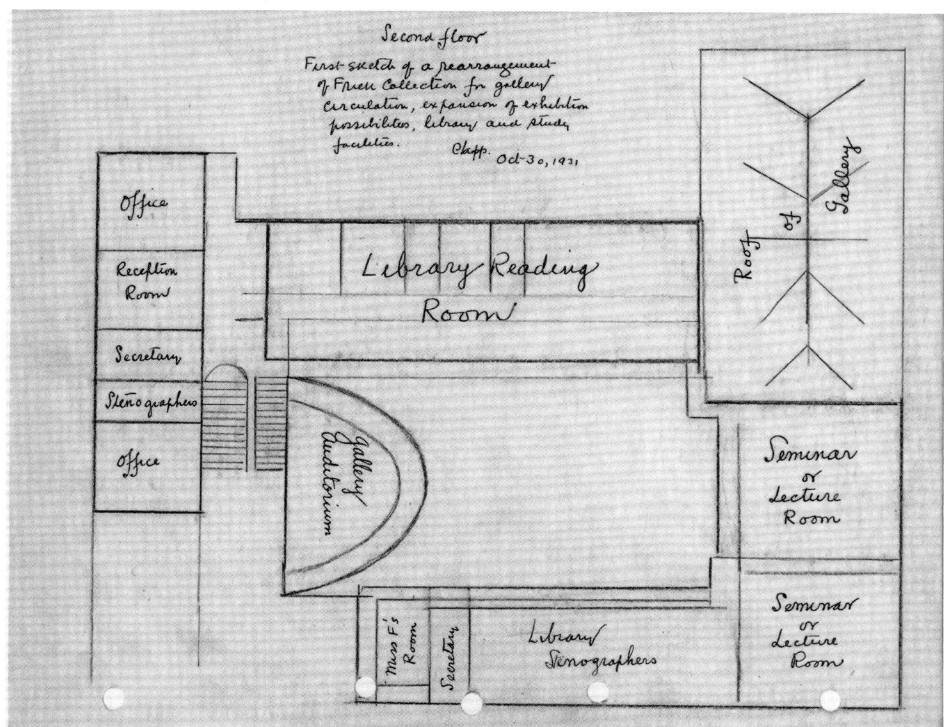

1.18 Frederick Mortimer Clapp's sketch for possible second floor layout of the Frick Collection, 1931. Clapp Notebooks, Courtesy of the Frick Collection/Frick Art Reference Library Archives.

(though neither connection is open to the public, preserving the "closed system of circulation for public" of point number four). As for the public entrance in the third point, option "c," the closed court, would be selected and would become the much beloved "Garden Court." Also in this period, Clapp himself experimented with potential arrangements and circulation schemes, even making sketches that survive in his notebooks (see figs. 1.17 and 1.18).

Architect John Russell Pope was selected to design additions to, and renovations of, the Frick house after he and the firm of Delano & Aldrich had been invited to submit proposals by the Board of Trustees of The Frick Collection. Pope's winning submission (see fig. 1.19) was to go through some evolution; for example, at this point, the plan was to keep the existing Frick Art Reference Library intact. However, he had already introduced many of the innovations that would form the basis of what was to be executed. Among these important decisions, the following stand out: the enclosure of the previously open courtyard and carriageway; the transformation of the porte-cochere into an enclosed entrance and reception hall; and a round gallery (the executed version is oval) on the north end of the covered court.

By late 1932 most of the eventual design solutions to the transformation from residence to museum had been reached. *A Report on the Plans for Alterations and Additions to The Frick Collection as Submitted by John Russell Pope, September 15, 1932* contains a concise summary of what would be done:

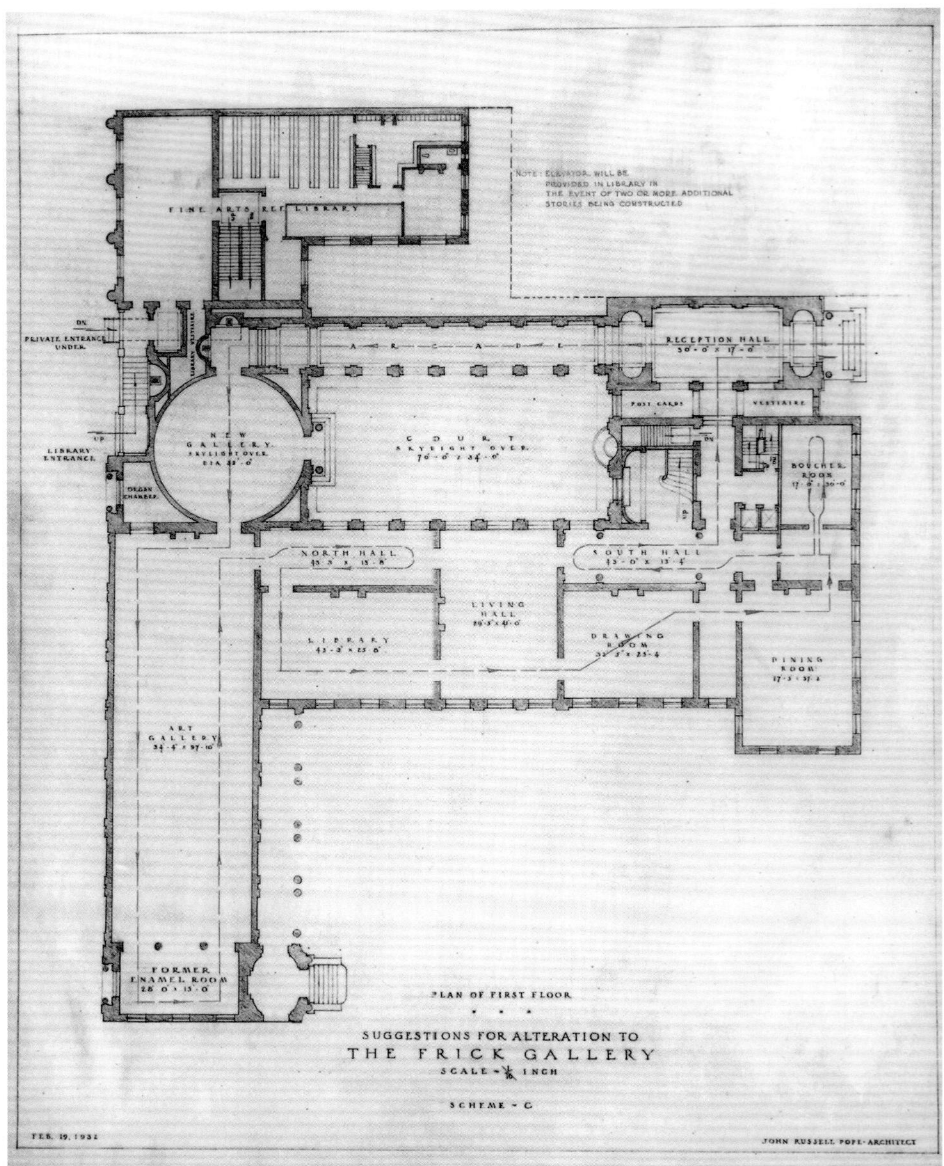

1.19. John Russell Pope's initial plan for proposed addition to the Frick residence to convert it to a museum, Scheme C, February 19, 1932. Courtesy of the Frick Collection/Frick Art Reference Library Archives.

The sketch plans for alterations in the Frick Collection property with a view to opening it to the public are now fairly complete, and, as they stand, solve most of the problems raised in the discussions of the Organization Committee since its inception.

They show: (1) the porte-cochere rebuilt as entrance, reception hall, cloak room, etc.; (2) the court glassed and colonnaded in a style that is harmonious with the architecture of the house; (3) the construction of a suitable room in the space between the house and the Frick Art Reference Library on 71st Street; (4) the construction of a second exhibition room on the site of the present Frick Art Reference Library reading room; (5) the construction of an exhibition room-auditorium on the site of the stacks and office of the present Frick Art Reference Library; (6) the erection of a separate building for the Frick Art Reference Library in which space is found for its future expansion. Final sketch plans for these are appended, as well as a separate report on the library plans.

The situation, as it now stands, is that a solution, as nearly ideal as possible, has been found for (1) entrance to, circulation in, and exit from the Collection, and (2) for the development of the Frick Art Reference Library as an integral part of an architectural whole and providing space for its adequate development in the future. All these matters have been worked out, as desired, by Mr. Pope's office during the summer.[7]

Indeed, looking at the final drawings and the executed building, these solutions remained intact. Another important and fascinating element in the evolution of the institution, particularly the Frick Art Reference Library, was the fact that Clapp and Pope were not the only ones sketching. Helen Clay Frick, who served as a trustee of the corporation and took a particularly proactive role in the undertaking, personally provided some preliminary sketches for the new Frick Art Reference Library. As the library had always been her own project, it is not surprising that she played a great role in its evolution; however, that a trustee and heiress would actually put pencil to paper would seem unusual in the design of American museums of the time[8] (see figs. 1.20 and 1.21).

THE COMPLETED COLLECTION
AND ITS OPENING TO THE PUBLIC

The Frick Collection was opened to the public on December 16, 1935. A press release, issued in a packet on December 11, 1935, introduced the new museum and its mission:

> The Frick Collection, including the works of art and residence at 1 East 70th Street of the late Henry Clay Frick, will open officially this afternoon with a reception between 4 and 7 o'clock to state and city officials, trustees of museums, museum directors and others especially interested in art, as well as people prominent in the life of the city. During the remainder of the week, final details in the organization of the Collection will be completed and on Monday morning, December 16 at 10 o'clock the Collection will be open to the public in accordance with the provisions of Mr. Frick's will. [. . .]
>
> The collection is recognized as one of the world's great treasuries of art. It was assembled by Mr. Frick not only as an art lover himself but for use as part of his home and practically every piece of it fitted into his conception of that home. It was his desire, too, that that conception be carried out in bequeathing the Collection to the public.

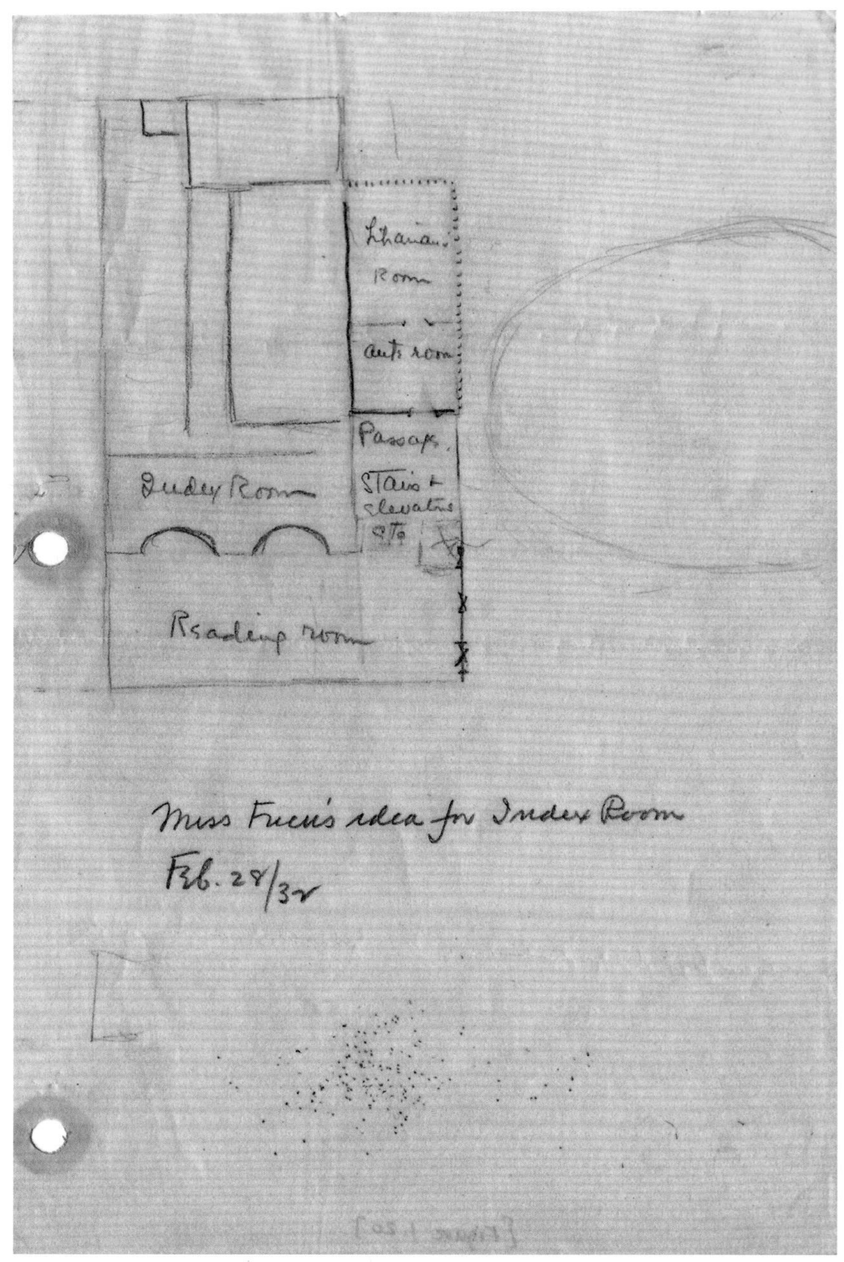

1.20. Helen Clay Frick's idea for Index Room, February 28, 1932. Courtesy of the Frick Collection/Frick Art Reference Library Archives.

In carrying out the provisions of Mr. Frick's will, the Trustees have maintained the residential character of the building. In order, however, to accommodate as many persons as possible at one time in a residential building of limited capacity, the area for the display of the objects of art has been more than doubled by new construction undertaken since the death of Mrs. Frick in 1931.[9]

The press release went on to detail how and when admissions tickets (issued free of charge) would be distributed and how the number of visitors could be controlled. Attached to the above press release were more general information

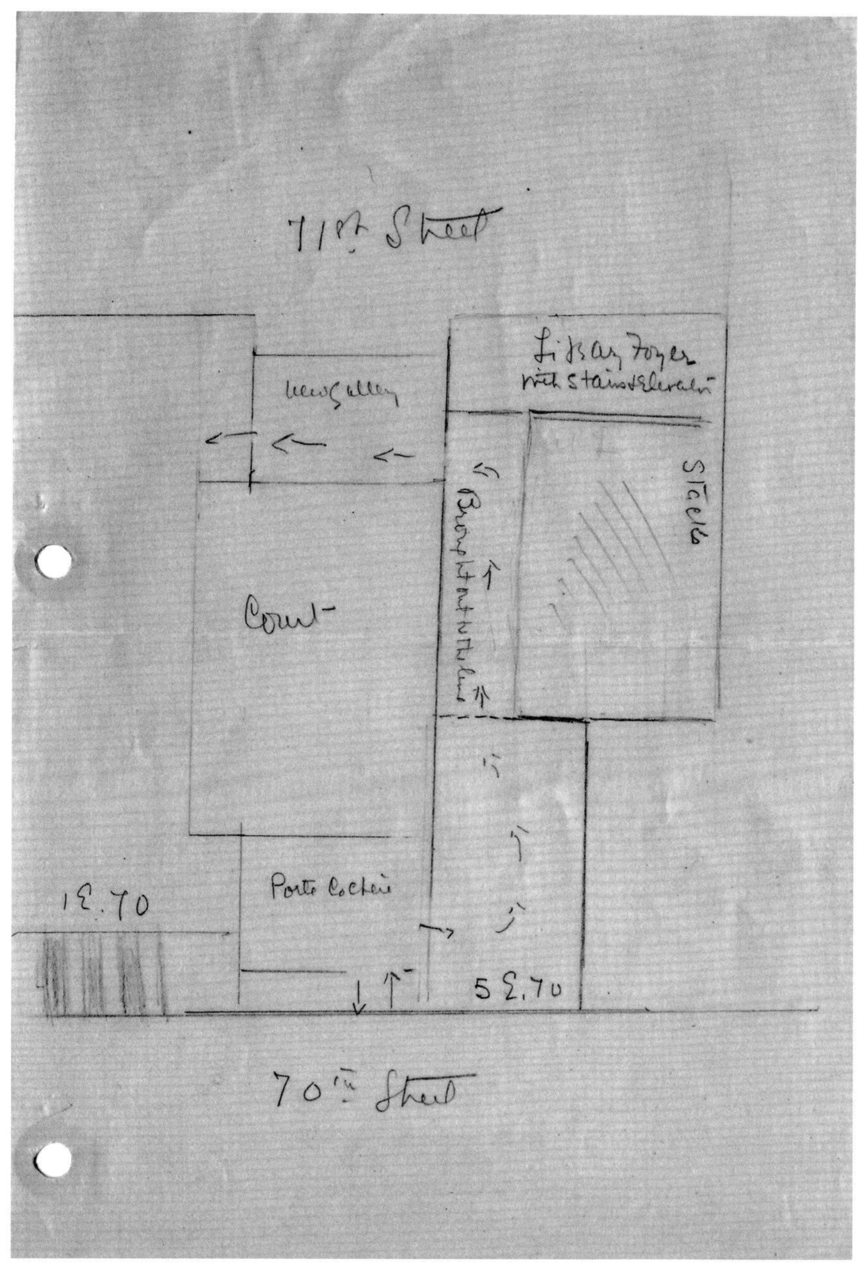

1.21. Sketch by Helen Clay Frick of her idea of possible arrangement for circulation with reference to the Library. Courtesy of the Frick Collection/Frick Art Reference Library Archives.

about the collection, descriptions of the galleries, a prescribed route for the visit (a plan with arrows indicating the path; see fig. 1.22), a checklist of works, rules and regulations, and a series of photographs of the newly opened galleries (see figs. 1.23–1.28).

Although the tight controls on the number of visitors, prescribed circulation, and advance ticket sales are all things of the past at The Frick Collection, a glance at the press photos issued ahead of the opening in 1935 show how little the experience of visiting the collection has changed. The document included in the press packet, under the title of "How to Visit The Frick Collection," stated a few other interesting points. Initially, "The Frick Collection will be open to the public, without charge, week days from 10:00 a.m. to 4:00 p.m. The Collection will be closed on Sunday and on legal holidays." Today, the collection is open on Sundays and, like most museums, is closed on Monday; hours are now 10:00 a.m. to 6:00 p.m. (Tuesday–Saturday), and 11:00 a.m. to 5:00 p.m. (Sunday). Unfortunately, admission to the collection is no longer "without charge." Another unusual policy of The Frick Collection was the provision in this same document regarding admission of children: "Children under 10 years of age will not be admitted and those under 16 must be accompanied by an adult." This policy remains intact to this day. Though to some extent necessitated by the domestic scale of the galleries and the display of decorative arts and furniture in their original or functionally appropriate locations, this policy has also helped to create the unique experience of visiting the Frick and establishing it as a serene haven in the city, unlike any other cultural institution in New York.

Through the use of the same high-quality materials, moldings, proportions and general aesthetic, the trustees and John Russell Pope were so successful in their expansion and transformation of the residence into a public museum that few visitors now realize that the Entrance Reception Hall, Garden Court, East Gallery, Oval Room, and Music Room were not part of the original house. Likewise with what is displayed inside the museum; while the vast majority of the works in The Frick Collection were collected by Henry Clay Frick, the collection continues to grow and acquire paintings, sculptures, and decorative arts. In collection development and acquisitions, as with the museum's architecture, the spirit and aesthetic of Mr. Frick's house and original collection has been carefully maintained.

THE NEW FRICK ART REFERENCE LIBRARY

The new Frick Art Reference Library opened to the public on January 14, 1935. As in its original founding in 1920 through its relocation to its 1924 site to the present, the library was open to all adults with an interest in art, free of charge. The three-floor façade of the library hides the fact that it is actually a twelve-floor building masquerading as an Upper East Side townhouse (see figs. 1.29 and 1.30). Of the twelve floors screened by the façade, eight of them were stack space. The following gains in square footage were made from the original purpose-built library:

Description	1924	1934	Percentage Increase[10]
Reading rooms	1,081 sq. ft.	1,992 sq. ft	84%
Working spaces	1,357 sq. ft.	2,183 sq. ft.	60%
Stacks and other	8,495 sq. ft.	41,875 sq. ft.	392%
Total	10,933 sq. ft.	46,050 sq. ft.	321%

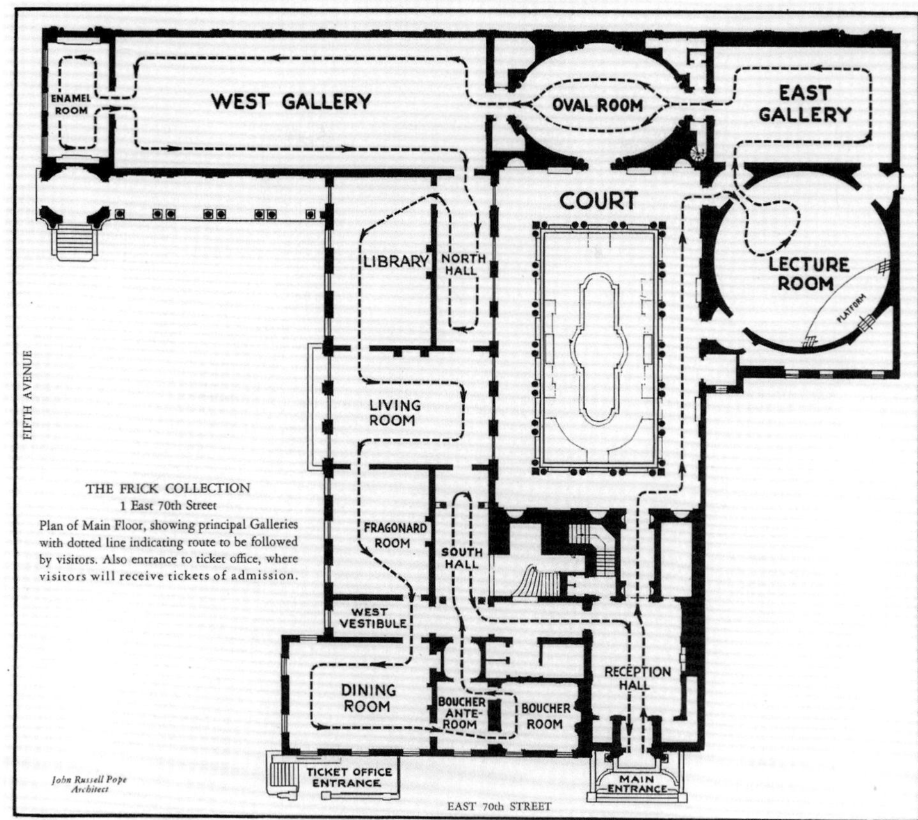

1.22. Plan of The Frick Collection with prescribed path for visit marked with dotted line and arrows, December, 1935. Courtesy of the Frick Collection/Frick Art Reference Library Archives.

As with the collection, the new Frick Art Reference Library was designed to be consonant with the old one. The fresco from the original reading room was relocated to the new one, and the aesthetic of the whole institution—that of Henry Clay Frick's residence—was intact (see fig. 1.31). The new library was intended to allow for the growth, expansion, and development of the collection. This it managed to achieve with a great deal of success; seventy-four years after its opening, although space is now scarce, all of its material is still stored on site (with the exception of some periodicals, which were stored off-site in September 2008). At this point the library houses over a quarter of a million books, the photoarchive now contains over one million images, and the collection of art auction catalogs is one of the largest in the world. Although there has been some rearrangement of nonpublic interior spaces, including the installation of a modern digital laboratory, the 1935 structure continues to house almost the entirety of the library's collections, staff, and services.

THE 1977 ADDITION TO THE FRICK COLLECTION

If few contemporary visitors to The Frick Collection realize that much of the gallery space was not part of Henry Clay Frick's original house, fewer still realize that

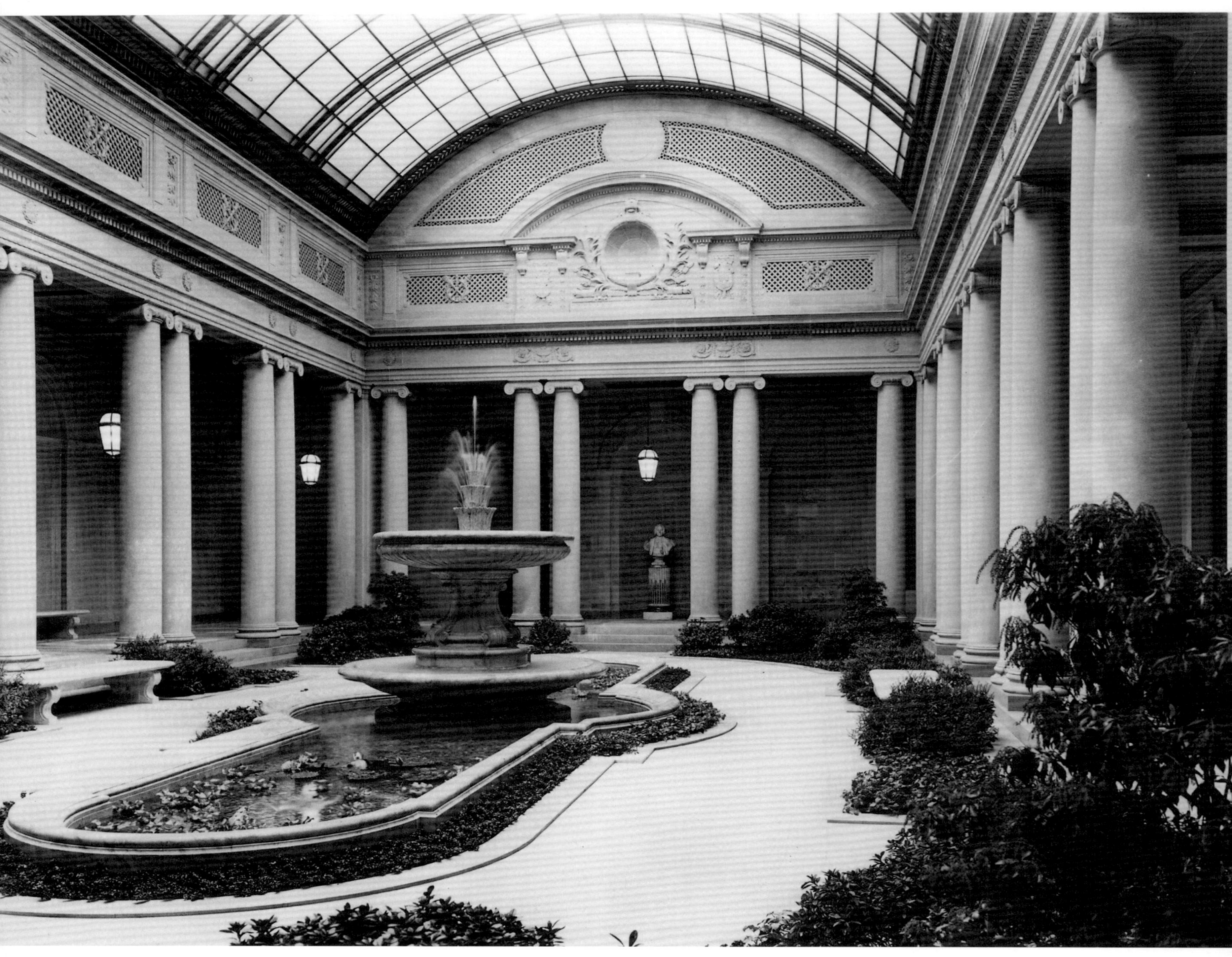

1.23. Garden Court, press photograph for the opening of The Frick Collection, December 1935. Courtesy of the Frick Collection/Frick Art Reference Library Archives.

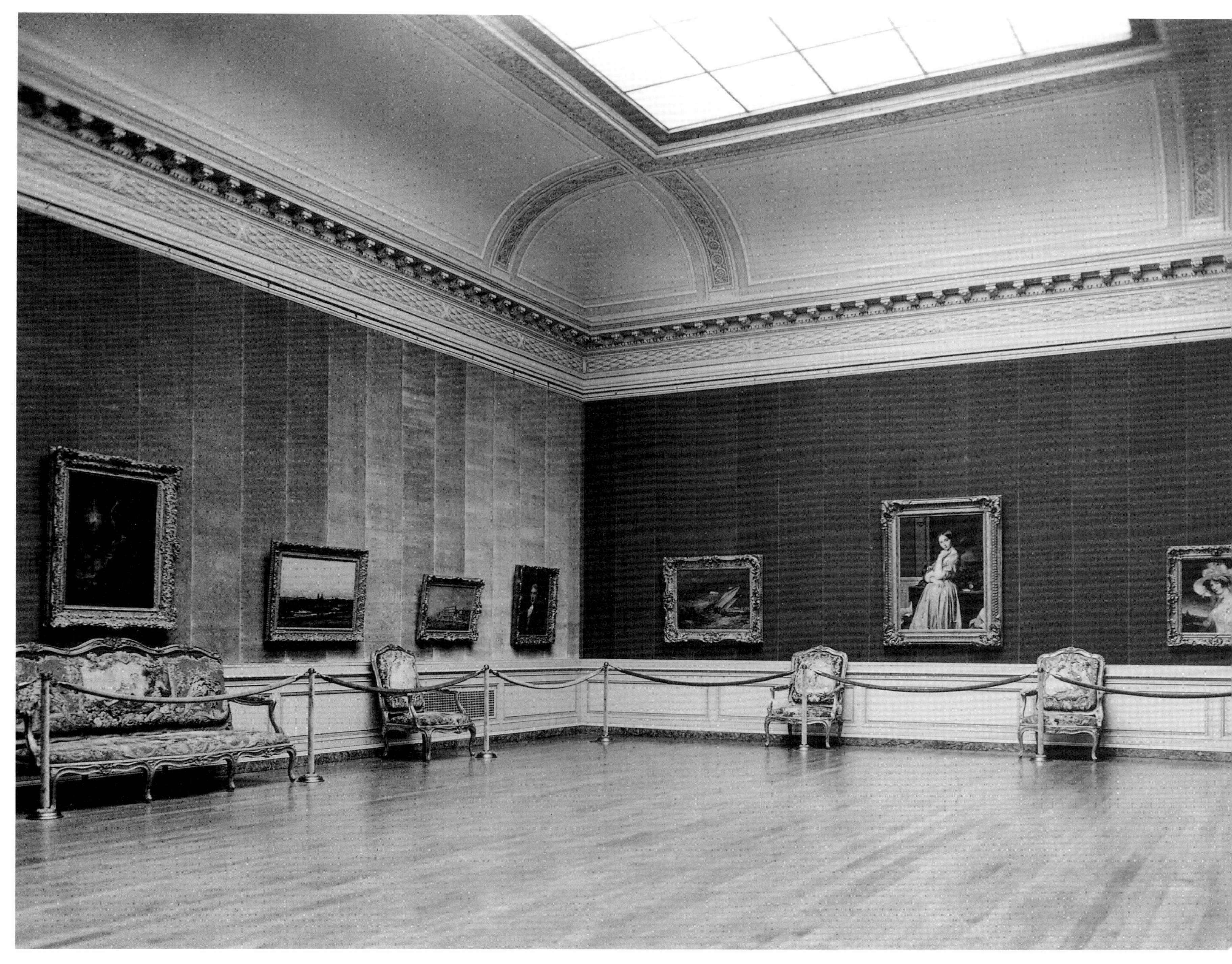

1.24. East Gallery, press photograph
for the opening of The Frick Collection,
December 1935. Courtesy of the Frick
Collection/Frick Art Reference Library Archives.

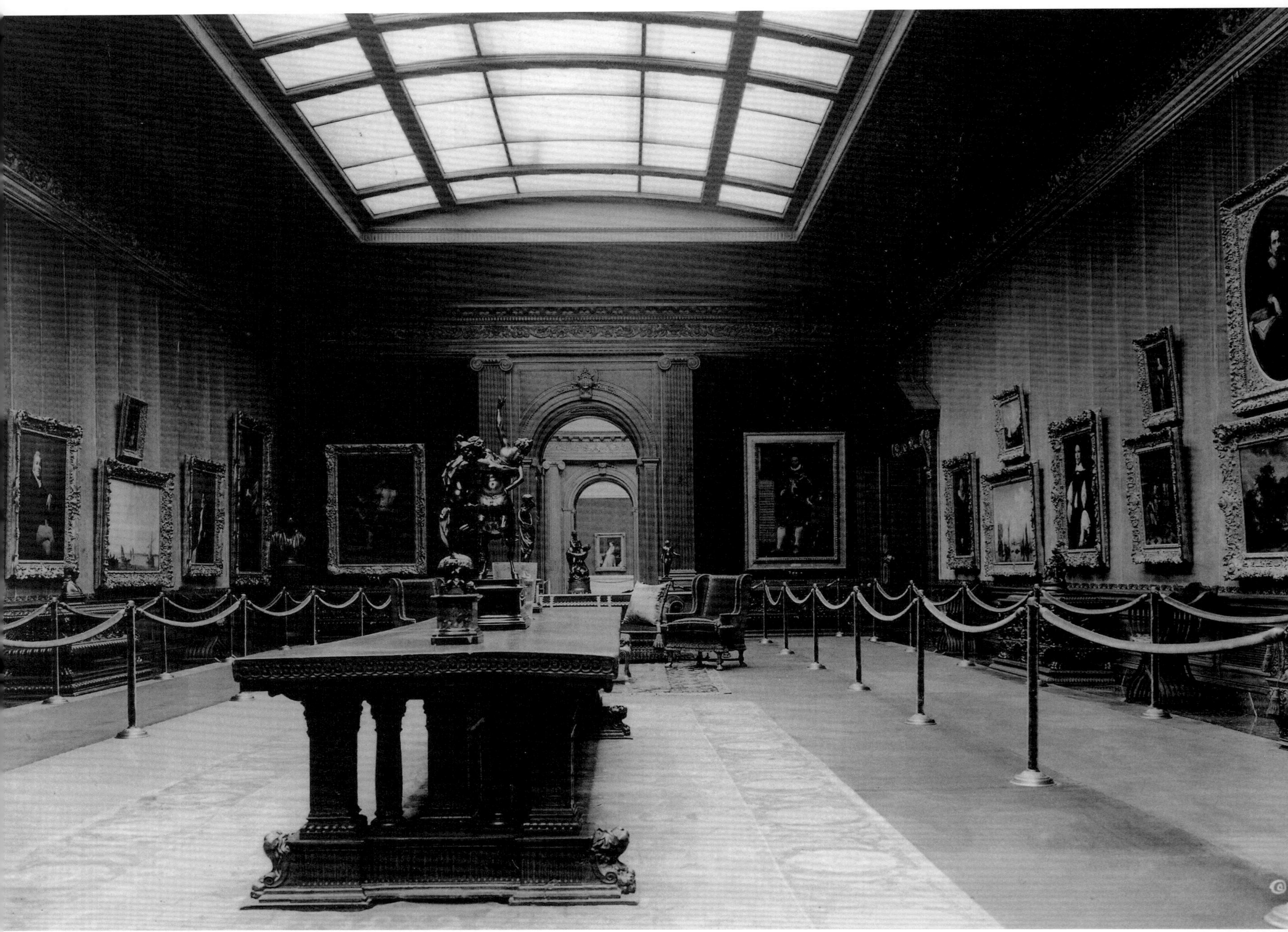

1.27. Picture Gallery (West Gallery
looking toward Oval Room and East
Gallery), press photograph for the
opening of The Frick Collection,
December 1935. Courtesy of the Frick
Collection/Frick Art Reference Library Archives.

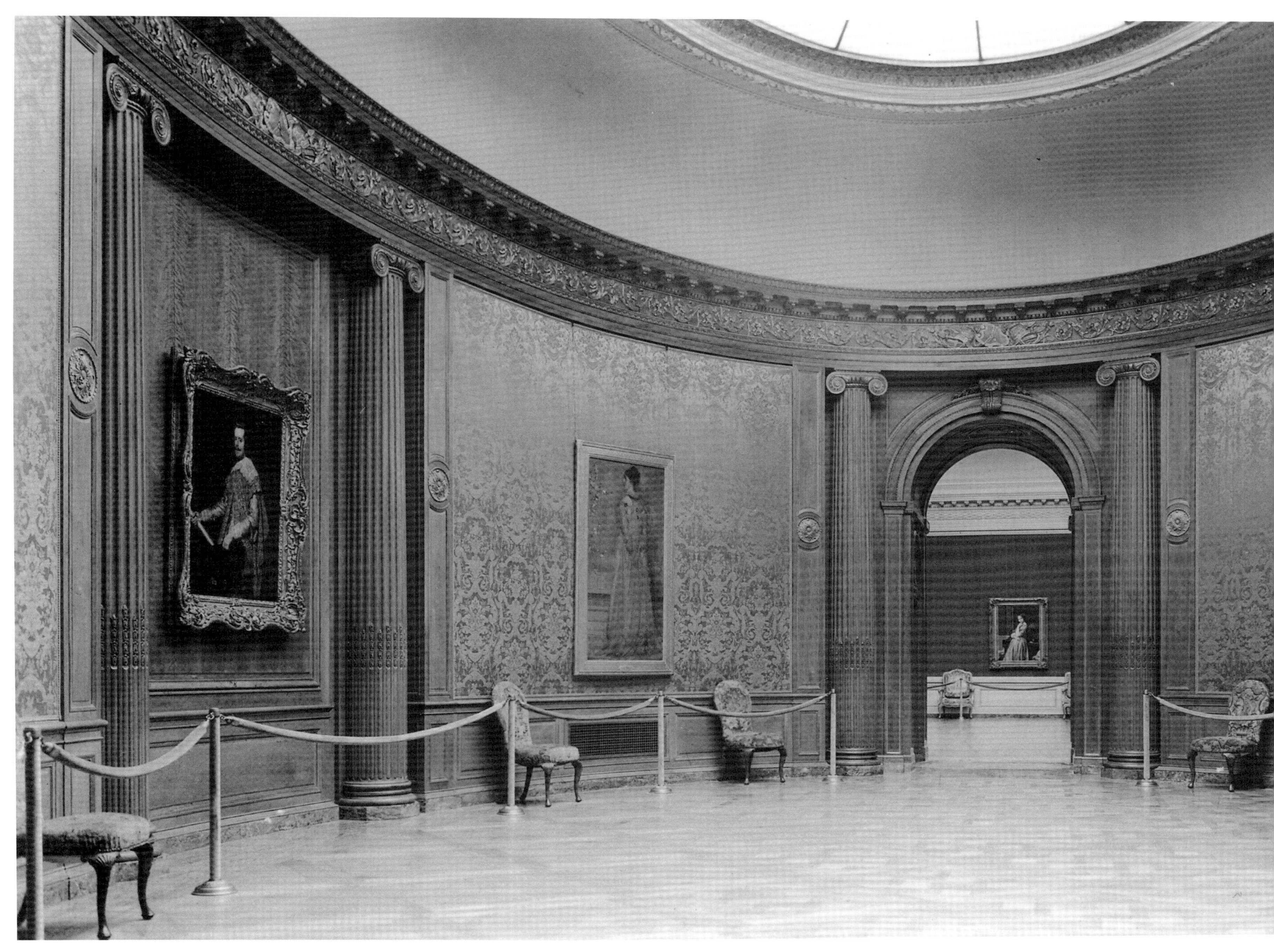

1.25. Oval Room, press photograph for the opening of The Frick Collection, December 1935. Courtesy of the Frick Collection/Frick Art Reference Library Archives.

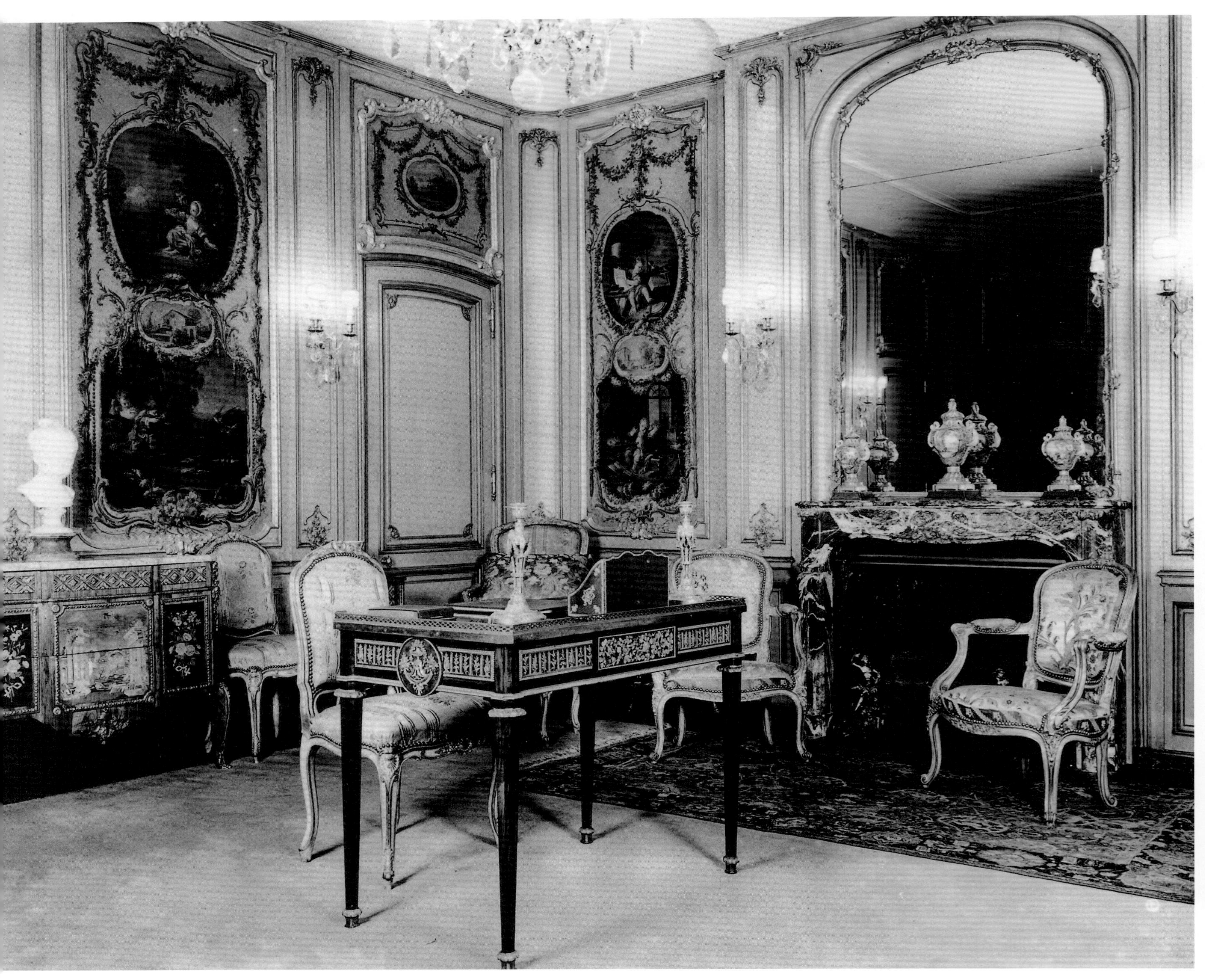

1.26. Boucher Room, press photograph
for the opening of The Frick Collection,
December 1935. Courtesy of the Frick
Collection/Frick Art Reference Library Archives.

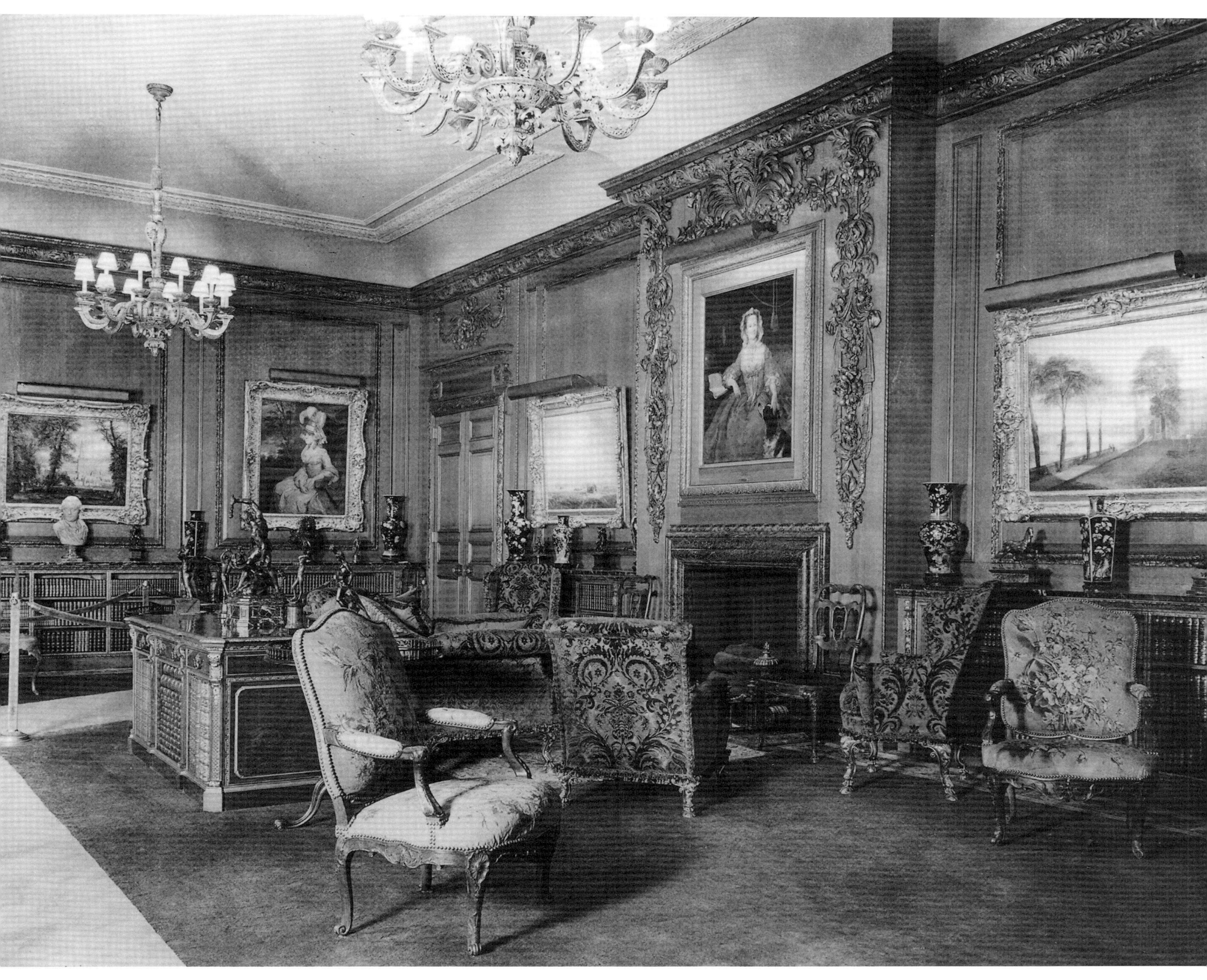

1.28. Mr. Frick's Library, press photograph for the opening of The Frick Collection, December 1935. Courtesy of the Frick Collection/Frick Art Reference Library Archives.

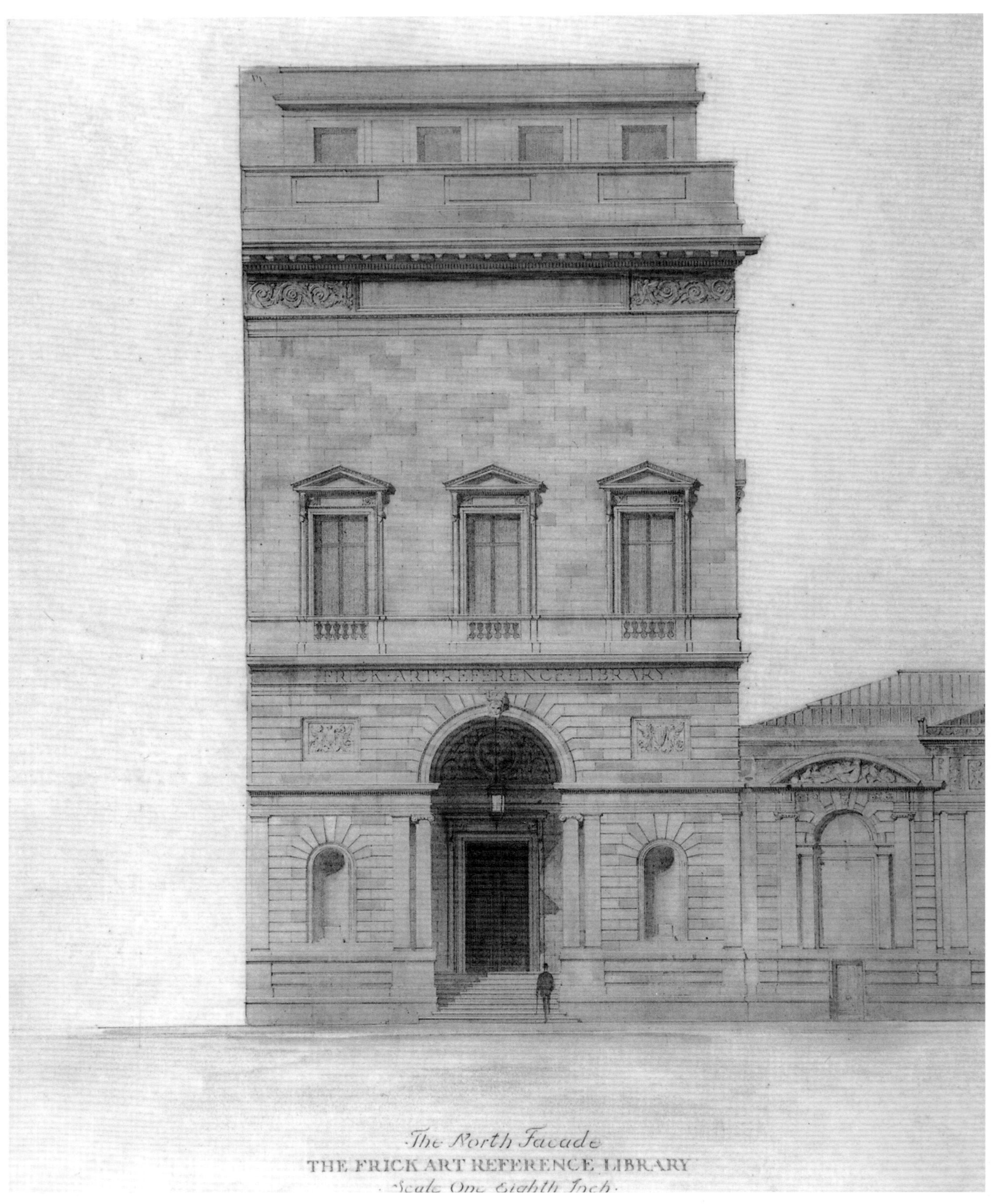
FRICK ART REFERENCE LIBRARY
The North Facade
THE FRICK ART REFERENCE LIBRARY
Scale One Eighth Inch.

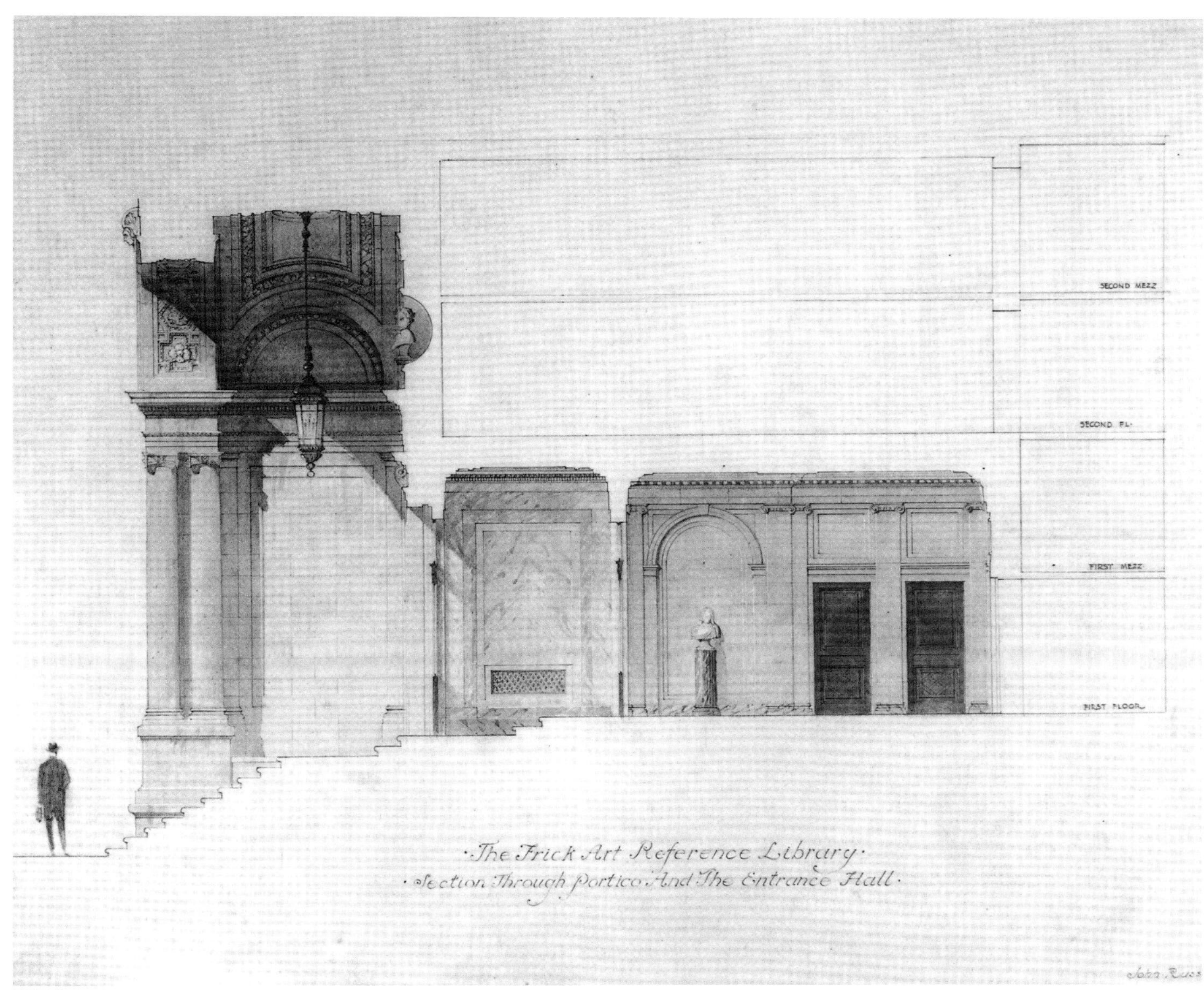

parts of the collection date from the 1970s. The trustees of the collection began acquiring the neighboring properties on East 70th Street in the 1940s and had obtained all three neighboring properties by 1972. These acquisitions allowed for the planning and execution of a modest and aesthetically all but invisible addition of a new wing and a lovely garden, intended for viewing from the street and the interior of the new addition. On the ground floor the new wing was to contain a reception hall, gift shop, and coat room. In the basement it would house two "study rooms," which were soon converted to special exhibition galleries; these galleries are now home to the many successful loan shows, particularly of drawings and smaller works that have become a signature of The Frick Collection. The architects of this project were John Barrington Bayley, Harry Van Dyke, and

FACING PAGE

1.29. Elevation of 71st Street façade (North Façade) of the Frick Art Reference Library, John Russell Pope, May 3, 1933. Courtesy of the Frick Collection/Frick Art Reference Library Archives.

ABOVE

1. 30. Partial north-south section of the Frick Art Reference Library (Section Through Portico and Entrance Hall), John Russell Pope, May 3, 1933. Courtesy of the Frick Collection/Frick Art Reference Library Archives.

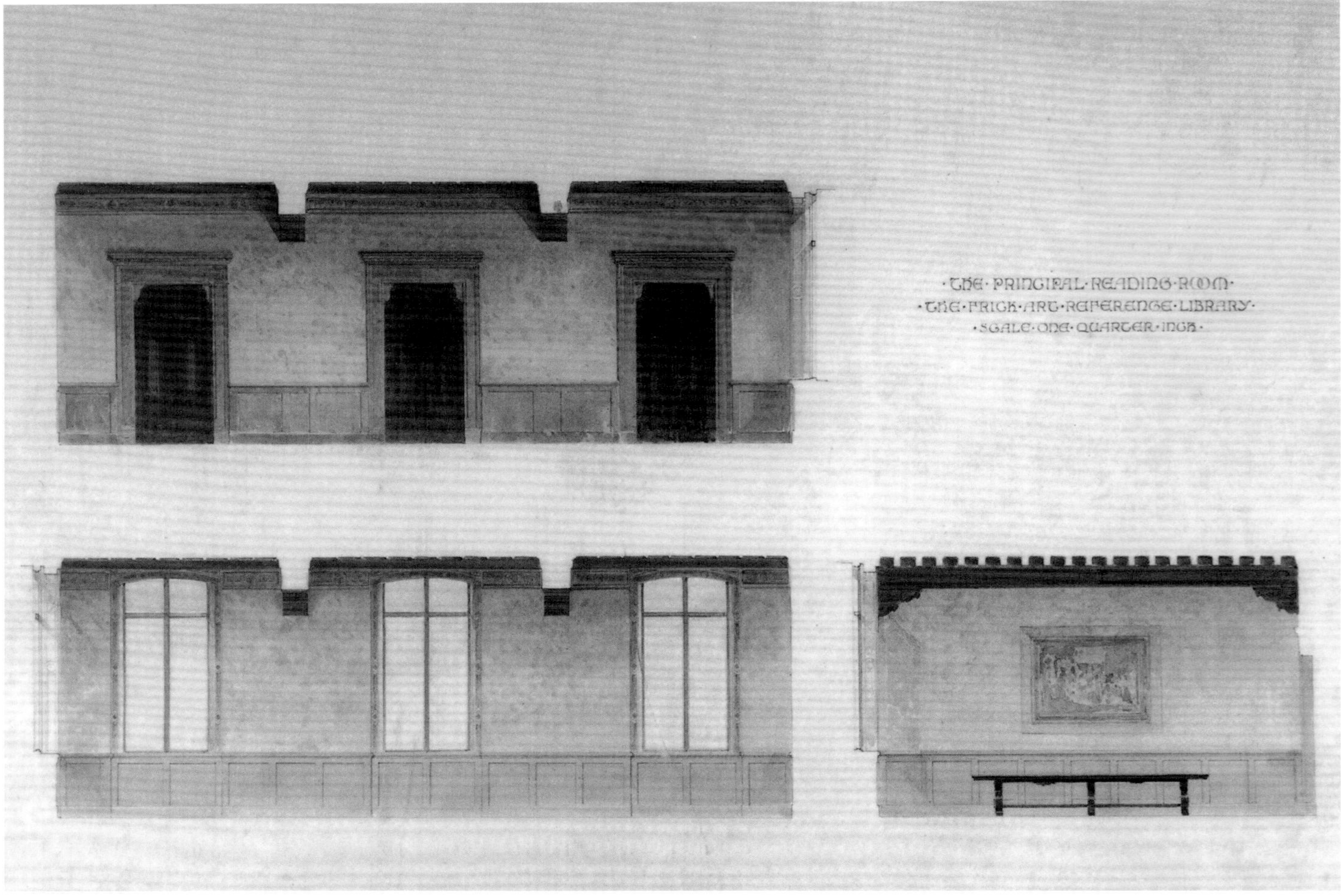

1.31. Interior elevations of the Main Reading Room, Frick Art Reference Library (The Principal Reading Room) John Russell Pope, May 3, 1933.
Courtesy of the Frick Collection/Frick Art Reference Library Archives.

G. Frederick Poehler, and the new wing was opened in 1977 (see fig. 1.32).

The centerpiece of the new addition was the creation of a garden to the east of the Reception Hall. Renowned English garden designer Russell Page was brought in to design this garden. The iron gate bounding the new garden on 70th Street was the original gate to the carriageway in Frick's original residence. The garden, complete with fountain, serves primarily as a backdrop to be viewed from the large round-headed French doors of the Reception Hall or from the sidewalk on 70th Street, and helps to enhance the serene atmosphere of The Frick Collection as a peaceful oasis in the urban chaos of Manhattan (fig. 1.33).

This addition maintains the institutional goal of The Frick Collection of preserving the feel and aesthetic of Henry Clay Frick's original residence and personal tastes rather than reflecting contemporary trends in museum design— a great contrast with most other museums, where new wings are usually designed to demonstrate that institutions are aware of, and have kept pace with, contemporary trends in architecture, design, and museological practice. An example of a similar institution that has a similar history but has opted for the opposite approach can be found at the Morgan Library and Museum, which recently completed a major expansion (designed by Renzo Piano) that creates a stark contrast with the original McKim, Mead & White designed Pierpont Morgan Library building. However, this conservatism in design is exactly what has allowed The Frick Collection to maintain its unique identity and to stay true to the vision of its founder, who so clearly spelled out his intentions and desires. Although the phrase "invisible museum" has entered the discussion of art museum architecture and design only recently (see Chapters 5 and 7 for further discussion of this concept), it is perhaps only at The Frick Collection where true "invisibility" of a museum has actually been achieved. The spirit and vision of Frick as a collector and the way he intended his art to be experienced are very, very well preserved for the general public today. This clear and complete adherence to mission and the intent of the collection's founder is rare indeed in the world of art museums.

THE FRICK COLLECTION'S MOVEMENT INTO THE FUTURE

Though The Frick Collection is committed to preserving the spirit and aesthetic of Henry Clay Frick's house and collection, it is also a living institution; it continues, as permitted by Mr. Frick's will, to acquire works of art, to reinstall and rotate paintings and objects, and to mount temporary loan exhibitions. Although the collection has earned a place in the New York museum world for its qualities not only as a sanctuary from the noise and bustle of the city but also from the constant state of flux in the art world, it cannot remain entirely static. When asked about her vision for the future of The Frick Collection, Director Anne L. Poulet first discussed the notion of responsibility: "In planning for the future of an institution it is important to keep an eye on its underlying financial health; in adding space or staff, adding to the endowment to support these efforts is essential. Trouble results in the mania to add new things. An institution must have the financial underpinnings to guarantee sustainability. Better to do less with sound financial support than to do more on shaky foundations." According to Ms. Poulet, the very will that dictated so much of what would comprise the collection also gave her a great deal of freedom: "Mr. Frick did not try to control the institution from beyond the grave, he left that to the Trustees—giving them the responsibility to maintain the museum's personality."

With this freedom granted her, Ms. Poulet, a former curator of decorative arts and sculpture at the Museum of Fine Arts, Boston (1980–1999), has sought to advance the decorative arts, always an integral part of Mr. Frick's collections, which have been previously somewhat neglected. To this end funds have been raised to endow a curatorship in the decorative arts. This effort has not been imposed from the top but is, rather, a natural area to expand, as The Frick Collection has significant holdings in this area, and it is supported by the entire curatorial staff. To this end the

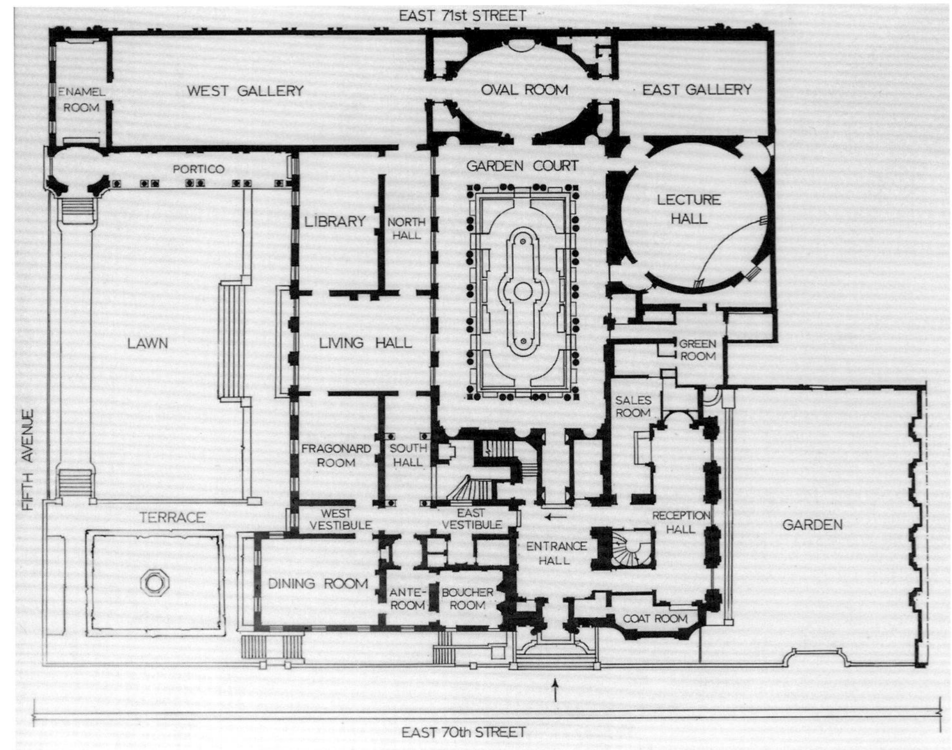

1.32. Plan of The Frick Collection as it now stands, after addition of Reception Hall and Russell Page Garden. Courtesy of the Frick Collection/Frick Art Reference Library Archives.

collection has won a challenge grant (four to one) from the National Endowment of the Humanities. A good curator in this position would not only "raise the profile of the institution in the decorative arts community, but would also attract a whole world of supporters among decorative arts scholars and collectors."

Regarding the Frick's virtually unique policy that excludes children under the age of ten, Ms. Poulet states:

> We intend to continue this policy; it contributes to the atmosphere people treasure most about the Frick—the "favorite museum," "serene, tranquil, oasis in the city." It is a tradeoff, but we feel by prohibiting children under 10, furniture can be exhibited without platforms, fragile objects without vitrines; we thus maintain the domestic atmosphere of a house. This is not possible with strollers and small children running around. On the other hand, we have hired a new head of education (from the Metropolitan Museum of Art) and are planning to expand educational programming—more on the Internet, CDs, and other virtual methods of access; more sensitive and focused programming for all age groups. There are also other demographics that we must pay attention to: the elderly, artists, people who work. We hope to bring back Friday evening hours, which will be pay-as-you-wish; we are investigating special programs in the evenings for young professionals and other groups. We can expand educational programming while remaining faithful to our mission and the unique atmosphere of the museum.

Group visits are not permitted during daytime hours, yet we have been experiencing a spike in requests. So we are accommodating groups on Monday afternoons (when the collection is closed to the general public). We are thrilled people want to come—the challenge is how to guarantee a good experience for them without compromising the experience of others— without changing the atmosphere of the collection.

Ms. Poulet attributes much of the success she has had in preserving the feel and spirit of the collection to this:

> The Board of Trustees has never made it a priority to increase attendance. The Frick has created a niche for exhibitions featuring important artists who are not well known in the United States, and for exhibitions that are not shown in other venues. There is no pressure to mount blockbuster exhibitions; there is a respect for the type of focused exhibitions and high standards of quality that the Frick strives to attain. This is all the result of the fact that there is complete agreement among members of the staff and members of the board on the standards of excellence of the place, and no one has ever tried to compromise these values. Museum visitors, perfect strangers, feel this without knowing why.

This rare and fortunate situation leads to the question of both short-term and long-term goals and agendas for the further development and expansion of the institution:

> In the short term we must conserve and upgrade the existing building. The Fragonard Room has just undergone the installation of new lighting, new wiring, and refinishing of surfaces. It looks great but is so subtle that it is not visible to most visitors. The skylights need to be replaced, particularly those that date back to 1914. It is important to carry out these projects gradually, so as never to have to close the entire collection (as the Pierpont Morgan Library had to do during their recent restoration). We need to upgrade public amenities: the restrooms must be brought up to compliance with the Americans with Disabilities Act codes; the entrance will need to be reconfigured, the bookshop is too small, presenting security problems, and coat check and restrooms are inadequate for current attendance.
>
> Reconfiguring and adding spaces comes later. The library presents many opportunities and challenges. First the definition of the library, its use and needs, has completely changed due to advances in areas such as digitization and institutional development such as the creation of the Center for the History of Collecting in America. Space can be obtained through moving certain parts of the collections that can be digitized to off-site storage, keeping on site those materials that are unique, fragile or archival. The study of the history of collecting increases the use of archives and may

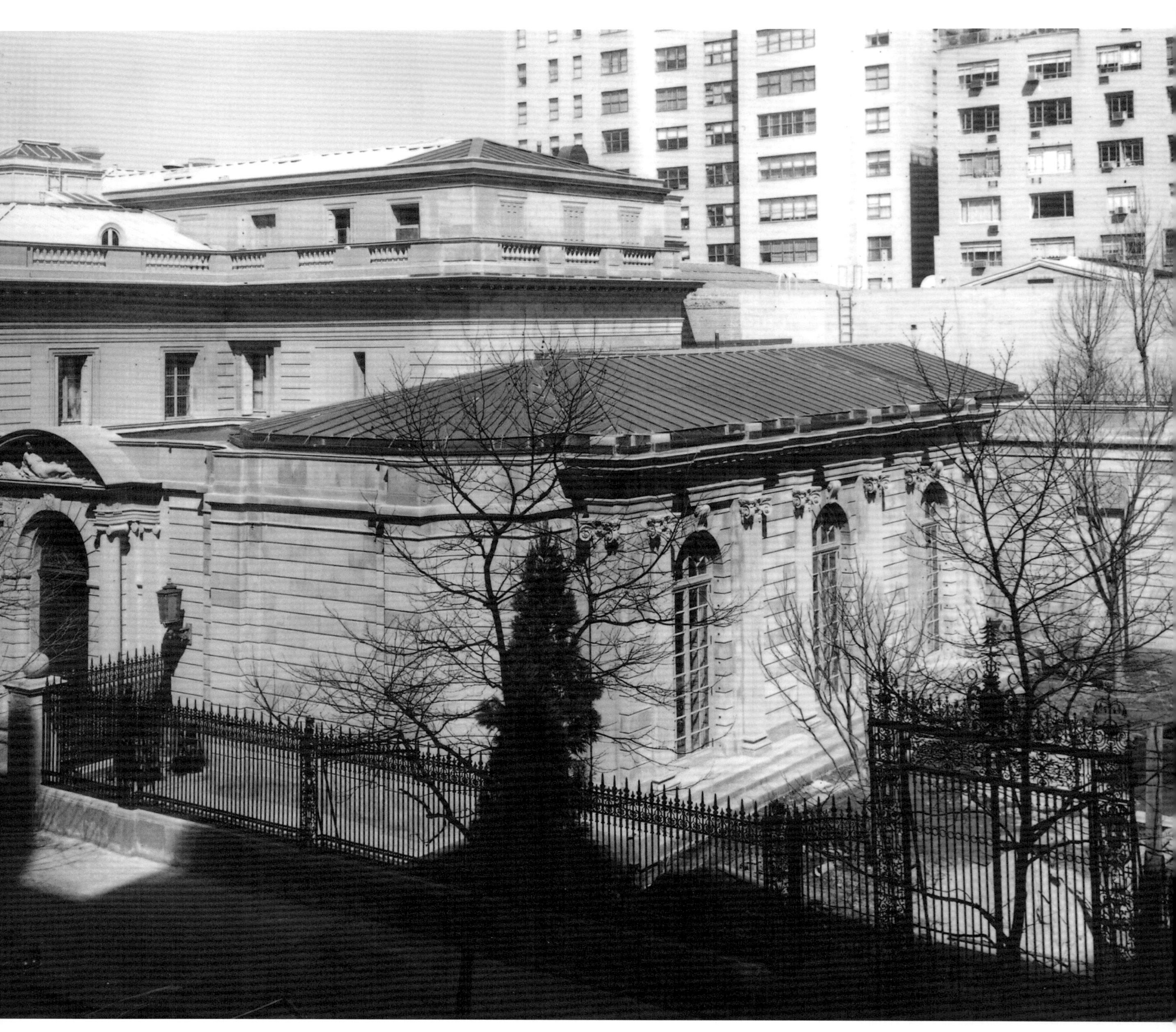

attract the donations of more archival collections to the Library. We need to find ways to house staff and fellows who work with these collections. This will lead to one of the most exciting, and potentially changed, parts of The Frick Collection.

Discussion of change at a place as beloved and historically specific as the Frick always begs the question of how one addresses the preservation of the spirit and institutional personality of Henry Clay Frick's original plans and intentions while staying current with important trends and developments in museology and museum design. To this question Ms. Poulet responds:

> That, in fact, is the challenge in running an institution like The Frick Collection, with such a well defined value system and such architectural distinction. How do we improve handicapped access, visitor amenities and meet expectations regarding exhibitions while preserving our unique atmosphere? We are now studying these very issues; we have completed a strategic plan and are looking at space implications. I have told the trustees, and it is true, that this institution has changed constantly. It is not if you change, but how you change that counts; John Russell Pope, who designed the addition to the home in 1935, is a perfect example. It is a tribute to both Pope as an architect and to the trustees who understood the difference between a museum and a house, that in making the addition, they were able to maintain a domestic feeling in the building. The key is to preserve that feeling—using the same noble materials that Frick used within a simple design. Unfortunately, the 1977 addition to the Frick had neither that simplicity nor the best materials and has caused some problems, but it is now part of the history of the institution.

> Important changes can be made that will be imperceptible to the public. Meeting code requirements, Americans with Disabilities Act compliance, better spaces for special exhibitions (the current galleries in the basement were intended as educational spaces) are all priorities. The landmark status of the building and block limit options, but the vision of Henry Clay Frick continues to give direction to the next steps. Further integration of the library with the collection can help spatially and programmatically. This did not happen previously, owing to animosity between John D. Rockefeller, Jr. and Helen Clay Frick. A greater interconnection could be achieved through creating needed new office space for the Library and the museum. This would allow us to open part of the second floor of the original house to the public as John Russell Pope and Helen Clay Frick originally intended to do. The second floor has smaller, more intimate, galleries ideal for the display of decorative arts and cabinet pictures.

In summing up, Ms. Poulet concisely stated what she felt was most important: "Maintaining the character and feel of the house." Her statements certainly resonate with the history and spirit of the collection and its founder.

1.33. View of the Frick Collection from the southeast with the 1977 addition and Russell Page Garden. Courtesy of the Frick Collection/Frick Art Reference Library Archives.

THE MENIL COLLECTION

"The building is to be of an intimate human scale rather than monumental, constructed of materials in accord with such a scale and the site surroundings. A balanced interplay between exterior and interior spaces will exist, with natural light used as a source of illumination in most areas. Spaces will not overwhelm the art displayed and will provide an environment more domestic than institutional in nature."

— Excerpt from "Project Information,"
December 16, 1981, Menil Archives

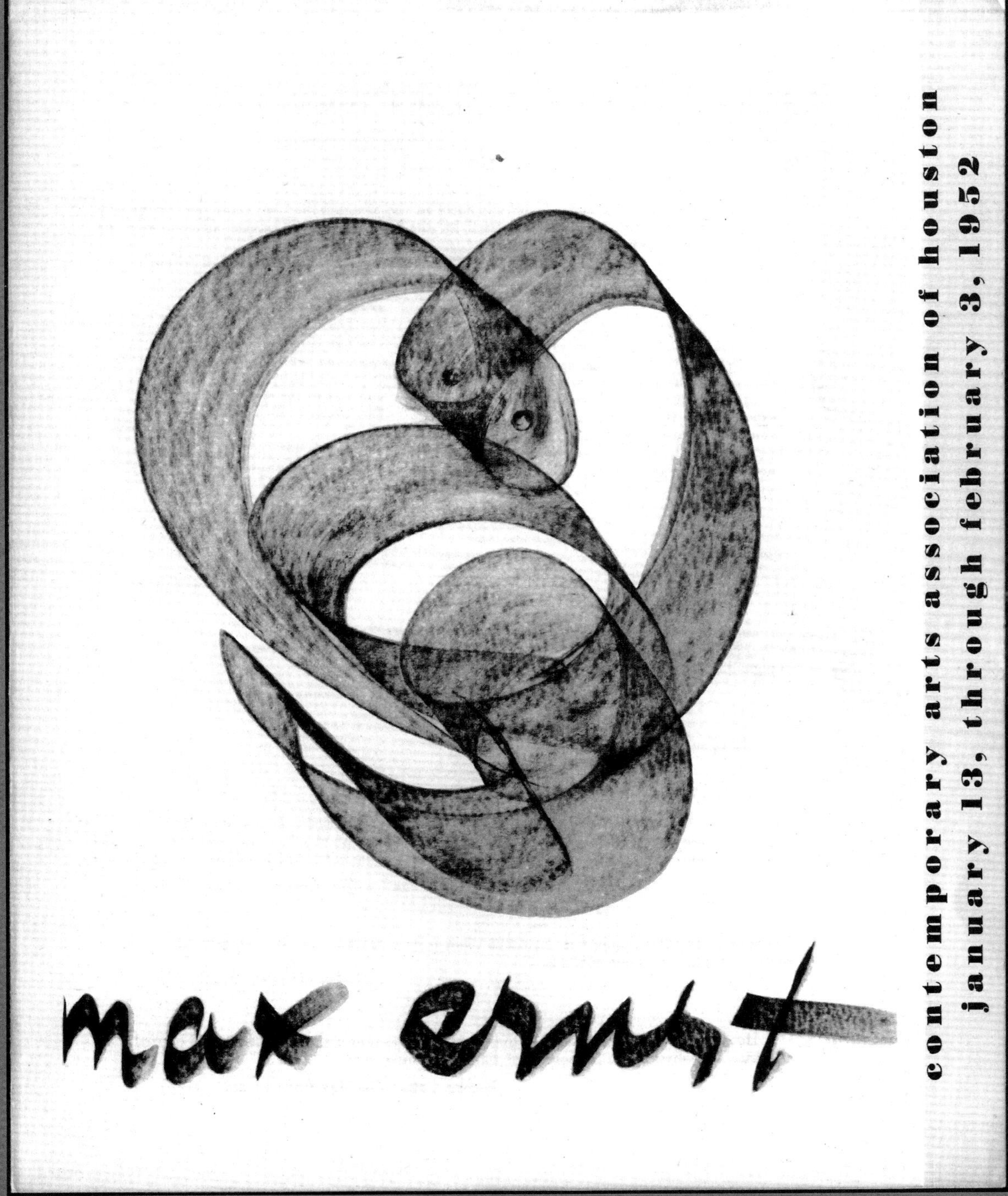

2.1 Exhibition catalog cover from
"Max Ernst," Jan. 13-Feb. 3, 1952,
Contemporary Arts Museum, Houston.
Courtesy of the Menil Archives, The Menil
Collection.

THE MENIL COLLECTION AT A GLANCE

Corporate name:	The Menil Collection
Address:	1515 Sul Ross Street, Houston, Texas 77006
Architect:	Renzo Piano
Opening date:	1987
Addition:	Cy Twombly Gallery
Architect of addition:	Renzo Piano
Opening date of addition:	1995
Addition:	Richmond Hall (Dan Flavin Installation Gallery)
Opening date of addition:	1996 (reuse of grocery store from 1930s)
Collecting scope:	Twentieth century, ancient, Byzantine, African, Oceanic, and the Americas
Related institutions:	The Rothko Chapel
	The Byzantine Fresco Chapel Museum
Amenities:	Bookshop

JOHN AND DOMINIQUE DE MENIL: THEIR ART COLLECTION AND PATRONAGE OF HOUSTON

Like that of Henry Clay Frick, the fortune of John (born Jean, 1904–1973) and Dominique (1908–1997) de Menil came from the energy industry. Where Mr. Frick's company dealt in coked coal, the fuel of the nineteenth century, the Menils' business dealt in the fuel of the twentieth century: oil. Dominique de Menil (née Schlumberger) was the daughter of the inventor of important oil-prospecting technologies. After their marriage, Dominique's parents hired their son-in-law to lead the family business (Schlumberger, still a leader in oil exploration technology). The business of oil prospecting sent the Menils (both of whom were French) to many parts of the world, including Eastern Europe and Latin America, before eventually landing them in what would become their permanent home of Houston, Texas.[1]

2.2. Installation view of "Mark Rothko," exhibition at the Contemporary Arts Museum, Houston, Sept. 5–Oct. 6, 1957. Photo by Maurice Miller. Courtesy of the Menil Archives, The Menil Collection.

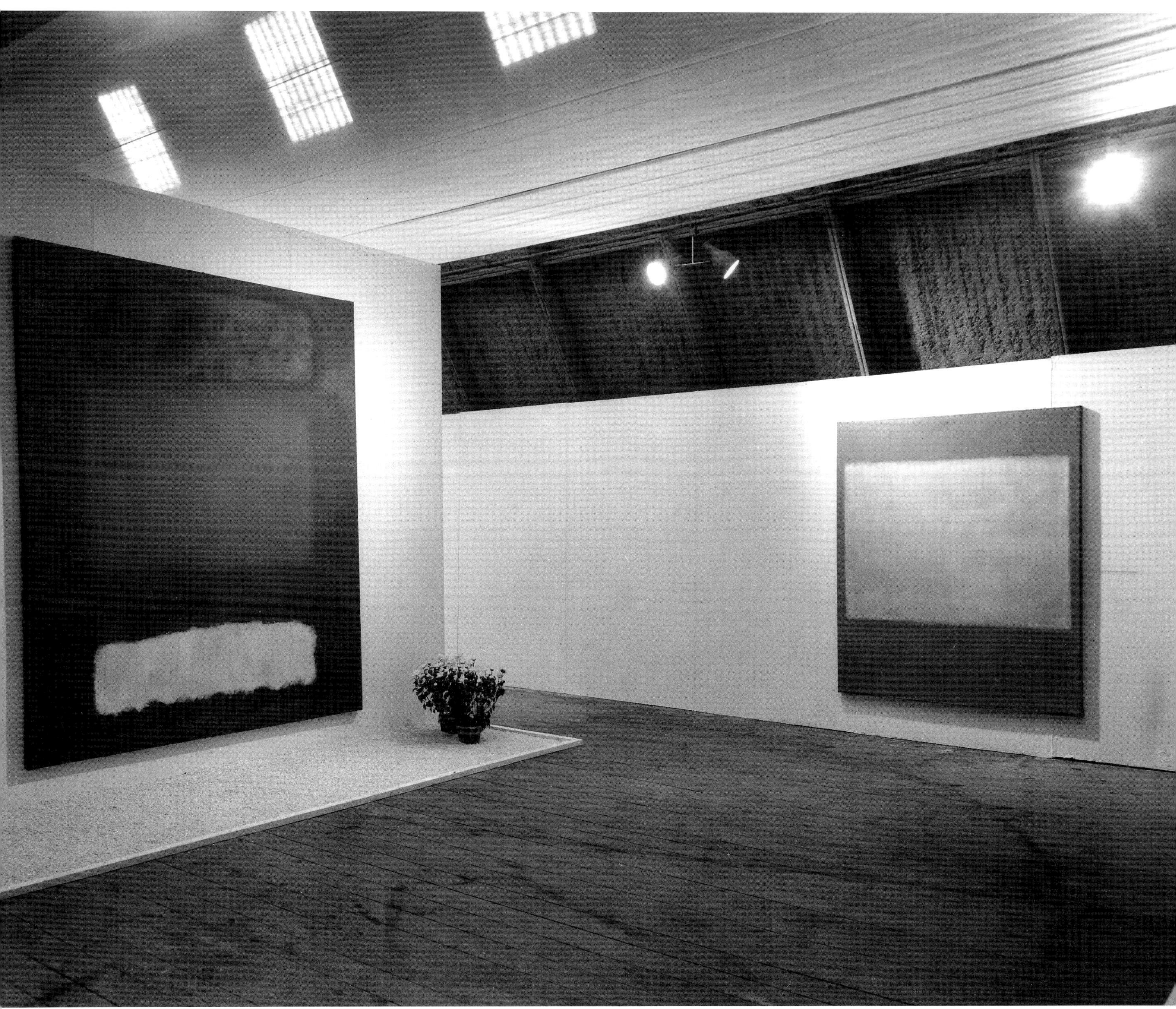

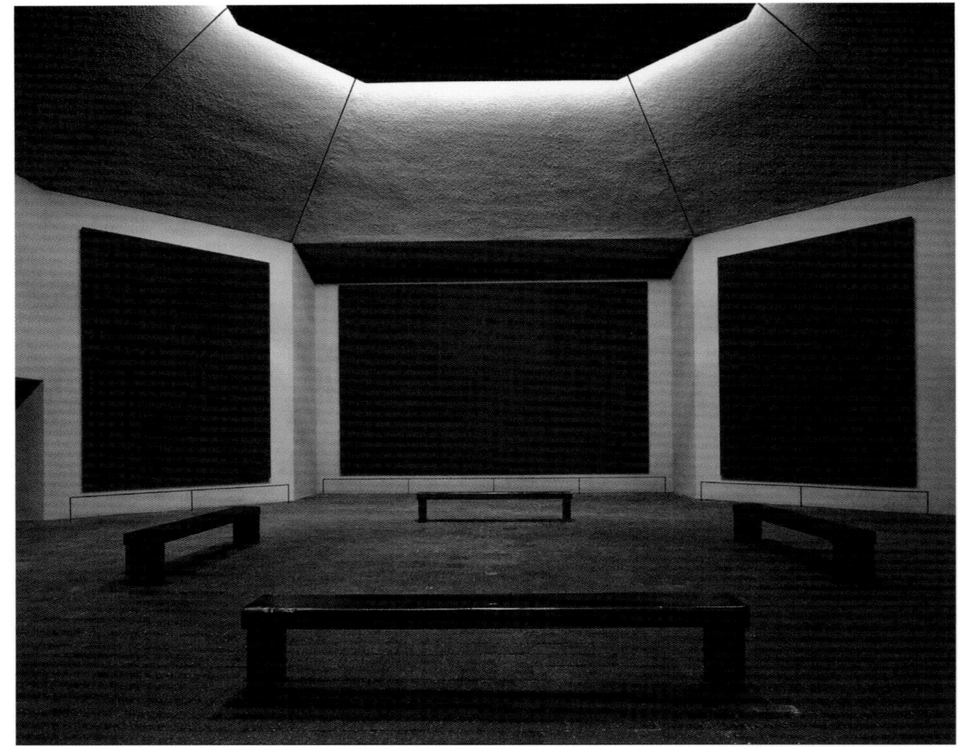

2.3. Rothko Chapel, interior view facing north. Courtesy of the Rothko Chapel. Photo by Hickey-Robertson, Houston. © 1988 Kate Rothko Prizel & Christopher Rothko/Artists Rights Society (ARS), New York.

Again, like Henry Clay Frick, the Menils became avid art collectors relatively early in their careers. However, the similarity between these two collectors and their collections ends with a fortune from the energy sector and a passion for collecting in the arts. Where Mr. Frick hired Thomas Hastings, the great architect of the Eastern establishment, to design his home in New York, the Menils hired Philip Johnson to design what would be one of the first houses in the so-called International Style in Texas (built in 1951). The Menils filled this house with what would become one of the country's best collections of modern and contemporary art. Additionally, they collected heavily in African, ancient, and Byzantine art. Although these areas of collecting might at first seem very disparate, they not only worked well together aesthetically, but were also often the types of art championed by the modern and contemporary artists whom the Menils favored (the fascination that the cubists and surrealists had with "primitive art" is well documented).

John and Dominique de Menil were not satisfied to merely collect great works for their own home, however. Between the first exhibition of their works at the Contemporary Arts Museum, Houston (where the Menils were extremely active, serving on the board as well as sponsoring many exhibitions and contributing works to them) and the opening of their own museum in 1987, the Menils organized and/or loaned works from their collection to over 160 exhibitions.[2] Most of these exhibitions were held in local Houston venues, and they often were the first major exhibitions of various twentieth-century artists and themes in the Houston area. Further, the Menils were major contributors to many of these institutions, giving

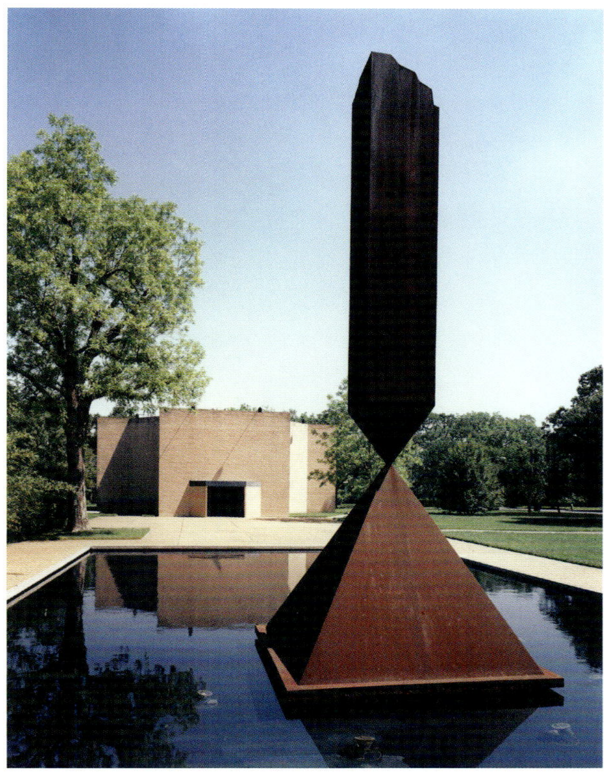

2.4. Rothko Chapel, Houston; exterior view with Barnett Newman, *Broken Obelisk*, 1963–1967. Courtesy of the Rothko Chapel. Photo by Paul Hester, Houston. © 2009 The Barnett Newman Foundation, New York/Artists Rights Society (ARS), New York.

the land for what would become the University of St. Thomas (later recommending that the university use Philip Johnson as architect) and founding the Art History Department at Rice University (triggering the foundation of the Institute for the Arts and the Rice Museum). Here are just a few representative exhibitions from this period:

- Max Ernst: Jan. 13–Feb. 3, 1952—Contemporary Arts Museum, Houston
- Mark Rothko: Sept. 5–Oct. 6, 1957—Contemporary Arts Museum, Houston
- Totems Not Taboo: An Exhibition of Primitive Art: Feb. 26–April 23, 1959—
  Cullinan Hall, Museum of Fine Arts, Houston
- Paul Klee: April 19–May 22, 1960—Museum of Fine Arts, Houston
- Rene Magritte in America: Feb 2–Mar. 1, 1961—Museum of Fine Arts, Houston
- Humble Treasures: An Exhibition of Tribal Art from Negro Africa: Oct. 15, 1965–
  Feb 20, 1966—Jones Hall Gallery, University of St. Thomas, Houston

The list goes on. Thus the Menils created a local audience for the art that they collected. Through close work with the local universities and art departments, they also sought to create a local public that was well educated in the arts.

Originally desiring to build a chapel for the University of St. Thomas, the devoutly Roman Catholic yet ecumenical John and Dominique de Menil commissioned abstract expressionist painter Mark Rothko to paint a series of canvases to adorn the chapel's interior. Philip Johnson, the architect of both Menil homes and the university, was to be the chapel's designer. Although the chapel would indeed be built, it did not proceed as planned. Disagreements between the Menils and the University of St. Thomas over issues of traditionalism versus modernism in design would lead to a break between the Menils and the university they helped to create. The chapel was transformed into a nonsectarian interfaith institution, built by the Menils on their own land, and it would eventually be incorporated as its own institution, run by its own board (though it is part of the "campus" of the current Menil Collection, it is a separate corporate entity). Conflict was not limited to issues of patronage and governorship, however.

The relationship between Mark Rothko's painting and Philip Johnson's architecture caused conflict between artist and architect. The Menils would side with Rothko, causing Johnson to leave the project in 1967.[3] Local architects Howard Barnstone and Eugene Aubry were brought in to complete the architectural design of the project, which they adapted from Johnson's original plans. Johnson was later brought back to complete the entrance and to design the reflecting pool around Barnett Newman's *Broken Obelisk*, a sculpture the Menils acquired in 1968, dedicated to Martin Luther King, Jr. and sited in front of the entrance to the chapel (figs. 2.3 and 2.4). The Rothko Chapel would be the last major project that John and Dominique de Menil would work on together, as John would pass away in 1973.

ENVISIONING THE MENIL COLLECTION

As early as the time of John de Menil's death, Dominique de Menil was thinking about the future of their collection. In *The Houston Post*'s obituary of John, published on Sunday, June 10, 1973, Dominique is quoted as saying:

> As long as I live I will keep certain paintings in our Paris, New York and Houston houses; however, the collection goes to the foundation. What will we do with it? We will circulate it, lend it, make it completely alive. I've seen so many collections that are not displayed correctly. This is what happened to the remarkable legacy of the Cone sisters in Baltimore until recently. Every institution goes through ups and downs. We can lend works for five years, even 10 years and will place no restrictions but we won't give all for nothing. We hope the work will serve as an inspiration.
>
> We are definitely not contemplating building a big museum. What we contemplate is a storage center. We want to keep everything visible when it is not on exhibit elsewhere. [4]

The same article mentions that "rumors have been rampant concerning a new museum structure to be built possibly near the Rothko chapel by the great Louis Kahn." Both Mrs. de Menil's quotation and the rampant rumors were partially, but

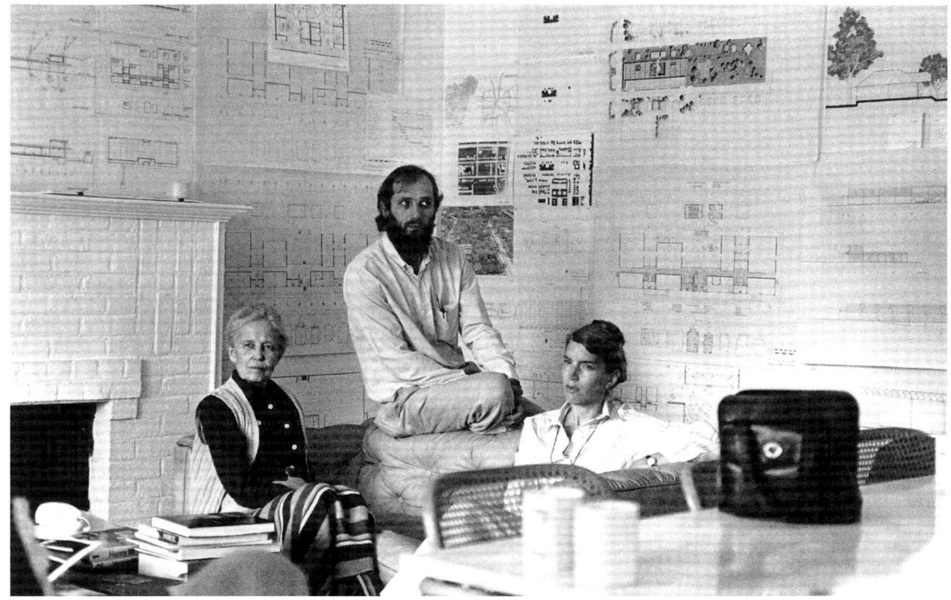

2.5. Dominique de Menil, Renzo Piano, and Kathryn Davidson at presentation of plans. Courtesy of the Menil Archives, The Menil Collection.

not entirely, prophetic. The architect of the project was not to be Louis Kahn, nor was it to be Luis Barragan, who was also considered to build a guesthouse on the site. The new museum was, however, to be built near the Rothko Chapel. While the Menil Collection would not be a "big museum," it would be far more than "a storage center" (though the idea "to keep everything visible" would remain, as seen below).

Dominique de Menil and the Menil Foundation worked quickly to establish their new institution. An internal memorandum titled "Museum Projections" of early 1981 stated their very ambitious schedule:

Scheduled below are estimated dates of necessary events implementing the proposed museum:

1. Creation of the museum as a legal entity by February, 1981.

2. Employment of the architect by February, 1981.

3. Secure schematic design by June, 1981.

4. Acquire title to, or commitment to sell, unowned properties by June 1981.

5. Secure design development drawings by November, 1981.

6. Secure working drawings and construction documents by May, 1982.

7. Secure and approve construction bids by August, 1982.

8. Vacating and demolition of site by August, 1982.

9. Completion of construction of building by February, 1984.

10. Occupancy and installation of collection and exhibits by September, 1984.

11. Public opening of museum by October, 1984.[. . .][5]

By October 10, 1981, the Menil Foundation was able to issue a press release to the public describing the project:

Dominique de Menil and the Menil Foundation announce plans to establish a permanent home in Houston, Texas, for the Menil Collection, the important collection of art that has been assembled by Mrs. de Menil and her late husband, John de Menil, over the past thirty years.

The Menil Foundation is joined in this venture by benefactors and concerned members of the Houston community.

A site in Houston's Montrose area, adjacent to a small park in which the Rothko Chapel is located, has been selected for the new building to house the collection. It is defined by Sul Ross, Mulberry, Branard and Mandell Streets. All properties required for the project have been acquired.

Mr. Renzo Piano has been engaged as chief architect for the project.[. . .] Schematic plans for the facility have been prepared and design development drawings will be presented in late November. It is anticipated that construction will commence in the fall of 1982.[. . .]

The new museum is being established as a non-profit, Texas corporation and will be called the Menil Collection. [6]

A glance at the names of the designers of prominent museum projects in the United States since the selection of Renzo Piano as architect of the Menil Collection reveals just how prescient and inspired Dominique de Menil's choice was—Mr. Piano has been the lead architect on the majority of major museum expansions and building projects over the past decade or so (examples already complete or under construction include the Art Institute of Chicago; the Morgan Library and Museum, New York; the High Museum, Atlanta; and the Los Angeles Country Museum of Art; in the design phase is the new branch of the Whitney Museum of American Art, to be built in New York). However, when hired by the Menil Foundation, the only museum building he had worked on was the Centre Georges Pompidou in Paris, France. That project was a collaboration with architect Richard Rogers. So the Menil Collection was Renzo Piano's first solo effort at designing a museum, and his first work in the United States. In 2010, the selection of Mr. Piano to design a museum to house an important collection would seem almost a conservative choice; in 1981, however, it was rather daring; the success of the project is largely responsible for Piano's incredible resumé of museum projects cited above.

Issued with the press release of October 10, 1981 was a summary of Renzo Piano's resumé and a statement summarizing the mission, purpose, and scope of the project:

The Menil Collection reflects the ideas and interests of those who have gathered it together, Dominique and the late John de Menil.

Assembled over the past thirty years, the collection numbers approximately 10,000 items and ranges from Paleolithic to Contemporary art. It represents many phases of Near Eastern, Mediterranean and European cultures, and those of Africa, Oceania and the Americas. An emphasis has always been placed on the individual work of art and the ideas it embodies.

Thus, art has been collected for its value to human understanding, as well as for beauty and delight.

It is a diverse collection with strengths developed in certain areas. Among these are antiquities from the Mediterranean world, artifacts of the Migratory people of Eurasia and Europe, and a broad body of African art. The collection of modern art is of great significance and includes an outstanding group of works by the Cubist painters, and extraordinary selection of Surrealist art, with particular depth in the work of Max Ernst and Rene Magritte, and a fine collection of American and European paintings and sculpture from the last four decades. A collection of drawings, prints and rare books has also been developed.

The new building to house the collection will embody ideas regarding the exhibition of art developed by Dominique de Menil over the past twenty years. The facility will be sympathetic to the presentation of art; this will be on an intimate human scale, in harmony with the environment. Interplay between exterior and interior spaces will be created, and natural light will be used as a source of illumination in many areas.

The public galleries of the facility will present selections from the permanent collection in changing installations. An innovative temporary exhibition program continuing in the tradition of Mrs. de Menil will draw from the Menil Collection and other sources in order to examine art and culture from varied points of view. Storage areas will be arranged in a unique way to allow easy access to all items for purposes of research and study. [7]

Interestingly, lacking in this important and very illuminating statement is any talk of monumental entrances, atria, restaurants, bars, cafes, auditoria, facilities for young children, or many other of functions so common in postwar museums in this country. The program outlined here is very innovative in its attempts to use natural light effectively, and, perhaps on the early side of attempting to be "in harmony with the environment" (not new in architecture, but in application to an art museum, ahead of the curve). In other ways, however, this program harkens back to an earlier moment in art museum design (discussed further in Chapter 5 on the Museum of Modern Art) when a more human, domestic scale was used for displaying art. Indeed, the contents of the Menil Collection and its architectural language are almost diametrically opposed to that of the Frick Collection, yet the intimacy of its scale and the visitor's direct engagement with the art exhibited within are similar. This notion is further elucidated in another early document regarding the Menil Collection, a document titled "Project Information" and dated December 16, 1981:

The building is to be of an intimate human scale rather than monumental, constructed of materials in accord with such a scale and the site surroundings. A balanced interplay between exterior and interior spaces will exist, with natural light used as a source of illumination in most areas. Spaces will not overwhelm the art displayed and will provide an environment more domestic than institutional in nature."[8]

The same document contains a very useful summary of the overall building program for the proposed museum:

> When items from the collection are not on display in the public galleries, they will be in storage areas designed in such a manner to allow easy access by students, scholars and researchers. Large groups of paintings will be presented in rooms which facilitate in-depth examination. Objects in storage will be highly visible and provide a comprehensive view of the material culture from many civilizations. The estimated net area of the proposed building is 70,000 square feet according to the following categorical breakdown: Exhibition Facilities—25,000 square feet; Exhibition Support Facilities—5,000 square feet; Collection Storage Facilities—12,000 square feet; Collection Support Facilities and Conservation Lab—6,400 square feet; Library Facilities – 3,200 square feet; Administrative Facilities—2,200 square feet; Curatorial Office and Research Facilities, 2,500 square feet; Public Facilities – 5,800 square feet; and Building Service Facilities—8,000 square feet.

As is illustrated in the next section, the final executed project would contain little variation from the building envisioned in these early foundation documents.

THE BUILDINGS OF THE MENIL COLLECTION

While the public opening date of October 1984 was not to be, virtually all the other criteria on Dominique de Menil's agenda brought forth in the documents in the last sections were indeed met. The Menil Collection opened to the public in 1987. It fit in very well with its surrounding environment, preserving the domestic scale and character of the Montrose section of Houston, a predominantly residential neighborhood, not far from the Museum District, Rice University's campus, and downtown. It formed the nucleus of a campus of projects with Menil patronage bounded to the east by the University of St. Thomas and containing the Rothko Chapel between the new building and the university (fig. 2.6). The Menil Foundation was able to acquire all of the houses adjacent to the block of the main building (delineated by Sul Ross Street to the north, Branard to the south, Mandell to the west, and Mulberry to the east) to ensure that the residential nature of the block would be preserved in the future. Furthermore, they had these houses, mostly pre-war bungalows, painted the same light gray color they would use for the new museum building. This color scheme gives the neighborhood a very subdued atmosphere, bringing out the green lawn, trees, and sculpture surrounding the Menil Collection. This campus would continue to grow throughout the remainder of Dominique de Menil's lifetime.

2.6. Aerial view of Menil Collection, showing downtown Houston skyline. Photo by Ben Smusz. Courtesy of the Menil Archives, The Menil Collection.

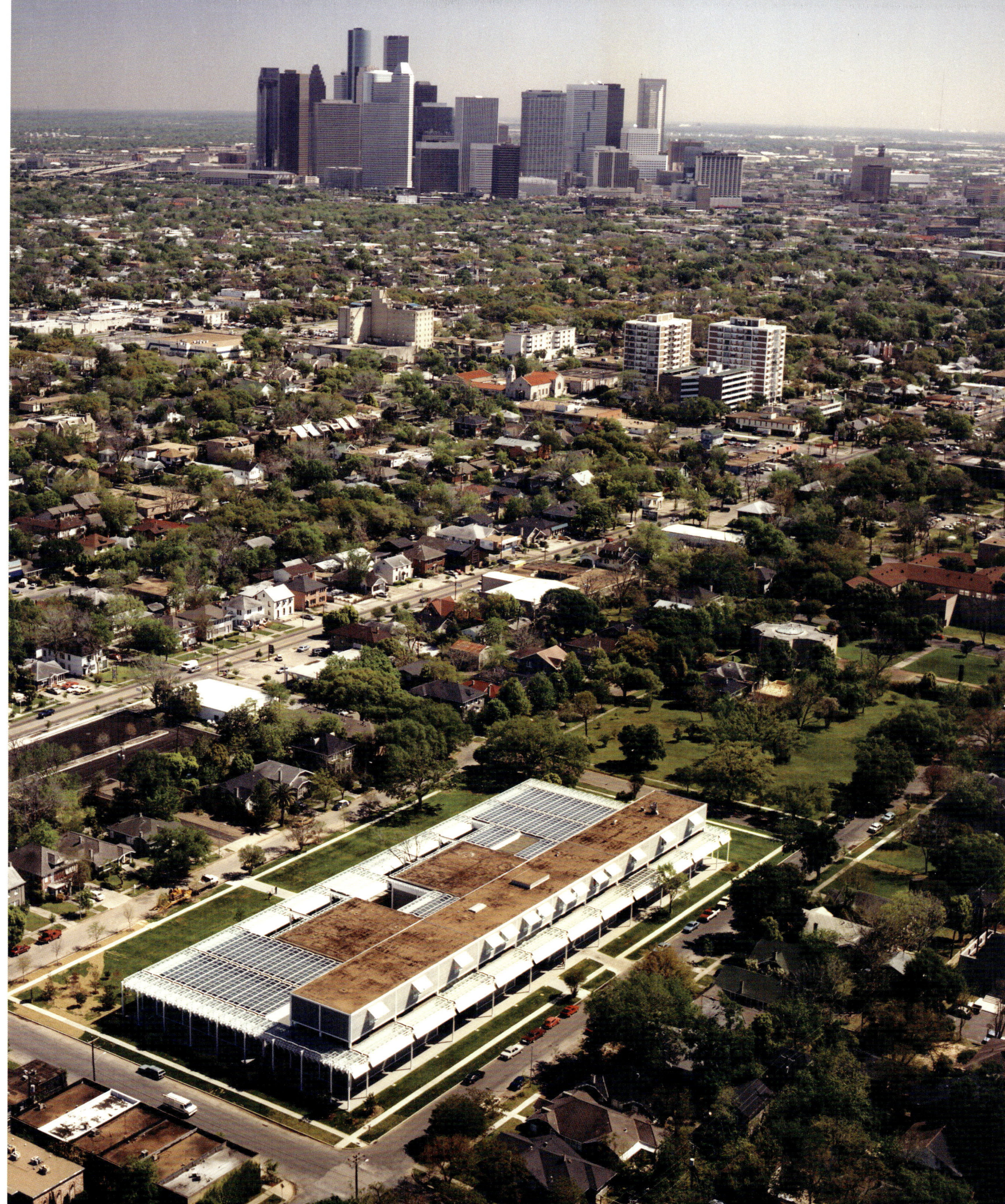

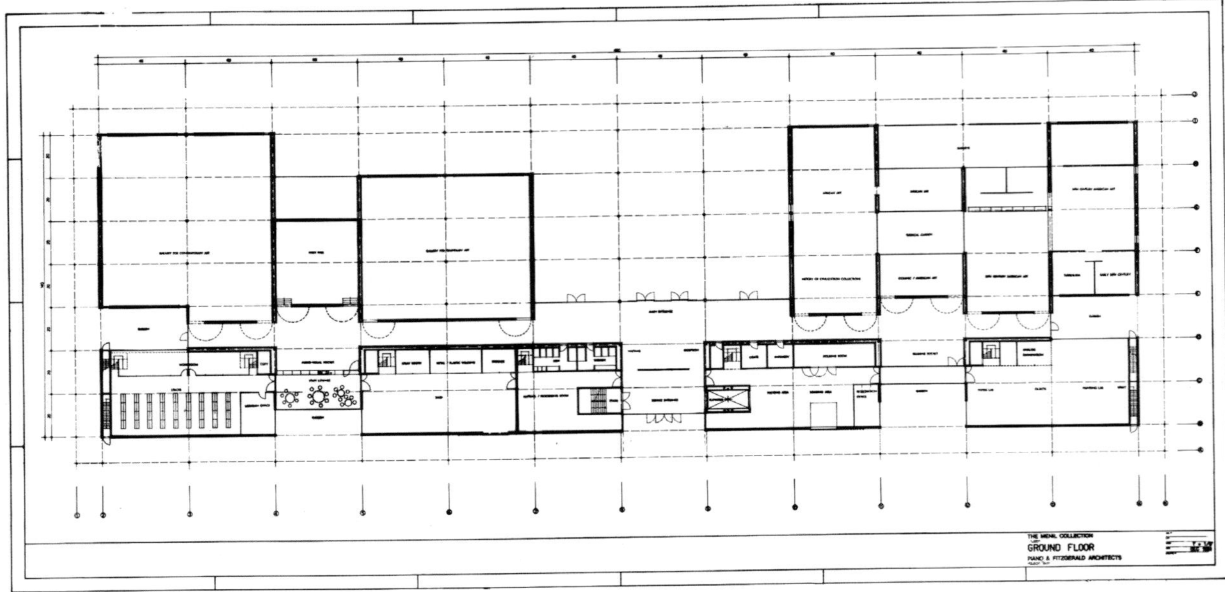

2.7. Ground-floor plan of the Menil Collection. Photo, Renzo Piano Building Workshop. Courtesy of the Menil Archives, The Menil Collection.

In a presentation at the Menil Collection on April 21, 2007, Renzo Piano stated that "the building is the portrait of Dominique de Menil."[9] He further stated "She was a stubborn lady. Everybody knows that. But she was actually the most stubborn lady I ever met in my life." So how was Piano able to design a building that would satisfy this "stubborn lady," preserve her requirements and vision, while still being able to project his own vision as a designer, realize a truly innovative museum, and create a model of the building type that would be universally admired and emulated in the future? A visit to the Menil Collection reveals that these two strong personalities made a very compatible team; Piano was the right designer to execute a home for the collection of Dominique and the late John de Menil.

Renzo Piano was able to create architectural solutions to the problems that his client presented, creating a product that was a physical embodiment of the ideas Dominique de Menil outlined in the section above. Analysis of his architectural plans for the Menil Collection reveals how he was able to translate Dominique de Menil's abstract ideas into concrete architectural spaces (figs. 2.7–2.10). The ground floor plan shows that the museum building is actually an irregular shape, determined by the various galleries and work spaces (library, conservation lab, loading dock, frame shop, and internal gardens). Externally, however, this irregular shape is regularized by a grid of I-beams supporting the rectangular and very innovative "leaved" roof that covers the entire rectangular footprint of the collection. These I-beams function as a colonnade surrounding the building and providing a shaded area—something essential in the hot, tropical Houston summers (see fig. 2.11, the entrance of the collection, showing the I-beams supporting the roof). The exterior is further regularized by the second floor, which contains collection storage and curatorial and administrative offices

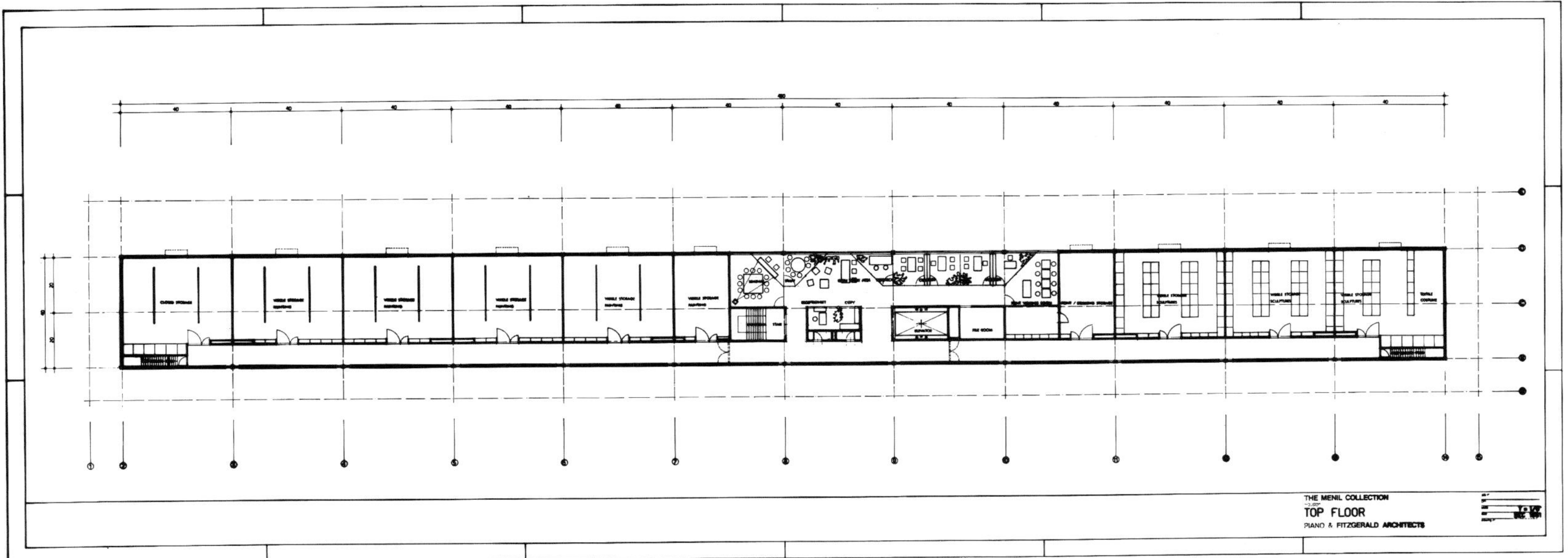

2.8. Second-floor plan of the Menil Collection. Photo, Renzo Piano Building Workshop. Courtesy of the Menil Archives, The Menil Collection.

and is a regular rectangle covering the northern half of the museum's footprint (see elevations, figs. 2.9 and 2.10).

This irregular ground plan is not merely an exercise in abstract architectural aesthetics. It is fundamental in realizing Dominique de Menil's desire to provide as much natural light in the galleries as possible. A look at the plan of the ground floor (fig. 2.7) shows that this undulation appears principally on the north side, the side of the central corridor that contains the bulk of the public gallery space (the south side chiefly houses nonpublic and semipublic functional areas such as a research library, conservation laboratory, frame shop, staff room, and kitchen). The irregularity therefore allows for more opportunities of direct natural lighting through strategically placed windows (see figs. 2.12 and 2.13). Further opportunities for indirect natural light come from the ingenious introduction of the "leaved" roof seen from the exterior. This structure is continued through the building's mass, not merely as a covering of the exterior colonnade but also to form the ceiling of the public spaces of the ground floor. It allows for diffused, indirect natural lighting of the galleries (figs. 2.14 and 2.15). This ceiling arrangement produces interesting changes in the lighting of the museum's interior throughout the day and the seasons (fig. 2.16), not unlike the effect of the diffused skylight in the nearby Rothko Chapel.

Unlike the clients of many museum buildings, Dominique de Menil demanded similar attention from her architect regarding the design of the building's semipublic and private spaces. The main building of the Menil Collection is virtually self-sufficient, containing within its own walls, not just the necessary galleries, reception areas, loading docks, amenities, and administrative areas necessary for the mounting of exhibitions, but also all of the ancillary, preparatory, research,

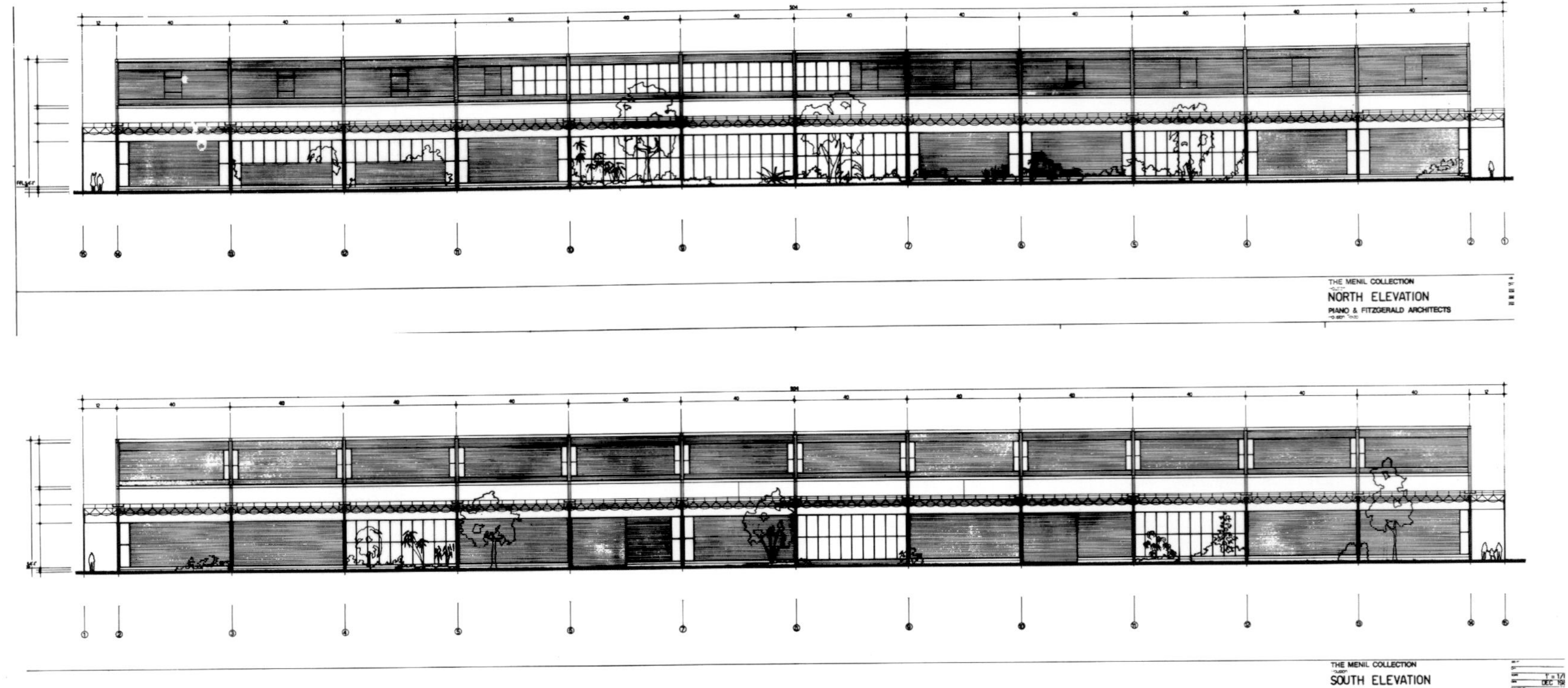

2.9. South and North elevations of the Menil Collection. Photo, Renzo Piano Building Workshop. Courtesy of the Menil Archives, The Menil Collection.

and conservation spaces required of an art museum. Although this is true of many institutions, rarely is the care in design and attention to detail put into these spaces of the same level as the public spaces. Such functions are usually shoehorned into basements, attics, and windowless corners and crevices; not so at the Menil Collection. If natural light is helpful for looking at art and enjoying the spaces of the galleries, it is equally so for the various staff members who must have workspace within the museum. However, this is rarely a priority of clients or architects when planning, designing, and building art museums. Here again, Dominique de Menil found the right architect in Renzo Piano to execute her vision and her values.

Most of the south side of the ground floor and the entire second floor of the museum are taken up by these semipublic and nonpublic spaces. The Menil Collection has its own conservation department, with most conservation work being done not only in-house but on-site. If any type of work demands large, obstruction-free spaces with lots of natural light, art conservation would have to be one of them. Contained on the south side of the building, the conservation laboratory is below the second floor and therefore does not have the leaf ceiling of the galleries (fig. 2.17). However, the east end of the north wall looks out onto one of the building's internal gardens (see plan, fig. 2.7). This positioning not only supplies the laboratory with useful natural light but also brings the garden and outside world into the space, without opening it to the outside, where passersby might distract conservators who perform extremely sensitive work that requires the utmost care and concentration. This garden also opens on the east end of the

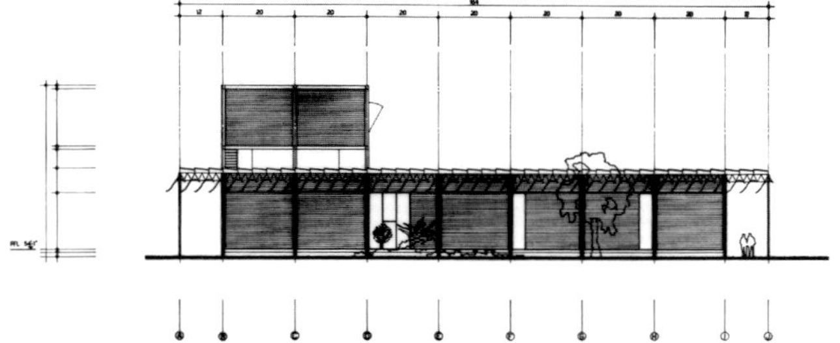

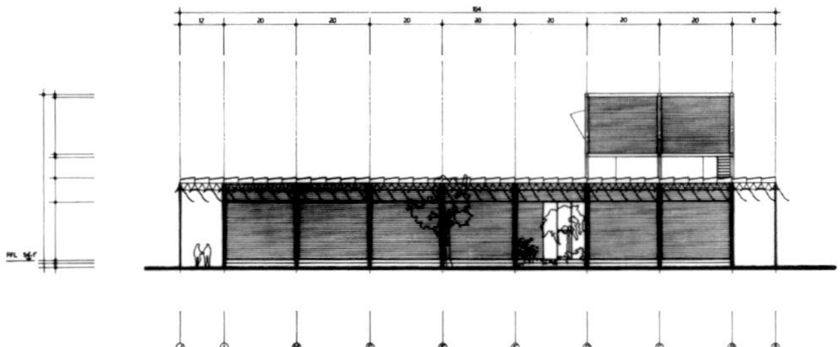

2.10. East and West elevations of the Menil Collection. Photo, Renzo Piano Building Workshop. Courtesy of the Menil Archives, The Menil Collection.

central corridor and the gallery to the north. A similar pocket garden on the west side of the building provides light to the central corridor, the gallery to the north, and the research library to the south.

If little attention is ordinarily given to the design of workspaces in museums, even less is typically spent regarding the design of collections storage facilities, beyond heating, ventilation, and air conditioning. However, as quoted above from the October 10, 1981 press release, one of Dominique de Menil's early requirements stated that "storage areas will be arranged in a unique way to allow easy access to all items for purposes of research and study." To make storage easily accessible, Piano arrived at the solution found in the second floor of the Menil Collection (see plan, fig. 2.8), creating the rooms known at the Menil Collection as the "treasure rooms." The second floor consists of a long corridor on its north side. Off the center of this corridor are the director's, curatorial, and administrative offices. To the east and west, however, is a series of windowless rooms, each containing art from a different area of the collection (the rooms are divided between twentieth century, African, ancient, Byzantine, etc.). Each room allows all of the objects that are not on public display or on loan to other institutions to be viewed. In other words, the art storage at the Menil Collection is curated (fig. 2.18). This arrangement allows easy and quick access to any work in the collection, which lack of gallery space prohibits from being on display, for visiting scholars, students, and researchers as well as museum staff. Although these rooms are not open to the general public, they are available to a much wider audience than typical museum storage facilities and in many ways anticipated the twenty-first-century trend of having publicly accessible "open storage" facilities seen at such institutions as the New-York Historical Society, the Greek and Roman Galleries at the Metropolitan Museum of Art, and the American Galleries at the Brooklyn Museum of Art.

EXPANSION OF THE MENIL CAMPUS

In keeping with the domestic scale of the main building and the residential nature of the surrounding area, expansion of the Menil Collection has not involved adding new wings to the main building. Rather, repurposing existing buildings and constructing small, modestly scaled structures has been the approach taken. From the beginning the Menil Collection was thought of as being built on a sort of campus, within walking distance of the Rothko Chapel, with Barnett Newman's *Broken Obelisk* and the reflecting pool designed by Philip Johnson, all of which were commissioned by John and Dominique de Menil. Other large-scale outdoor sculpture has been displayed on this campus. Some of the bungalows in the surrounding blocks (all of which are owned by the Menil Collection and painted the same gray as the museum building) are used by the museum for additional office space; the bungalow directly across Sul Ross Street from the main (north) entrance of the museum is currently the museum's book and gift shop.

The only purpose-built addition to the Menil Collection is the Cy Twombly Gallery, which, like the main building, was designed by Renzo Piano (figs. 2.19 and 2.20). It opened in 1995 and is located across Branard Street, immediately south of the main building. Built of concrete blocks in contrast to the wood siding of the main building, its massing, scale, and color are in harmony with both the main building and the surrounding neighborhood. All of the gallery space inside is dedicated to the work of the abstract painter and sculptor Cy Twombly, whom Dominique de Menil began to collect and champion later in her life.

The last expansion to the Menil Collection in Dominique de Menil's life, and to date, is the Dan Flavin installation in Richmond Hall, entered on Richmond Avenue, three blocks south of the main building. Dan Flavin was an installation artist who worked with white and colored fluorescent light tubes that seem to alter their surrounding environment in unexpected ways through various lighting effects. Unlike the Cy Twombly Gallery, Richmond Hall was not purpose-built; rather, it is a reuse of an existing building, built in 1930 as a grocery store, with fine art deco detailing on its exterior (fig. 2.21) and a large, open interior, ideal for the display of one of Flavin's last and largest installations. The gallery actually contains one Flavin installation in three parts: one part on the building's exterior (west side, below top molding), the other two located in the two galleries inside (fig. 2.22). Dan Flavin passed away in 1996, the same year this gallery opened. Dominique would pass away the following year in 1997.

2.11. Exterior entrance to the Menil Collection with Michael Heizer, *Charmstone*, 1987. Photo by Hickey-Robertson. Courtesy of the Menil Archives, The Menil Collection.

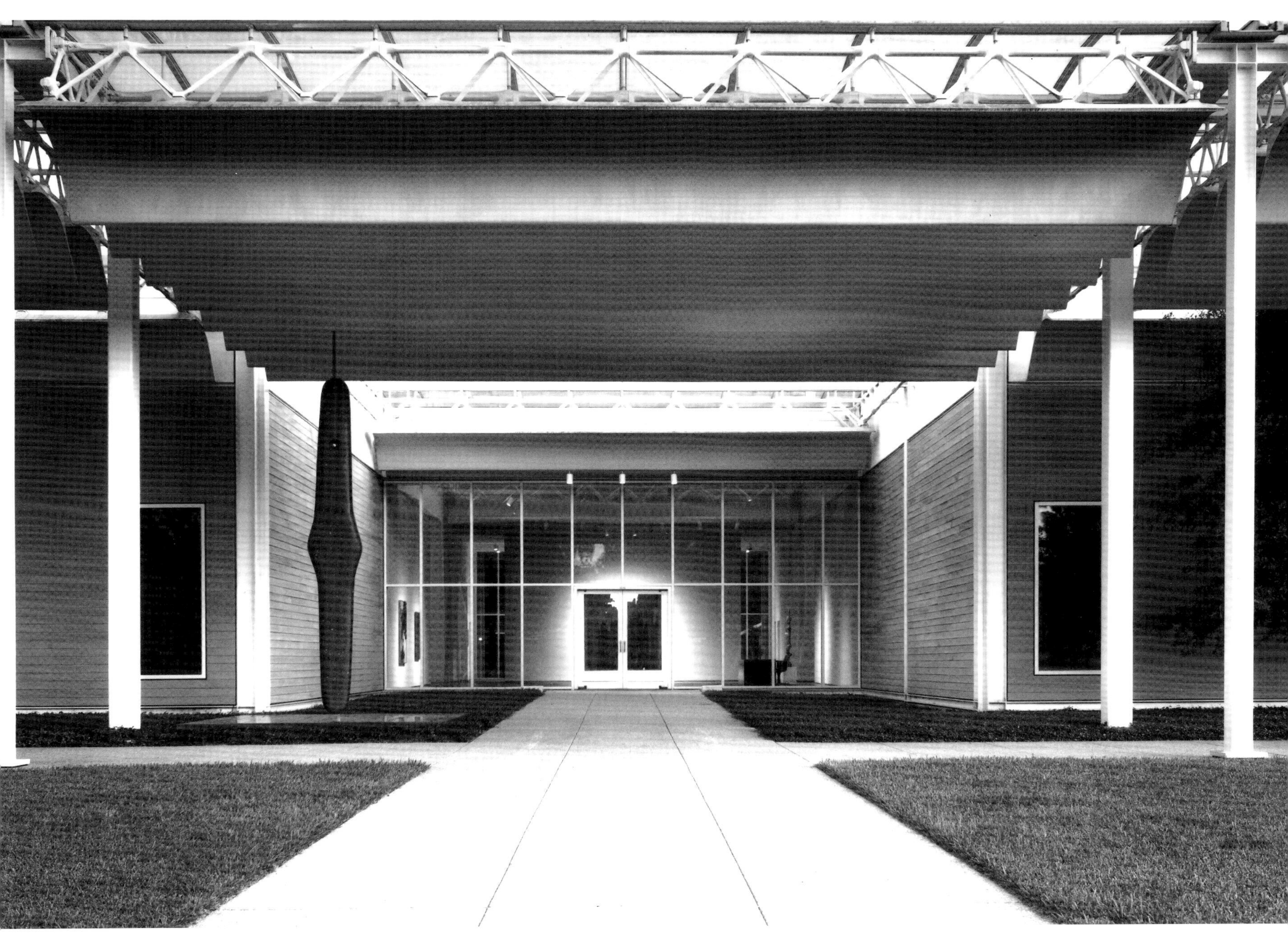

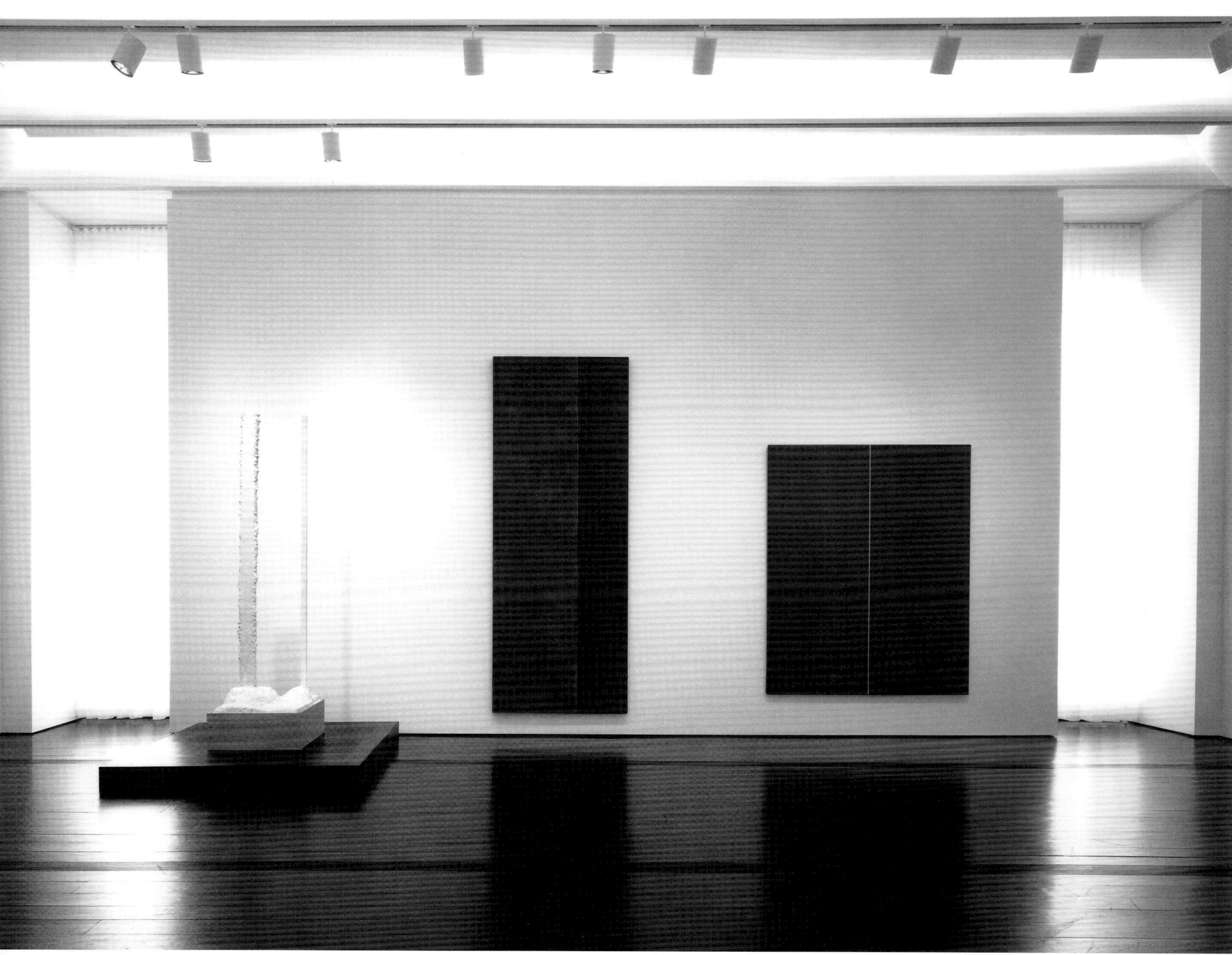

2.12. Twentieth-century galleries,
showing Barnett Newman painting and
windows providing natural light, 1987.
Photo by Paul Hester. Courtesy of the Menil
Archives, The Menil Collection.

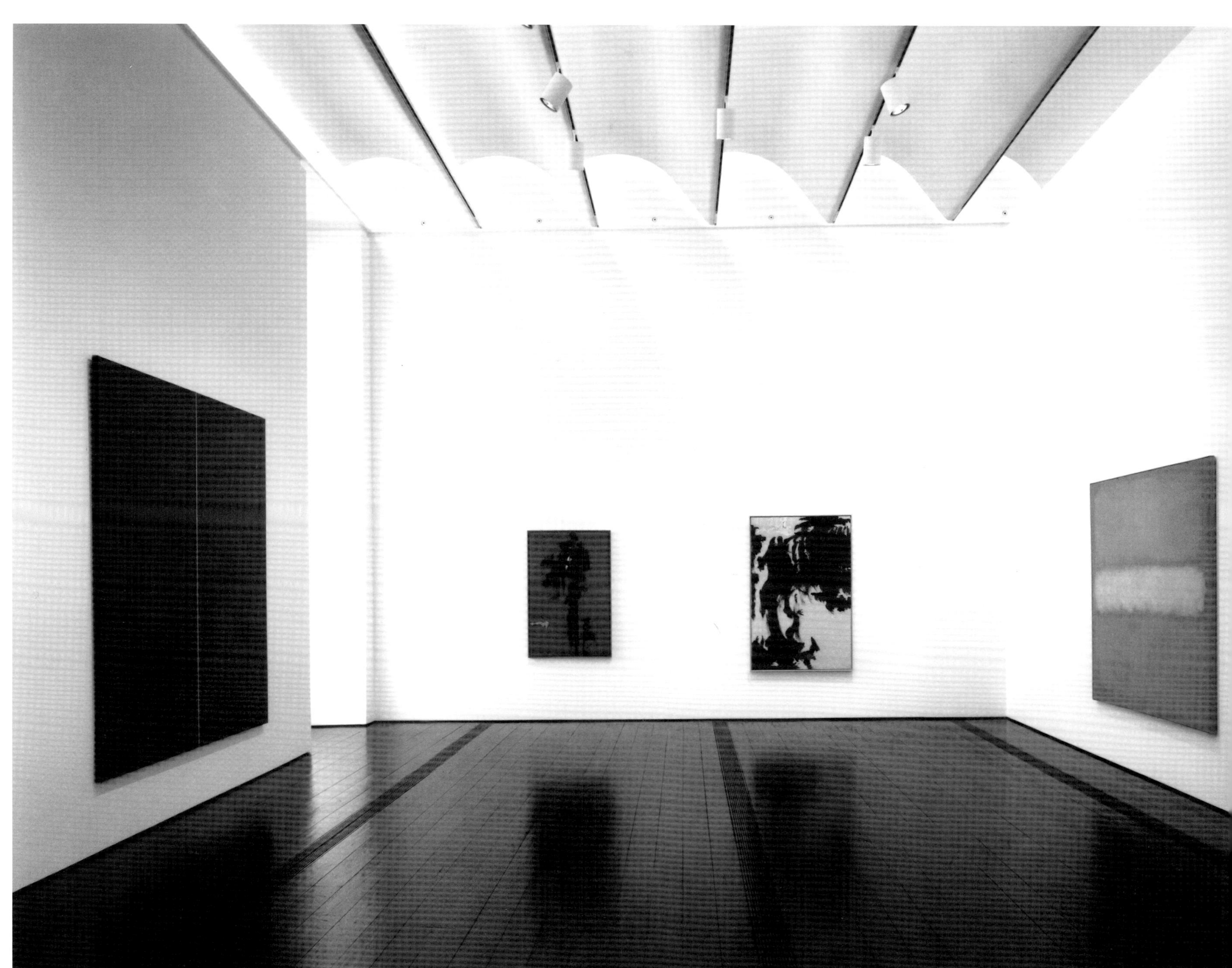

2.13. Twentieth-century galleries with natural light coming from the west end of the central corridor through the gallery entrance, 1987. Photo by Paul Hester. Courtesy of the Menil Archives, The Menil Collection.

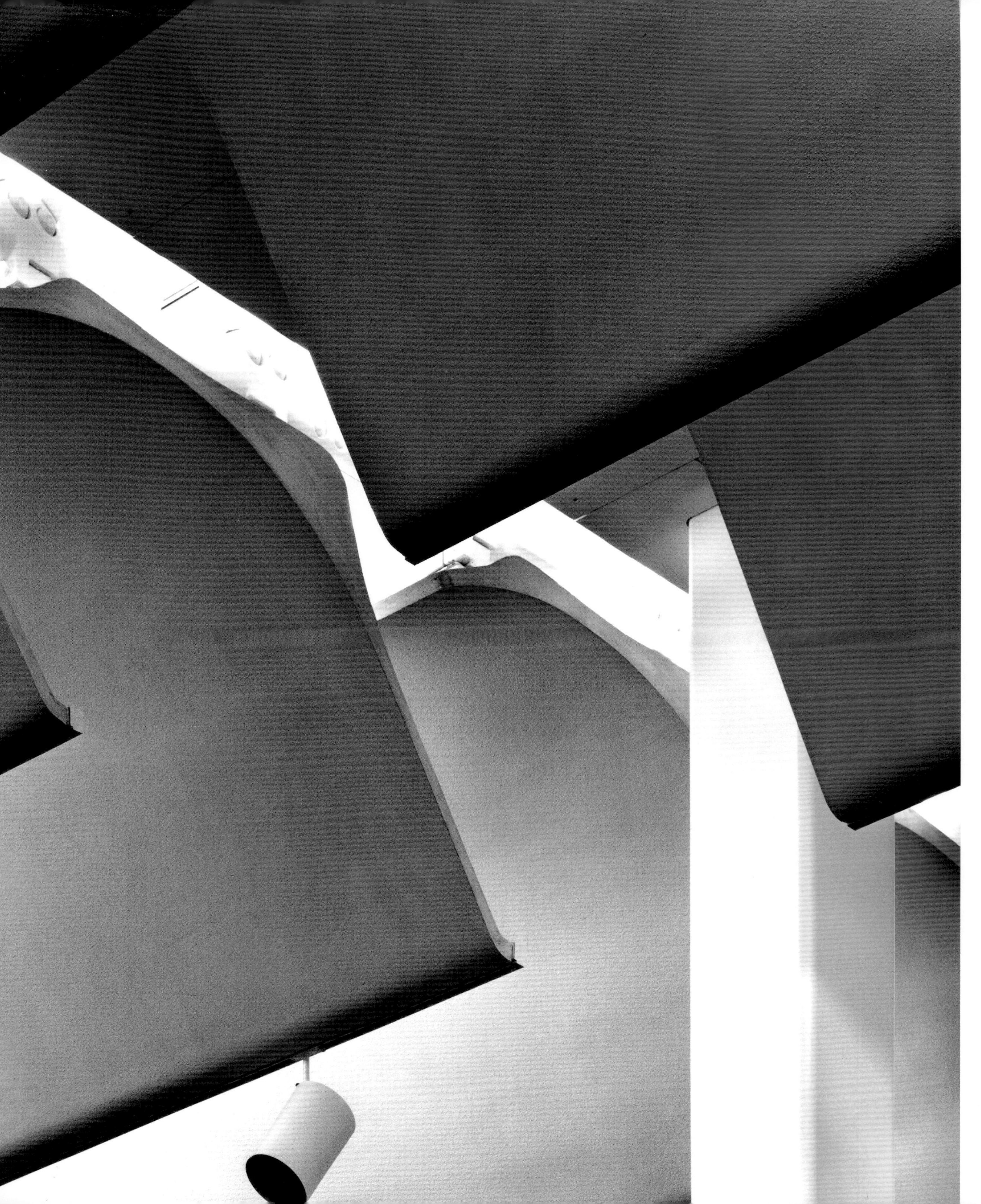

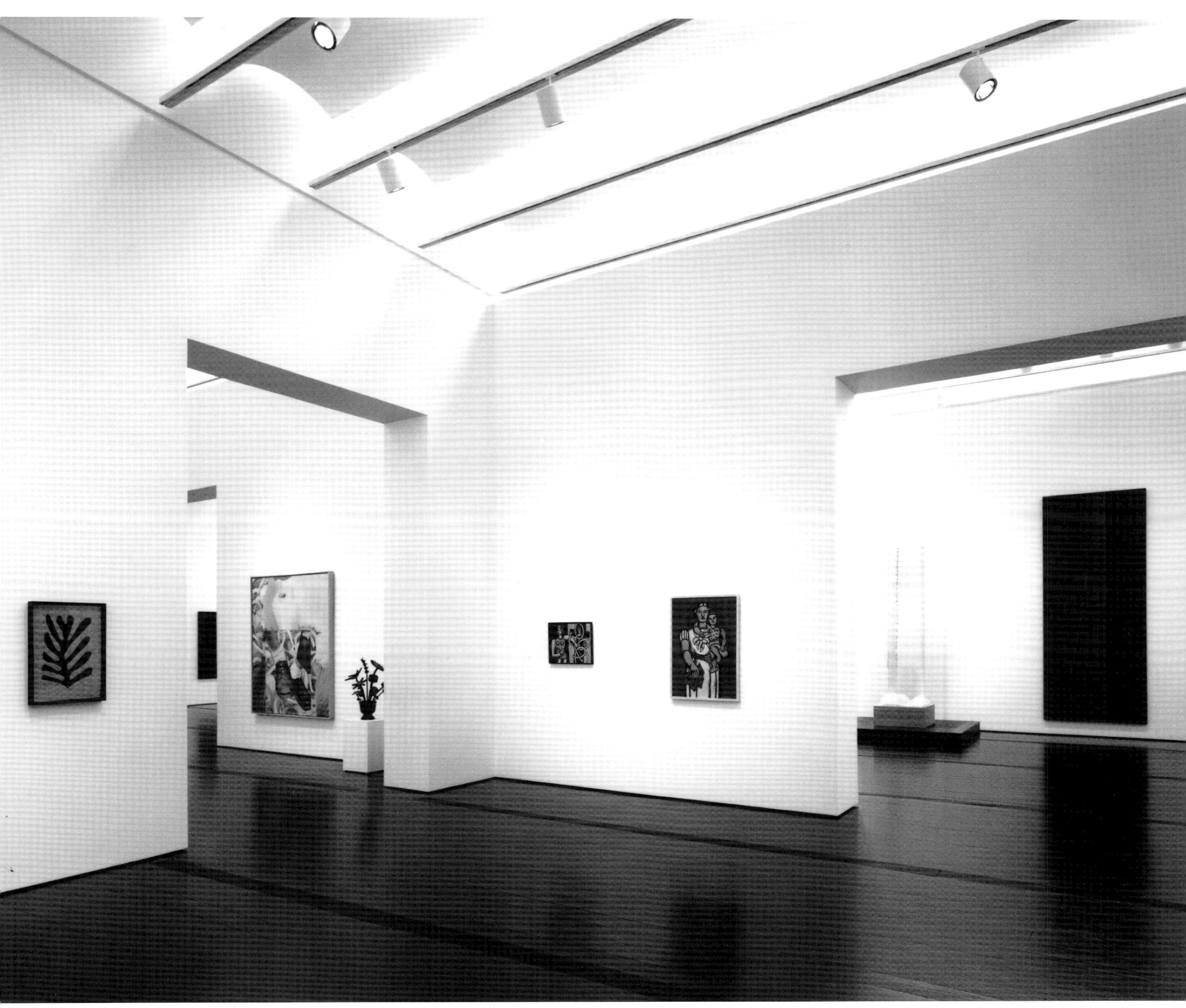

2.14. Detail of interior leaves. Photo by Richard Bryant. Courtesy of the Menil Archives, The Menil Collection.

2.15. Oblique view of twentieth-century galleries, 1987. Photo by Paul Hester. Courtesy of the Menil Archives, The Menil Collection.

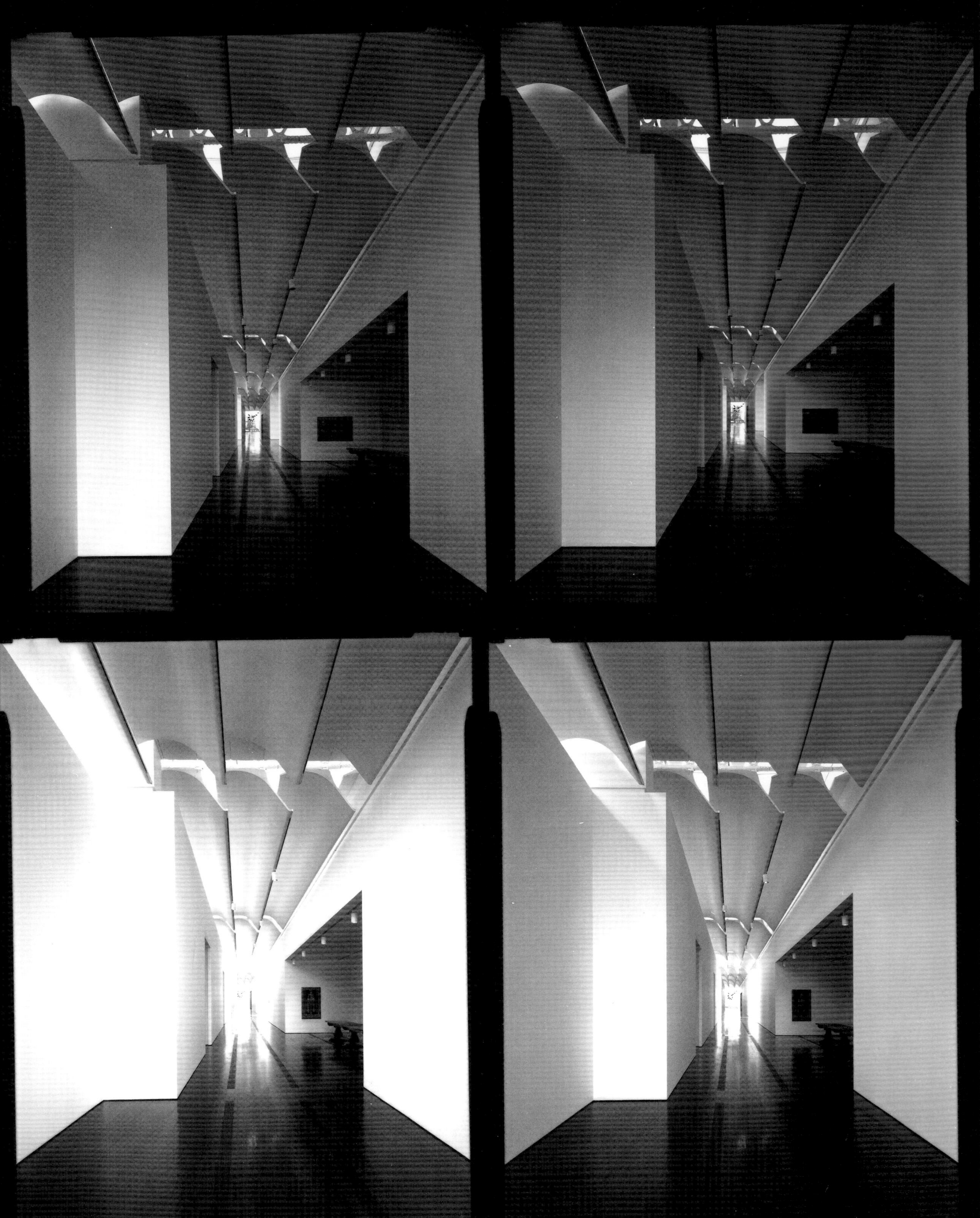

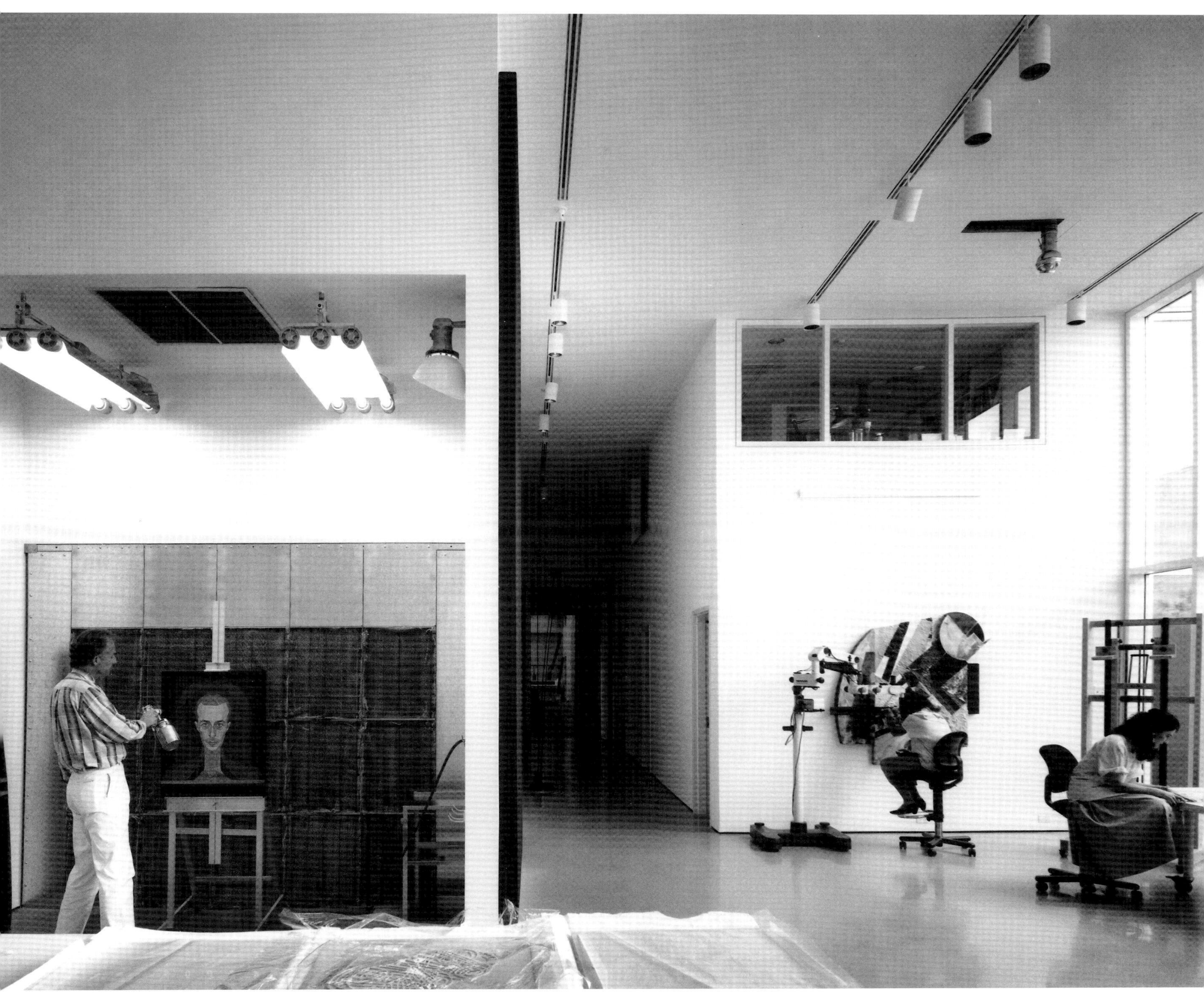

2.16. Four photographs showing changing light at different times of day, hallway and west pocket, 1987. Photo by Paul Hester. Courtesy of the Menil Archives, The Menil Collection.

2.17. Interior view of the Conservation Department, 1987. Photo by Paul Hester. Courtesy of the Menil Archives, The Menil Collection.

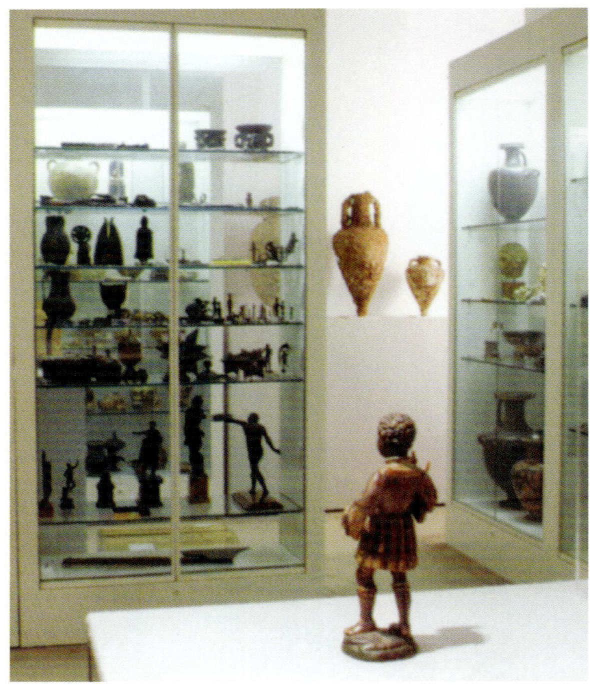

2.18. Interior view of one of the "treasure rooms": Antiquities storage area. *Courtesy of the Menil Archives, The Menil Collection.*

Though not a part of the Menil Collection, like the Rothko Chapel, the Byzantine Fresco Chapel Museum was commissioned by the de Menils and lies on the Menil campus. The chapel was envisioned, designed, and built to give context to Byzantine frescoes from the island of Cyprus, which were brought to the United States by Dominique de Menil and are on loan from the government of Cyprus. The chapel was designed by Francois de Menil, son of John and Dominique de Menil, and is a consecrated Greek Orthodox church, governed by its own board (figs. 2.23 and 2.24). This chapel was the last gift of John and Dominique de Menil to Houston, Texas and the art world at large and was the last component of their art campus in the Montrose neighborhood.

LEGACY AND FUTURE

Dominique de Menil's will left no clear instructions or limitations on the board of the Menil Collection, leaving the institution to continue to grow in any fitting direction. However, in the more than a decade since her passing, the Menil Collection has stayed true to the spirit she and her husband fostered. To this day the Menil Collection still charges no admission fee. In an era with admissions charges at museums with similar-quality collections and programs typically ranging between $15.00 and $20.00, this is no small detail. Further, the experience of visiting the Menil Collection is still what it was on opening day: a chance to engage directly with the finest examples of the diverse periods of art that John and

Dominique de Menil collected, on an intimate, human scale, without many of the distractions found in other institutions. The Menil experience is entirely about direct engagement with the work on exhibition; there is no ambient noise from cafes or soundtracks from introductory films or videos as one enters the galleries. Indeed much of the art on display was originally collected and displayed in their home, and the scale of the galleries, particularly the smaller ones, still gives that domestic interior context to much of the work—a context that is harder and harder to recreate in many of today's larger-scaled venues.

The vision of the current director of the Menil Collection, Josef Helfenstein, is consonant with that of the museum's founder. [10] When asked about the major challenges facing the director of an institution that is so closely associated with the collecting of two personalities as strong as John and Dominique de Menil, Mr. Helfenstein replied as follows:

> Their vision has always been quite broad—and given the expansive vision of the founders, there will always be room to continue and develop this mission. The Menil is more than an art museum, it incorporates a spirituality and humanism that is the basis of everything. That philosophical foundation expresses itself even in architecture—through the intimacy and contemplative character of the existing museum buildings. The Menil Collection is not just a museum, but a neighborhood. There is something holistic about the Menil experience, including its collection, which has evolved over time. John and Dominique de Menil surrounded themselves with scholars and experts to whose advice they listened, creating a broad and idiosyncratic collection. A director and our curators need to be sensitive of this history; within this larger framework we can collect in a way that makes sense.

Dominique de Menil left no restrictions on what the collection could acquire or exhibit. When asked about the policies of the Menil Collection regarding the acquisition of new work and planning exhibitions, Mr. Helfenstein replied:

> It would be arbitrary to stop collecting with the death of the founders. The museum has and will continue to collect. The staff and Board thought deeply about this and, after my arrival, we had an intense internal discussion about mission, legacy, and core values. This led to the creation of a strategic plan. We also discussed how to build the collection without a narrow, constricting acquisitions policy. We continue to concentrate on certain areas (and do not try to be encyclopedic); we are committed to the collecting in depth of certain individual artists knowing others will be missed. Over the past years, we have collected Rauschenberg and now have probably the most comprehensive museum collection in the country, although we still have important gaps. We do not only seek masterpieces; the Menil lacks such resources. The Menil Collection has always been and hopefully will remain intellectually independent; our collecting should not be driven by trends. We often collect

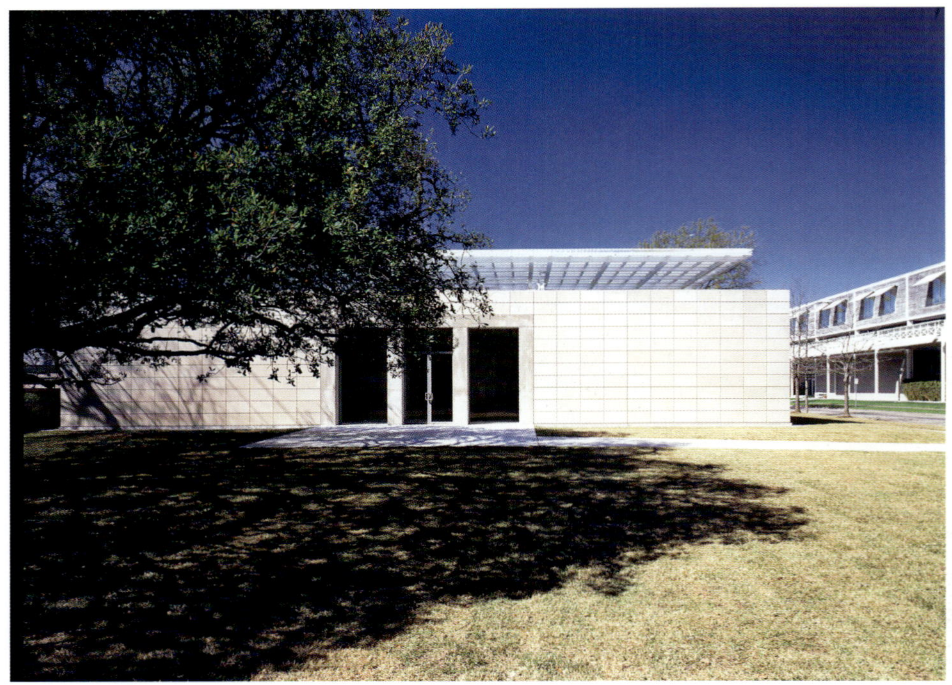

2.19. Cy Twombly Gallery, east façade at entrance. Cy Twombly Gallery, courtesy of The Menil Collection, Houston. Photo: Hickey-Robertson, Houston.

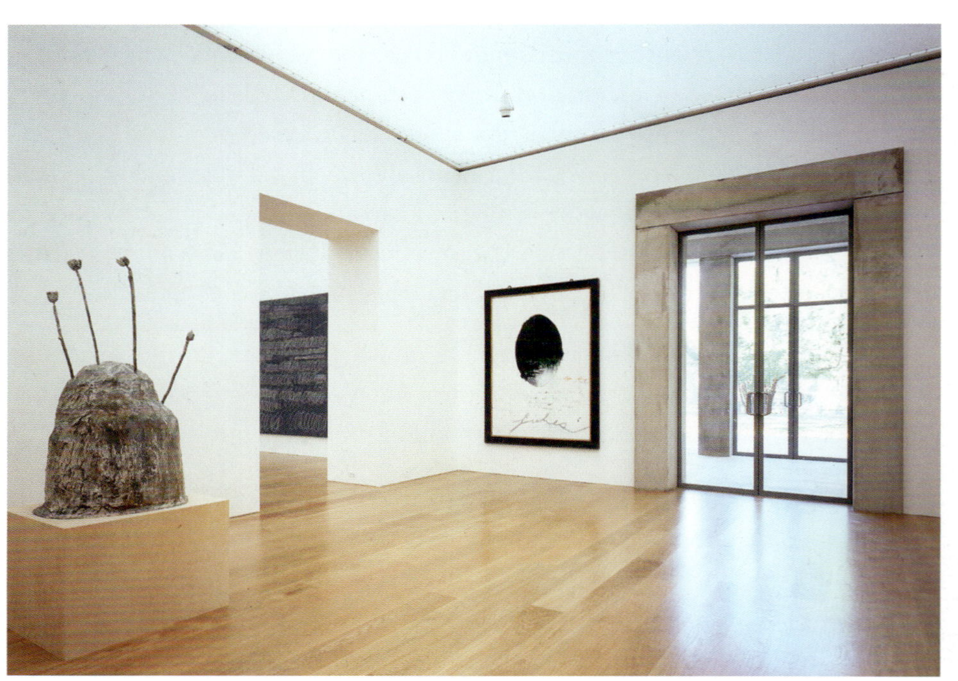

2.20. Cy Twombly Gallery, interior view of entrance gallery; left to right: *Thermopylae*, 1991, bronze; *Untitled*, 1984. Cy Twombly Gallery, courtesy of The Menil Collection, Houston. Photo: Hickey-Robertson, Houston.

artists and curate exhibitions on material that other institutions will not. I have always been fascinated by the dialogue between different periods and parts of the collection. This is unique and important to understand going forward.

The Menil campus, including the allied institutions of the Rothko Chapel and Byzantine Fresco Chapel Museum, is ideally scaled and preserves the proportion

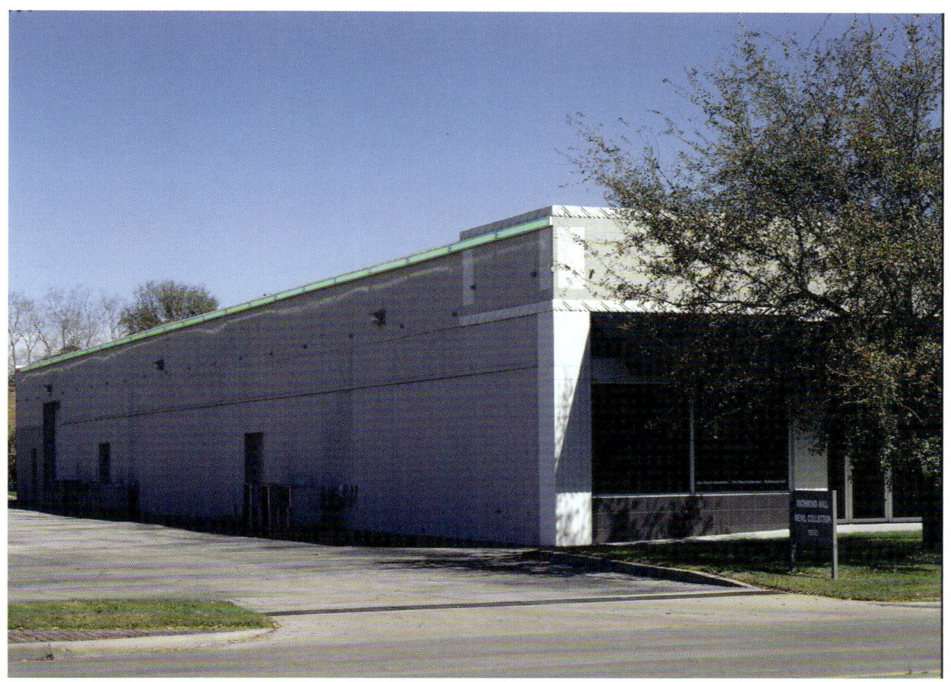

2.21. Dan Flavin, *Untitled*, (an installation of twenty-two encased fixtures mounted below the parapet cap on the east and west exterior walls of Richmond Hall), 1996. The Menil Collection, Houston. Photo: Hickey-Robertson, Houston. © 2009 Stephen Flavin/Artists Rights Society (ARS), New York.

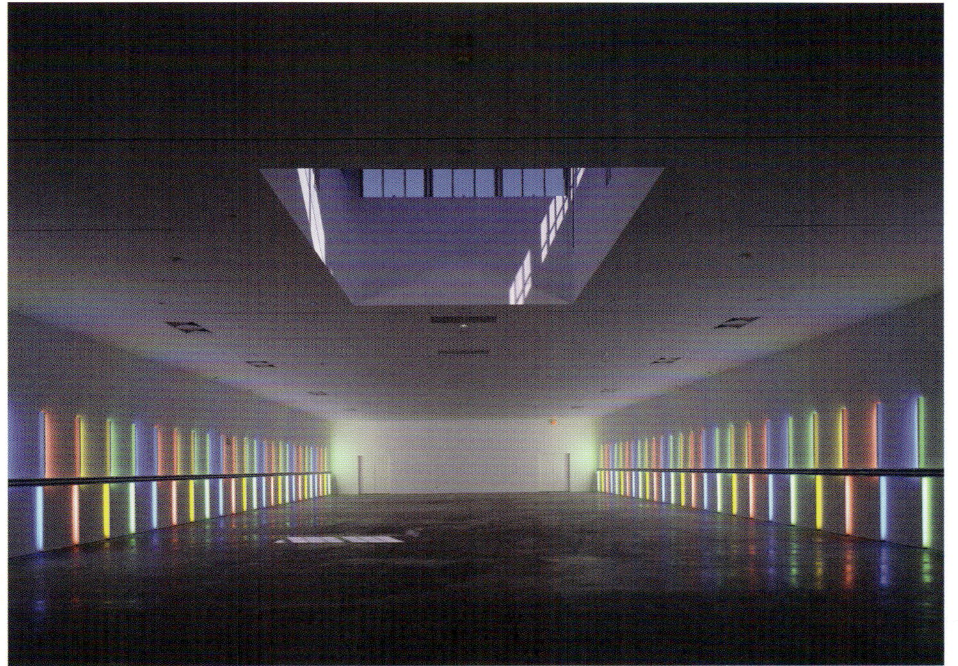

2.22. Dan Flavin, *Untitled* (an installation of 4-foot fixtures in two opposing banks for the east and west interior walls of Richmond Hall), 1996. The Menil Collection, Houston. Photo: Hickey-Robertson, Houston. © 2009 Stephen Flavin/Artists Rights Society (ARS), New York.

that many great museums have lost (e.g., the Museum of Modern Art in New York); it also fits well in its surroundings and maintains a domestic scale in its galleries for viewing art. When asked if further physical expansion is ruled out, Mr. Helfenstein stated:

> Of course not, the Menil's atmosphere is more about scale than size. Change, including physical expansion, is inherent to an intellectually lively project.

I see the Menil Collection as a work in progress, not a monument—like a utopian vision. The collection will grow, but not for the sake of growth. The existing sense of scale should inform expansion. The main building is like a motherhouse surrounded by satellites. Expansion could add more pavilions, but should always preserve the experience of the environment and neighborhood. The museum is kind of an organism for me. The better I know it, the more I find it unique; its spirit must be protected. There is something completely nonhierarchical about the existing Menil campus; it is understated, not loud: the museum buildings, the bungalows, the outdoor art, the simple landscaping, the trees—an informal beauty, there is no other place in the world like it. This unique, nonmonumental quality of informality must be maintained.

The Menil Collection, with its holdings from the ancient world and Africa through modernism and up to the work of Dan Flavin, represents a narrative of art history that is closely linked to that advanced by the Museum of Modern Art in its first fifty years (one thinks of Alfred Barr's famous diagrams, with the roots of modern art in primitive art, etc.).[11] In a sense, the terminus of the current collection with abstract Twombly and Flavin is a logical end to this narrative. When asked if this narrative was something that he, as the director, felt was necessary to maintain, or whether he would like the type of works collected to be left open-ended, reflecting contemporary interests and practices, he replied:

I don't think the de Menils followed a vision of collecting that is as linear as Barr's. They may have started that way, but their intellectual interests changed. The de Menils understanding of collecting became increasingly influenced

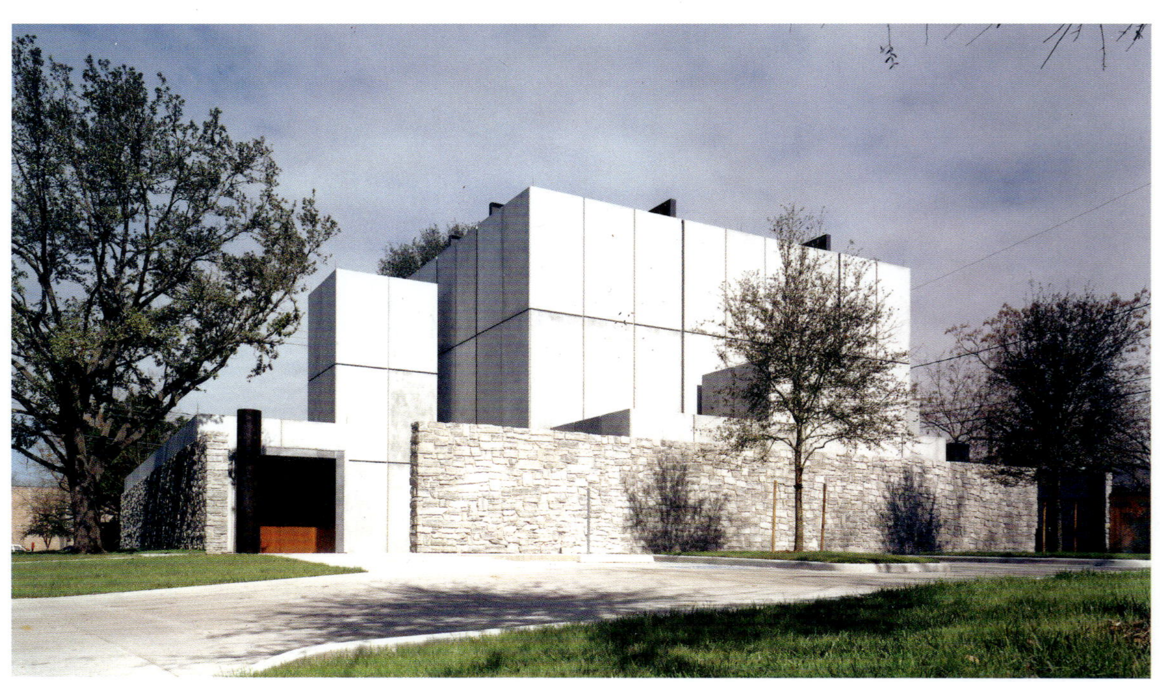

2.23. Byzantine Fresco Chapel Museum, exterior view. Courtesy of the Byzantine Fresco Chapel Museum. Photo: © Paul Warchol Photography Inc.

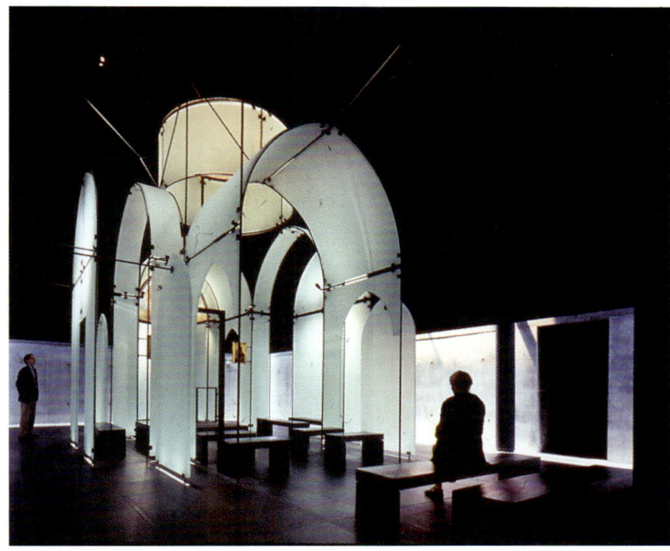

2.24. Byzantine Fresco Chapel Museum, interior view. *Courtesy of the Byzantine Fresco Chapel Museum. Photo: © Paul Warchol Photography Inc.*

by Surrealism, which is by definition less hierarchical and more idiosyncratic than MoMA's [Museum of Modern Art] linear approach. The Menil collection is based on the chance encounter. It is a fundamentally different approach to collecting, both more contemporary in its open-endedness and pluralism and at the same time, there is something ancient and spiritual about it. It is antidogmatic, in a sense it is the very opposite of Barr's understanding of modern art.

When asked to briefly discuss his own vision for the future of the Menil Collection, Mr. Helfenstein replied:

> My goal is to keep up that kind of broad vision—a humanistic, idealist concept that is the basis of the Menil project. An institution of such a generous and visionary nature must be protected—protected from being commercialized or trivialized. I hope the Menil will always continue to believe in art in the most radical way. It is a place of contemplation and a research facility rather than a platform for parties. My goal is to keep its integrity in every way, artistically and intellectually.

When asked what he found most interesting and challenging, and, conversely, what was most frustrating and difficult in running the Menil Collection, Mr. Helfenstein stated:

> What is most surprising and challenging is that everything here is charged with history and meaning. Every bush and tree around the Menil is charged with history. There are private stories attached to everything. How can things be done while respecting this? The challenge is to find balance between the future and the past; between openness to change and preservation of the history without becoming an uncritical, naïve admirer of the past.

CHAPTER 3

THE WHITNEY MUSEUM OF AMERICAN ART

"Since its opening the Whitney has set the pattern in this country for what a museum can do for the art of its own period. From its Whitney Studio Club days, through its various developments, up to the present, it has been the greatest single force in support to the living art of the United States."

— Excerpt from letter to Mrs. G. Macculloch Miller, signed by 168 artists and dated February 3, 1944, Whitney Archives

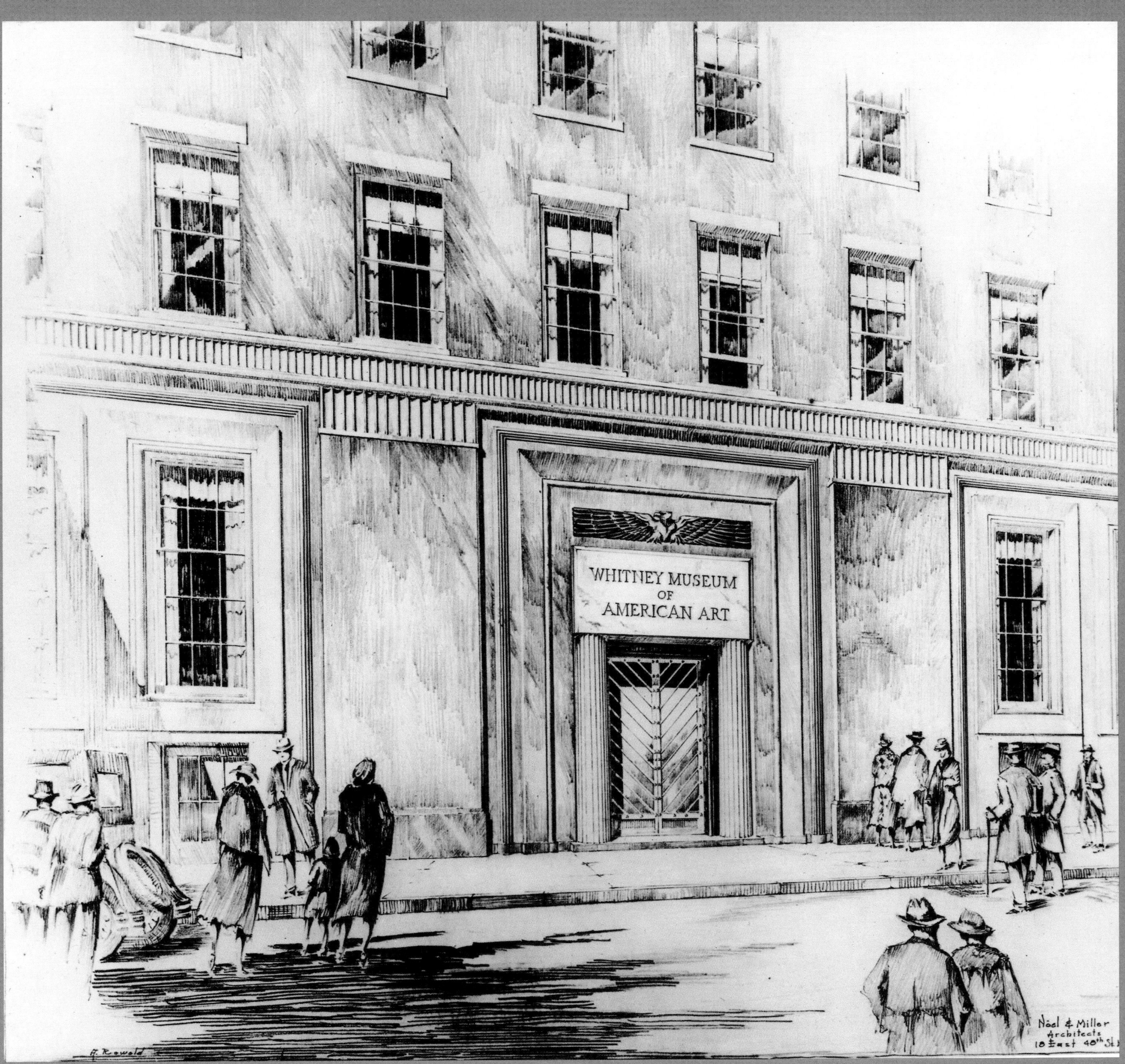

3.1. Rendering of Whitney Wing of the Metropolitan Museum of Art, unexecuted, drawn by Hugh Ferriss, 1944. Image © The Metropolitan Museum of Art.

THE WHITNEY MUSEUM OF AMERICAN ART AT A GLANCE

Corporate name:	The Whitney Museum of American Art
Address of current venue:	945 Madison Avenue, New York, New York 10021
Opening date of current venue:	1966
Architect of current venue:	Marcel Breuer
Address of original venue:	10 West 8th Street, New York, New York
Opening date of original venue:	1931
Architect of original venue:	Noel & Miller
Address of intermediate venue:	22 West 54th Street, New York, New York
Opening date of intermediate venue:	1954
Architect of intermediate venue:	Philip Johnson, Auguste Noel (Noel & Miller)
Address of future expansion:	Gansevoort Street (between 10th Avenue and Washington Street)
Projected opening date of future expansion:	2012
Architect of future expansion:	Renzo Piano
Collecting scope:	American Art, emphasizing modern and contemporary
Special programs:	Whitney Biennial
Amenities:	Bookstore, gift shop, restaurant

GERTRUDE VANDERBILT WHITNEY
AND THE BEGINNINGS OF THE WHITNEY MUSEUM

Gertrude Vanderbilt Whitney (born January 9, 1875, New York City; died April 18, 1942, New York City) was not only an heiress to the steamship and railroad fortune of her great-grandfather Cornelius Vanderbilt, but also a collector of American art. Thus, like Henry Clay Frick and John and Dominique de Menil, the fortune upon which a great museum would be built was from industry (though this time

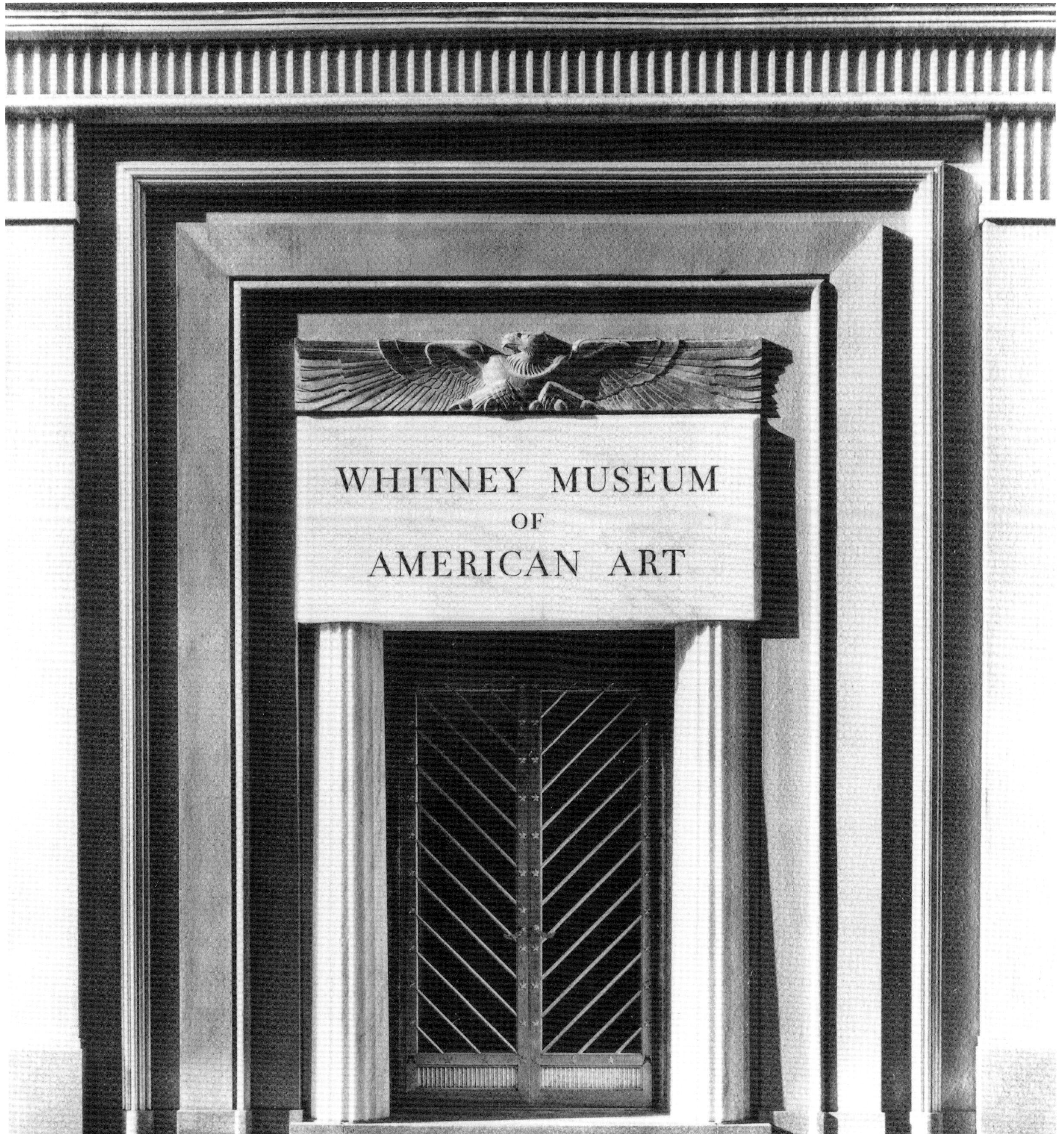
WHITNEY MUSEUM
OF
AMERICAN ART

transportation rather than energy); however, unlike the museum founders discussed above, Mrs. Whitney's fortune was inherited. Furthermore, her interest in the arts was not merely that of a collector but also that of an accomplished practitioner— she was a sculptor—successful enough to have an exhibition of her work at the Art Institute of Chicago in 1928.

Her role in the contemporary art world of her time was still greater than that of a practicing artist and collector; she was also an active patron of young artists and those having trouble financing their careers. To this end she opened the Whitney Studio Club in 1918 in Greenwich Village to provide an exhibition venue for the artists she supported. This institution would become the foundation for the eventual establishment of the Whitney Museum of American Art around her growing collection and interest in contemporary American art. Gertrude Vanderbilt Whitney's strong interest in contemporary American art remains the basis of one of the Whitney's most important functions in the American art world: since 1933 the museum has hosted the Whitney Biennials (the Whitney Museum opened in 1931), the most important such exhibition of contemporary American art in the world and perhaps the most important recurring museum-sponsored contemporary art show in the country.

THE ORIGINAL WHITNEY MUSEUM

The first venue of the Whitney Museum was in a series of neighboring, connected townhouses, entered through 8 West 8th Street in Greenwich Village, which had previously been the home of the Whitney Studio Club (the houses had a unified street façade but were formerly separate structures—numbers 8, 10, 12, and 14 West 8th Street; see figs. 3.1 and 3.2). This building is largely preserved and is today the home of the New York Studio School. When the Whitney (and all of its collections) opened in 1931, it was entirely the private property of Mrs. Gertrude Vanderbilt Whitney. It was not until November 27, 1935 that ownership was transferred to a trust with a board consisting of herself, her daughter Flora Whitney Miller, her son Cornelius Vanderbilt Whitney, Juliana Force (the first director of the Whitney Museum), William Adams Delano, and Frank L. Crocker.[1] The Deed of Trust lists this personal property as being transferred from Mrs. Whitney to the trustees:

> 1. The paintings, drawings, statuary and furnishings now located in her galleries at Nos. 8, 10 and 12 West Eighth Street, in the Borough of Manhattan, City, County and State of New York, and particularly described in an inventory delivered to the Trustees by the Founder contemporaneously herewith.
> 2. A lease of all the parts of the premises Nos. 8, 10, 12 and 14 West Eighth Street, in the Borough of Manhattan, City, County, and State of New York, now occupied

by the Founder as a gallery and exhibition rooms, for paintings, statuary and other works of art, under the name of *"WHITNEY MUSEUM OF AMERICAN ART"*; which said lease shall run for the term of ten years at a rental of One Dollar ($1.00) per year.

3. Twenty thousand (20,000) share of Common "B" stock of R. J. Reynolds Tobacco Company, which is of the present market value of approximately One million, one hundred and twenty thousand Dollars ($1,120,000), and the income from which is Sixty thousand Dollars ($60,000) per year.

4. One hundred thousand Dollars ($100,000) in cash.

Further, this Deed of Trust discusses the purpose of this new institution:

The nature, object and purpose of the institution to be founded, endowed and maintained are as follows:

To maintain a public art gallery and exhibition rooms for the purpose of presenting examples of the fine arts created by American artists, on the premises of which a lease is hereby granted, and upon such premises as the Trustees may hereafter select in addition thereto or in lieu thereof, for the use and benefit, free of expense to them, of all persons whomsoever, subject only to suitable rules and regulations; to preserve, protect, and put on public view, the paintings, drawings, and sculpture hereby acquired and hereafter to be acquired; to sell, exchange, and dispose of the same, and to acquire new works of art by American artists, from time to time as the Trustees may see fit; to render the said works of art available, under suitable regulations and restrictions, to artists, scholars, educators, and persons interested in art and literature; and to contribute to the encouragement and development of art and artists, generally, in America, and to the education of the public in art, literature, and kindred subjects.

The name by which the institution shall be known is "WHITNEY MUSEUM OF AMERICAN ART".

The fact that this Deed of Trust empowers the trustees to carry out the Whitney's mission "upon such premises as the Trustees may hereafter select in addition thereto or in lieu thereof" the venue on West 8th Street reveals that Mrs. Whitney never considered the original venue of the Whitney Museum to be in any way its permanent home. Further, it suggests that the physical consideration of the venue, museum architecture, was not of great importance to her (a very different attitude from that of Henry Clay Frick or Dominique de Menil). Further, the permission to "sell, exchange, and dispose of" works of art in her collection and "to acquire new works of art by American artists, from time to time as the Trustees may see fit" suggests that Gertrude Vanderbilt Whitney's interest was always in establishing an organic, evolving institution rather than a collection and venue that would memorialize her own collecting tastes and aesthetic preferences.

THE WHITNEY AND THE METROPOLITAN MUSEUM OF ART COALITION—TO BE OR NOT TO BE?

Following the death of Gertrude Vanderbilt Whitney in 1942, the will and dedication of the trustees she had appointed would indeed be tested. With the Second World War raging in Europe and Asia and a Whitney family divided in its commitment to the Whitney Museum of American Art, 1943 saw the closing of the galleries and the beginning of a long and serious discussion over the future of the institution and its collections. After much debate, it was decided that the Whitney Museum would form a "coalition" with the Metropolitan Museum of Art; the Metropolitan would build a new wing (on the south side of the existing museum, in roughly the position that the galleries dedicated to the Arts of Africa, Oceania, and the Americas on the first floor, and European nineteenth-century art on the second floor, now inhabit) to be known as the Whitney Wing.[2] This agreement was official and public, being released to the press immediately and announced in all of the major New York City newspapers the next day. Here is an excerpt from a representative article in the *New York Herald Tribune,* dated January 19, 1943:

> Plans for the coalition of the Whitney Museum of American Art with the Metropolitan Museum of Art were announced yesterday at the annual meeting of the Corporation of the Metropolitan Museum. The Whitney Museum, at 10 West Eighth Street, was founded by the late Gertrude Vanderbilt Whitney, sculptor and widow of Harry Payne Whitney.
>
> Mrs. Flora Whitney Miller, President of the Whitney Museum, and William Church Osborn, president of the Metropolitan Museum, who made the announcement jointly at the end of the meeting at the Metropolitan, said that removal of the Whitney Museum's artworks to the Metropolitan would begin after the close in February of the Gertrude V. Whitney Memorial Exhibit. The artworks will be stored at the Metropolitan, and it is expected that from time to time certain sections of the Whitney Collection will be put on display.
>
> But the first full-fledged exhibits of the collection at the Metropolitan will not take place until April, 1944, when the Whitney Annual Exhibition of painting, watercolors, sculpture and the graphic arts will be held.
>
> Museum officials also announced yesterday that plans are now being made to erect after the war at the site of the Metropolitan Museum, Fifth Avenue at Eighty-second Street, a Whitney Wing to house the Gertrude V. Whitney collection as well as the Metropolitan's other collections of American art.
>
> Though the site of the new wing has not been determined, museum officials said that the planning of the Whitney Wing would be a part of the general architectural program for the rearrangement and improvement of the museum's buildings after the war. Architectural details of the improvements,

which are expected to cost $4,000,000, will be announced later this year. The Museum's building program has already been approved by the City Planning Commission.

What will be done with the buildings at 10 West Eighth Street has not been decided, museum officials said. [3]

From the beginning of this intended coalition, the Whitney tried to establish continuity with its own history. As stated in the above newspaper article, the Whitney would continue its important biennial (at that time it was an annual) exhibition of contemporary American art. It would continue to acquire contemporary American art for its permanent collection (now belonging to the Metropolitan) and to fulfill its mission of encouraging the development of contemporary art in America. An undated document in the Whitney Museum's files (probably from early 1943) reveals how the Whitney envisioned this continuity being manifest in the architecture of the new Whitney Wing:

> In general, as has already been agreed upon by the Trustees of both organizations, the Whitney Wing should recreate something of the atmosphere of charm and the intimate character of the present building [i.e., at West 8th Street].
>
> This can be accomplished by keeping the galleries moderate sized and with sufficient variety in shapes and dimensions. This will avoid monotony.
>
> Ceilings should be about fifteen feet high and the lighting directed toward the walls and not in the eyes of the spectator. Galleries should range in size from 18' by 22' to 25' by 48'.
>
> As the general number of exhibits will be temporary, all suggestion of "period" should be eliminated. This would include all elimination of wainscoting, decorative molding and trim except in the entrance hall and stairways.
>
> *Ground Floor*—By placing the main entrance at ground level the impractical and formidable steps could be avoided. The entrance doorway could be similar to that of the present building, on a larger scale of course.
>
> The *Entrance Hall*, as in the present building, to be circular or oval in shape with curving stairs to the right and left with a bank of elevators conveniently placed. If the ceiling on this level proves too low, it could be carried up to include two floors.
>
> The ground floor should provide space for check-room, toilets, information desk, switchboard and sales room. A comfortable lounge and reading room might be a feature of a combined publications sales-room and information bureau.
>
> The ground floor should also contain offices (at least for the operating staff), storage and receiving and packing space. A storage room arranged for

easy access for the study of the collections not on public exhibition at the time. Service elevators should connect the storage and shipping rooms with the permanent and temporary galleries.

If possible, receiving and shipping rooms could be provided and these should be independent of the Metropolitan. This would require a separate service driveway and loading platforms.

Second Floor—(which is equal to the Metropolitan main floor)

Galleries for sculpture, watercolors, drawings and prints, administrative offices, board and reception rooms.

The stairways leading from the main entrance hall might open directly into the sculpture gallery. This gallery to have a higher ceiling than fifteen feet. Most of the material on this floor would be from the permanent collection and need not necessarily be confined to the mediums given above.

With combined fluorescent and incandescent light placed above glass ceilings, as already installed in the sculpture gallery or the present building, it would be possible to simulate the effect of daylight.

Third Floor—(Equal to Metropolitan second floor)

Galleries for paintings from the permanent collection and temporary exhibition galleries.

The galleries for temporary exhibitions should be easily accessible from storage by way of the freight elevator, and should be placed so that they can be closed to the public without interfering with free access to the galleries containing the permanent collection.

The galleries for temporary exhibitions should contain space enough to show 250 items at one time.

An auditorium seating about 400 should be adjacent to the temporary exhibition galleries as most lectures and other programs would relate to the exhibitions on view at the time.

A smaller and more informal lecture room could be placed in this area where movies could be shown, talks given for the benefit of gallery visitors, and where material relating to the current exhibitions could be on view. [4]

Thus, at this point, the Whitney saw this new Whitney Wing at the Metropolitan as a physically as well as programmatically autonomous unit; truly a museum within a museum rather than as an integrated part of the Metropolitan Museum of Art. Architectural drawings and models were commissioned, and the Whitney's architects, the firm of Noel & Miller, delivered a scheme for the entrance with an American eagle and doors reflecting those of the 8th Street building (figs. 3.3–3.5). [5]

From the beginning, this proposed coalition brought about considerable resistance from the art world. Following the announcement that the then-closed Whitney Museum on West 8th Street would reopen for the biennial of fall 1943, a

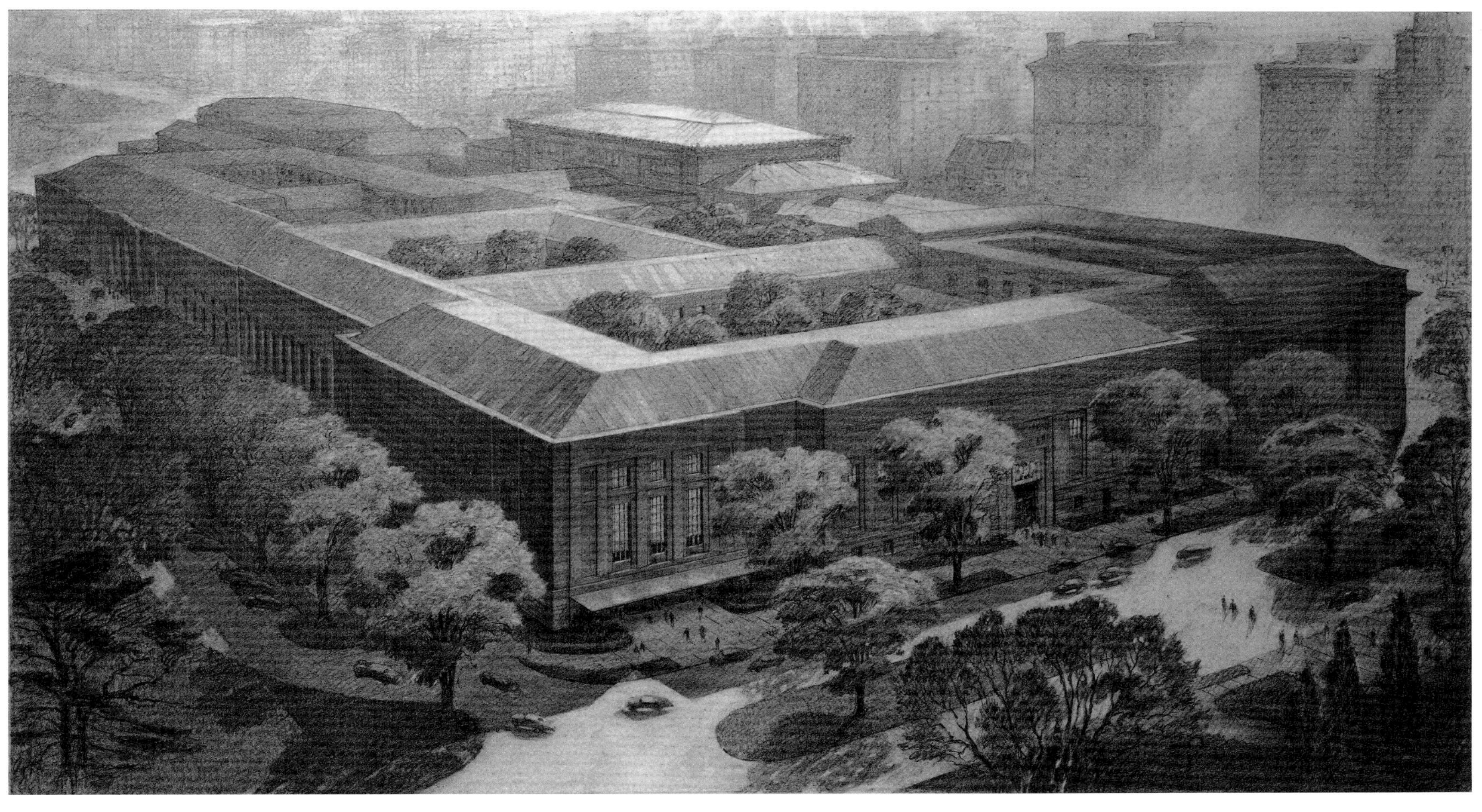

3.3. Rendering of Whitney Wing of the Metropolitan Museum of Art, unexecuted, drawn by Hugh Ferriss, 1944. The Metropolitan Museum of Art. Image © The Metropolitan Museum of Art.

letter signed by 168 contemporary American artists was sent to Mrs. G. MacCulloch Miller. This letter revealed the importance of the Whitney's place in the art world from the perspective of the artists that Gertrude Vanderbilt Whitney worked so hard to advance. It is worth quoting this letter in its entirety:

Dear Mrs. Miller:

When the announcement came last year of the closing of the Whitney Museum of American Art each of us experienced a deep sense of disappointment and loss. The unexpected reopening of the Museum this fall brought back to us a renewed sense of the Whitney's significance and it was marked by extraordinary feeling of sentiment and affection. It was as though we adventitiously found ourselves back in a home which we thought we had lost.

The tie between most museums and the living artist is usually a tenuous and impersonal one. The traditional role of the museum has so long been that of a repository for the art of the past that the existence of the artist has been recognized only with seeming reluctance or not at all. Now museums exhibit his work, sometimes award him a prize and more rarely, make a purchase. But the pervasive feeling which the average museum has tended to communicate to the living artist has been one of aloofness and relative lack of interest.

With the Whitney this has never been the case; and to the Whitney belongs the major share of the credit for the more liberal treatment which contemporary American Art has received from most other American museums. Since its opening the Whitney has set the pattern in this country for what a museum can do for the art of its own period. From its Whitney Studio Club days, through its various developments, up to the present, it has been the greatest single force in support to the living art of the United States.

The Whitney has always treated American artists with sincerity and respect. It did not reward [*sic*] prizes. Instead, it set aside a fund each year, within the limits of its resources to buy as many works of art from its exhibitions and outside these exhibitions as it could. No living American artist was excluded from participation in its activities because of his aesthetic direction and schools shared its advantages without discrimination. This democratic policy, wherein merit alone was the consideration, had an inspiring effect on the young artists of America and an invigorating effect on American art as a whole. By this procedure Mrs. Whitney and Mrs. Force [Julianna Force, founding director of the Whitney Museum] did more than found a museum. They helped to build faith in living American art. Mrs. Whitney's love of art and the wisdom shown in the form taken by her patronage has had incalculable results upon the present and future of our aesthetic culture. The country has made great strides forward since the days which marked the beginning of the work of Mrs. Whitney and Mrs. Force. We artists understand the great debt which the country owes to the Whitney for this advance.

As a group of artists we take this occasion to express our deep appreciation of the Whitney Museum. We have been privileged to feel that it is so much a part of our lives that its future is of vital importance to us. Should the trustees and director consider that our cooperation might be of service in furthering the interests of the museum we should welcome such an opportunity. We sincerely hope that, whatever changes are deemed necessary to guarantee the continuance of the museum, they may never interfere with its unique functions and the ideals established and carried on by Mrs. Whitney and Mrs. Force. [6]

The 168 signatories to this letter included such important and diverse artists as Thomas Hart Benton, Paul Cadmus, Alexander Calder, Stewart Davis, Arshile Gorky, Edward Hopper, Isamu Noguchi, Charles Sheeler, and David Smith.

Although it took some time for the trustees of the Whitney to get there, they too would realize the unique and important role the Whitney had played in the American art world—*after* they were unable to secure the levels of autonomy for the Whitney collection that they desired from the Metropolitan Museum. The institutional commitment of the Whitney to the often-controversial content of

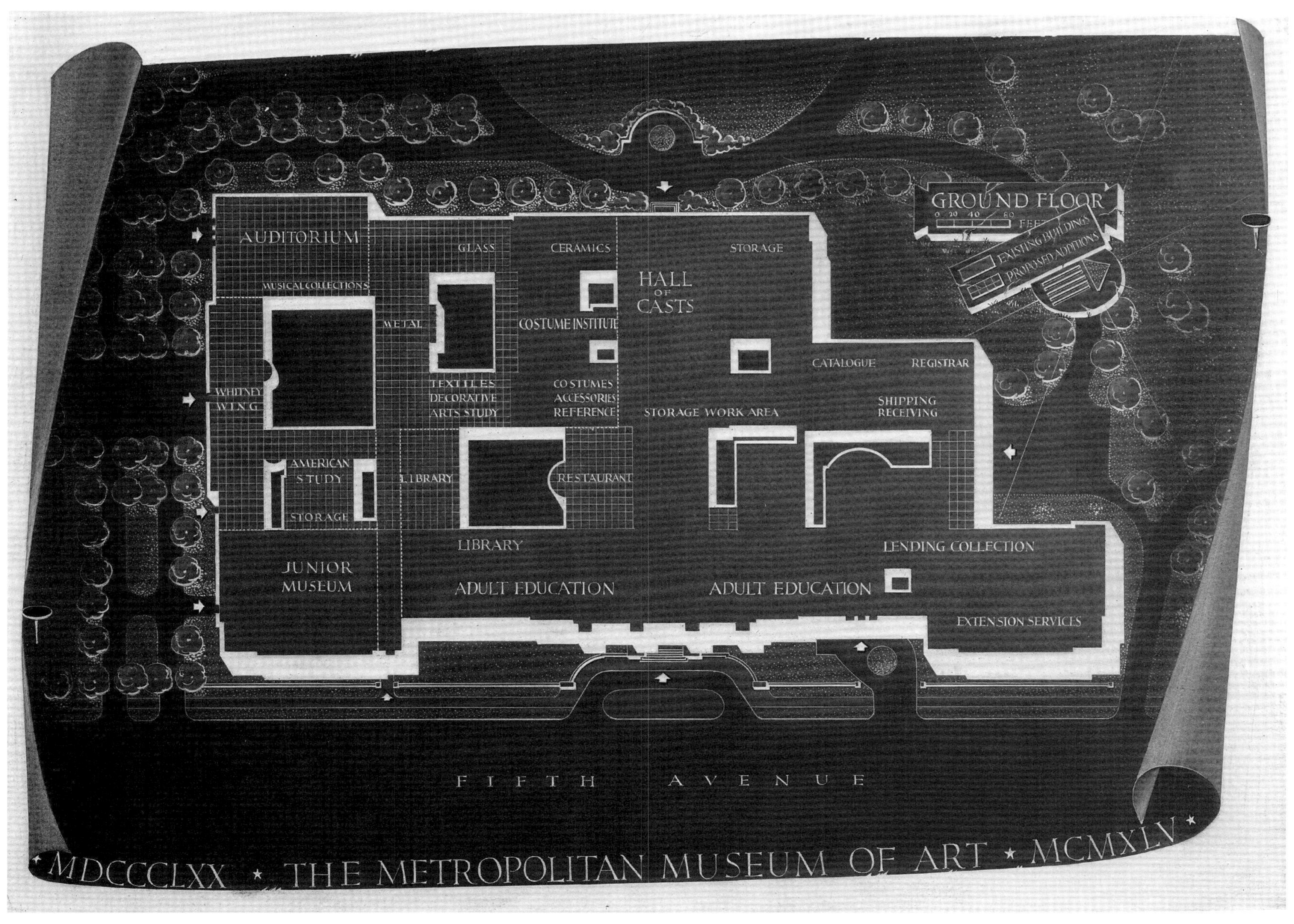

3.4. Plan of proposed addition to the Metropolitan Museum of Art, including Whitney Wing, unexecuted, Robert B. O'Connor and Aymar Embury II, 1945. Image © The Metropolitan Museum of Art.

contemporary American art could not easily be enacted in the face of the relative conservatism of the Metropolitan Museum of Art of the 1940s. On October 1, 1948, after repeated attempts to reconcile their differences and negotiate a series of agreements, the Whitney would announce the termination of the attempt at forming the coalition with the Metropolitan Museum of Art. The similarity of this announcement to the letter written by the artists, quoted above, is striking:

> A short time after the death of Gertrude Vanderbilt Whitney, the founder and sponsor of the Whitney Museum of American Art, the Trustees of the Museum and the Trustees of the Metropolitan Museum of Art reached a

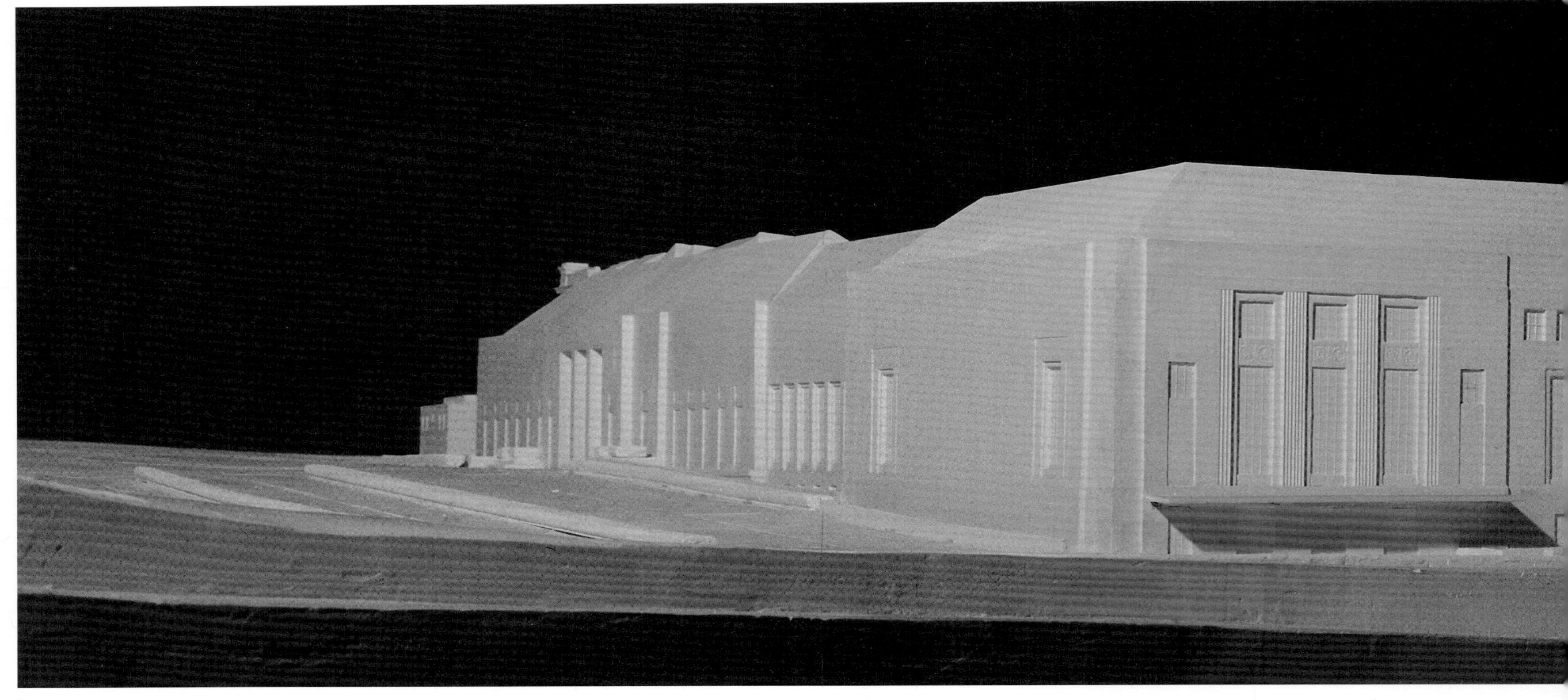

3.5. Model of proposed southwest addition to the Metropolitan Museum of Art, including Whitney Wing, Robert B. O'Connor and Aymar Embury II, unexecuted, 1945. Image © The Metropolitan Museum of Art. Photograph by John H. Heffren.

tentative agreement looking toward the eventual coalition of the two museums. The Trustees of the Whitney Museum looked forward to this coalition, which would have combined the two most important collections of American art and housed them in a suitable wing of the country's largest museum, and at the same time would have continued the original purposes of Gertrude Vanderbilt Whitney in founding the Whitney Museum. Since 1943 the staffs of the two museums have endeavored to integrate their activities as a preliminary to this coalition. However, the aims of the two institutions in relation to contemporary art have proved to be so divergent that the Trustees of the Whitney Museum have decided to abandon the plans for coalition.

The Whitney Museum represents a long tradition of liberalism in contemporary American art. The Museum's origins go back forty years to 1908, when Mrs. Whitney founded the Whitney Studio Gallery to provide a place where progressive artists, excluded from the academic art world, could exhibit and sell their work. For many years the Gallery and its successor the Whitney Studio Club were important centers of liberal art in the country. With the founding of the Whitney Museum in 1930 this liberal tradition was embodied in permanent form.

The Museum, which is primarily concerned with contemporary art, has

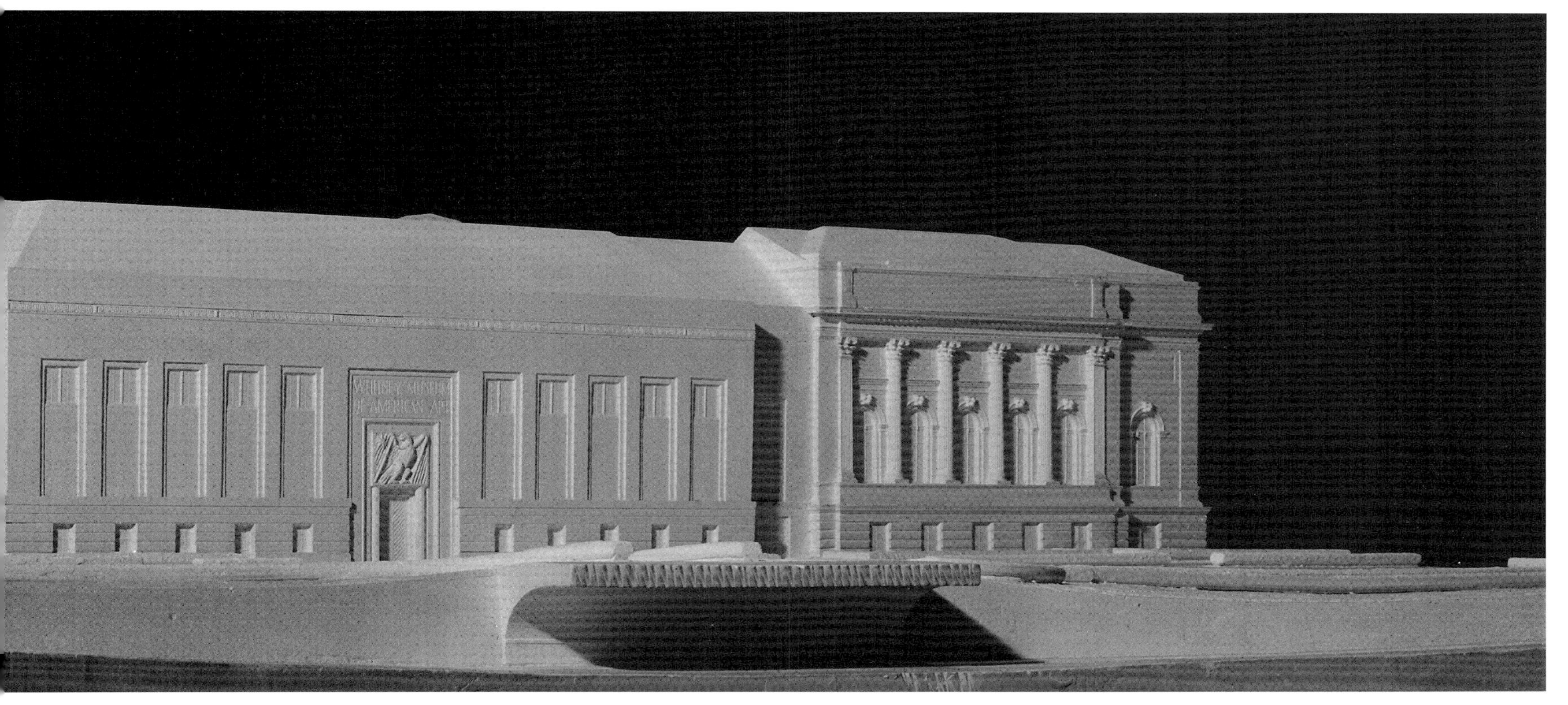

always aimed impartially to represent the many diverse tendencies of the art of our time.[. . .]

In the years of contact between the staffs of the Whitney Museum and of the Metropolitan Museum since the first announcement of the proposed coalition in 1943, it has become increasingly apparent that there were serious divergences in the attitude toward contemporary art of the two institutions, especially with respect to the showing of advanced trends in the art of today. This disagreement in fundamental principles raised grave doubts in the minds of the Trustees of the Whitney Museum whether the Museum's liberal tradition could be preserved after coalition. This consideration outweighed the many advantages of the coalition. Therefore after careful deliberation they have decided reluctantly and with sincere regret to abandon the plans for the coalition.[. . .][7]

If the tone and language of this announcement seem much more in accord with the mission and collecting interests of the Museum of Modern Art (though with an American rather than a European focus), it will not come as a surprise that it was to the Museum of Modern Art that the Whitney would look for a partner. However, the trustees had clearly learned a lesson from their failure to reach an agreement with the Metropolitan, so the agreement made with the Museum of

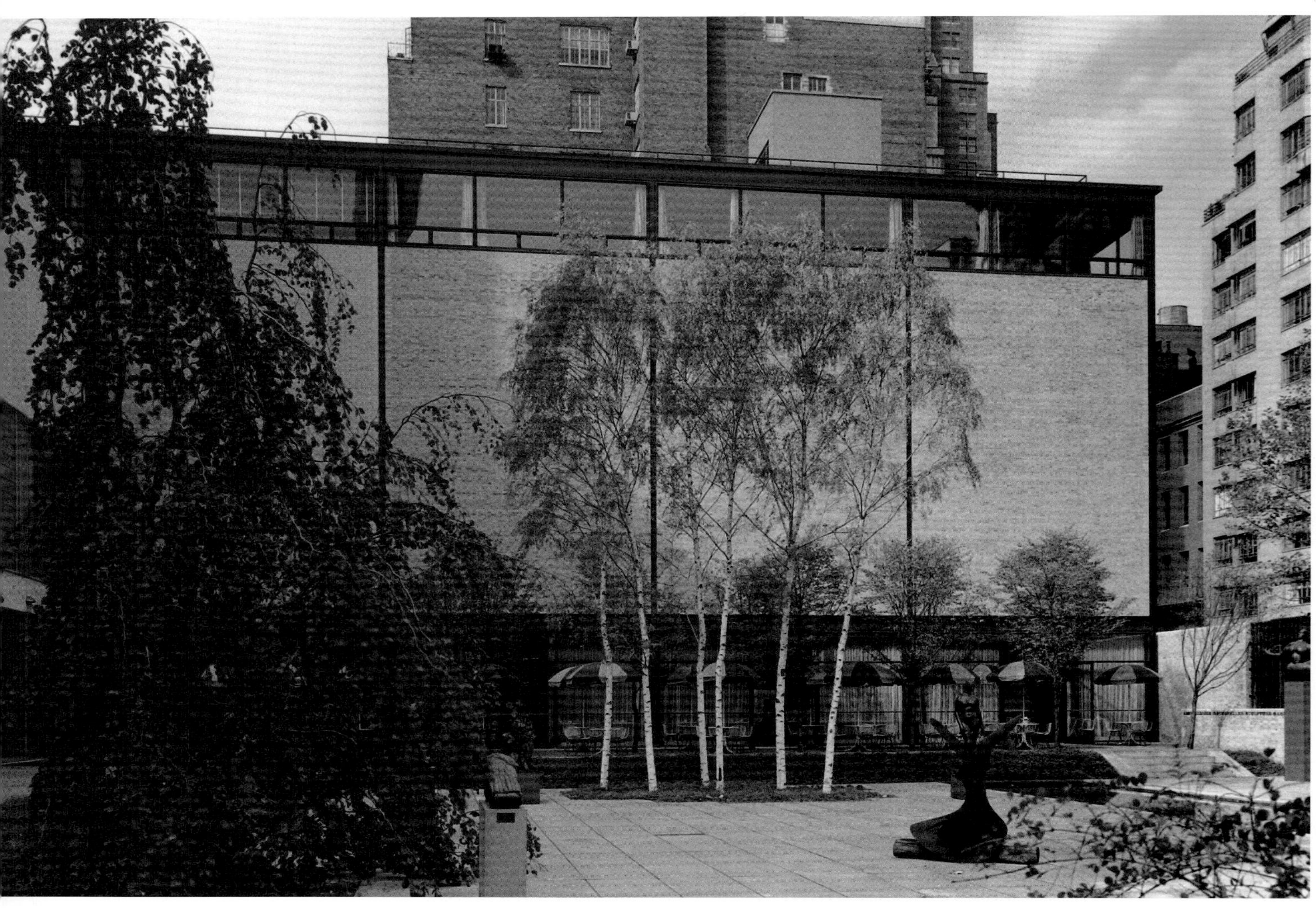

3.6. East façade of the Whitney Museum of American Art at 54th Street, seen from the Museum of Modern Art's Sculpture Garden, Philip Johnson, Auguste L. Noel, 1954; note the ground floor was the restaurant of the Museum of Modern Art. Ezra Stoller © Esto.

Modern Art for a new building and some coordination between institutional goals and collecting policies would be much less ambitious; it would also actually reach fruition.

THE WHITNEY MOVES UPTOWN— THE FIFTY-FOURTH STREET BUILDING

As is explored further in other sections of this book, as early as 1933 the Museum of Modern Art was interested in reaching agreements with both the Whitney Museum

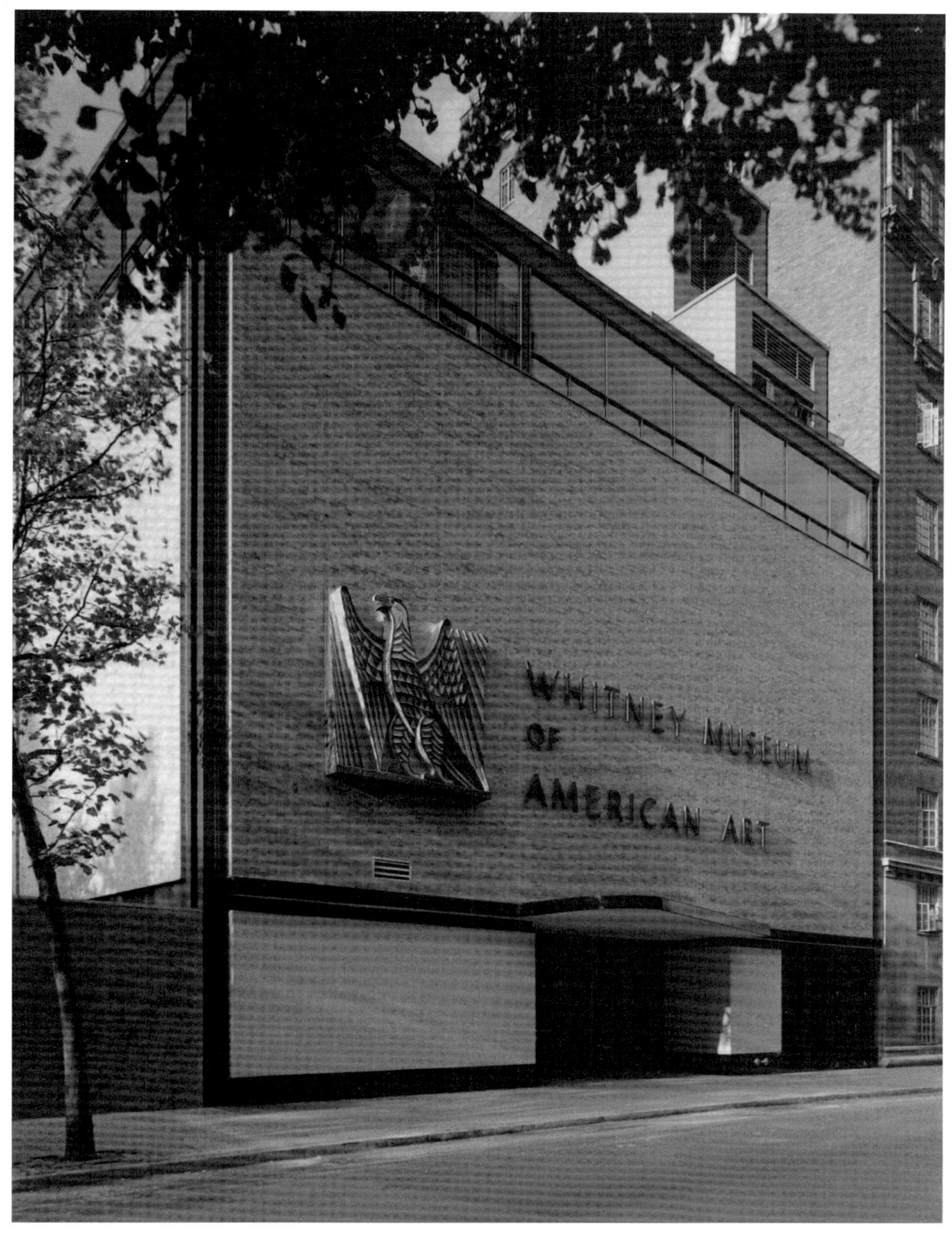

3.7. The 54th Street façade of the Whitney Museum, 1954. Ezra Stoller © Esto.

of American Art and the Metropolitan Museum of Art regarding the coordination of collection policies and the redistribution of some of the works owned by each institution to better fit each museum's relative advantage in existing collections, method, and overall philosophy.[8] Although some basic agreements between the institutions were signed in 1947, the abandonment of the coalition between the Whitney and the Metropolitan required that those agreements be reevaluated and renegotiated in 1948. The final agreement between the Metropolitan Museum and the Museum of Modern Art was signed in 1948, though it would have only limited ramifications, as it was discontinued in 1953.

As with most proposals and agreements, so too with those between important museums: those that are signed quickly with little argument are

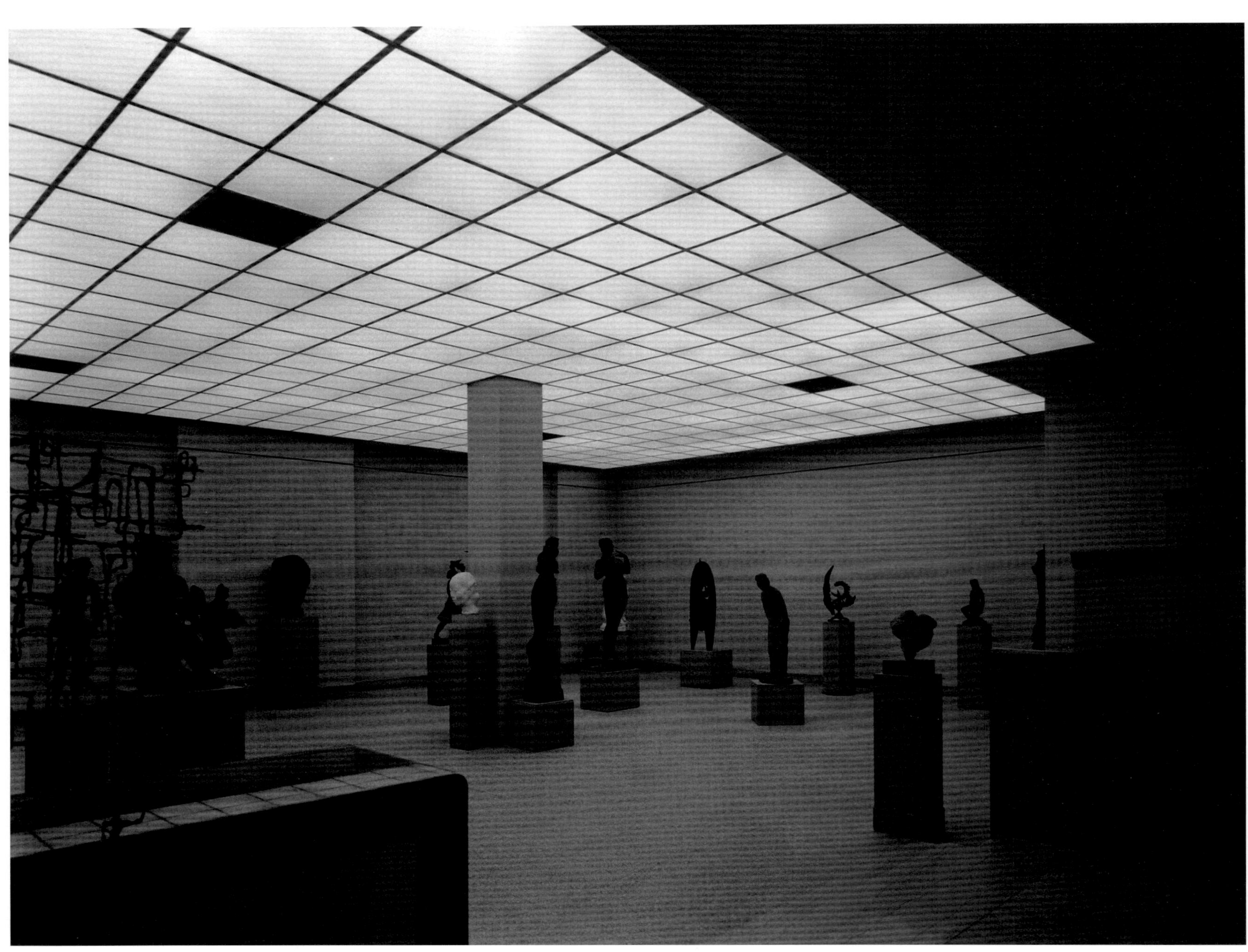

3.8. Interior of galleries, Whitney
Museum, 1954. Ezra Stoller © Esto.

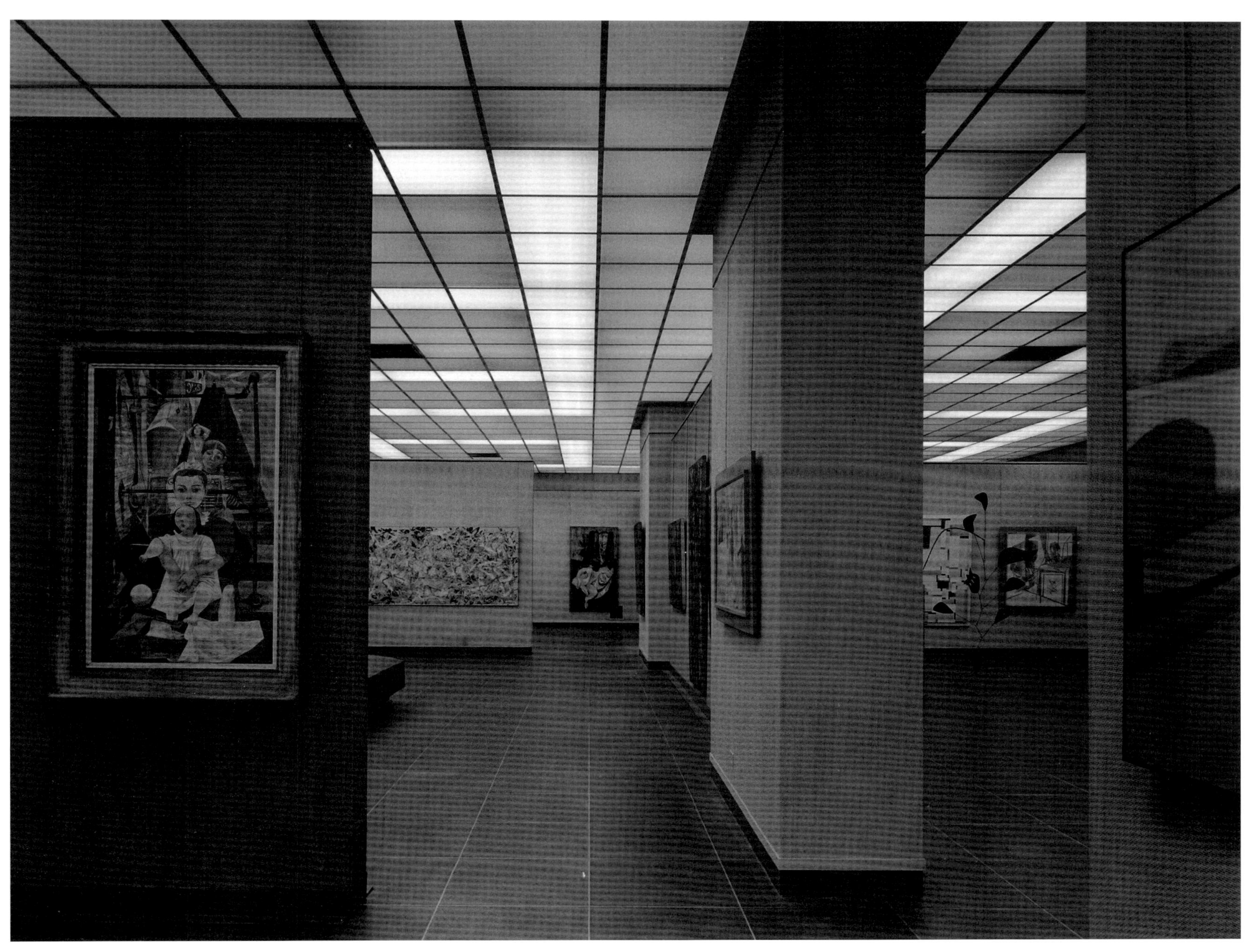

3.9. Interior of galleries, Whitney Museum, 1954. Ezra Stoller © Esto.

those that actually get implemented. By May 31, 1949, agreement between the Whitney and the Museum of Modern Art had been reached; the Museum of Modern Art would transfer land adjacent to their museum to the Whitney, to be the future home of a fully independent Whitney Museum of American art. [9] No time was wasted in announcing this agreement to the public; the same day that the land deed to the property on 54th Street, adjacent to the existing Museum of Modern Art was conveyed to the Whitney, the two museums issued a joint press release:

> Mrs. G. Mcculloch Miller, President of the Board of Trustees of the Whitney Museum of American Art, and Mr. John Hay Whitney, Chairman of the Board of Trustees of the Museum of Modern Art, announce that an agreement between the Boards of Trustees of the two museums has been reached by which the Museum of Modern Art will transfer by gift a plot of land 50 x 100 feet in the west portion of its property on 54th Street for a new building for the Whitney Museum.
>
> The agreement will not affect the current art policies of the two museums and their complete independence of one another. The Whitney Museum will continue to devote its activities entirely to American art and will not exhibit foreign works; and the Museum of Modern Art will not arrange shows comparable to the Whitney Museum's annual exhibitions of American painting and sculpture. [10]

Thus, from its conception, the new Whitney would have complete autonomy from the Museum of Modern Art. The prohibition against collecting and exhibiting foreign art was hardly a restriction, as the very mission of the institution had always been restricted to American art. Further, the agreement protected the Whitney's signature event, the biennials and annuals.

The condition in this agreement that the new building would be "in harmony" with the Museum of Modern Art and subject to its board's approval was very important, however. Unlike the abandoned project at the Metropolitan, the new Whitney would not be a stripped-down classical building with major architectural allusions to the Whitney building on 8th Street; rather it would be a modernist building, more consistent with the contemporary art that the Whitney advanced, collected, and exhibited. The eastern façade of this building would form the western boundary of the Museum of Modern Art's sculpture garden and would even contain the restaurant of the Museum of Modern Art. Architecturally, it would therefore be fully integrated with the structures of the Museum of Modern Art. (In fact, when the Whitney moved to its current location in 1966, this building was incorporated into the Museum of Modern Art [see below Chapter 5] and was used by the Museum of Modern Art until the building of the Taniguchi addition, which opened in 2004.)

Though the architect of record for the new Whitney Museum was still the Whitney's architect, Auguste L. Noel of Miller & Noel, Philip Johnson, the

3.10. Trustee Meeting Room/Conference Room (4th Floor), Whitney Museum of American Art, 22 West 54th Street, New York, NY. Frances Mulhall Achilles Library, Whitney Museum of American Art, N.Y. Photograph by Alexandre Georges, Hewlitt, N.Y.

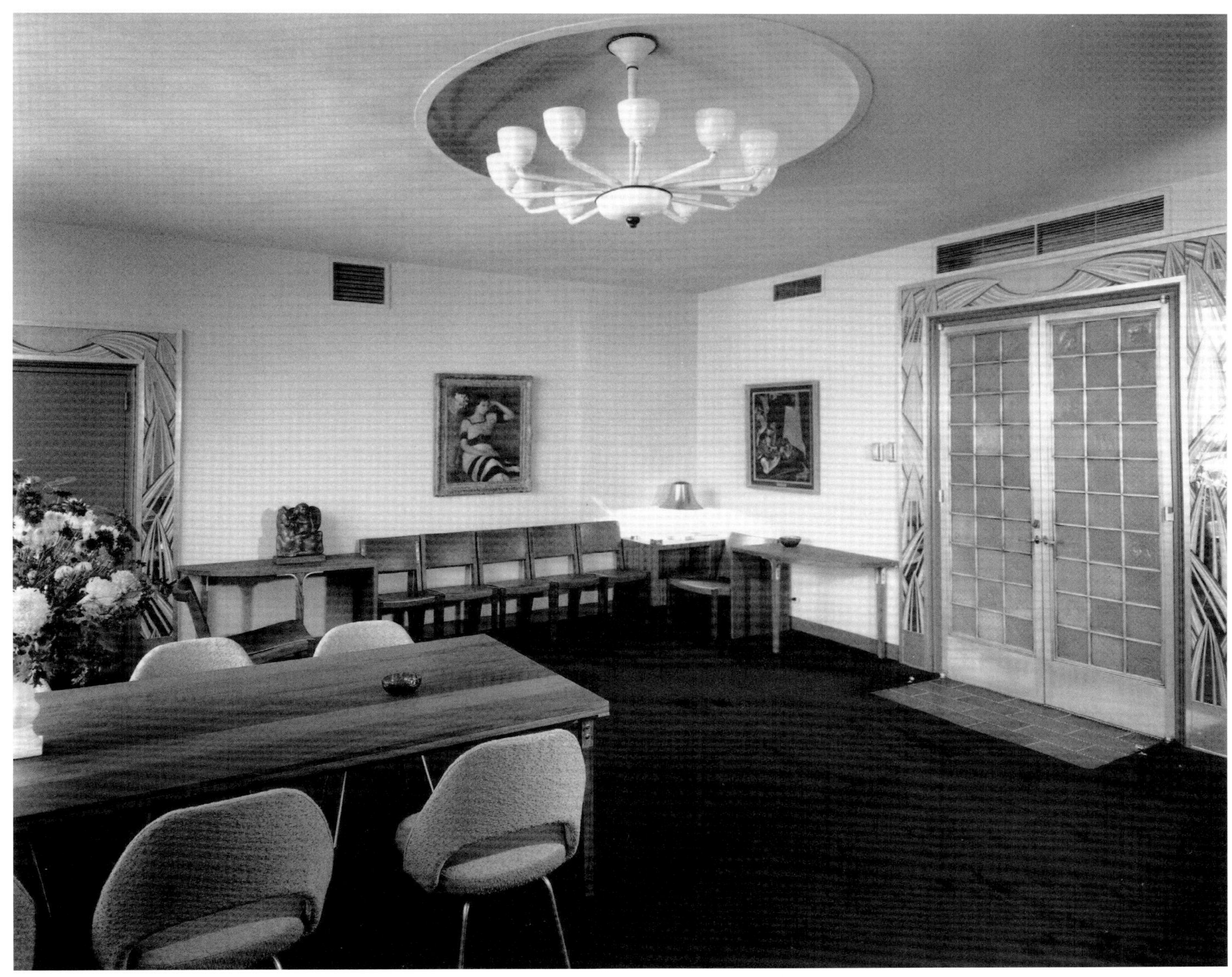

Museum of Modern Art's curator of architecture and unofficial architect played a critical role in the design of the building.[11] A portion of the ground floor of the new building—that facing the Museum of Modern Art's sculpture garden—would belong to the Modern and serve as their restaurant. Johnson would also be responsible for the entire eastern façade of the new Whitney, which served as the western terminus of the Modern's garden and formed a coordinated composition with the original Museum of Modern Art building on the south side of the garden. This façade would dictate the rhythm, scale, proportion, and detailing of the main 54th Street entrance façade designed by Noel, but clearly following Johnson's lead (see figs. 3.6 and 3.7). The only reference to the 8th Street Whitney façade on the new one was the placement of a relief of an American eagle, then the symbol of the Whitney, on the eastern end of the entrance façade (the south side of 54th Street).

To fill the new, much more spacious, white cube galleries that replaced the domestic spaces that had been converted to galleries on 8th Street, the Whitney raised money to continue acquiring contemporary art through the deaccessioning and sale of all of its nineteenth-century art (see figs. 3.8 and 3.9). As is the usual practice among collecting institutions, money raised through the sale of works is used only for the purchase of new works for the collection.[12] This collection included paintings, watercolors, drawings, prints, and sculpture by such artists as Eakins, Homer, and Audubon. The new, modern galleries would therefore be used principally for the exhibition of modern and contemporary art, the only art that would be collected by the Whitney from this point forward.

THE WHITNEY MOVES FURTHER UPTOWN: THE MARCEL BREUER BUILDING

The 54th Street building succeeded in increasing the gallery space of the Whitney Museum and giving it a physical environment more in keeping with the modernist aesthetic of the contemporary art that it championed. The Trustees' Room (fig. 3.10) and the movable partitions employed in the galleries also allowed it to keep a trace of the domestic scale that was part of the tradition of the original 8th Street venue. However, the Whitney's close proximity to, and smaller scale than, the Museum of Modern Art diluted its feel of independence and individual identity:

> The 54th Street building took five years to realize, opening only in 1954; six years later the Whitney was ready to abandon it. While attendance had increased, the Museum had come to look like an annex, perhaps a poor cousin, of its mighty neighbor. Moreover, in 1956 a patron's group had been founded, the Friends of the Whitney Museum of American Art, whose members wanted a more public presence for the institution. Friends acquired works for the collection, sponsored exhibitions, and—having bought a stake in the Museum—demanded a share in its policy making: in 1961, the Board of Trustees was reorganized to include supporters outside the family, its advisors, and staff. The search for a new, independent home that would assert a clear identity was the first order of business. [13]

The institutional dangers of the close association with the Museum of Modern Art were becoming apparent, and the Whitney sought to reestablish its own identity, program, aesthetic, and unique place in the art world of New York City.

On June 17, 1963 the Whitney announced to the public its plans to build a new facility in a new location:

> The Whitney Museum of American Art announces today (Monday, June 17) that it has contracted to sell its present building at 22 West 54 Street to the Museum of Modern Art and that it would erect a new one, approximately

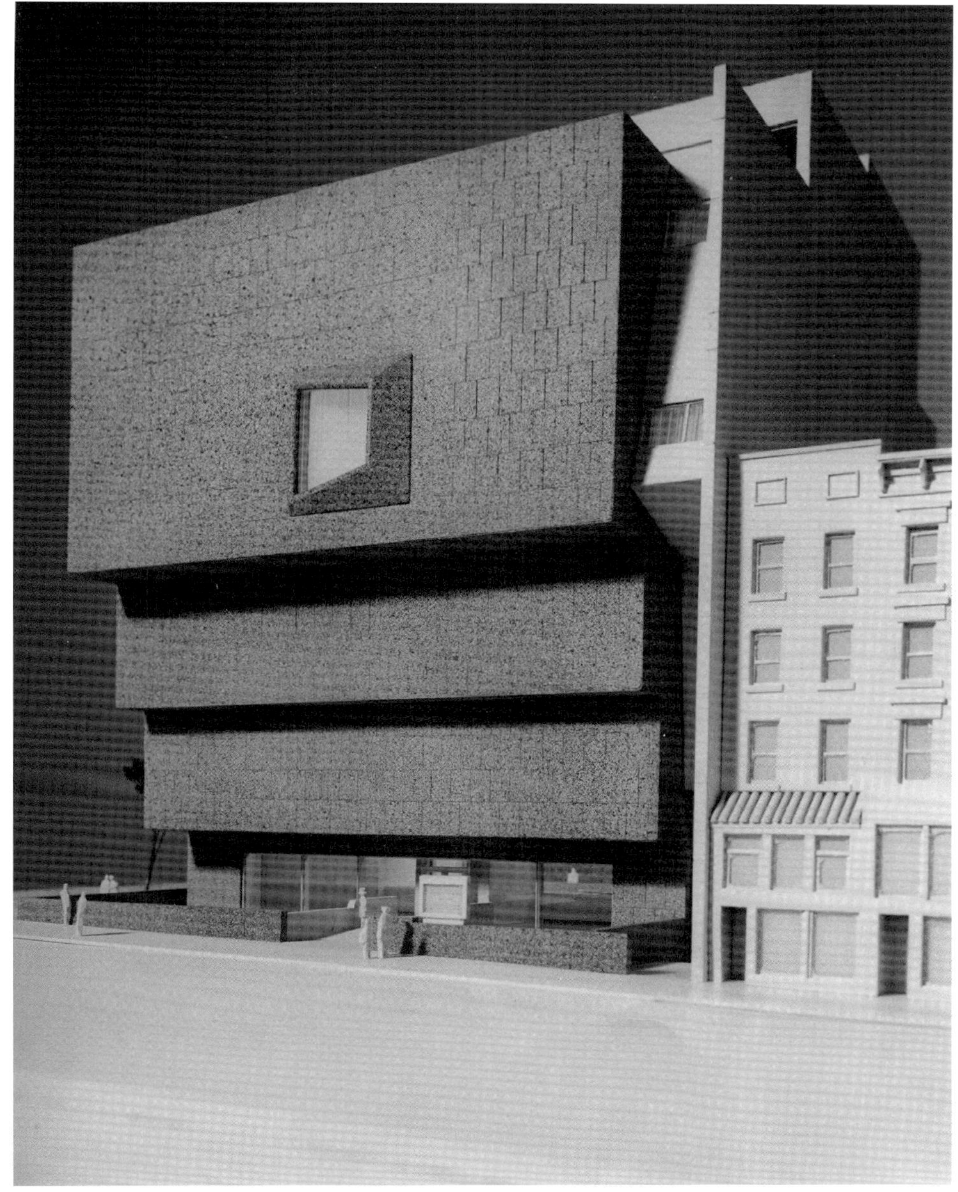

3.11. Model of the Whitney Museum, 1964.

three times as large on a site at the southeast corner of Madison Avenue and East 75th Street. Marcel Breuer, the noted architect, will be retained to design the new museum, which will he his first work erected in Manhattan. Michael E. Irving will be the consulting architect. [14]

This new project would become the Whitney Museum of American Art that we know today. Not only a radical design, Breuer's building would become an architectural icon of New York City and a symbol of the radicalism and controversy that would surround much of the Whitney Museum's activities and commitment to often controversial trends in contemporary art (perhaps best encapsulated in the Whitney's biennials).

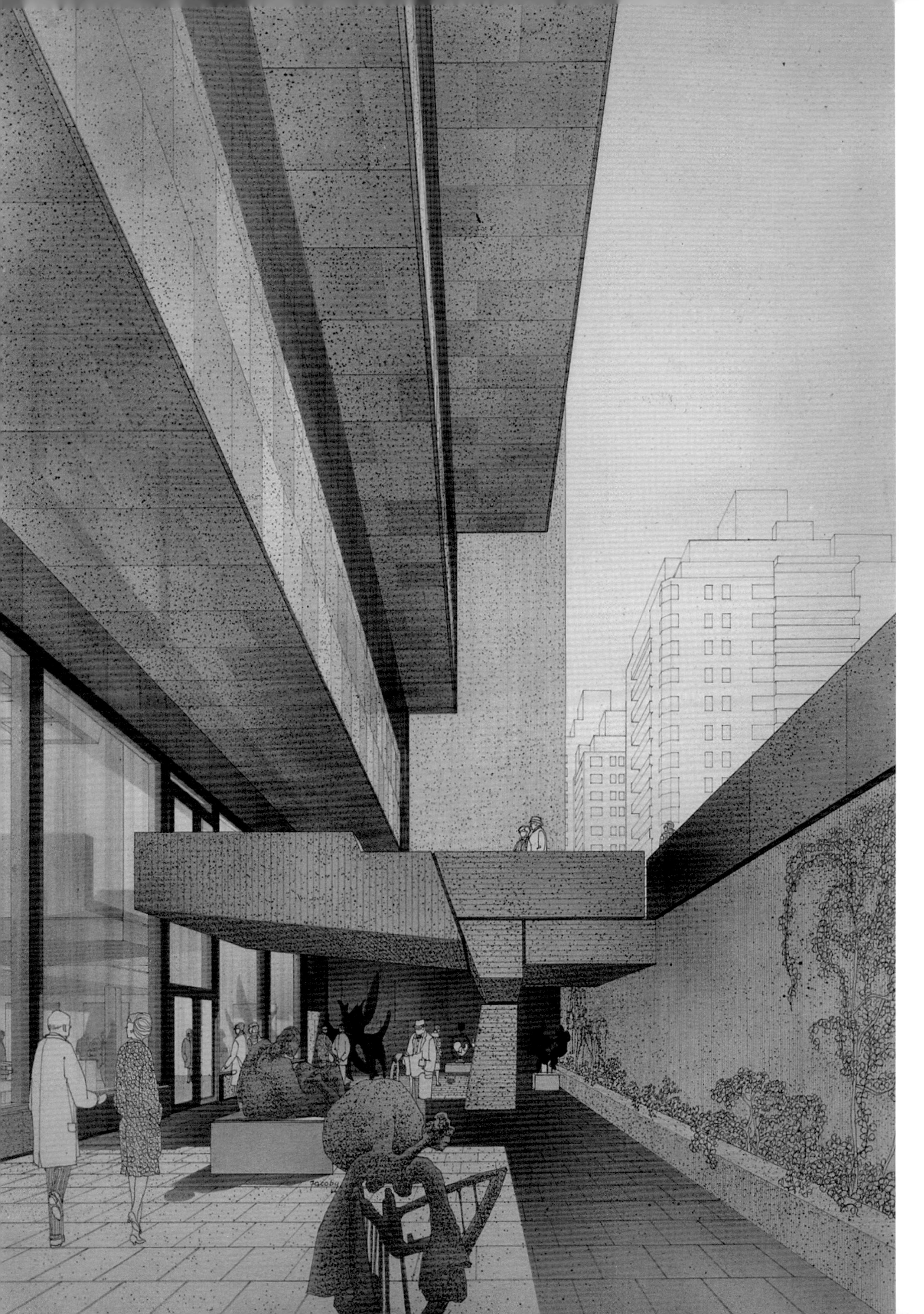

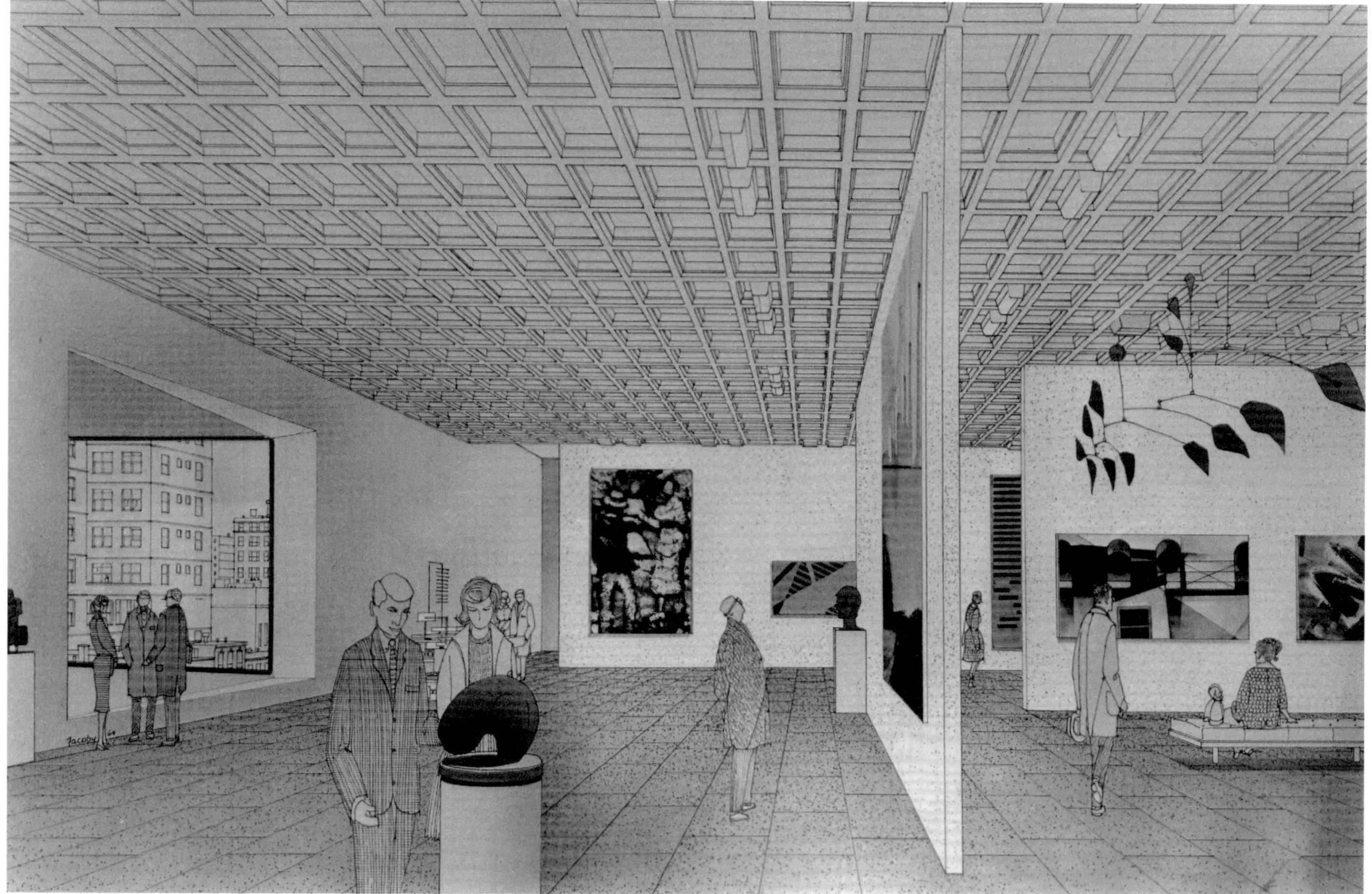

3.12. View of sunken sculpture garden, showing entrance bridge and projecting floors overhead. Marcel Breuer. From *A Program for the New WHitney Museum of American Art*, c. 1965–66. Whitney Museum of American Art.

3.13. Partial view of the fourth floor gallery, showing movable floor-to-ceiling partitions and large window alcove. Whitney Museum, Marcel Breuer. From *A Program for the New WHitney Museum of American Art*, c. 1965–66. Whitney Museum of American Art.

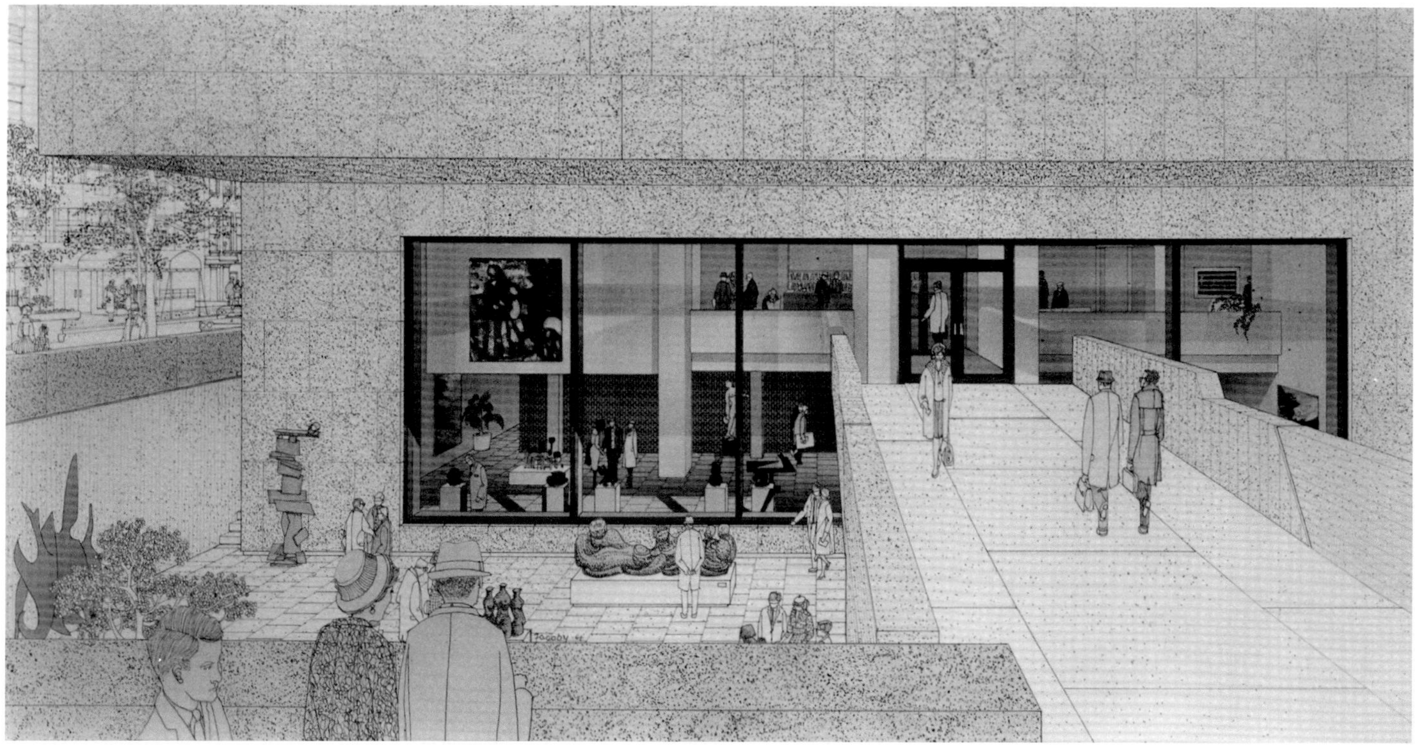

3.14. Entrance of the new Museum, showing the sidewalk-parapet and sunken sculpture garden, which continues to the interior through a two-story-high glass wall. Whitney Museum, Marcel Breuer. From *A Program for the New WHitney Museum of American Art*, c. 1965–66. Whitney Museum of American Art.

The new location on the Upper East Side would place the Whitney Museum in the "Museum Mile" district of Manhattan. Though one block east of the "mile" itself (the Whitney would be on Madison Avenue rather than Fifth Avenue), it would be five blocks north of the Frick Collection on 70th Street and Fifth Avenue (more or less the southernmost of the museums of the district) and seven blocks south of the main entrance of the Metropolitan Museum of Art on 82nd Street. It would also be located very near to the Guggenheim Museum and the Jewish Museum, two institutions that, at that time, had major commitments to contemporary art. However, it was far enough from all of these institutions to reassert its own identity and autonomy.

Before the new building design was begun, careful consideration of special needs was undertaken. Here is a summary of a comparison of the 54th Street venue to the projections for the Madison Avenue building:

Function	Existing Square Feet	Square Feet Recommended
Storage	2,588	5,176
Work areas	1,814	2,935
Exhibition space	9,939	19,899
Office space	1,808	2,926
Library and files	700	700
Lounges/meeting rooms	1,089	1,584
Total	**17,938**	**33,220**[15]

Thus the program that would be given to Breuer to guide his design would be 85% larger than the existing museum on 54th Street. The only space not expanding in this basic program was the library and files (though the library would expand greatly in the eventual expansion undertaken in the 1990s).

By 1964 Marcel Breuer had come up with a definitive design for the new Whitney, which was published in a fundraising report for the museum with the title *A Program for the New Whitney Museum of American Art: In the Service of American Art*.[16] The model, renderings, and plans published in this pamphlet were virtually identical to what would be executed on the building site (see figs. 3.11–3.15). This very bold inverted ziggurat would become, along with the Solomon R. Guggenheim Museum, one of the most recognizable museum buildings not only in America, but the world. The successive outwardly projecting floors and central window on the fourth-floor gallery would form one of the façades in New York City that would be loved most by some while reviled by others. The Whitney would be a radical departure from the staid white steel and glass "international modernist" buildings and would be one of the great monuments of a more personal interpretation of modernism. Breuer's use of richer materials would differentiate the Whitney from the "brutalism" that was becoming more and more dominant in the modern architecture of the time, though the general massing and use of projecting higher floors like inverted steps would be themes explored by that movement. Its galleries, based on a free plan with movable floor-to-ceiling partitions, would also become some of the most versatile and flexible spaces for displaying successfully a very wide variety of artistic media and practices. This was, naturally, perfectly suited to the mission and needs of the Whitney, an institution firmly committed to contemporary art and therefore in need of such flexibility to exhibit the ever-changing types of work in that always unpredictable world.

As designed and built, the Whitney was originally completely self-contained in the Breuer building. The space where today's fifth-floor galleries are located was originally a courtyard, open to the sky and surrounded by the museum's offices. This floor was not accessible by the general public. The mezzanine, still only reachable from the fifth floor, was originally home to a Publications Office at the foot of

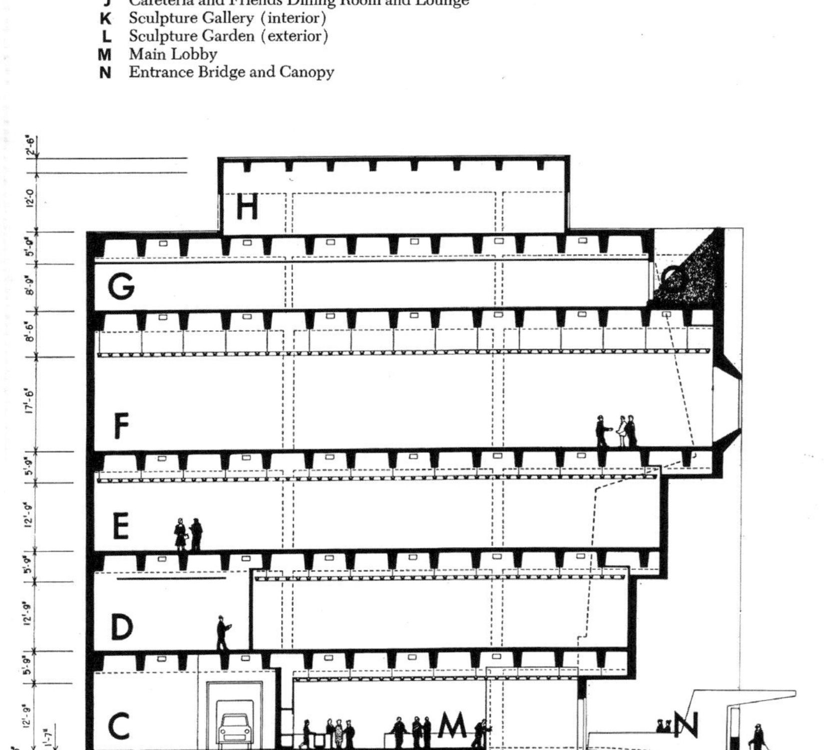

3.15. Longitudinal Cross Section. Whitney Museum, Marcel Breuer.

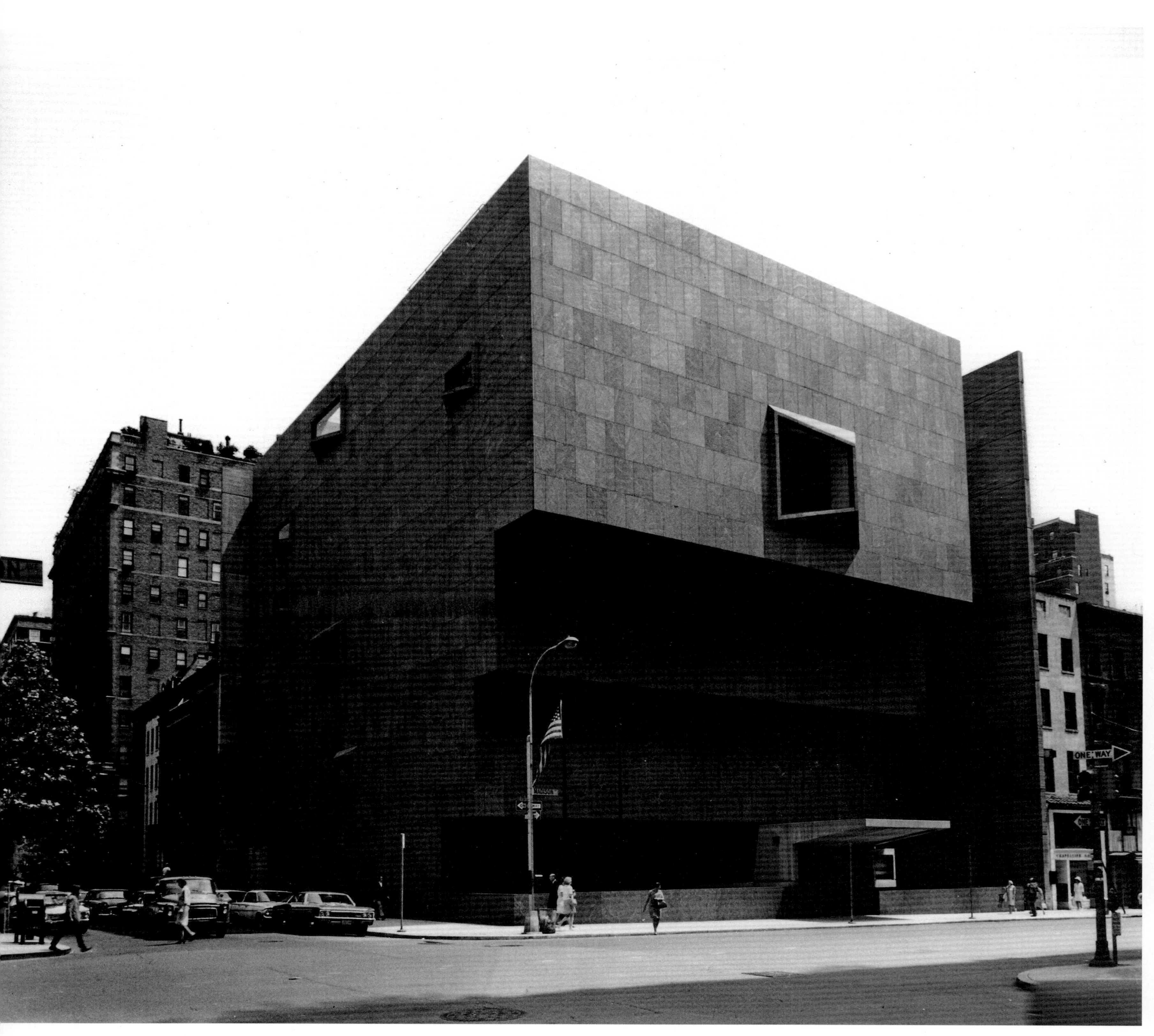

3.16. Whitney Museum, exterior, seen
from the northwest, Marcel Breuer.

3.17. Whitney Museum, exterior,
Madison Avenue façade, Marcel Breuer.
Ezra Stoller © Esto.

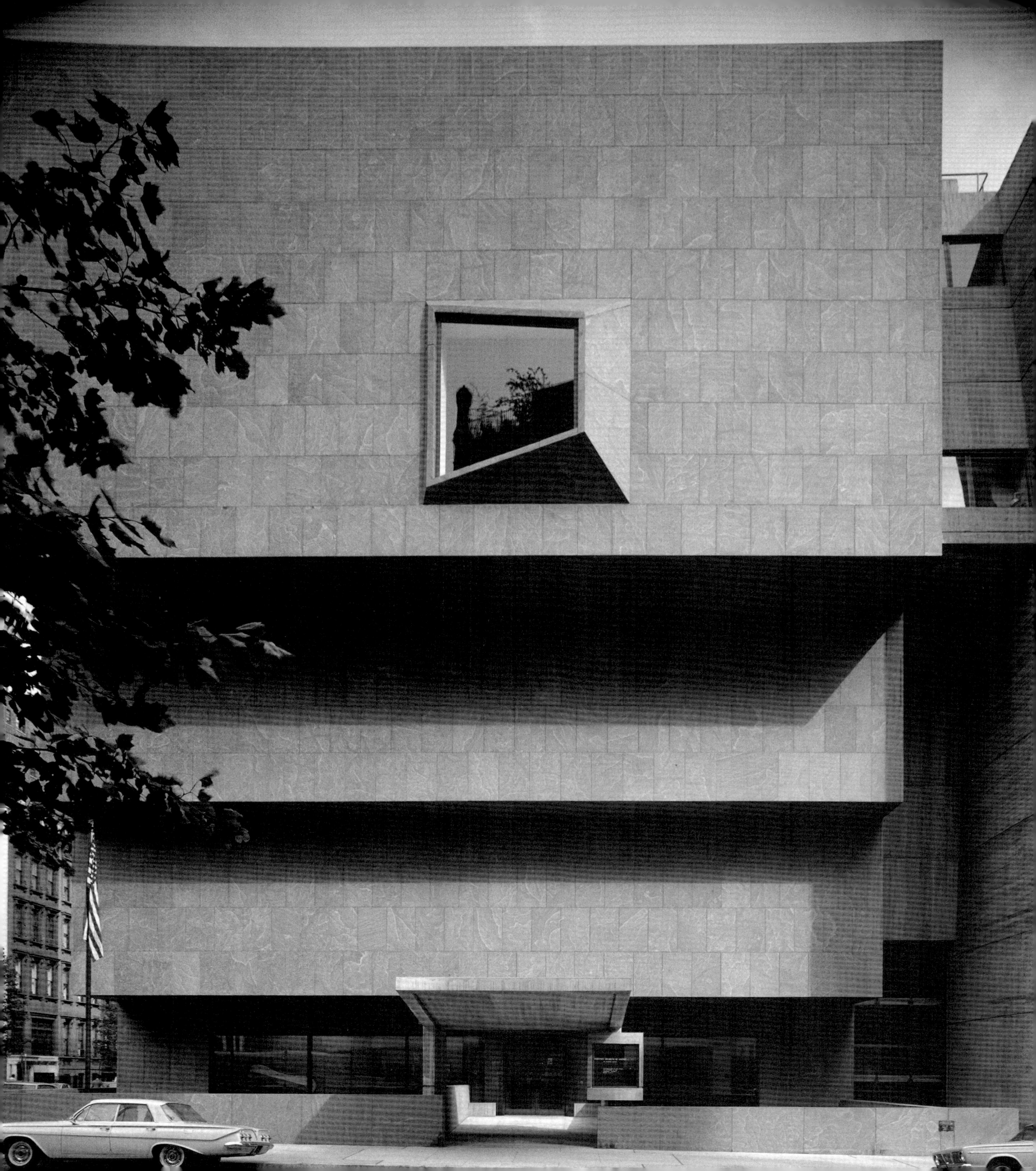

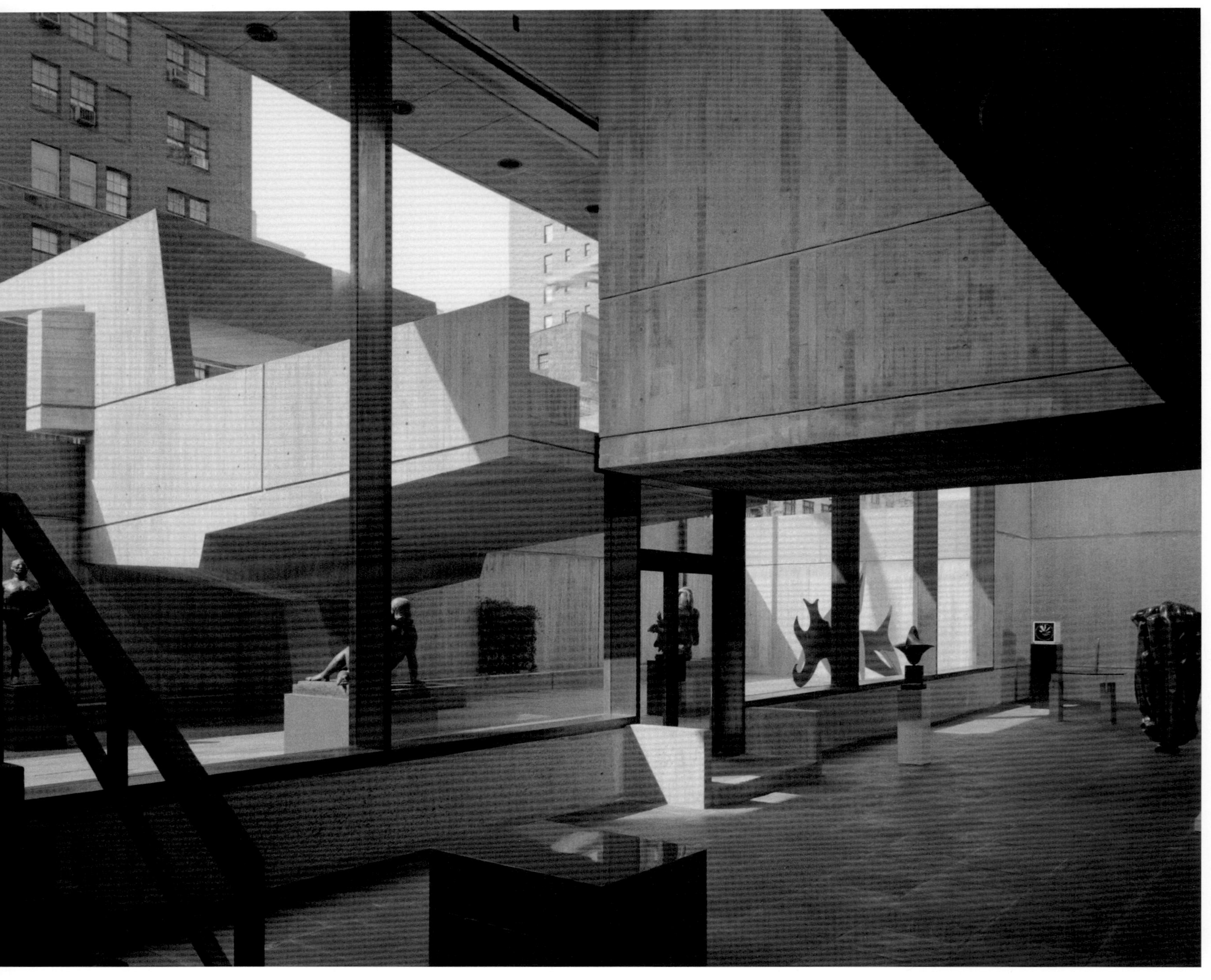

3.18. Entrance bridge, Whitney Museum,
Marcel Breuer. Ezra Stoller © Esto.

3.19. Bookstore counter with built-in
display for books, Whitney Museum
lobby, Marcel Breuer. Ezra Stoller © Esto.

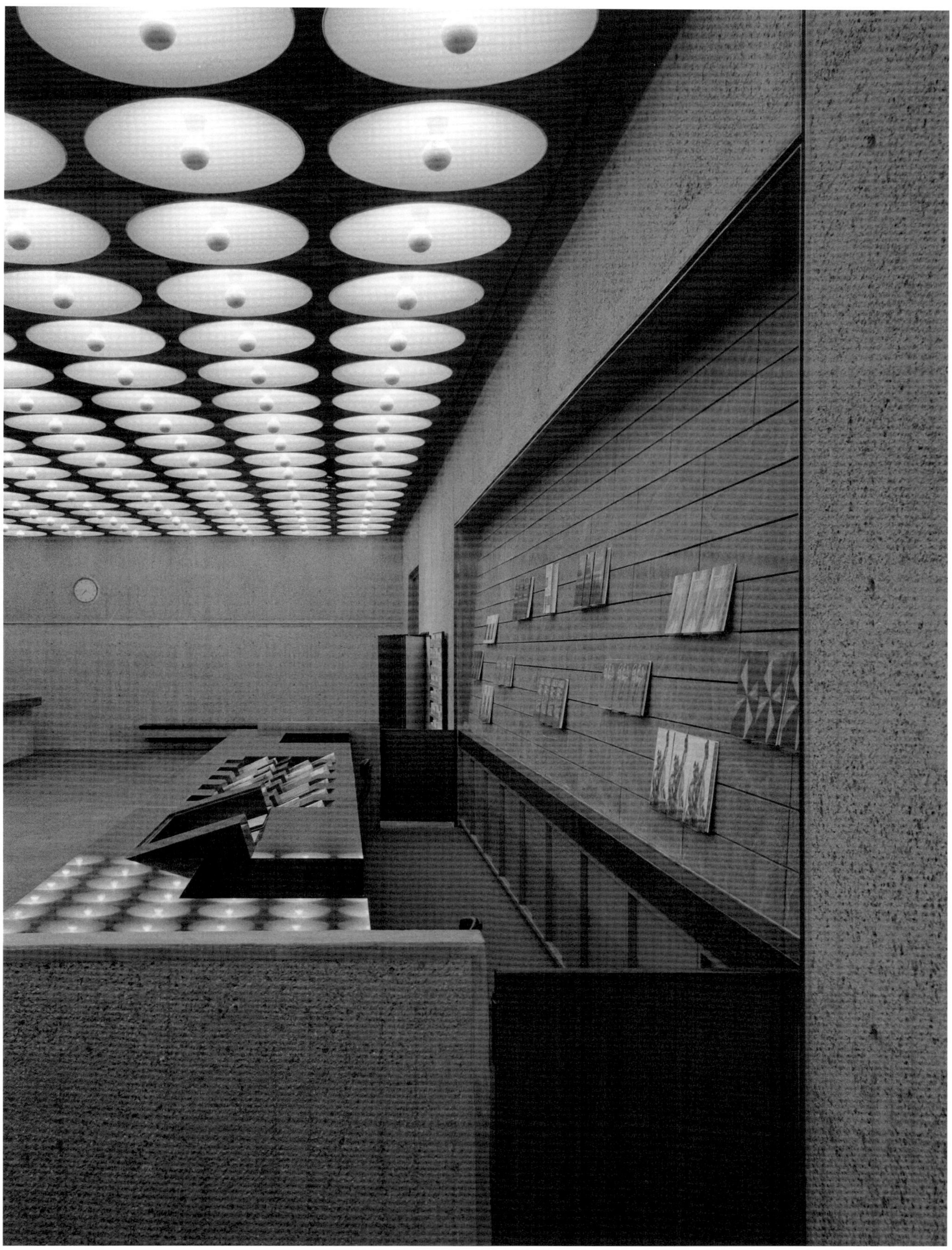

the staircase, followed by the Museum Library, in the space now occupied by the Gillman Photography Gallery. The basement, with its opening on the western (front) side to the ground floor, which today houses the restaurant and gift shop, was originally used as a sculpture gallery (double-height and continuous with the sunken sculpture court fronting Madison Avenue), with a smaller restaurant situated behind it.

With the exception of the alterations mentioned above, the Breuer building today is much the same as it was when it opened in 1966 (figs. 3.16 and 3.17). The museum is entered by crossing a bridge over the sunken sculpture garden (fig. 3.18), leading into the lobby that contains ticket sales, membership and information desks, bookstore and coat check (fig. 3.19). On the south side are the elevators (including a large freight elevator that doubles as a public elevator during open hours), main staircase, and stairs leading down to the restaurant and gift shop. The southeast corner contains a small exhibition gallery. The loading dock is in the northeast of the floor and completely separated from the public areas. Collection storage is housed behind the restaurant in the basement and subbasement. The second through fourth floors house the large exhibition galleries, all built on a free plan with movable partitions (figs. 3.20 and 3.21). The different floors have varying ceiling heights allowing for the optimum display of works in all media and scales. The second floor contains a small auditorium on the south side that now serves as the Film and Video Gallery.

CHALLENGES OF EXPANDING THE WHITNEY

Like most collecting institutions, the Whitney soon faced the problem of finding enough space to exhibit, store, and care for its collections, as well as provide workspace for its staff and other vital functions. As early as 1974, a mere eight years after the opening of the Breuer building, the Whitney's trustees appointed a Planning Committee to "articulate the goals of the Museum and make recommendations about its future."[17] This committee's report was approved by the trustees in 1978. The report stated that the present building "is too small to function as the major center for the permanent exhibition of American art of the 20th century, as a showcase for temporary exhibitions, and as an educational center." The necessary adjoining properties were purchased (already beginning in 1968 for the possibility of expansion), the last property being acquired in 1980. Consistent with the Whitney Museum's commitment to advancing contemporary trends in the arts, the pioneering Postmodernist architect Michael Graves was hired in October 1981 to be the architect of the expansion project.

Always a controversial designer, Graves is one of the designers most associated with the backlash against orthodox modernism that favored an approach to contemporary architecture which mixed modern technologies and programming

3.20. Interior of galleries on the 4th floor, Whitney Museum, Marcel Breuer. Ezra Stoller © Esto.

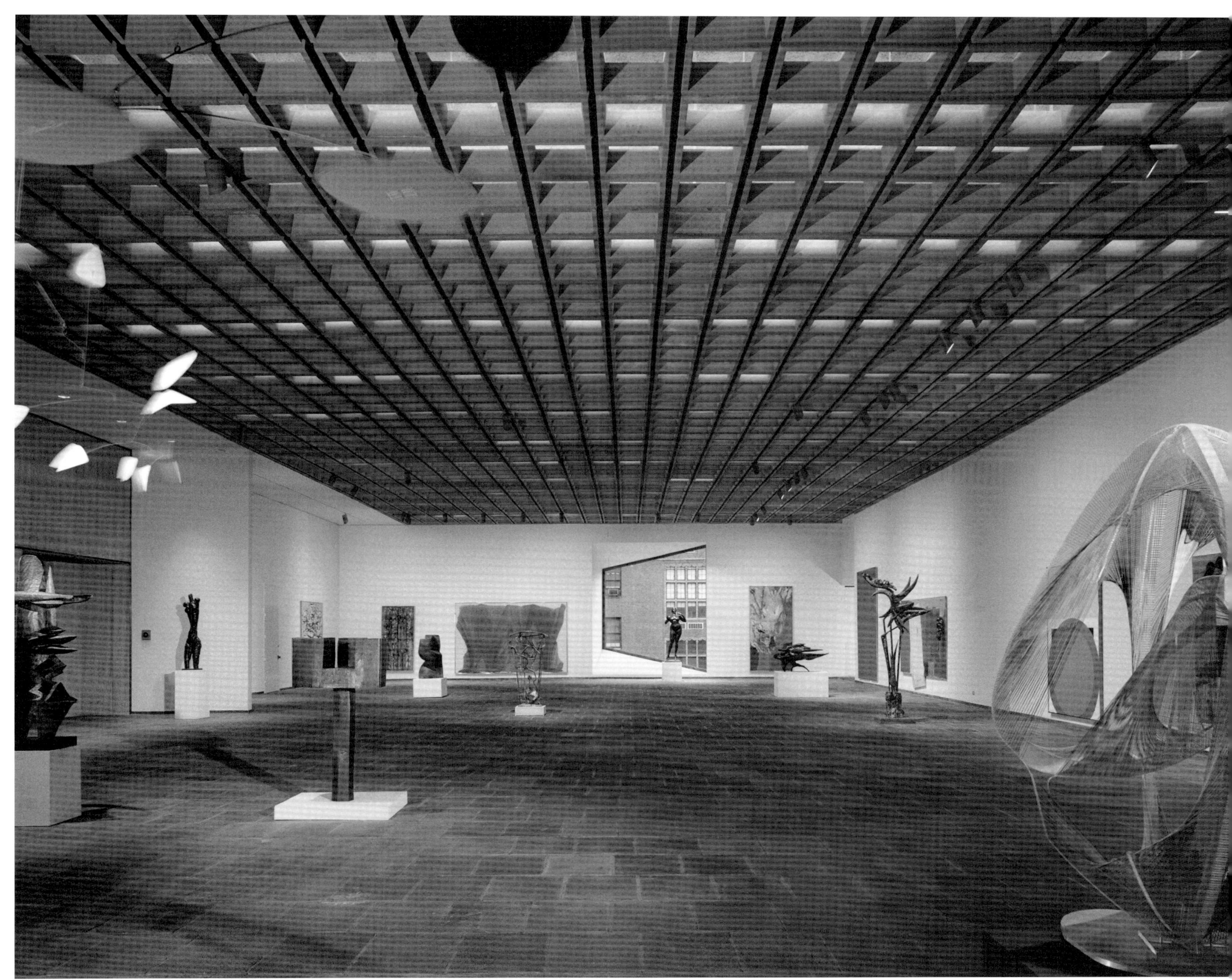

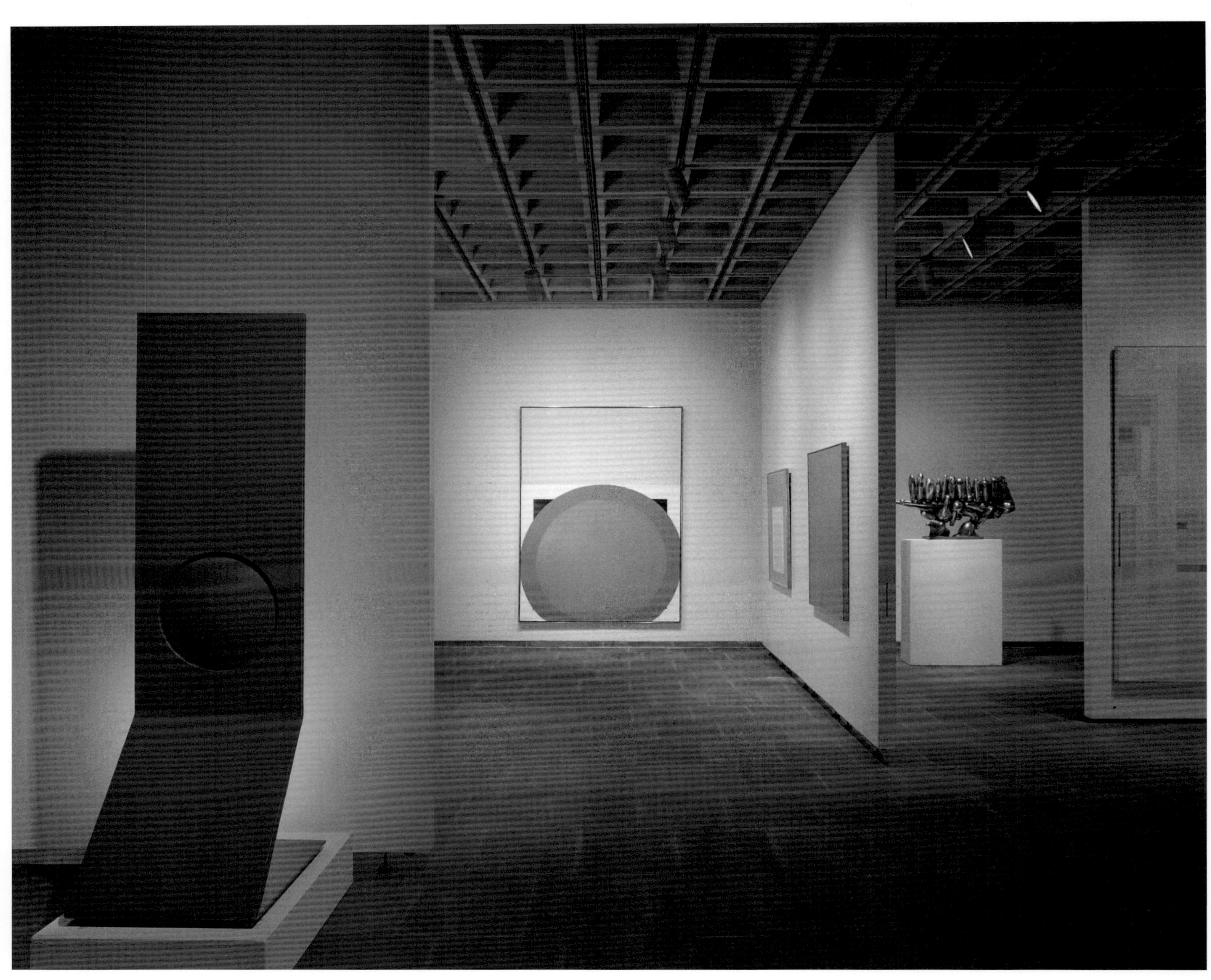

with an interest in quotations and play with forms and architectural languages from the history of architecture. Eschewing the whites, blacks, and colors of modernism and its steel, glass, and concrete materials in favor of a pastel palette and polychrome stones, Graves's scheme caused huge controversy throughout the world of art and architecture in New York and beyond. Because the Whitney Museum, its building, and collections were closely associated with the modernism it had advanced, many saw this project and the choice of designer as disrespectful to the building, the institution, and its collections. However, the institution, Breuer's building, and the Whitney's collection and very mission had always been at the forefront of both radical and reactionary artists, movements, and works. The choice of an architect and a design as polarizing as Graves and his proposal was thus entirely in keeping with the history and tradition of the Whitney Museum of American Art.

The postmodernism of the 1980s perhaps has not aged as well as Breuer's modernism; it was, nonetheless, an important moment in the history of American architecture. Further, unlike modernist architecture, with its distinctly European origins, postmodern architecture was entirely homegrown and American, its two most important protagonists being Michael Graves and Robert Venturi. This fact, which is hard to dispute, makes the choice of the architect entirely suitable for the Whitney Museum of American Art.

However, the choice of designer and the design he delivers are two disparate elements. Graves's proposal (fig. 3.24) was not merely a new wing connecting to the Breuer building on one side. Rather it completely enveloped and dominated Breuer's building, with new floors added above the roof on the old building, a projecting "hinge" in the center of the block becoming the fulcrum of the Madison Avenue elevation, and a southern wing of the same dimensions as the original building. The scheme looked like Breuer's building had been conquered more than expanded. The thought that this addition was disrespectful to Marcel Breuer's building and the very modernist philosophy underlying it, coupled with the predictable "NIMBY" (Not In My Backyard) response of the Whitney's Upper East Side neighbors, were enough to prevent this project from ever being executed. Though Graves and the Whitney board would continue to advance and alter this scheme until 1988, it would ultimately be abandoned.

The controversy surrounding the Graves project also scared off donors, forcing the Whitney to scale back its still-needed plans for expansion. In 1996 the Whitney hired Richard Gluckman of Gluckman Mayner Architects to design a much less ambitious scheme, though a scheme that had the virtue of being all but invisible to the outside world. Two adjoining townhouses on East 74th Street were converted into museum offices that were linked to the Breuer building on three levels. The rear garden of one of the townhouses was enclosed to form the reading room of the new, vastly expanded library (fig. 3.22). The concrete southern wall of the Breuer building was left exposed in the new reading room.

In the Breuer building itself, Gluckman enclosed the roof garden on the fifth floor, creating an additional floor of galleries, used for the continuous display of

3.21. Interior of galleries, Whitney Museum, Marcel Breuer. Ezra Stoller © Esto.

the permanent collection. The offices previously housed there were moved to the 74th Street townhouses. The publications office and library were moved from the mezzanine, which became a small gallery (usually used to house Alexander Calder's *Circus*) and the Gillman Photography Gallery; the original Breuer staircase was left in situ to provide access. The only space completely preserved on the fifth floor was Breuer's boardroom (still not open to the public, now entered through the old glass doors from the original Whitney Museum on West 8th Street; fig. 3.23). These alterations were made so seamlessly as to prevent their being detected by an uninformed visitor.

THE PRESENT AND FUTURE OF THE WHITNEY

Although Gluckman's more modest addition solved the immediate problems facing the Whitney Museum by moving the administrative offices and creating an additional floor of galleries, it was far smaller than the earlier scheme they had hoped to build and which conformed, in scale and size, to the recommendations of the institution's Planning Committee. So, by the twenty-first century, the Trustees were already looking to expand; further, the Whitney already had control of all of the property fronting Madison Avenue from the Breuer building to the corner of 74th Street as well as the two townhouses around the corner that now contained their offices and library. Rem Koolhaas was brought in to offer a proposal, but in 2004 the trustees decided to hire Renzo Piano for the project. The Piano project was intended to be constructed on the same land that was designated twenty-five years earlier for the Graves project.

Piano, a more modernist architect than Graves, designed a building that would be set back from the Breuer building and much more consonant with it (fig. 3.25). Nonetheless, the neighborhood voiced great concerns about the project. In the end, with alterations to the Madison frontage that would preserve two of the brownstones currently there, the Whitney won approval to move forward. However, with land becoming available in Downtown Manhattan, the board reconsidered and abandoned this project in favor of building a second branch. The site of the new project is on Gansevoort Street, west of Washington Street in the trendy Meatpacking District, just south of Chelsea, the center of New York's contemporary art gallery district (figs 3.26 and 3.27). Based on the state of the project, as published in the *New York Times*, the new satellite branch would actually be larger than the Breuer building, with 50,000 square feet of gallery space (as opposed to the 32,000 square feet in the Madison Avenue building).[18] The new building would connect with the High Line, a former section of elevated railroad tracks, now a park. Section 1 of the High Line, which runs from Gansevoort Street to 20th Street, opened to the public, to great acclaim, in June 2009. The project is currently anticipated to open in 2012.

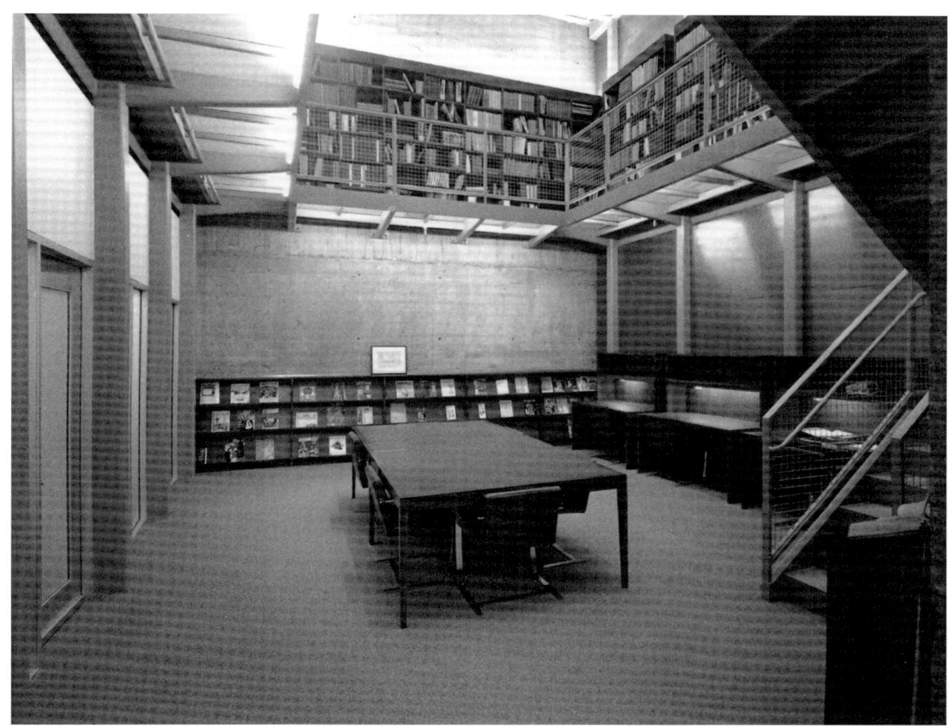

3.22. Reading Room of Frances Mulhall Achilles Library, Whitney Museum of American Art, Annex, 33 East 74th Street, New York, N.Y. Gluckman, Mayner Architects, 1997.
Photograph by Geoffrey Clements.

CONTINUITY AND CHANGE AT THE WHITNEY: ONE MISSION AND MANY BUILDINGS

Unlike many institutions, the Whitney Museum of American Art has not stayed in the same building or even in the same district of New York. It has existed downtown, midtown, and uptown. It contemplated being a wing of a larger institution and was once physically connected to another; currently it contemplates splitting itself into two disparate locations. Its biennial exhibitions, though contained mostly in the Whitney's own premises, have used outside venues, from Central Park to the Seventh Regiment Armory.

From the beginning, founder Gertrude Vanderbilt Whitney and her chief lieutenant, founding director Juliana Force, sought to advance contemporary American art and the artists who were often marginalized by the larger established institutions such as the Metropolitan Museum of Art (which was more concerned with the art of the past) and the Museum of Modern Art (which was primarily concerned with European modernism). Although venues have changed, this commitment has endured. The Whitney biennial continues to be one of the premier exhibitions of contemporary art, and perhaps the single most important such exhibition concentrating on American art. The buildings that the Whitney has inhabited over the years reflect this commitment. The original Whitney Museum of American Art evolved from the Whitney Studio Club and expanded in an ad hoc manner. The modernist elevations of the 54th Street Whitney were very much in

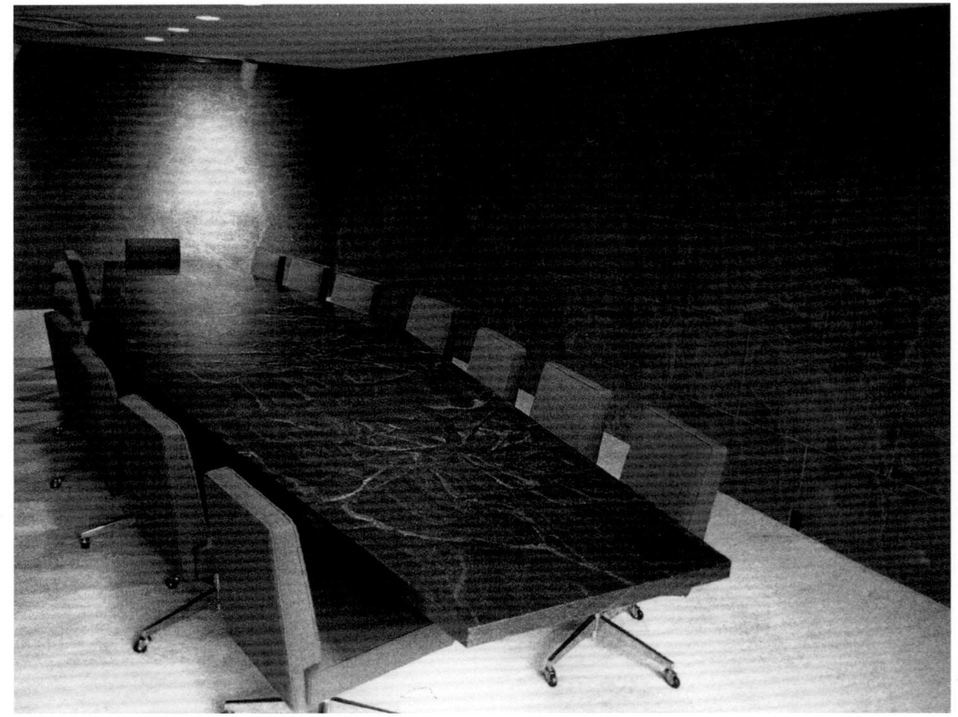

3.23. Boardroom, Whitney Museum of American Art, Marcel Breuer. Frances Mulhall Achilles Library, Whitney Museum of American Art.

3.24. Madison Avenue elevation study of proposed Whitney Museum extension, Michael Graves, July 1980. Frances Mulhall Achilles Library, Whitmey Muesum of American Art.

keeping with the high modernism of the time, while (under contractual obligation) forming a harmonious whole with the neighboring Museum of Modern Art. The Breuer building was a radical design in its time, and it remains an icon of the modernism of the 1960s. Though unexecuted, Michael Graves's project was even more radical in its challenging of the modernist orthodoxy that had reigned as the norm in American museum architecture since the 1950s, thus in keeping with the Whitney's goal of representing contemporary trends, no matter how controversial they might be. Only time will tell what will come of the Whitney's current plans for a downtown satellite.

Through all of these moves and expansions, the original commitment to contemporary American art has remained. This commitment was reinforced and clarified with the publication of a Mission Statement in 1992:

> The Whitney Museum of American Art is dedicated to collecting, preserving, interpreting, and exhibiting American art. We exist to serve a wide variety of audiences and to celebrate the complexity, heterogeneity, and diversity of American art and culture.
>
> The Whitney is by definition a historical museum. Its permanent collection of 20th-century American art is the Museum's key resource, and will be the basis for curatorial and museological innovation in programs and education.
>
> At the same time, programs will continue to support the new. As we move into the 21st century, the Whitney will collect and present all forms of contemporary American art and establish linkages between the new and

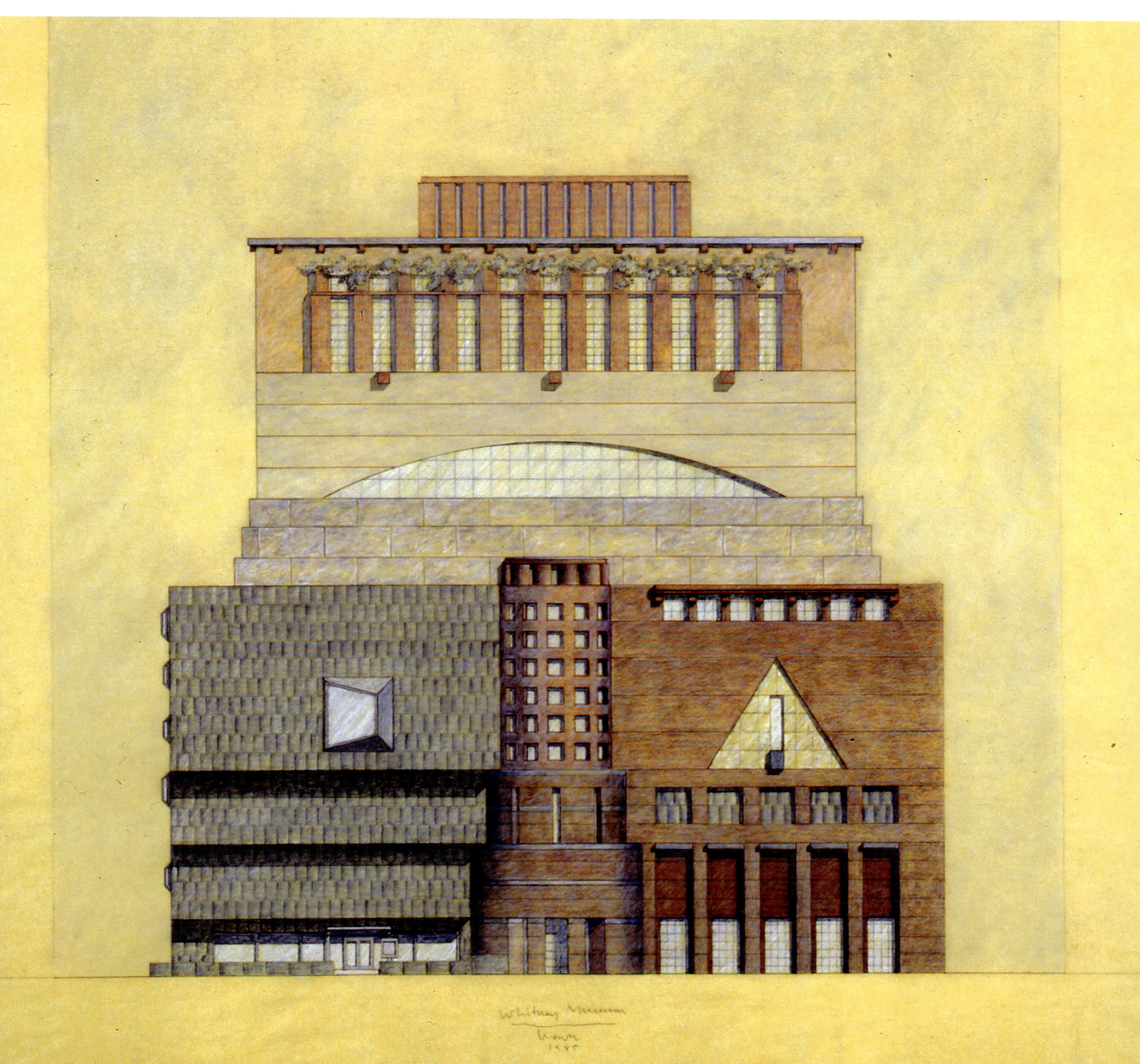

Whitney Museum
1985

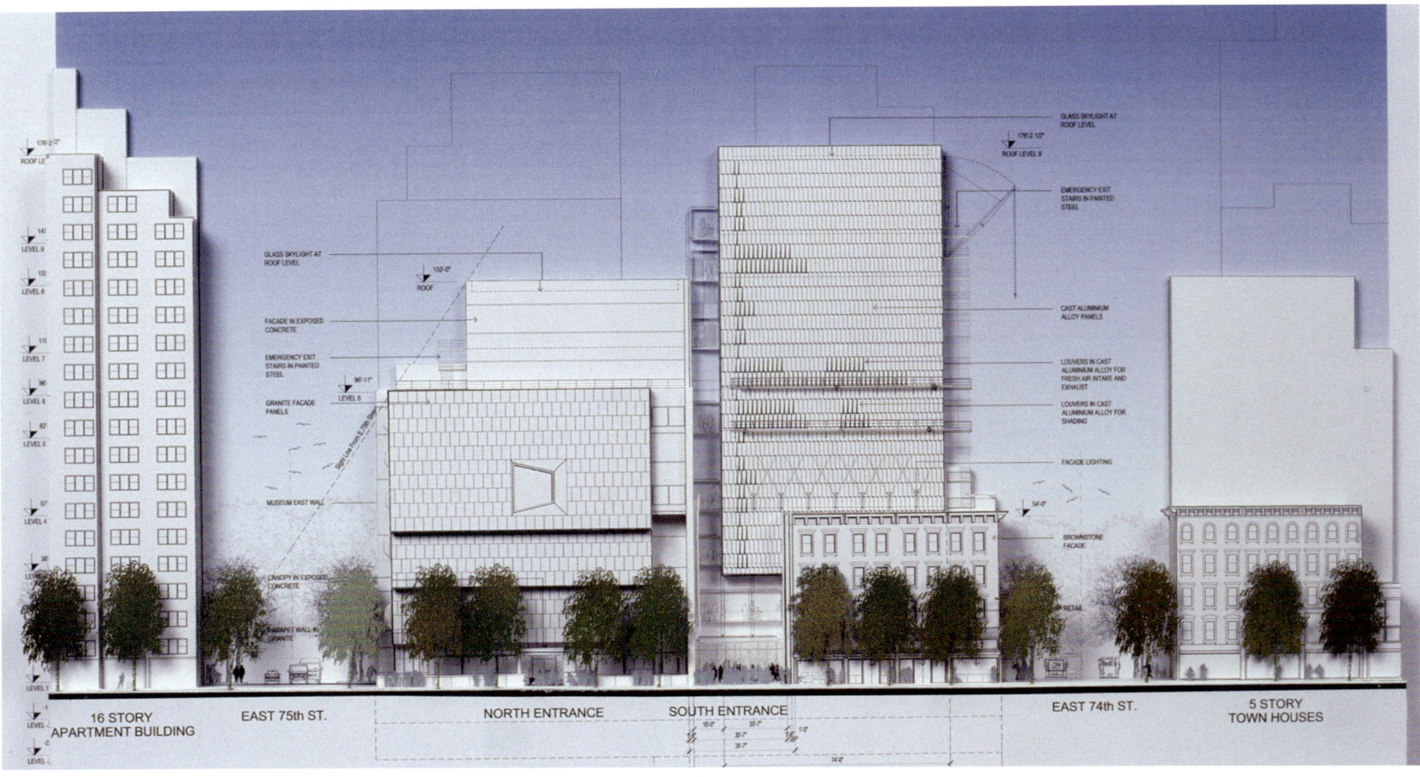

3.25. Plan for expansion of Whitney Museum on Madison Avenue, Renzo Piano, 2004.

the historical, the art of other countries and our own. This way, the Whitney's permanent collection and its identity, like the history of American art itself, will never be fixed and final but will always be in the making.

In carrying out our responsibility to the past and our commitment to the present, the Whitney reaffirms the values and practices that have made it the preeminent museum of American art: (1) the ideal of America as an inclusive, pluralistic nation with the possibility of a common identity and culture, and (2) the practice of connoisseurship—critical curatorial judgments of quality including the application aesthetic, artistic and theoretical standards—in an intellectual tradition of open, skeptical analysis and scholarly detachment. [19]

Through all of its moves and changes, this mission seems very healthy. The various buildings that have housed the Whitney are indeed outward signs of the proper execution of this mission. As contemporary American art has changed, so have the Whitney's various venues. From the domestic interiors of the original building on 8th Street to larger galleries with movable partitions on 54th Street, to still larger, more flexible gallery spaces uptown on Madison Avenue, to plans for the largest venue yet back downtown, changes in both the scale and diversity of art produced in the United States have forced the Whitney to repeatedly alter and enlarge its physical plant to stay true to its commitment to representing all that is new and current in American art.

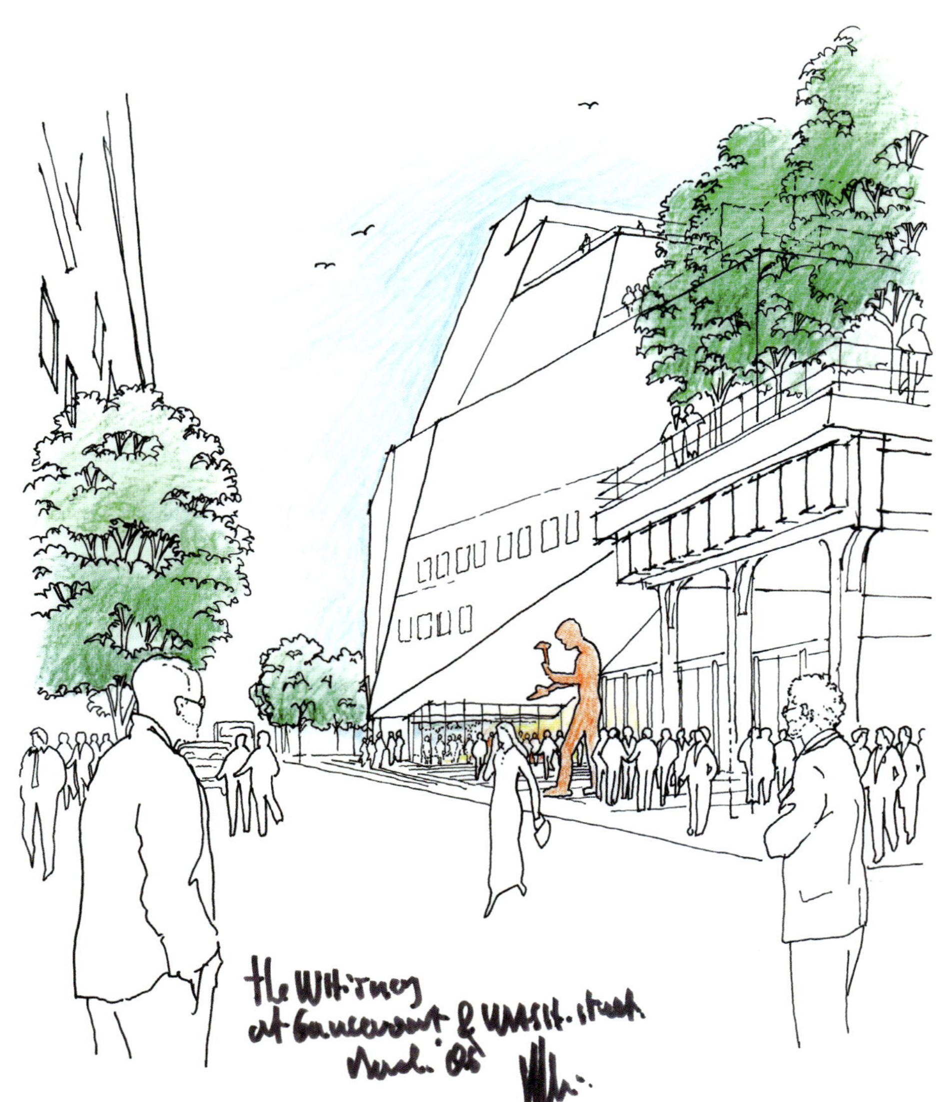

3.26. Preliminary rendering of Whitney Museum satellite facility located in downtown Manhattan, Renzo Piano, 2008.

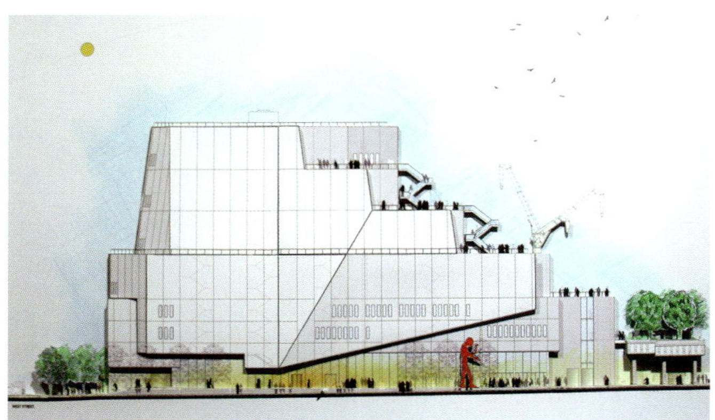

3.27. Preliminary rendering of Whitney Museum satellite facility located in downtown Manhattan, Renzo Piano, 2008.

CHAPTER 4

GEORGIA O'KEEFFE MUSEUM

"Devoted to preserving and presenting the life work of one of America's preeminent artists, the 13,000 square-foot museum will house a permanent collection of O'Keeffe's art unsurpassed by any museum in the world. The new museum, situated in an adobe building being renovated by Richard Gluckman, will bring to downtown Santa Fe an outstanding selection of work by the artist most closely identified with the city and the Southwest."

— Excerpt from press release, "Grand Opening of the Georgia O'Keeffe Museum set for July 1997 in Santa Fe," Georgia O'Keeffe Museum Research Center Institutional Archives

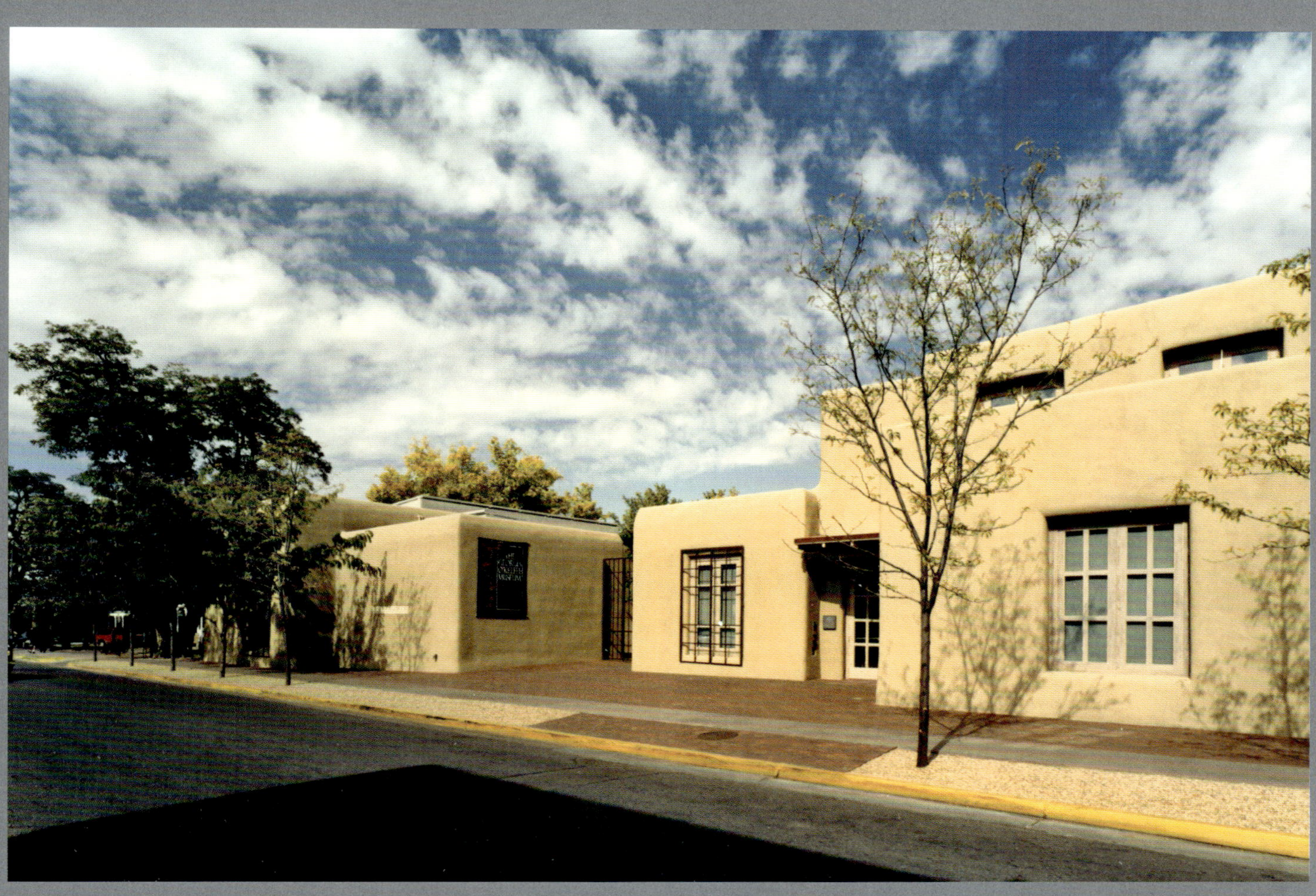

4.1. Exterior of the Georgia O'Keeffe
Museum, Santa Fe, New Mexico.
Copyright Georgia O'Keeffe Museum.
Photograph by Robert Reck.

GEORGIA O'KEEFFE MUSEUM AT A GLANCE

4.2. Georgia O'Keeffe's Ghost Ranch
House patio, Ghost Ranch, New Mexico.
Copyright Georgia O'Keeffe Museum.
Photograph by Malcolm Varon.

Corporate name:	Georgia O'Keeffe Museum
Address:	217 Johnson Street, Santa Fe, New Mexico 87501
Opening date:	July 17, 1997
Architect:	Richard Gluckman (Gluckman Mayner Architects)
Collecting scope:	The Work of Georgia O'Keeffe, related work
Exhibition scope:	Georgia O'Keeffe and American modernism
Other major units:	Georgia O'Keeffe Museum Research Center
	Ghost Ranch House
	Abiquiu House
Scholarly program:	Scholarships for research on American modernism
Amenities:	Bookstore/gift shop, café, film screening room

THE SINGLE-ARTIST MUSEUM: GEORGIA O'KEEFFE AND NEW MEXICO

Not only is the Georgia O'Keeffe Museum the youngest museum analyzed in this book, it is also the only institution dedicated to the work of a single artist. The notion of the single-artist museum is not unusual in Europe (in France alone one can find many examples; there are museums dedicated to the work of Rodin, Picasso, Delacroix, Ingres, and Toulouse-Lautrec, just to name a few). In America, however, such museums are rare, if not without precedent (the Noguchi Museum in Queens, New York comes to mind, though it lies inside of the late artist's studio and was not a purpose-built structure). The O'Keeffe Museum realistically bills itself as "America's first art museum dedicated to the work of a woman of international stature."[1]

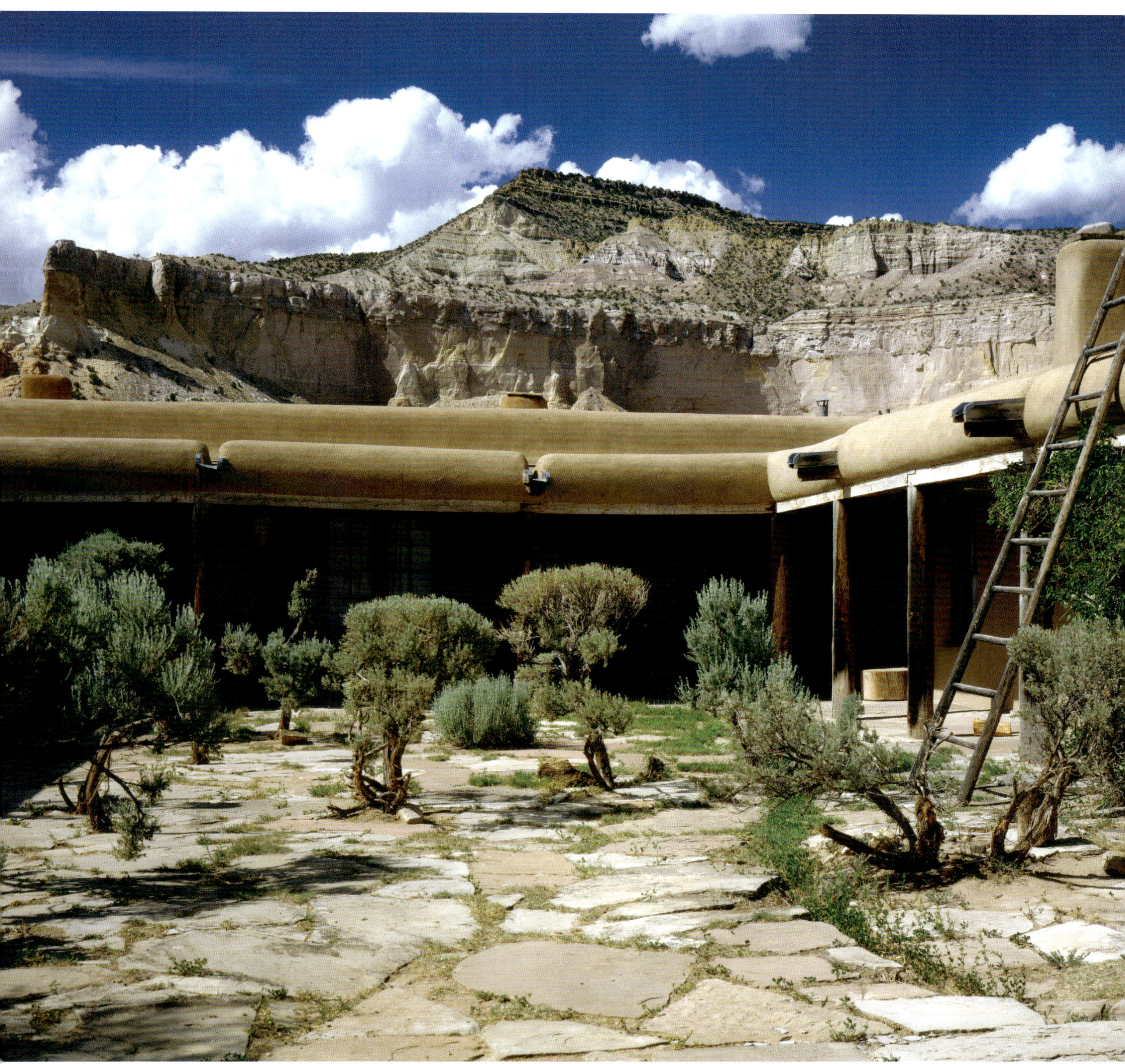

Georgia O'Keeffe benefits from this single-artist approach for a number of reasons. Though she was born in the Midwest (November 15, 1887, Sun Prairie, Wisconsin) and lived, studied, taught, and worked in Chicago, Virginia, South Carolina, and Texas, O'Keeffe would be identified most closely with the art scene of New York, where her career began, and New Mexico, to which she started making what would become regular visits in 1929 and where she lived permanently from 1949 until her death in 1986 at the age of 98. The influential photographer and art impresario Alfred Stieglitz took an interest in her work, promoted it heavily through his New York galleries, and in the process engaged in a romance with O'Keeffe that resulted in marriage. Although this promotion by, and identification with, Stieglitz yielded extraordinary recognition, acceptance, and appreciation of her work, it also created an image of the artist outside of her own control. The interpretations of her work advanced by contemporary critics and the context in which they placed her work were not necessarily consistent with her own aspirations and intentions as an artist.

In New Mexico Georgia O'Keeffe found sanctuary from the New York art world's scrutiny, as well as a natural landscape that appealed to her aesthetic sensibilities, allowing her to find a working environment in which she was more comfortable, and her art to grow in new directions. The combination of modernist abstraction and representation of the unique, heroic topography of the American West led her to refine her artistic idiom into something highly personal, yet with a very broad appeal. The result is an artist with a distinctive aesthetic, who is not easily associated with any specific movement in twentieth-century art. New Mexico was thus transformative for O'Keeffe in both her practice as an artist and in the creation of the image she presented of herself to the world; this engagement with New Mexico also led to changes in how art critics interpreted her work— all ends that she desired. As her work was so closely based on the surrounding landscape of New Mexico, she began to be universally associated not only with that landscape but the place itself (see fig 4.4). New Mexico allowed her to be an artist on her own terms in a way that the New York would not.

Few artists are as closely identified with specific geography in the popular imagination as O'Keeffe is with New Mexico. Though she lived in Santa Fe itself only at the very end of her long life, she lived in the surrounding countryside for nearly forty years, and Santa Fe is, without a doubt, the cultural capital of the state of New Mexico. Strangely, before the creation of the Georgia O'Keeffe Museum, there were relatively few O'Keeffe paintings to be seen in a region where tourists expected to see many—after all, many considered the region "O'Keeffe country." The fact that she is so closely identified with New Mexico and that New Mexico was central to the image of herself as an artist that she advanced make Georgia O'Keeffe the perfect candidate for a single-artist museum—provided that this museum is built in New Mexico, and built following the basic aesthetic she had worked so hard to advance.

4.3. Georgia O'Keeffe's living room, Abiquiu House, Abiquiu, New Mexico. © 2009 Hester & Hardaway.

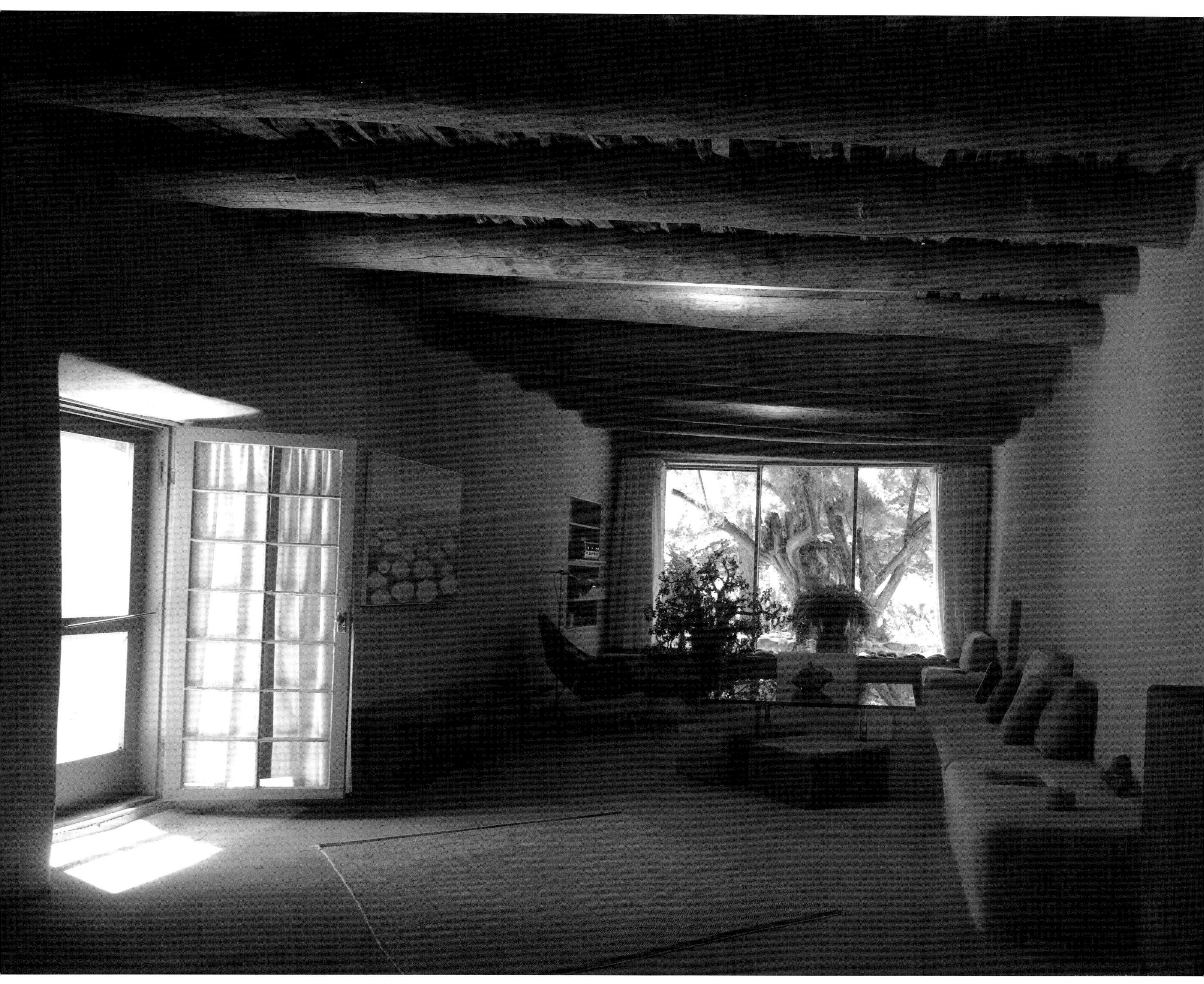

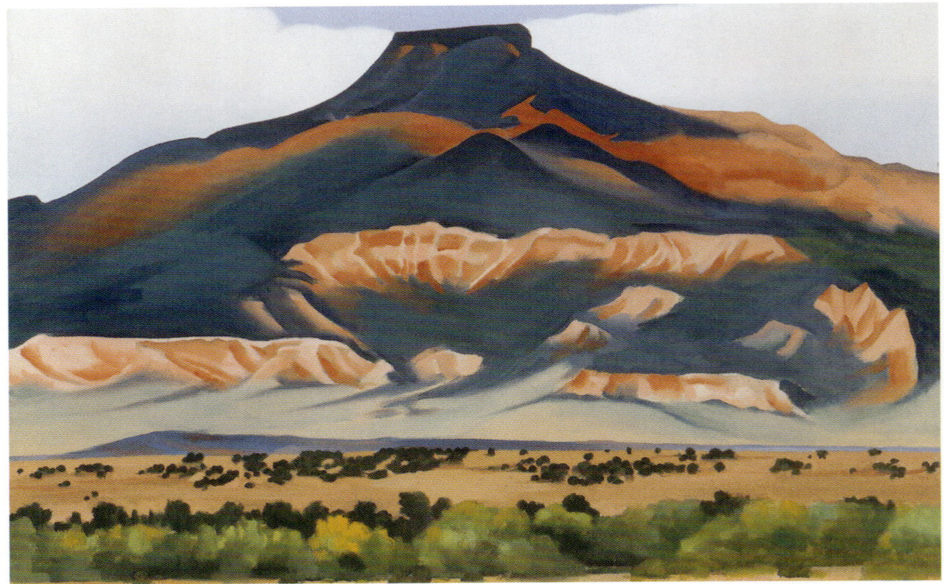

4.4. Georgia O'Keeffe, *Pedernal*, 1941, oil on canvas, 19 x 30 ¼ in., Georgia O'Keeffe Foundation, CR 1022, Georgia O'Keeffe Museum, Santa Fe, New Mexico. © 2009 Georgia O'Keeffe Museum/Artists Rights Society (ARS), New York.

THE FOUNDING OF THE GEORGIA O'KEEFFE MUSEUM

The Georgia O'Keeffe Museum was founded in November 1995 by Anne and John Marion, who had been part-time residents of Santa Fe and collectors and advocates of Georgia O'Keeffe and her work. As with the other institutions discussed in this book, the family is closely tied to an industrial fortune. Mrs. Marion was the great-granddaughter of Texas rancher and oilman Samuel Burke Burnett. She went on to become the chairman of Burnett Oil Company, Inc. and president of its philanthropic arm, the Burnett Foundation of Fort Worth, Texas. Mr. Marion was president and later chairman of Sotheby's auction house, where he continues as honorary chairman.[2]

When opened, the O'Keeffe Museum boasted the largest collection of O'Keeffe's work in a single collection. The Marions' own collection was enhanced through a major gift of thirty-three works donated jointly by The Burnett Foundation and The Georgia O'Keeffe Foundation, which was then charged with distributing the works of the artist that were in her own possession at the time of her death.[3] Thus at the time of the opening, the museum had a permanent collection of over 80 paintings, works on paper, and sculptures by the artist. The press release announcing the opening of the museum also states its mission:

> The mission of the O'Keeffe Museum focuses on three major areas: the presentation and continuing development of the museum's permanent collection of paintings, drawings, and sculpture by O'Keeffe, as well as archival material related to her life and work; the support and creation of traveling exhibitions and educational programming that illuminate aspects

of O'Keeffe's art, her lasting contribution to American culture and that of her contemporaries; and the support of new scholarly work on O'Keeffe.

CORPORATE EXPANSION OF THE GEORGIA O'KEEFFE MUSEUM

he Georgia O'Keeffe Museum opened the Georgia O'Keeffe Museum Research Center in July 2001. Located two blocks from the main building, the Research Center houses a small research library (which includes the books the artist herself collected at her Ghost Ranch House) as well as the collection of her sketches on paper, archival material, her collections of paint samples of the colors she used in her own works, and many of the found objects she collected and used in her painting (e.g., bones, shells, stones). These collections were donated to the Research Center by Anna Marie and Juan Hamilton. The Research Center also contains the facilities for its scholarship program, including offices for its visiting scholars. The purpose of the Research Center is described as follows:

> The Georgia O'Keeffe Research Center opened in July 2001 as a component of the Georgia O'Keeffe Museum. As the only museum-related research facility in the world dedicated to the study of American Modernism (1890s to the present), it sponsors research in the fields of art history, architectural history and design, literature, music, and photography through its annual, competitive scholarship program. Six, three-to-twelve month scholarships are available to applicants at the pre- and post-doctoral levels, one of which can be awarded to a museum curator or an otherwise qualified individual

4.5. Architectural rendering of the Georgia O'Keeffe Museum, Richard Gluckman, 1997. Rendering by Greg Allegretti, Architect of Record for The Georgia O'Keefe Museum.

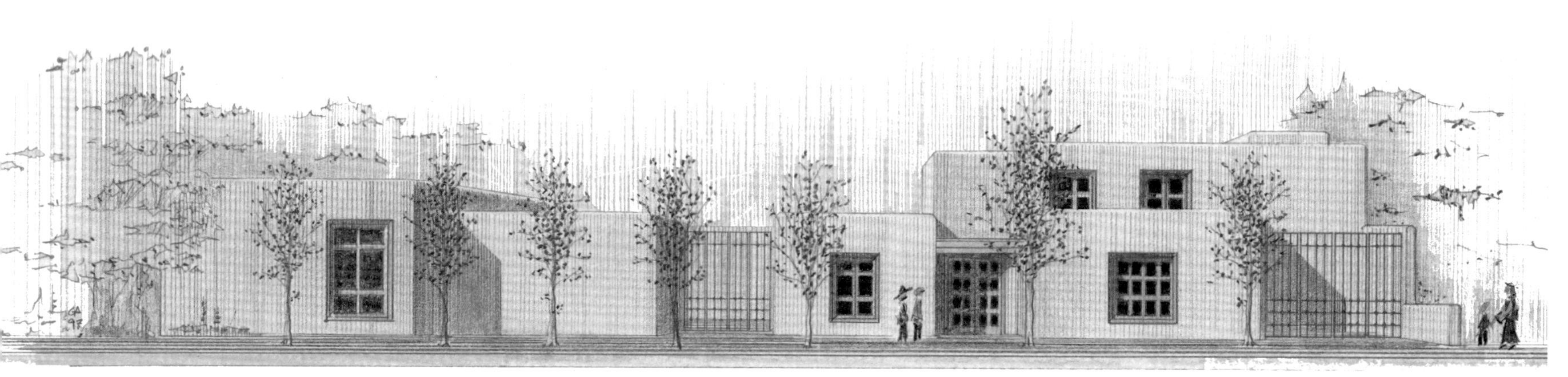

interested in organizing an exhibition pertaining to American Modernism for the Georgia O'Keeffe Museum.[4]

This important unit of the museum is not open to the general public but is integral to the mission of the Georgia O'Keeffe Museum, as it sponsors scholarship not just on O'Keeffe but also on her position within the broader context of American modernism.

In 2006 the then nine-year-old museum reached an agreement with The Georgia O'Keeffe Foundation, by which its remaining assets would be transferred to the museum.[5] These assets included the foundation's collection of more than 800 O'Keeffe artworks and extensive archival materials as well as Georgia O'Keeffe's house and studio in Abiquiu, New Mexico. This agreement settled, once and for all, the various conflicts and difficulties surrounding the execution of the artist's contested will and made the O'Keeffe Museum the principal repository for all of the artist's personal and archival material still in the possession of her estate.

By 2006 the museum owned, in addition to its main public facility, the Research Center, the two New Mexico houses of Georgia O'Keeffe (Ghost Ranch and Abiquiu; figs. 4.2 and 4.3) as well as their contents, and the largest collection of the artist's works of art in the world. It had succeeded in becoming the leading institution for the exhibition and study of an extremely important artist with a close connection to its location. The museum was in a unique position to advance and preserve a very significant portion of not only Georgia O'Keeffe's artistic production, but also her personal history through control of her two houses and personal effects.

THE MUSEUM BUILDING

The museum's founders selected Santa Fe for the location of the institution because they felt that it provided a proper context for experiencing O'Keeffe's work: it was, after all, a location and a landscape that the artist herself loved. Georgia O'Keeffe's homes and studios in New Mexico, at Ghost Ranch and Abiquiu, were traditional New Mexico adobe buildings. So it was logical for the Georgia O'Keeffe Museum to be designed along similar lines, though on a scale and with a program consistent with its purpose as a public art gallery. To this end, the board of the museum hired Richard Gluckman of Gluckman Mayner Architects to design the Georgia O'Keeffe Museum.

The project was actually a renovation and addition to a building that had originally been constructed as a Spanish Baptist church, which had previously been remodeled to serve as a contemporary art gallery.[6] Like most buildings in central Santa Fe, its design recalled traditional New Mexico adobe architecture. This reality presented the architect with the challenge of designing a building in keeping with the general aesthetic of the Santa Fe architecture without appearing

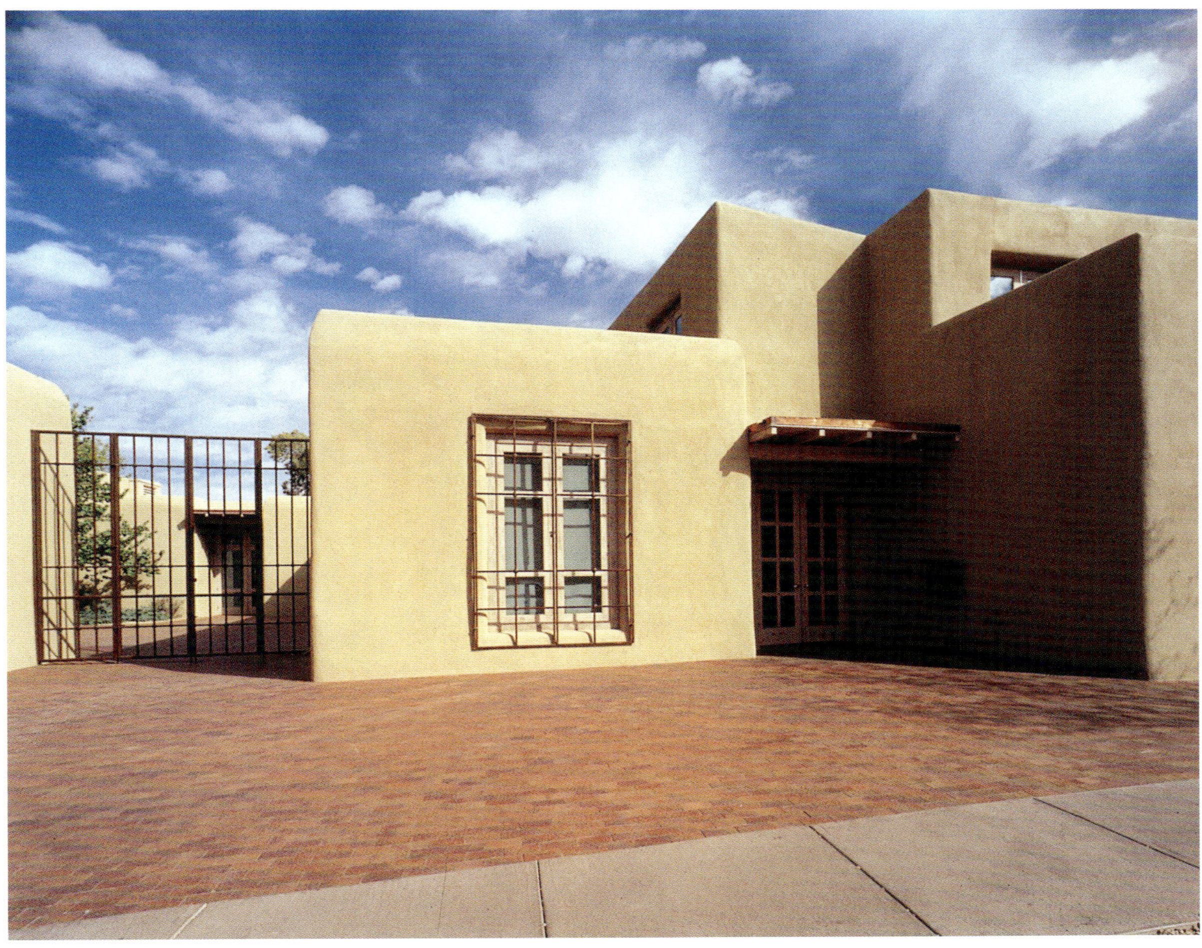

false or theme-park-like. Evoking the artist's houses without trying to recreate them and designing a museum that could give the feel of domestic space without resorting to kitsch were essential considerations.

Perhaps an even greater challenge arose from the fact that Georgia O'Keeffe and her work are rightly associated with New Mexico and its aesthetic; particularly her New Mexico landscapes and paintings of animal skulls and bones were unique to her time in the area. However, other aspects of her work, such as her large-scale flower paintings and abstractions (two of her most important and well-known idioms) were clearly established well before 1929 and therefore before she had ever been to New Mexico. So although the architect would be required to evoke the Southwestern aesthetic that was so important in O'Keeffe's work and self-image, he would have to design galleries neutral enough not to create a false context for the earlier, most formative phases in her career—she was already in her forties and well established as an artist in 1929. Finding a compromise between creating a sense of place and the importance of New Mexico in the museum's design and creating a space that did not overly contextualize the works on display in that location was thus critical.

4.6. Exterior detail of the Georgia O'Keeffe Museum, Santa Fe, New Mexico. Copyright Georgia O'Keeffe Museum. Photograph by Robert Reck.

To some extent, the location of the museum in central Santa Fe made some of the architect's decisions simpler; virtually every building in the area has an exterior evoking traditional adobe New Mexican architecture, with the same muted palette of colors derived from desert mud. Hard edges and bright colors would have made the museum clash with its surroundings. That the museum's exterior would fit in nicely with its traditional New Mexico surroundings was helpful in evoking the essence of Georgia O'Keeffe's two area houses, as they were also built in the same traditional adobe idiom. The solution adopted gracefully evokes the massing and materiality of native area architecture without resorting to such literal quotations as projecting ends of beams and joists below roof lines, wooden ladders, and such (figs. 4.4–4.6). This abstraction of the native regional architecture is further consistent with the approach Georgia O'Keeffe herself took to the built environment of New Mexico in her painted representations of it (fig. 4.7).

The floor plan of the museum reveals how the previously existing structures (now containing the galleries) are linked to the new construction (containing the entrance, shop, receiving area, and offices) around an open courtyard (fig. 4.8). This solution works very well, with the courtyard providing an outdoor venue for public presentations (which, given the climate of Santa Fe, is very pleasant and effective) in addition to a space for the exhibition of sculpture (fig. 4.9). The galleries distributed around the courtyard are of different sizes, shapes, and scales, allowing for the proper display of works of various sizes, proportions, and media (figs. 4.10 and 4.11). This variation in size and scale not only produces a visually interesting procession between galleries, but serves well for the display of O'Keeffe's works, which range in size from small works on paper to very large-scale oil paintings. Further, the diversity of gallery spaces serves the museum's broader mission of contextualizing O'Keeffe within the broader realm of American modernism by providing spaces that work well for the display of photography—not merely an important medium in American modernism, but a medium of fundamental importance in the work of the Alfred Stieglitz circle to which O'Keeffe belonged.

Whereas the museum's exterior rightly evokes native New Mexico architecture, the interior is, again appropriately, much more neutral. The galleries are essentially a series of well-linked white cubes of various dimensions and proportions, allowing for works to be viewed without a fixed (Southwestern) architectural context. This is critical to the proper appreciation of O'Keeffe's work, as much of her personal idiom was developed well before her time in New Mexico. Further, such galleries allow for a great deal of curatorial freedom in how works can be displayed and contextualized. Neutral and noninvasive as the galleries are, they are not without some consistency and evocation of the museum's exterior and Southwestern influences. The natural light in the larger galleries enters through skylights supported by narrow parallel beams that, despite being plastered over and painted white and flush with the surrounding ceilings, do evoke the wooden beam ceilings ubiquitous to New Mexico's traditional adobe architecture. However, such elegant allusion is quite subtle and in no way affects the prevailing neutrality of the

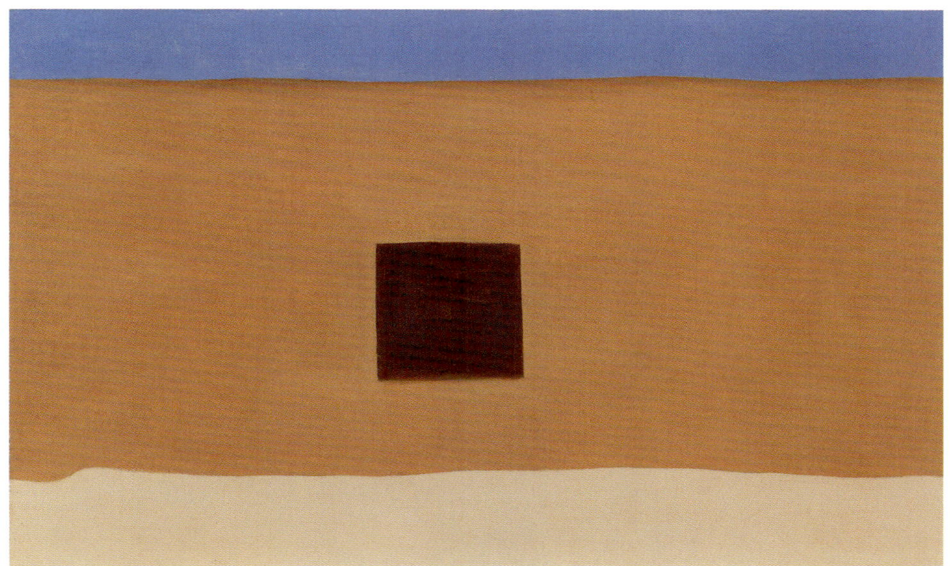

4.7. Georgia O'Keeffe, *In the Patio III*, 1948, oil on canvas, 18 x 30 in. Gift of Georgia O'Keeffe Foundation, CR 1160, Georgia O'Keeffe Museum, Santa Fe, New Mexico. © 2009 Georgia O'Keeffe Museum/Artists Rights Society (ARS), New York.

gallery spaces. The generally small, human scale of the entire museum is indeed suggestive of the domestic qualities of O'Keeffe's houses, without a literal or overly interpretive quality, providing an appropriate scale and backdrop for her works and those of her contemporaries, without putting severe limits on curators and exhibition designers.

GEORGIA O'KEEFFE MUSEUM RESEARCH CENTER

The Georgia O'Keeffe Museum Research Center, which opened in 2001, is housed in a nineteenth-century historic house (the Bergere House, 135 Grand Street) around the corner and a block away from the main building of the museum. This house, like the museum itself, was a renovation and expansion of an existing building and was designed by Richard Gluckman of Gluckman Mayner Architects (fig. 4.12). The house contains the offices for the Research Center, and for visiting scholars, and the center's research library. A stated goal of the Research Center is to provide an "environment of quiet contemplation and study, echoing the atmosphere of Georgia O'Keeffe's houses in Abiquiu and Ghost Ranch."[7] Like the museum itself, this goal is accomplished through an exterior that is very consistent and harmonious with its surroundings, containing interiors that are subtle, modern, and full of natural light.

The elevation presented to the street preserves the form of a nineteenth-century Santa Fe historic house. The new structural additions to the rear of the original structure are all but invisible from the street. The old house contains offices for both staff and visiting scholars. The addition contains the library and archives of the institution. Outside the walls of the Research Center is a garden containing poppies, calla lillies, and the other plants and flowers that O'Keeffe painted, adding to the atmosphere of contemplative serenity the center fosters for its scholars, researchers, and staff.

The centerpiece of the Research Center is its library, located in the rear of the building, away from the noise and bustle of the street, with a view of a lawn and garden (fig. 4.13). Though small in size, the library is very efficiently designed, maximizing the productive use of space by following all of the latest ideas in library planning, from compact shelving for books (which include the personal library of the artist from her New Mexico houses at the time of her death) to pleasant work areas with sufficient light, both natural and artificial. Perhaps the most compelling feature in the design of the library is the built-in flat files, located below the windows looking onto the garden and containing personal possessions of the artist from the time of her death (fig. 4.14). This well-curated collection includes labeled, dated paint chips with the pigments used in each of her oil paintings; paint brushes and art supplies; shells, bones, and rocks she collected and used in her painted compositions; drawings and sketchbooks dating as far back as her childhood and previously unknown in the art world; and one of her famous black dresses with which she is so closely identified, thanks to the iconic photographs of her New Mexico years. This unique collection is without precedent in archival collections dealing with artists of her level of importance and influence. It further allows researchers to reconstruct exactly the pigments, brushes, and art supplies she used in making her works and allows for the precise dating of her oeuvre.

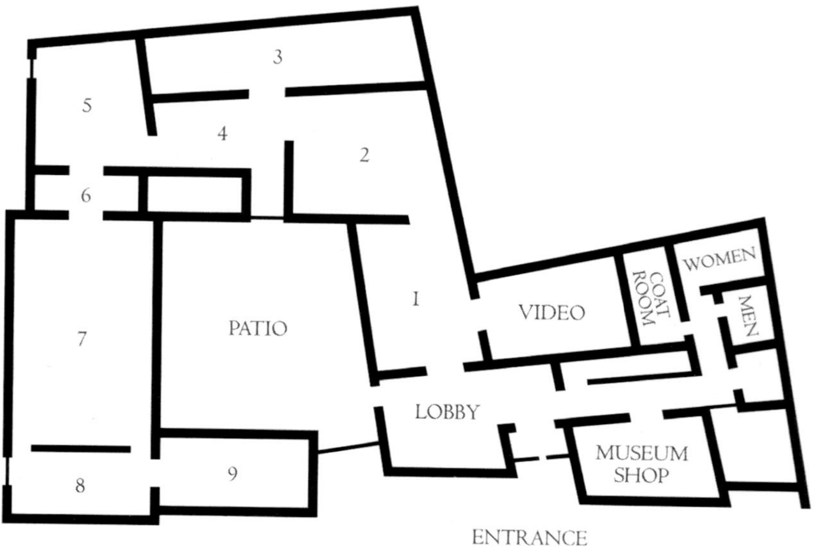

4.8. Floor plan of the Georgia O'Keeffe Museum, Santa Fe, New Mexico. Copyright Georgia O'Keeffe Museum.

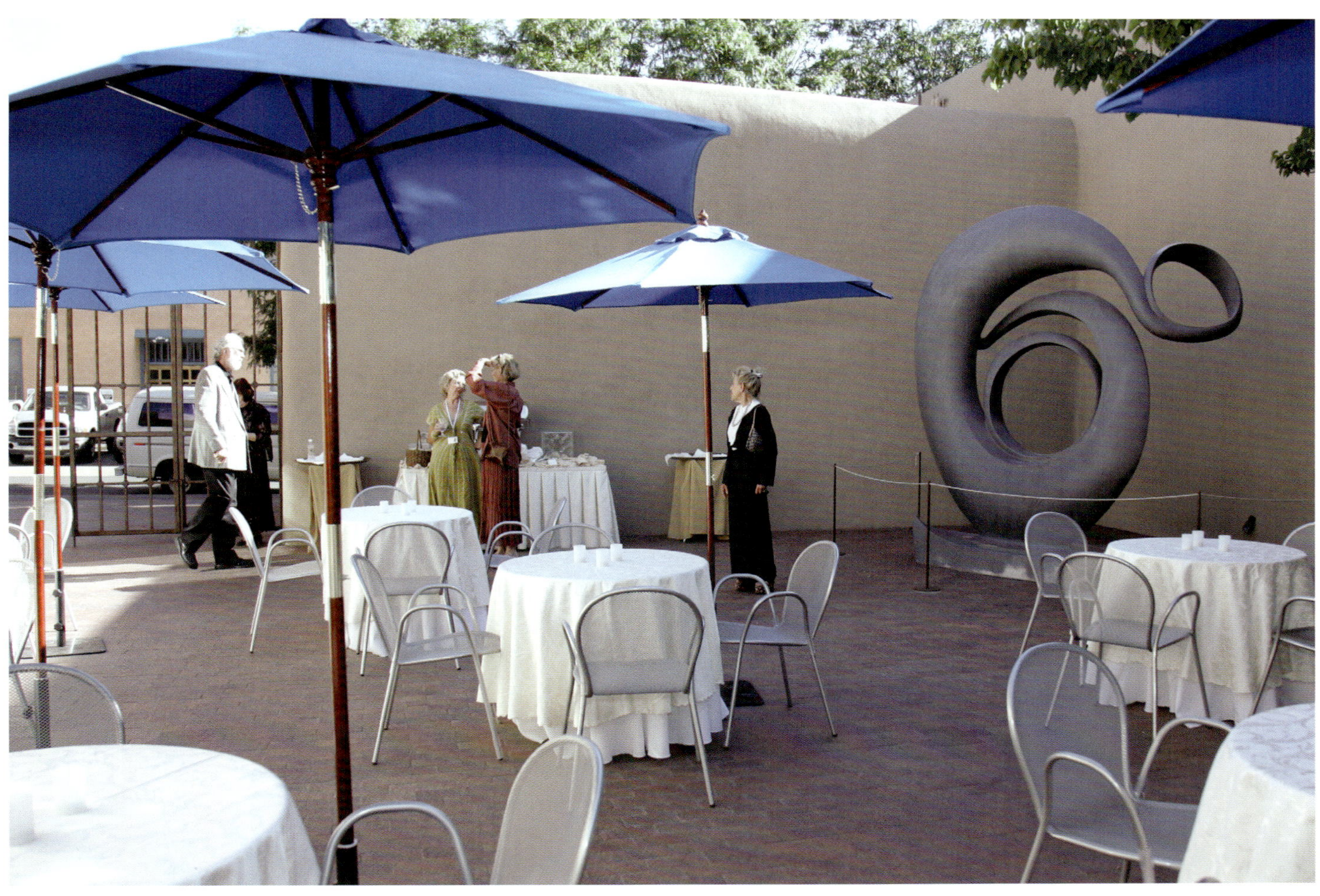

A DIFFERENT APPROACH TO, AND VISION OF, AMERICAN MODERNISM

The design, location, and museological philosophy of the Georgia O'Keeffe Museum does far more than contextualize her work within the landscape and region where she worked and that she loved best. It provides a different lens through which to view not only Georgia O'Keeffe and her work but American modernism itself. So much of the orthodox view of the subject was determined by the unprecedented success of the mission and program of the Museum of Modern Art in New York City in the 1930s and 1940s that the narrative, artists, and canon that it advanced had become mainstream by the late twentieth century.[8] Though the Museum of Modern Art always maintained a Eurocentric view of modernism, it would profoundly influence how modernism in America was developed, interpreted, and exhibited, to the point where even the Whitney Museum of American Art would select Marcel Breuer, a Bauhaus-educated German native (though one who resided in the United States at the time) as its architect.

4.9. Outdoor courtyard, Georgia O'Keeffe Museum, Santa Fe, New Mexico. Copyright Georgia O'Keeffe Museum. Photograph by Robert Reck.

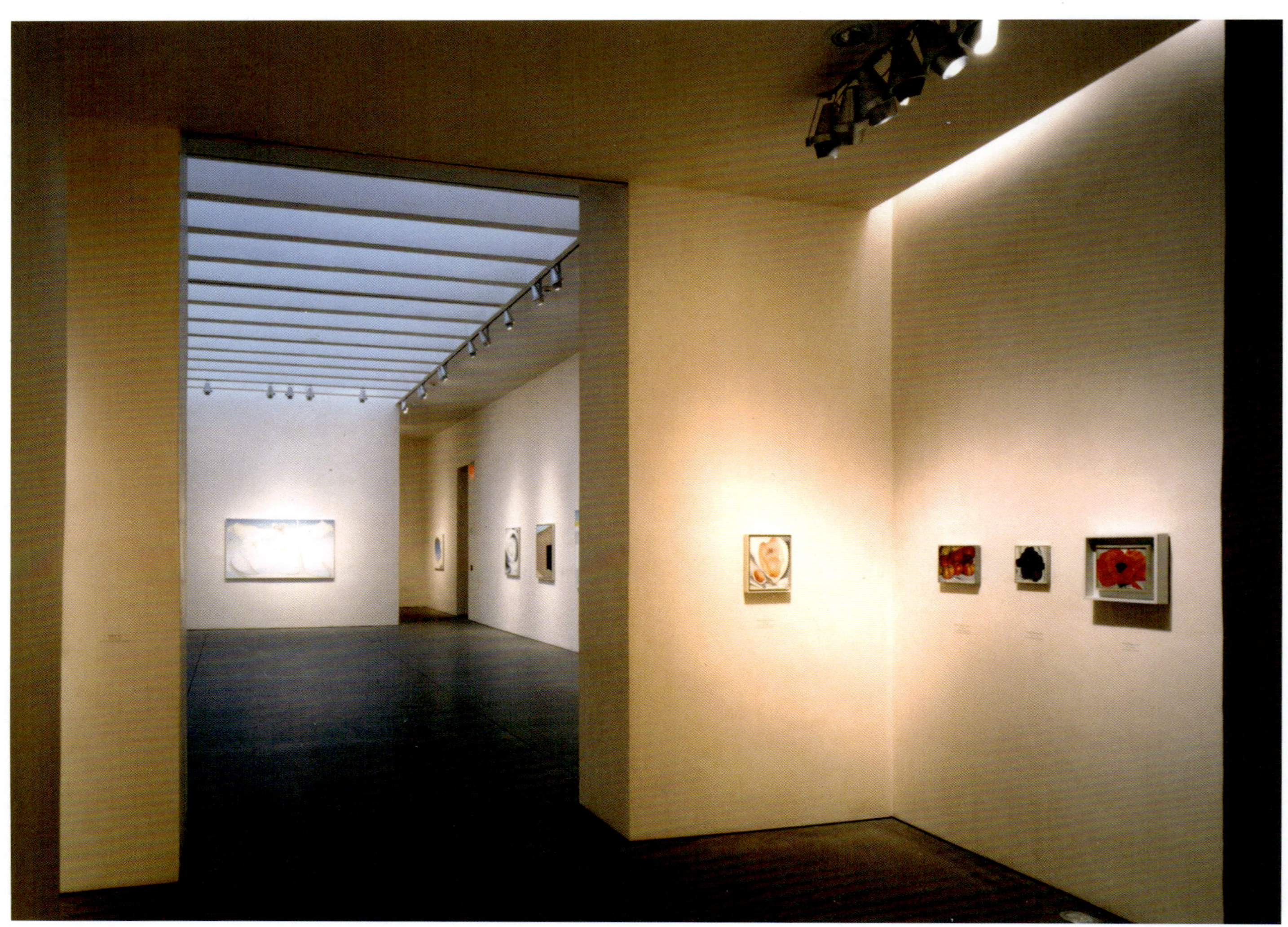

4.10. Galleries 6 and 7, Georgia O'Keeffe Museum, Santa Fe, New Mexico. Copyright Georgia O'Keeffe Museum. Photograph by Robert Reck.

Placing the O'Keeffe Museum and its Research Center far from New York City, the center of the Northeastern art establishment (where the Stieglitz circle that was so important to O'Keeffe's own formation and advancement as an artist was firmly rooted) allows for other important and very real influences on the formation of American modernism to be explored outside of the bubble of orthodoxy. The importance of the American West is a particularly salient factor in the development

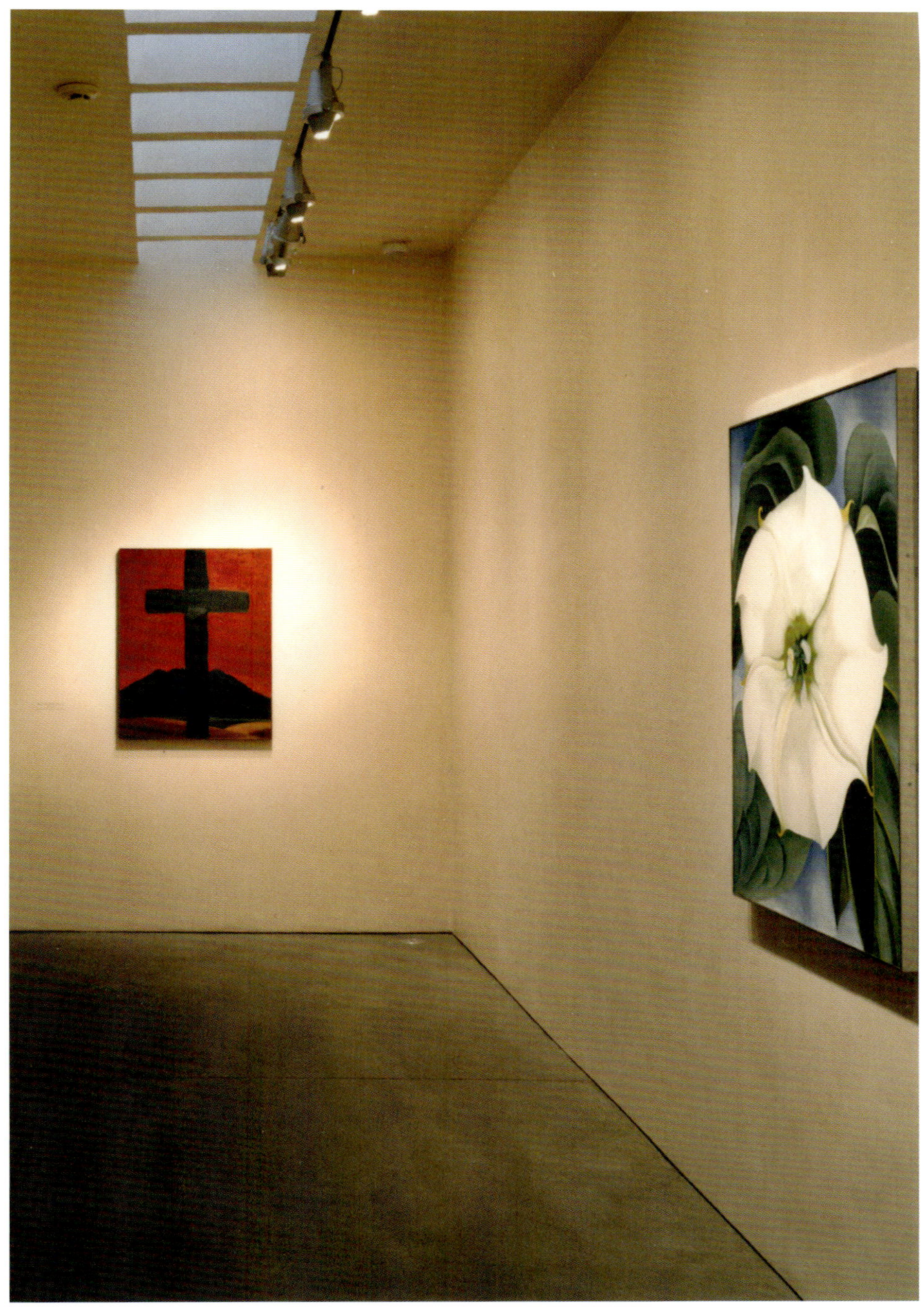

4.11. Gallery 1, Georgia O'Keeffe
Museum, Santa Fe, New Mexico.
Copyright Georgia O'Keeffe Museum.
Photograph by Robert Reck.

of American modernism that was neglected in the narrative advanced by Museum of Modern Art and other institutions of the Northeast; the continued importance of the West, with its many different regions and cultures, can be clearly seen in practices as diverse as those of Ansel Adams and Ed Ruscha. The career and artistic corpus of Georgia O'Keeffe is perhaps a perfect bridge between the Northeastern establishment and the art and atmosphere of the American West.

This broader view of American modernism is not merely embraced by the mission of the Georgia O'Keeffe Museum but is advanced by the scholarship sponsored by its Research Center and clearly manifested in its record of exhibitions. In addition to continuous display of works by O'Keeffe from its permanent collection, the Georgia O'Keeffe Museum has had many exhibitions contextualizing her work among those of her contemporaries and has had many exhibitions of other artists exploring both related and contrasting themes in American modernism, including a Living Artists of Distinction series. Here is a sampling of such exhibitions:

Eye of Modernism	March 23–Sept. 4, 2001
Edward Weston: Photography and Modernism	Jan. 25–May 12, 2002
Georgia O'Keeffe and New Mexico:	
A Sense of Place	June 11–Sept. 12, 2004
Photography by Alfred Stieglitz	May 2, 2003–Jan. 25, 2004
In the American Grain: Dove, Hartley,	
Marin, O'Keeffe, and Stieglitz	Sept. 24, 2004–Jan. 2, 2005
The Photography of Charles Sheeler:	
American Modernist	Jan. 14–May 1, 2005
Georgia O'Keeffe and Andy Warhol:	
Flowers of Distinction	May 13, 2005–Jan 8, 2006
Paul Strand, Southwest	Sept. 22, 2006–Jan. 14, 2007
Sherrie Levine: Abstraction	Jan. 26–May 13, 2007
Georgia O'Keeffe and the Women	
of the Stieglitz Circle	Sept. 21, 2007–Jan. 13, 2008
Marsden Hartley and the West:	
The Search for an American Modernism	Jan. 25–May 11, 2008
Georgia O'Keeffe and Ansel Adams:	
Natural Affinities	May 23–Sept. 7, 2008[9]

Unlike most single-artist museums in the world, the Georgia O'Keeffe Museum thus strives to do more than make a monument to an important and beloved artist; it uses the example of Georgia O'Keeffe to examine, expand, and critique the accepted narrative of American modernism, and it uses its location and architecture as part of this vital program and mission.

THE GEORGIA O'KEEFFE MUSEUM MOVING FORWARD

The Georgia O'Keeffe Museum has the largest collection of the works of O'Keeffe in the world. Its Research Center is becoming a leading institution in the study of American modernism. The museum is relatively small in comparison to the other

4.12. Georgia O'Keeffe Museum Research Center, Santa Fe, New Mexico. Copyright Georgia O'Keeffe Museum. Photograph by Malcolm Varon.

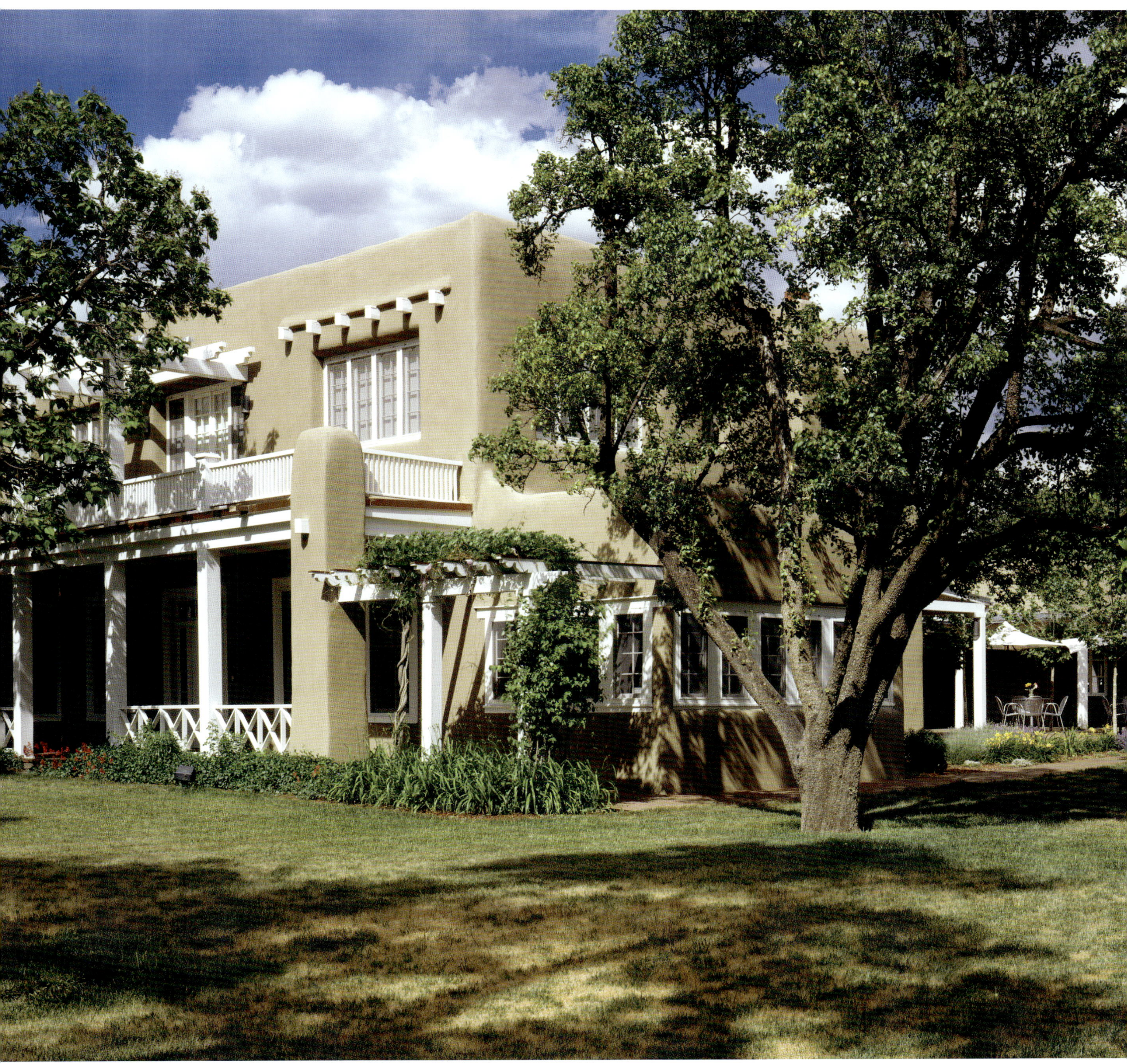

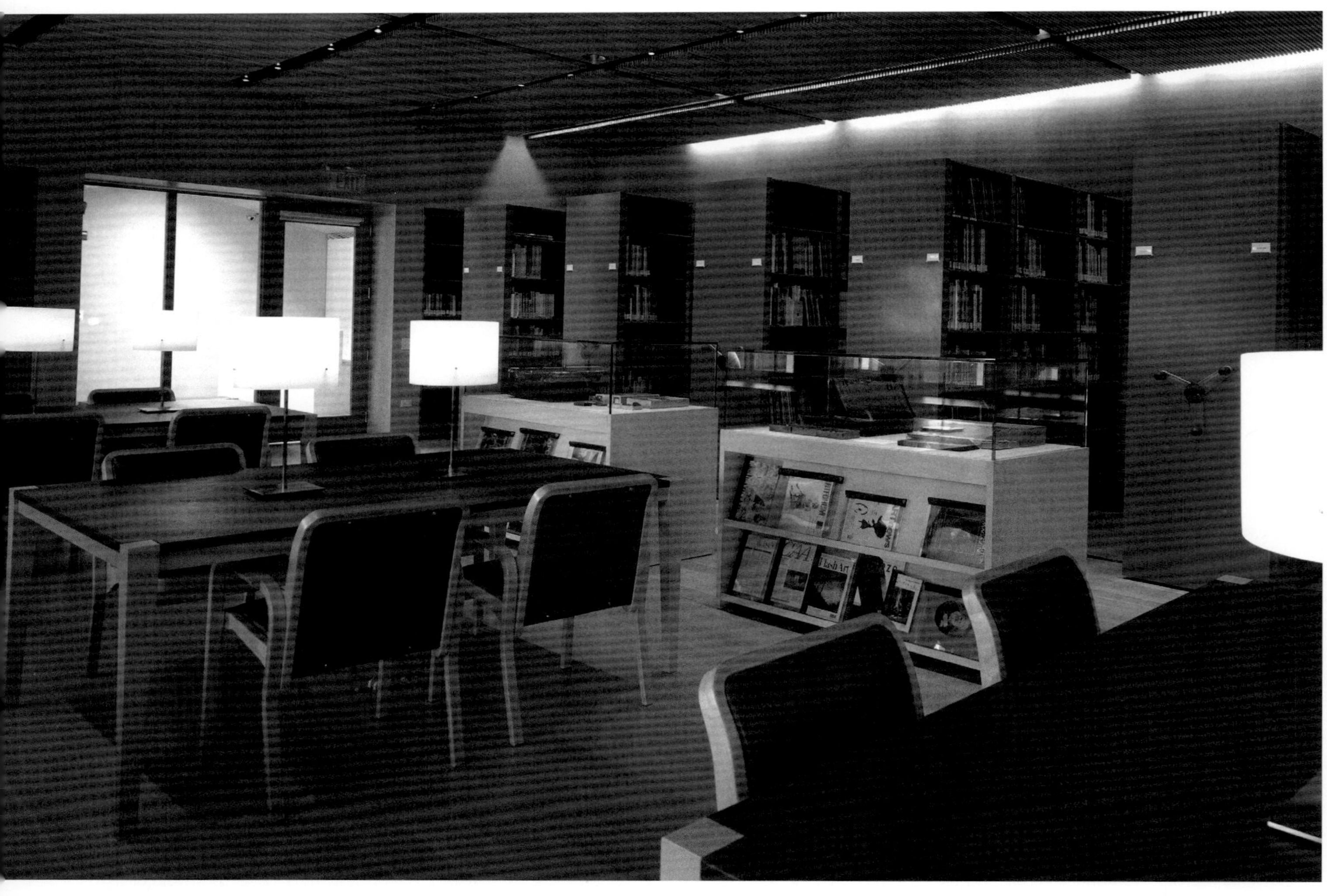

4.13. Georgia O'Keeffe Museum
Research Center Library, Santa Fe,
New Mexico. Copyright Georgia O'Keeffe
Museum. Photograph by Malcolm Varon.

institutions highlighted in this study. According to Barbara Buhler Lynes, chief curator of the museum and The Emily Fisher Landau Director of the Research Center (who has been with the museum since 1999 and is the leading scholar on Georgia O'Keeffe and the author of her Catalogue Raisonné), the maturing Georgia O'Keefe Museum does, however, seek to continue expanding its collections of works by O'Keeffe, her close circle of contemporaries, and other artists from the period of modernism defined as 1890 to the present. [10]

Through its exhibitions and the scholarship and projects of the Research Center's fellows and symposia, Dr. Lynes endeavors to continue the O'Keeffe Museum's successful project of exploring not only O'Keeffe's work and its place in the creation of American modernism, but also the history and significance of American modernism itself:

> This is a two-way dialogue, with O'Keeffe existing in a broader art world, but also participating and shaping this dialogue—having created a place in the

art world for women artists, not just in her own time, but still serving as an example and role model for women artists today. This includes investigation of Georgia O'Keeffe's image and how it has changed from her lifetime through her death to today. This image can be both literal (in the many photographs of her from some of America's foremost photographers) and figurative—how she is conceived of and represented in the literature of art history and criticism and in the popular imagination.

Using Georgia O'Keeffe, her work, the circle in which she moved, and the reception of her work, both in her own times and since by other artists and the art world, the museum adds another strong voice to the discussion and history of American modernism. The publications of the scholars of the Research Center as well as the center's symposia shape this history and further its continuity.

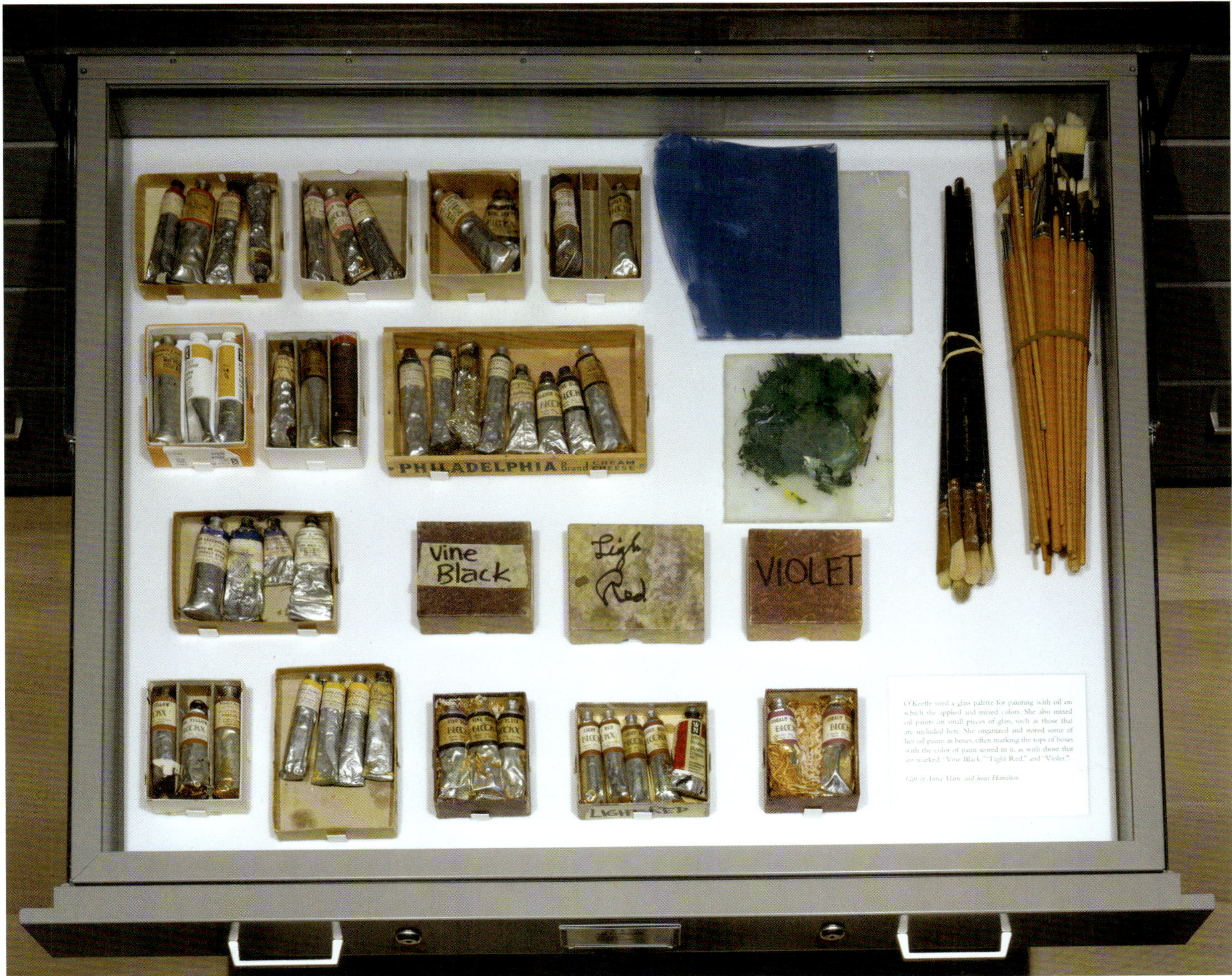

4.14. Georgia O'Keeffe Museum Research Center Library, O'Keeffe painting materials, display drawer, Santa Fe, New Mexico. Copyright Georgia O'Keeffe Museum. Photograph by Malcolm Varon.

CHAPTER 5

THE MUSEUM OF MODERN ART

"When the Museum was founded in 1929, it was predicated on a radical, and repeatedly courageous, departure for the 19th century concept of a museum. It devoted itself to art that was neither established nor, necessarily, recognized. It took risks no museum had taken before. Its perceptions were immediate rather than reflective."

— Excerpt from *New Directions for the Future* by John B. Hightower, Director, Museum of Modern Art, April 1970, MoMA Archives, Reports and Pamphlets 1970s (5)

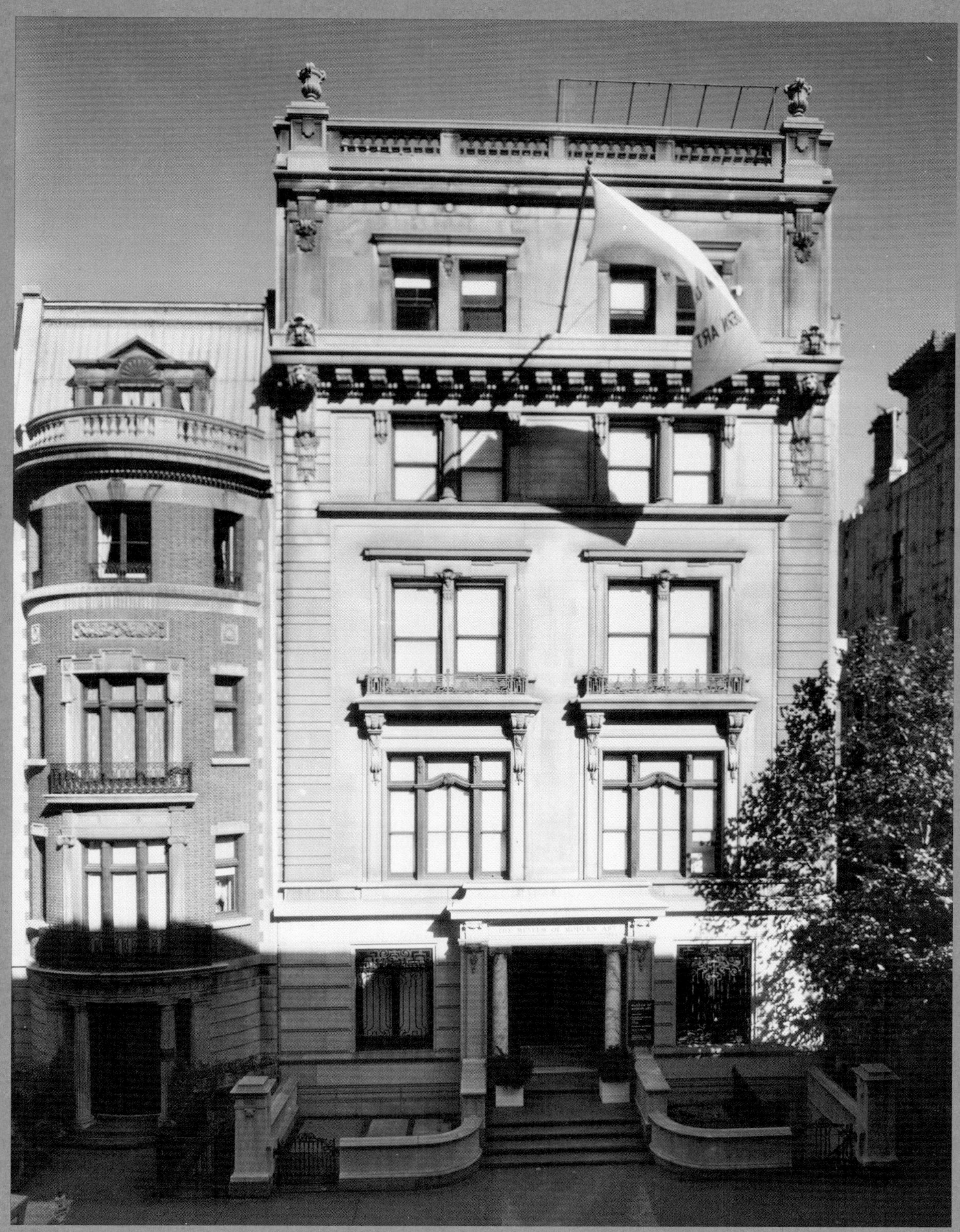

5.1. Townhouse at 11 West 53rd Street, the first permanent home of the Museum of Modern Art at its current location. 1937. © Digital Image © The Museum of Modern Art/Licensed by SCALA / Art Resource.

THE MUSEUM OF MODERN ART AT A GLANCE

Corporate name:	The Museum of Modern Art
Address:	11 West 53rd Street, New York, New York 10019
Opening date:	November 7, 1929
Opening date of current location:	May 10, 1939
Architects of original building:	Philip Goodwin and Edward Durrell Stone
Architects of major additions:	Philip Johnson, Cesar Pelli, and Yoshio Taniguchi
Dates of major expansions:	1951, 1964, 1984, 2004
Previous venues (before purpose-built museum):	Rented floors in the Heckscher Building, 730 Fifth Avenue, New York, New York; Former townhouse on current site
Collecting scope:	Modern and contemporary painting, sculpture, drawing, prints, photography, film, architecture, and design
Special programs:	Film series, lecture series, educational programs
Major units:	Library, archives, study center
Amenities:	Bookstore, design store, restaurant, bar, cafés, reading room, theaters

THE MUSEUM OF MODERN ART
AND THE CASE FOR MODERN ART IN AMERICA

The Museum of Modern Art (MoMA) may well be the most important and transformative cultural institution of the twentieth century. The museum was not merely the first American institution to collect the art of the European avant-gardes from the period before and after World War I (often considered the high-water mark of twentieth-century art, this period included such seminal movements as expressionism, cubism, dada, surrealism, etc.), it was the first art museum to

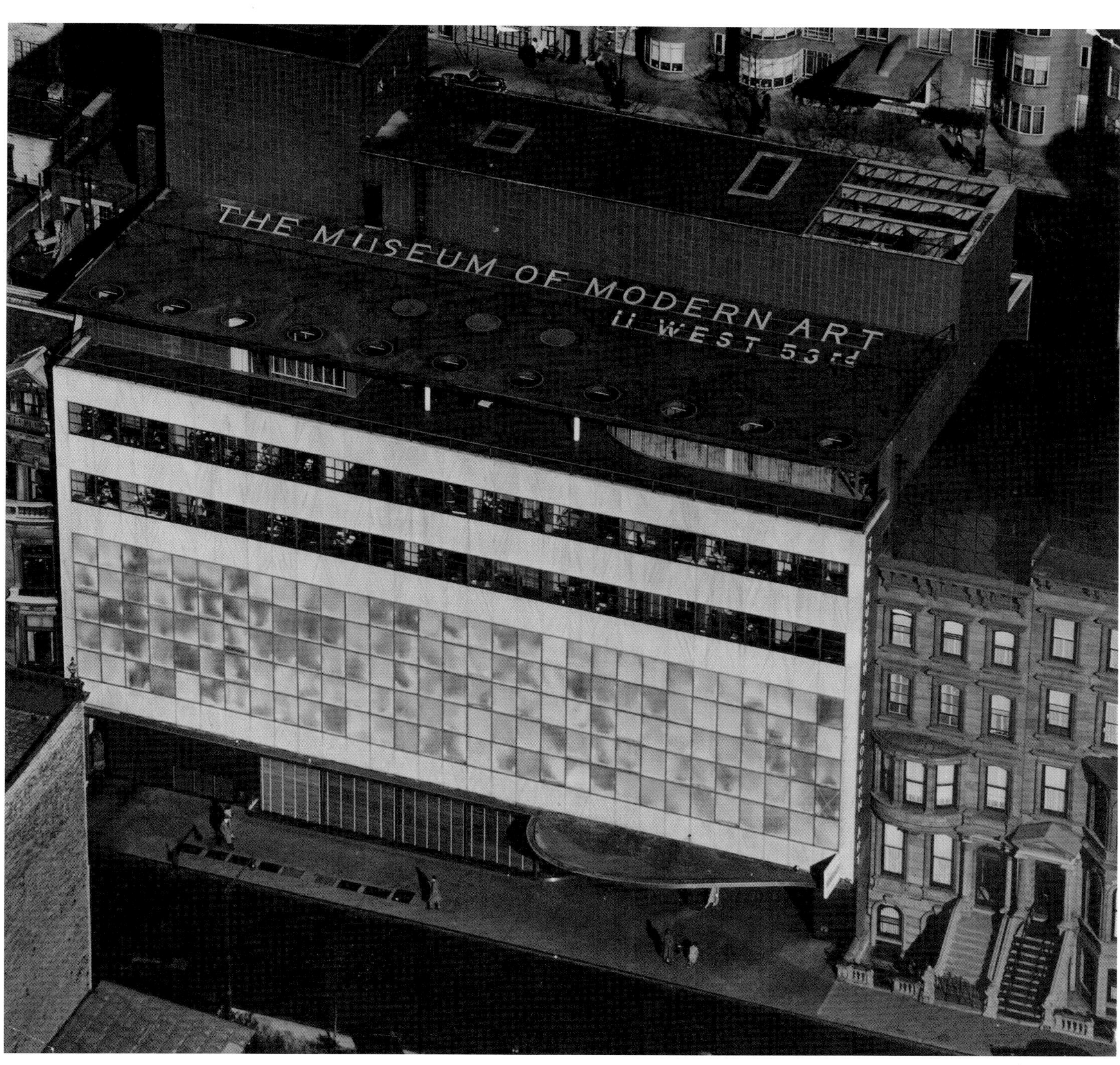

THE MUSEUM OF MODERN ART
11 WEST 53rd

establish curatorial departments in film, architecture, and design, and the first American museum to have a Department of Photography. In the artistic climate of the early twenty-first century, where contemporary art claims some of the highest prices on the art market and where names such as Cézanne, van Gogh, Matisse, and Picasso are more widely known and accepted than Raphael, Ingres, Verocchio, or David, it is difficult to overstate the importance and radicalism of MoMA's mission and program. The overwhelming success of this institution and its founders makes for great difficulty in appreciating the profundity and scope of what they were able to achieve at a time when contemporary art was anything but accepted by both the general public and major collecting institutions, both in the United States and abroad.

The Museum of Modern Art has become a symbol of American high culture to an extent that no other institution can claim. From cartoons in *The New Yorker* magazine to scenes in the films of Woody Allen, the museum has come to symbolize sophistication and intellectualism; it has also succeeded at making these attributes, often considered elitist, accessible and open to a broad public. Unlike other museums of the 1920s and 30s, the Museum of Modern Art always set out to be educational—to make an argument for modern and contemporary art forms and their relevance in life. It was not merely a place to ponder the great works of the past, but rather a "laboratory" for the investigation of current art and the times, culture, and intellectual climate that produced it.

If there is anything that most historians of modern art can agree on, it would be the importance of the "Armory Show" (or the "International Exhibition of Modern Art," as it was officially known) of 1913 in the formation of the canon of modernist art and its acceptance in America.[1] This show was the first major American exhibition of European avant-garde art, featuring the works of such artists as Picasso, Leger, Matisse, and Duchamp. At the time, however, the show was not so universally praised, and the triumph of the art and artists it advanced was by no means inevitable. Speaking in 1949, Museum of Modern Art Founding Director Alfred H. Barr, Jr. would credit the Armory Show with being the very origin of the museum:

> In a sense, the epoch-making Armory Show was the real beginning of the Museum; everyone thought and hoped that the exhibition of more than a thousand paintings and sculpture held in a New York Armory would be the beginning of a permanent institution. But possibly because of the war in Europe, possibly because New York was not ready, no such institution developed.[2]

This statement is certainly consistent with the mission that Barr and the founders of the Museum of Modern Art wished to advance; however, the Armory Show took place in 1913 and the Museum was not to be founded until 1929, sixteen years (and more than three-quarters of a "generation") later. The "everyone" mentioned in the quotation is comfortably left undefined. Mr. Barr himself, born in

1902 and thus a mere eleven years old at the time, was clearly not speaking from his own memory of the Armory Show; rather he was speaking from his position as the director of the institution that played such a vital role in making what was once shocking and controversial in 1913 already a part of the established and accepted canon of modernism a mere thirty-six years later in 1949. While the Armory Show did indeed lay out the canon that MoMA would advance, it was largely MoMA that finally made the Armory Show and what it stood for into something that would be accepted by "everyone."

It is important to emphasize that this acceptance and supremacy of the art from immediately before and after the First World War were by no means inevitable; there were currents in contemporary art available in 1913 other than the European avant-gardes advanced by the Armory Show; further, by 1949, when Barr was speaking, that work was already a third of a century old and no longer the "leading edge" of contemporary art, which was beginning to be dominated by abstract expressionism and its American practitioners—the center had already moved from Paris and Berlin to New York, though the Museum of Modern Art did not immediately recognize this shift (though it soon would; today the Museum has one of the premier collections of both the work from the earlier period and from the abstract expressionist era).

The Museum of Modern Art did far more than champion European avant-garde art, however. Its early embrace of motion pictures as worthy of inclusion in a museum committed to modernism would contribute not only to the acceptance of film as a fine art in America, but would result in the museum receiving an Academy Award. The collection and exhibition of modernist architecture and design would help to win the acceptance of these then-radical forms not just in the minds of a broader public, but would lead that public to commission modernist homes for themselves and to fill these homes with the very objects popularized through exhibition and collection by the museum. The Museum of Modern Art did more to shape tastes and create demand for the types of works it exhibited than any museum has ever done before or since. How MoMA and the various buildings that have housed it contributed to the writing of the story of modern art and its eventual acceptance will be discussed throughout this chapter.

FOUNDING AND EARLY HISTORY

Whereas the Armory Show of 1913 may have been the spiritual or mythical beginning of the Museum of Modern Art, its actual birth as an institution occurred on September 19, 1929. On that date the museum received its formal charter. Unlike the other institutions profiled in this book, the Museum of Modern Art was incorporated as an educational institution, receiving its charter from the Board of Regents of the University of the State of New York Education Department.[3] From its very beginning, the museum saw its mission as a didactic one. Today all museums tend to share an educational mission; however, in 1929 museums were still the domain of those who already appreciated the "high culture" contained within their walls—the institutions themselves did not necessarily feel that it was their duty to educate or enlighten a broader public.

Even before its incorporation, the museum had rented six rooms in the Heckscher Building at 730 Fifth Avenue to serve as galleries and offices. On November 7, 1929, less than two months after its incorporation, the Museum of Modern Art opened its first exhibition (a loan show, as the museum had not yet begun to acquire works and form its own collection), "Cézanne, Gaugin, Seurat, van Gogh." In January of 1930, the museum acquired its first painting, *House by the Railroad* by Edward Hopper, painted in 1925.[4] The museum's founders were working quickly. A pamphlet of October 1929 clearly lays out the goals and plans of the nascent Museum of Modern Art:

> The immediate purpose of the Museum of Modern Art is to hold, in its gallery at the Heckscher Building, 730 Fifth Avenue, New York, some twenty exhibitions during the next two and a half years.
>
> These exhibitions will include as complete a representation as possible of the great modern painters—American and European—from Cézanne to the present day, but will be devoted primarily to living artists, with occasional homage to the masters of the Nineteenth Century.
>
> With the co-operation of artists, collectors and dealers, the Trustees of the Museum hope to obtain for these twenty exhibitions, paintings, sculptures, drawings, lithographs and etchings of the first order.
>
> The ultimate purpose of the Museum will be to acquire, from time to time (either by gift of by purchase) a collection of the best modern works of art. The possibilities of the Museum of Modern Art are so varied that it has seemed unwise to the organizers to lay down too definite a program for it beyond the present one of a series of frequently recurring exhibitions during a period of two and a half years.[5]

Much of the actual (and still current) program of the Museum of Modern Art and the scope of its collecting would develop in the decade between its opening in November 1929 and the opening of its first purpose built home in 1939.

Perhaps surprising to the contemporary reader is the fact that the opening of the Museum of Modern Art was received with ambivalence and some skepticism by the popular press of the day. Here are some excerpts from a representative article from *The New York Times*:

> Nothing has recently stirred more interest in art circles—and outside of them for that matter—than the project to establish in this city a modern art museum. The plans are as yet tentative, but promising. Artistic direction and financial backing are already assured.[. . .] Its collections will at first be modest, though

select, and ought to do for New York what has been done in Paris and Berlin and London and other cities in setting up small but fine museums alongside the great national and municipal repositories.

This modern art museum would in no sense be antagonistic to the Metropolitan. The prospectus, with not too great modesty, speaks of its hope to be to the Metropolitan what the Luxembourg is to the Louvre. It surely will have some distance to travel before arriving at the Luxembourg—much further, in fact, than the Metropolitan has to go before catching up with the Louvre. It also seems to be something of a misapprehension to speak of the new museum as a place of approbation for modern art. The main thing is to get it shown. Whether or not it later passes from Purgatory to Paradise, whether the public understands it or not, there should be ampler facilities for its exhibit. [. . .]

Loan collections, it is stated, will be the basis of the activity of the new museum for a year or two. It must occasion a little surprise, not to say regret, that the first exhibition is to be French. American artists will feel that they might well have been given the earliest chance in an American museum of contemporary art to show what they can do. [. . .][6]

This review is historically fascinating for a number of reasons. Although it is enthusiastic about having a venue to display modern and contemporary art, it is skeptical about interest among the general public for such work. The regret voiced over the decision to open with an exhibition of French art would seem to deny the existence of such institutions in New York City at the time as the Whitney Studio Club (which was to become the Whitney Museum of American Art in 1931) that already focused on exhibiting contemporary American art. The above article is prescient in identifying the educational or instructional nature of the Museum of Modern Art's early exhibitions and collecting, however.

The strangest position advanced by this 1929 newspaper piece is the notion that the Metropolitan Museum of Art had less distance to travel to "catch up" with the Louvre than the new Museum of Modern Art would have to match the Luxembourg in Paris. How the Metropolitan, or any American institution specializing in the art of the past, particularly European art, could ever be seen as matching or overtaking the oldest, deepest, and richest collection of this art in the world is puzzling. When collecting modern and contemporary art, surely the playing field was much more level—why couldn't a young institution with firm private-sector financial backing easily compete with similar institutions abroad? What this article reveals, above all, is the climate of hostility and philistinism of much of the art world and the general public in the late 1920s toward the arts of the European avant-gardes specifically, and to much of modern and contemporary art generally. These are the very attitudes that the museum's founders sought to address through the creation of the Museum of Modern Art. It is truly amazing how quickly and completely they would succeed.

The first decade of the Museum of Modern Art was full of so many important and groundbreaking decisions that this study can present only the highlights; specifically the important decisions that would shape the future physical plant of the institution. Already by 1932, the museum had outgrown its rented space in the Heckscher Building (see fig. 5.1), acquiring a townhouse at 11 West 53rd Street (on part of the site of the current museum complex) and moving there by May of that year (see fig. 5.2). Interestingly, the last exhibition held at the original Fifth Avenue venue was "Modern Architecture: International Exhibition," the first exhibition by the Department of Architecture founded that year, and the first exhibition at the Museum of Modern Art dedicated to a medium other than painting or sculpture. The curator of this exhibition was Philip Johnson, who along with collaborator Henry-Russell Hitchcock, would coin the term "the International Style" in the exhibition's catalog: *The International Style: Architecture since 1922*. Johnson, of course, would become the museum's architect, designing and executing many later additions to MoMA as well as curating countless shows in the Department of Architecture and Design. Also in 1932 the museum's library was founded, initially with holdings of 2,000 books.

In 1935 another very important department was founded, the Film Library (later upgraded to Department of Film). This department was the first film collection at an art museum, giving recognition to this very modern, important, and previously neglected medium as a fine art. The importance of this department would be recognized in 1938 by the Academy of Motion Picture Arts and Sciences by their awarding MoMA with an Oscar, a special award to the Film Library "for its significant work in collecting films dating from 1895 to the present and for the first time making available to the public the means of studying the historical and aesthetic development of the motion picture as one of the major arts."[7]

The most fundamental element of any collecting institution is clearly its collection. Unlike the four museums discussed in the previous chapters, at the time of its opening the Museum of Modern Art had no permanent collection (the Frick Collection, the Menil Collection, the Whitney Museum and the Georgia O'Keeffe Museum were all built on the private collections of their founders). As stated in the October 1929 pamphlet quoted above, the museum always intended to assemble a permanent collection; however, it did not see this as prerequisite for its initial function.

For a museum dedicated to modern art to have a collection, it is of paramount importance for it to define clear parameters for what it considers "modern art" to be. After much debate and many internal documents, a policy was adopted by the museum and formalized at the meeting of the trustees of May 28, 1936:

> The Collection of works of art owned by the Museum of Modern Art shall at all times be made up principally of works produced within the previous fifty years, with a smaller number of works of earlier periods to illustrate the sources and aid in the understanding of contemporary arts. [. . .] From time to

5.3. Installation view of the exhibition "Modern Architecture: International Exhibition." The Museum of Modern Art, New York, the last exhibition held at the original home of the Museum of Modern Art at the Heckscher Building on 5th Avenue. February 10, 1932 through March 23, 1932. © Digital Image © The Museum of Modern Art/Licensed by SCALA / Art Resource.

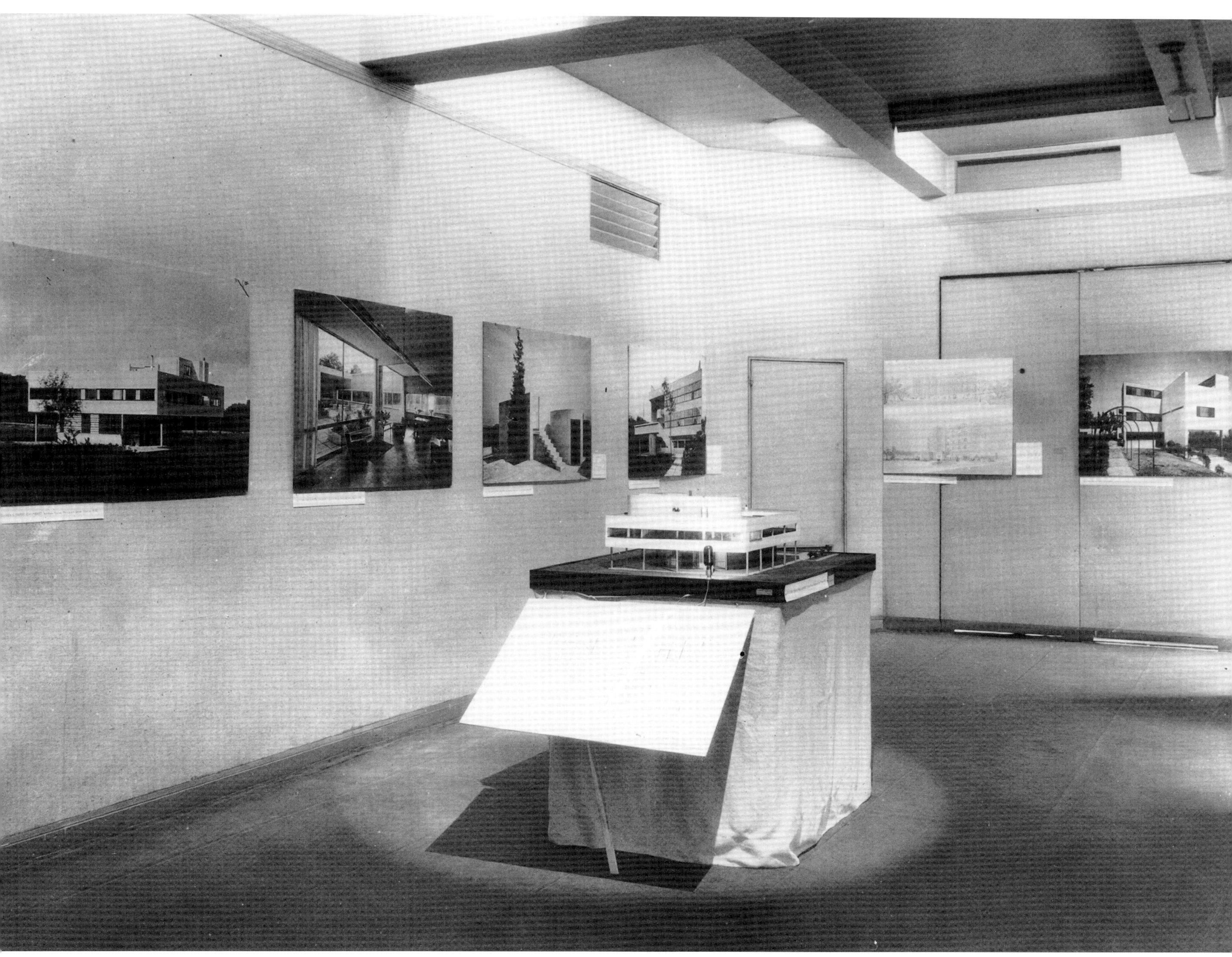

time works from the Collection may be distributed to other public institutions through loan, gift, sale, or exchange, by vote of the Trustees or may be sold on their direction, providing such action is not contrary to the terms of a deed of gift or bequest transferring such works to the Museum."[8]

This policy clearly established a collecting scope based in time, with fifty years being the age at which a work ceased to be in the scope of the main collection, though it could be part of a smaller collection used to illustrate important sources for contemporary art. Further exploration of this idea is found in then Director Alfred H. Barr, Jr.'s extremely important "Report on the Permanent Collection," which is reproduced in full in Appendix B. Unlike other museum collections and as clearly graphically illustrated in Barr's famous "Torpedo Diagram" (see Appendix B, fig. B.1), the Museum of Modern Art's "permanent" collection would thus always be changing and in flux, as works were sold to other institutions or otherwise deaccessioned when they reached that mandatory retirement age of fifty to make way for truly contemporary works.

As anyone who has visited the museum and enjoyed its permanent collection knows, this policy would not be carried out for very long, though it was adopted in earnest. From the late 1930s to as late as 1952, the Museum of Modern Art was trying to make it work, through hard negotiation with the Metropolitan Museum of Art and the Whitney Museum (see Chapter 3). Actual agreements regarding the practice of transferring older works were signed (in 1947 and 1948), though they would all be vacated in 1952. It is truly fascinating to speculate what the respective collections of the Museum of Modern Art and the Metropolitan Museum of Art might look like today had these two institutions been able to reach agreement on an automatic plan for the Museum of Modern Art to deaccession its "senior citizens" to the Metropolitan Museum of Art after they reached fifty—by 2008 there would be no works by Jackson Pollock, let alone Picasso, Matisse, or Cézanne, left in the Modern's collection, and the most popular galleries at the Metropolitan might well be those exhibiting early twentieth-century painting and sculpture!

THE GOODWIN AND STONE BUILDING
AND THE ESTABLISHMENT OF THE MODERN CANON

By the mid-1930s the Museum of Modern Art was making its argument for modern and contemporary art. It had the beginnings of a permanent collection (though it was still debating what the word *permanent* might mean); it had, through its Departments of Architecture and Film, successfully expanded the nature of the types of works and exhibitions one might expect to find in an art museum. What the museum still lacked was a proper home; a building that itself would participate in the institution's mission of advocacy for the modern. As the museum had done so much to bring European modernist architecture to an American audience, it

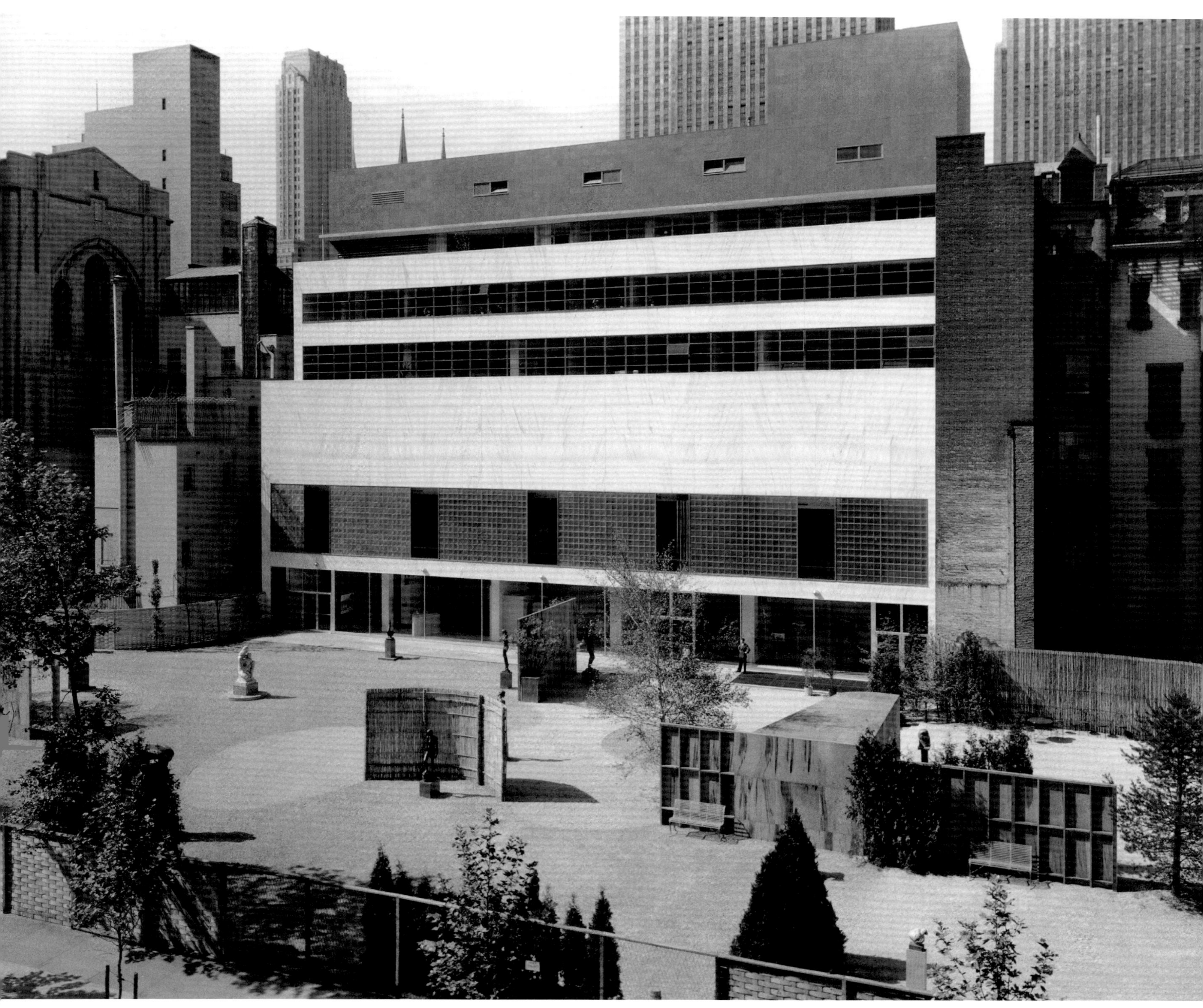

was only natural that its own building should follow the aesthetic and design philosophies that its curatorial staff worked so hard to advance.

By February 1936, the trustees had acquired the properties adjoining the Museum of Modern Art's townhouse at 11 West 53rd Street. Not surprisingly, Alfred Barr advocated hiring one of the top European modernist architects to design the new building. Names floated included Le Corbusier, Walter Gropius, and Ludwig Mies van der Rohe.[9] However, the trustees did not share Barr's enthusiasm for having the flagship institution in America devoted to modern and contemporary art designed by a foreigner. They selected architects Philip Goodwin (himself a trustee of the museum) and Edward Durrell Stone to design the project. A compromise suggesting collaboration between Goodwin and a major European architect was considered, but in the end failed to reach fruition.

A disappointed Barr resigned from the museum's Building Committee over the disagreement. This struggle reveals how the perceptions of the trustees—and, one can assume, the American art world in general—had changed toward Europe as an intellectual center between the late 1920s, when the museum was being founded, to the mid to late 1930s, when the museum was planning its new building. In the late 1920s Europe was a beacon of hope and radical ideas for general enlightenment; by the mid-30s, it had become associated, in the minds of many, with the reactionary right wing and the rise of fascism and Nazism. As the likelihood of war loomed ever larger, a distaste for recognizing Europeans as being on the vanguard of modernism—the art and architecture of tomorrow—naturally grew among many.

Despite the difficulty and disagreements regarding the choice of designer, the end result was both well received and thoroughly modern. The traditional Beaux-Arts training of Goodwin did not show in the edifice he designed for the Museum of Modern Art, which fit squarely into the modernist architecture that the museum's curators labeled "the International Style" (figs. 5.3 and 5.4). The museum's façades were constructed of white marble over a glass wall at street level. The 53rd Street elevation had translucent glass on the two gallery floors and long window strips, recalling those of Le Corbusier's domestic architecture, on the above-office floors. A terrace opened off the Members' Club on the penthouse level. The entrance (contrary to the Beaux-Arts principles on which most museum buildings were constructed) was at street level and off axis with the center of the façade, articulated only by a curving overhang (fig. 5.5). This placement and design of the entrance symbolically made the museum less intimidating and more accessible, as visitors would be enticed to enter from the views of the interior afforded by the glass walls surrounding the doors. This design, in short, encouraged people to enter without equating the experience with going to a church, temple, courthouse, or government building. This notion of accessibility and the idea that art could belong to everyday life rather than hover somewhere above it, beyond the quotidian, was in sharp contrast to the Beaux-Arts architecture in which most museums were housed. The rear elevation

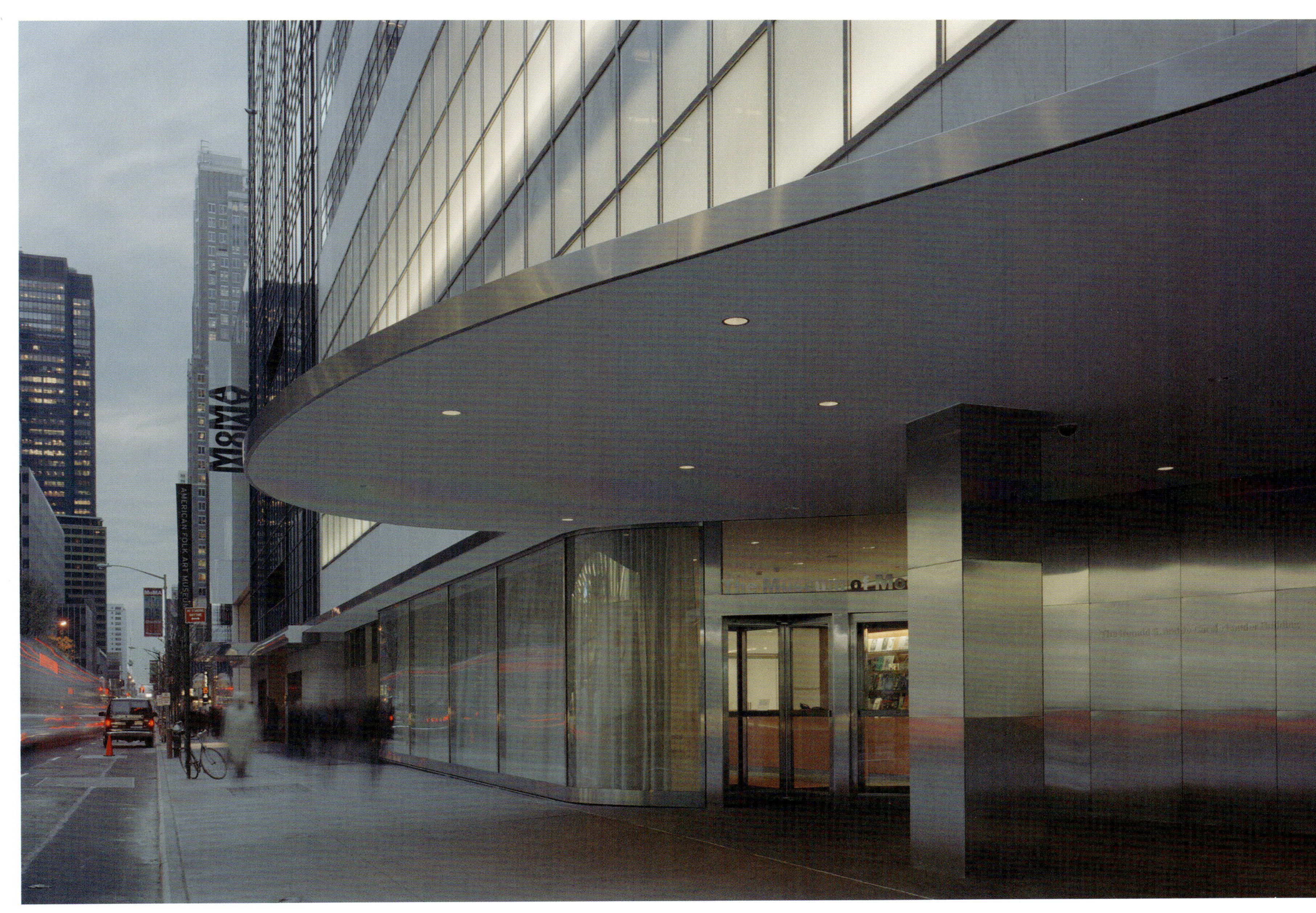

5.5. The entrance to the Museum's theaters, on 53rd Street, with its "piano" canopy (restored from the original design of 1939). New York, Museum of Modern Art (MoMA). Photograph © Timothy Hursley. © Digital Image © The Museum of Modern Art/ Licensed by SCALA / Art Resource.

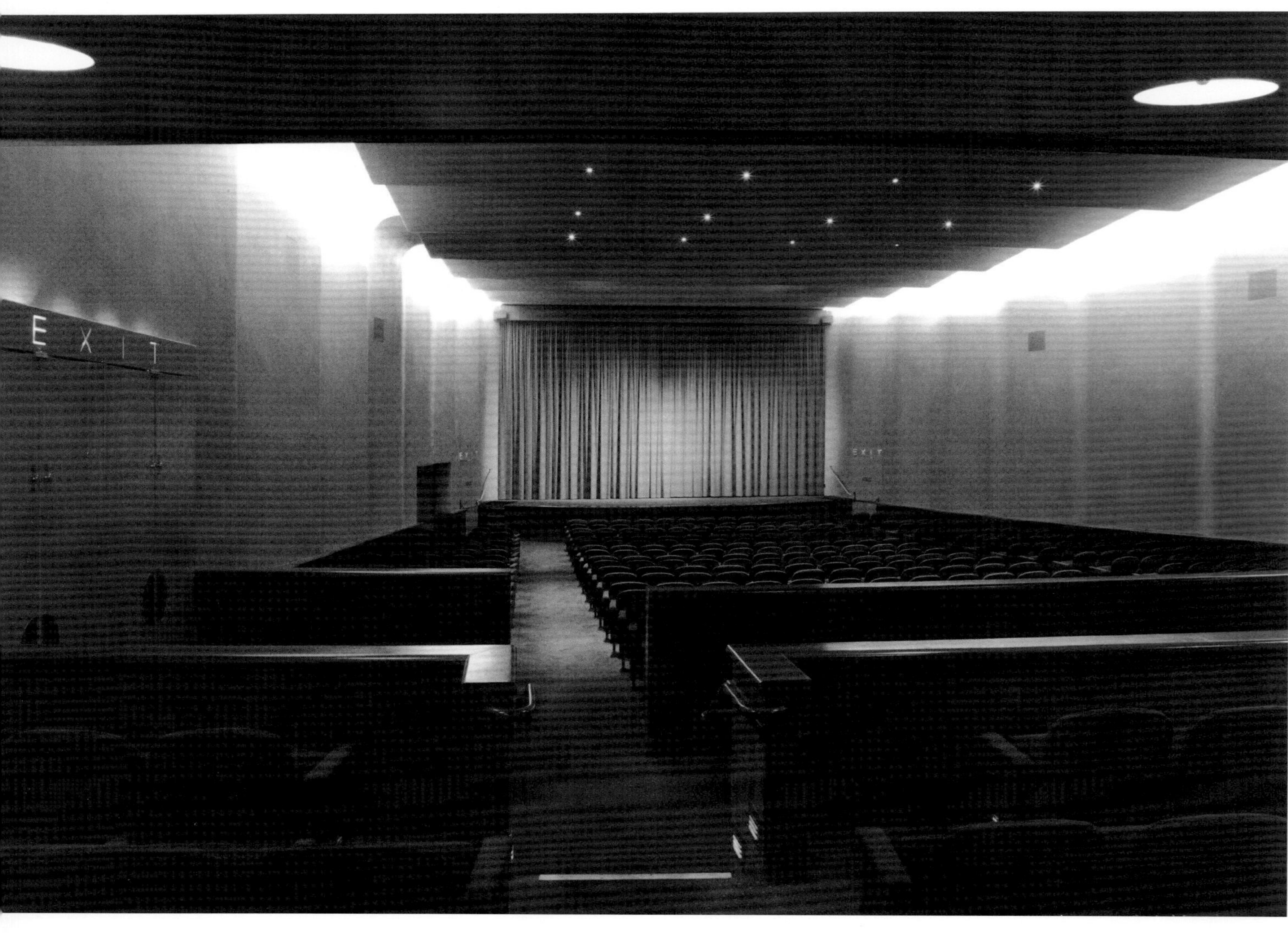

5.6 Titus 1 Theater, The Museum of
Modern Art, New York, original design
by Philip Goodwin and Edward D. Stone,
1939. Photographed January 4, 1989.
© Digital Image © The Museum of Modern
Art/Licensed by SCALA / Art Resource.

of the museum opened onto an outdoor sculpture garden (in the same space that
the current sculpture garden now occupies).

If the exterior elevations of the new Museum of Modern Art seemed different to
the average museumgoer, the interiors would appear even more original and well-
integrated with the museum's mission. From the spacious auditorium for lectures
and film screenings (fig. 5.6) in the facility's basement to the members' clubrooms
in the penthouse (fig. 5.7), patrons would be (many for the first time) inside
thoroughly "modern" spaces; further, all the furniture, fixtures, and appointments
were of the type that the museum's Department of Architecture and Industrial Arts
(now Architecture and Design) collected and displayed in its exhibitions. These
and other public spaces of the museum were all examples of modernism in the
applied arts of architecture and design, creating a proper context for the display
of contemporary art (figs. 5.8–5.10) and exposing New Yorkers to the experience

of being within a modernist interior. Today, in the early twenty-first century, it is difficult to imagine how strong the impact of this first entry into such a space would have been on a typical middle-class American, who had seen such interiors, furniture, lighting, and appointments only in pictures, if at all.

Indeed, though modernist architecture and interiors could be found in the United States since the 1920s, virtually all examples were residential (and therefore private), and usually found on the West Coast (such as the houses of Richard Neutra and Rudolf Schindler). The Museum of Modern Art thus also served as a national showroom for modernism (then, only figuratively; later, in the 1980s with the opening of the MoMA Design Store, it would serve as a literal one as well). It is likely not a coincidence that the Museum of Modern Art's location in Midtown Manhattan, one of the busiest, most important business centers of the world, helped familiarize quite a few corporate executives with modernist architecture and design, which, in the post–World War II era, became the preferred idiom for the high-rise corporate headquarters that still dominate the area. It can be assumed that many of the executives who chose modernist architects and designers for their corporate offices (as well as their homes) received their education at the Museum of Modern Art.

The new building did more than provide an example of modern architecture and design in Midtown Manhattan. It also created an ideal context for the display of modern and contemporary painting and sculpture. The scale of the galleries was smaller and more intimate than the typical museum gallery of the time. This reduction in scale allowed the galleries to provide a similar viewing context to the domestic interiors for which these works themselves were originally intended (fig. 5.11). Perhaps this was a useful lesson learned from the museum's former home in a New York City townhouse, but more likely it was another well-thought-out element in the museum's program to explore modernism as an integrated, cross-disciplinary movement, with a coherent aesthetic and philosophy.

Consistent with the entrance to the museum on street level rather than atop a high staircase, the smaller-scaled galleries also strove to make the art on exhibit more accessible, both actually and metaphorically. The Museum of Modern Art was conceived and incorporated as an educational institution, not as a temple; it was therefore scaled and designed around the principle that it should help to explain the art on display—work which director Alfred Barr repeatedly stressed was difficult for the uninitiated to understand and appreciate. The Goodwin and Stone building succeeded in becoming part of the lesson plan of this educational museum. The typical museum building of the first half of the twentieth century followed the tradition that began with the conversion of the royal palace of the Louvre in Paris into a public museum—the museum as a large public building, similar to a palace, government building, or other type of structure of authority, and usually looking to Greco-Roman antiquity for its architectural language. In contrast, the Museum of Modern Art was among the first collecting institutions to seriously question this tradition, to develop an architecture more closely allied with the works collected, and to provide a coherent philosophy for their display.

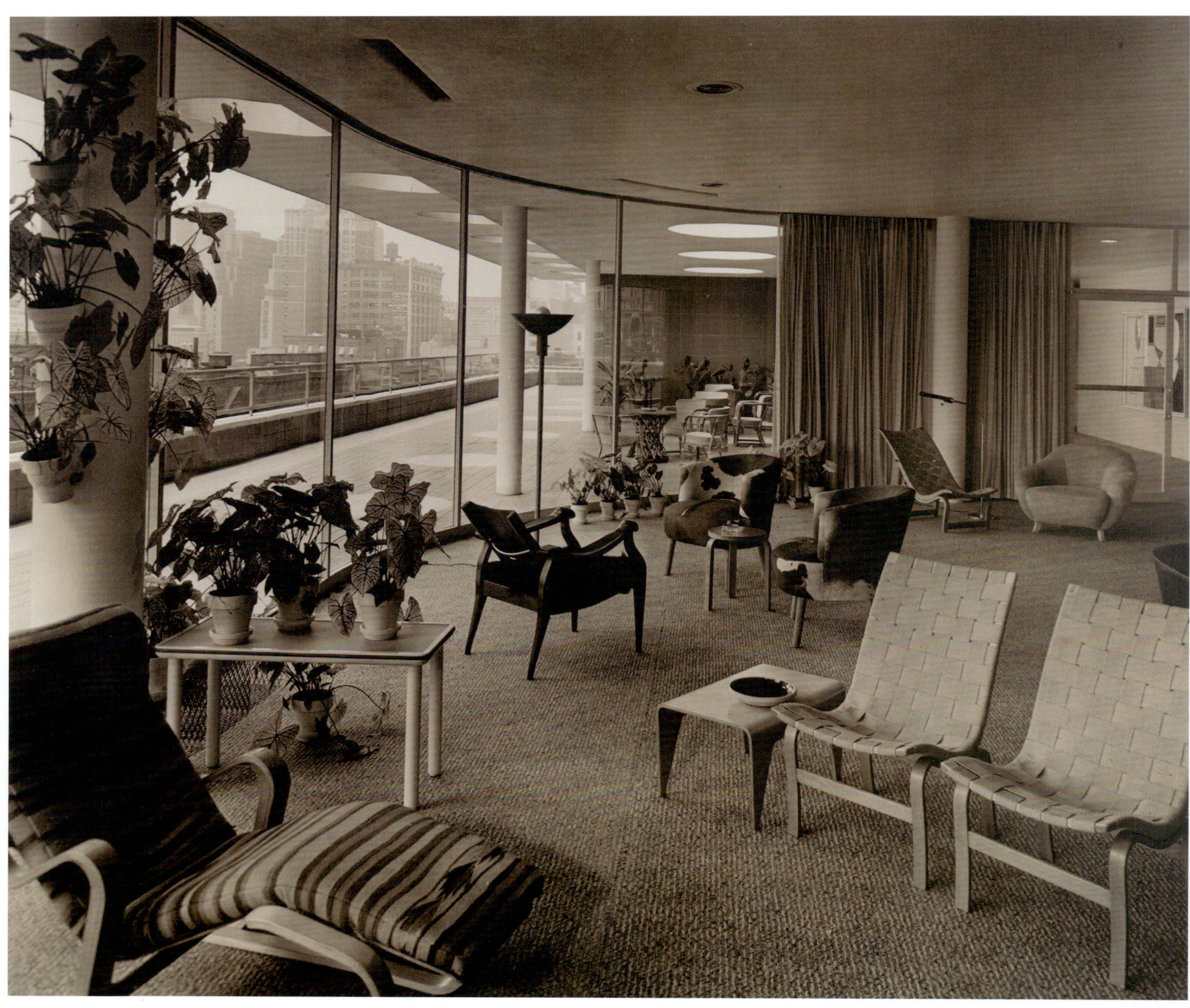

5.7. Interior of Member's Lounge,
penthouse, Museum of Modern Art,
Goodwin and Stone, New York, 1939. ©
Digital Image © The Museum of Modern Art/
Licensed by SCALA / Art Resource.

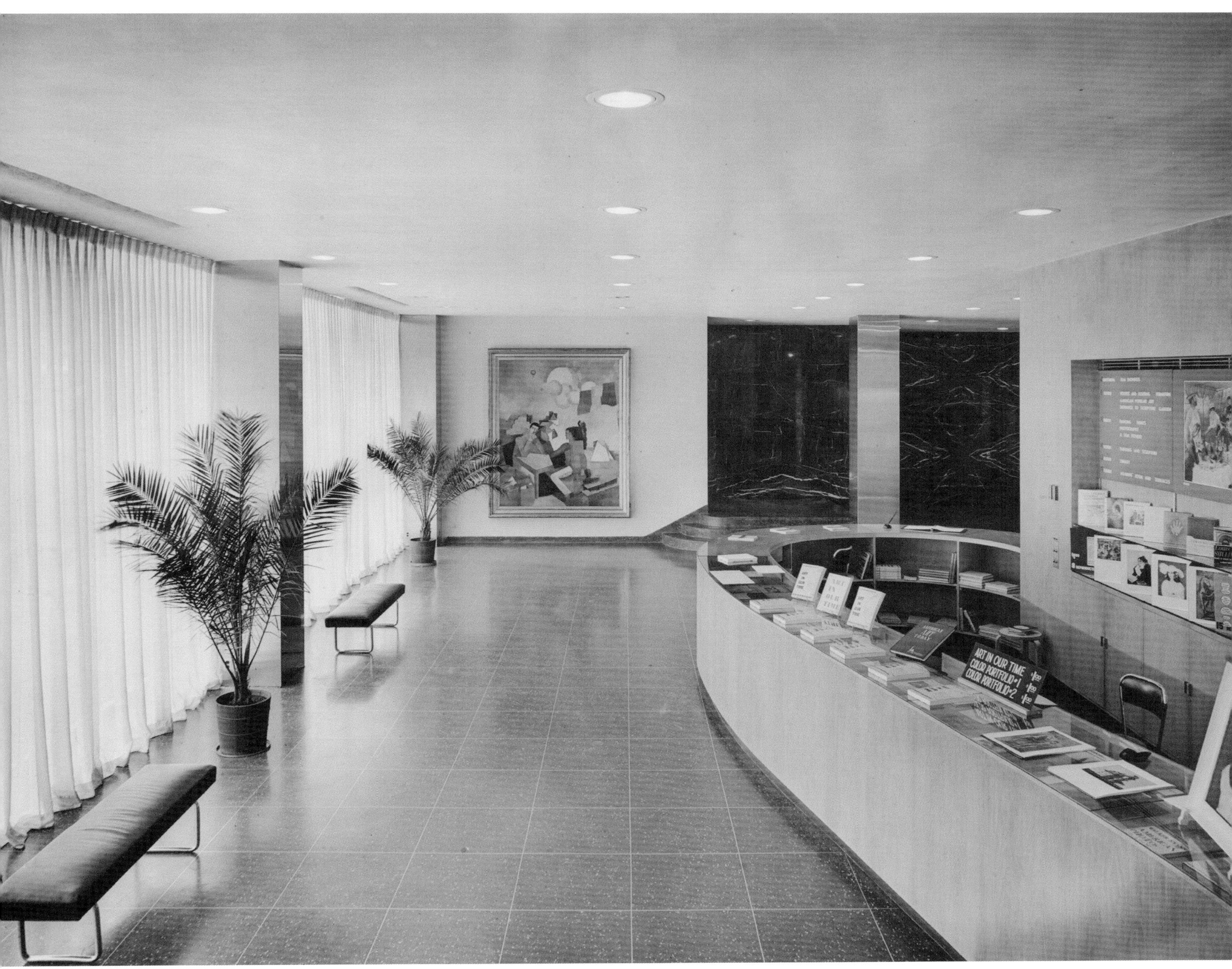

5.8. Interior view of the lobby, The Museum of Modern Art, Goodwin and Stone, New York, 1939. Lobby. © Digital Image © The Museum of Modern Art/Licensed by SCALA / Art Resource.

and interpretation.

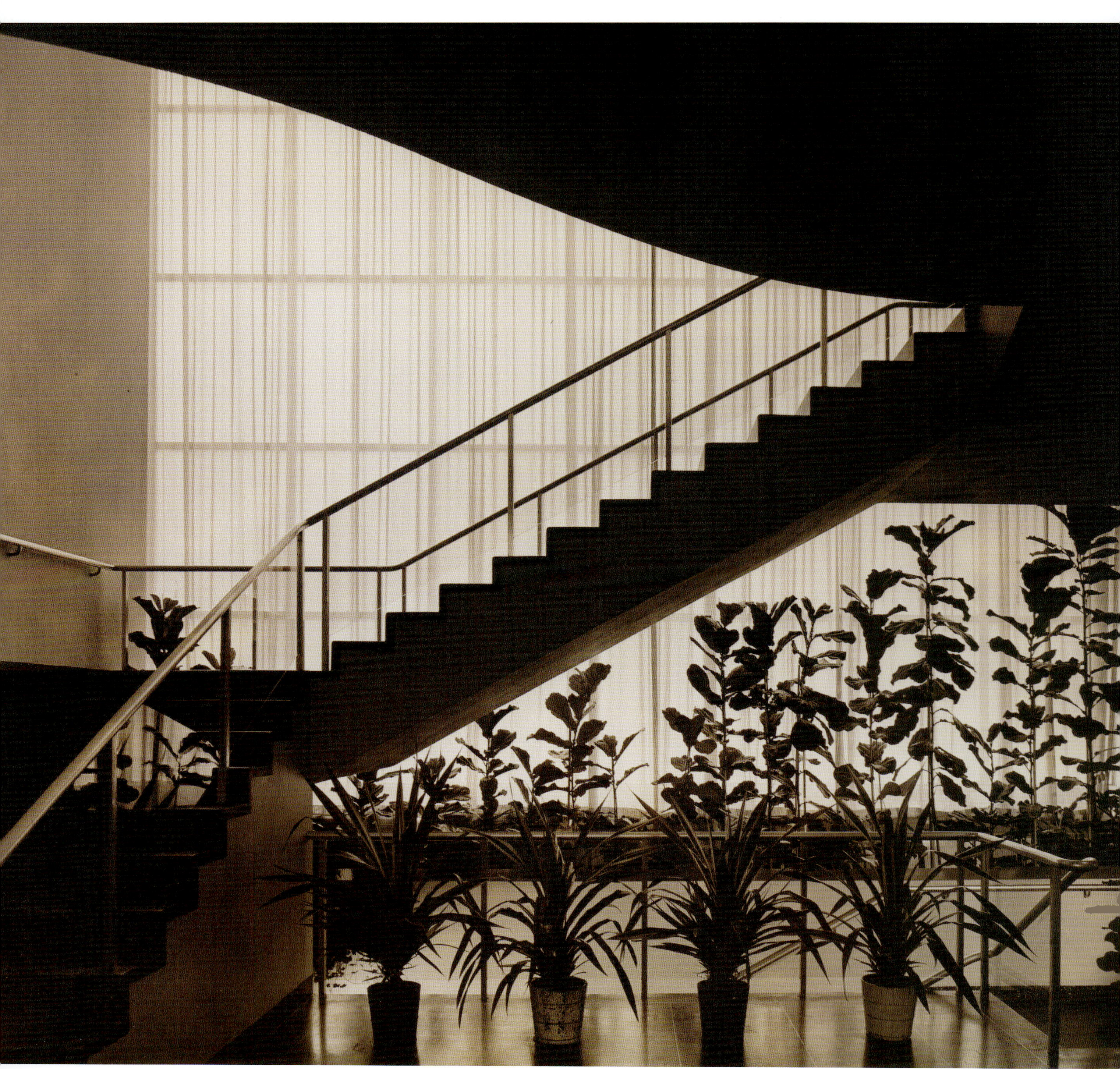

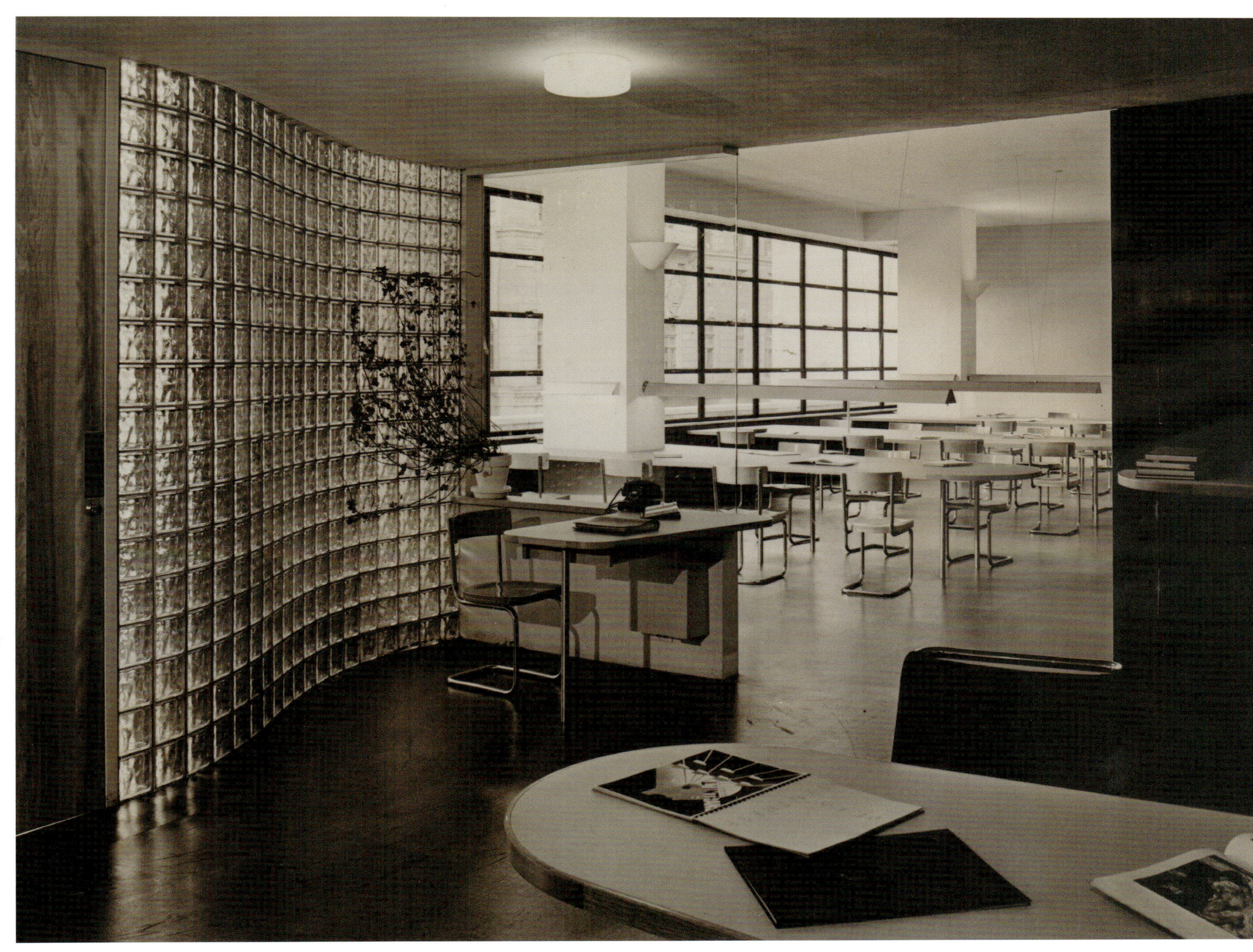

5.9. Staircase, Museum of Modern Art, Goodwin and Stone, New York, 1939. © Digital Image © The Museum of Modern Art/Licensed by SCALA / Art Resource.

5.10. Library Reading Room, Museum of Modern Art, Goodwin and Stone, 1939. © Digital Image © The Museum of Modern Art/Licensed by SCALA / Art Resource.

THE SUCCESS OF THE PROGRAM AND ADDITIONS,
BUILT AND UNBUILT

The first ten years of the Museum of Modern Art, from its founding 1929 to the opening of the Goodwin and Stone building in 1939, were certainly the most important years in defining what the museum would be, from its scope of collecting and exhibiting to the aesthetic of its buildings. Indeed, it is a credit to the vision of the museum's founders that already, in those first ten years, MoMA had become an important and unique cultural institution. The confidence of the 1929 pamphlet (quoted above) was not misplaced; and the author of the *New York Times* article of the same year (excerpted above) would likely admit he was wrong about how hard it would be for MoMA to surpass the Luxembourg, versus the Metropolitan Museum of Art surpassing the Louvre. In fact, a recurring theme in the rest of this chapter is the difficulty of building on the type of unmitigated success that the museum encountered in its early years.

The struggle to build on a continuous record of success and the fear of failure to maintain the same standards and critical reception bring challenges of their own. Particularly difficult for an institution such as the Museum of Modern Art, which was created with the goal of making an argument for artworks that were not broadly accepted by the public and the art world, is maintaining its place as an advocate for the new and radical after it has succeeded in its initial project. Already in the 1940s, the place of the artists for whom the museum had advocated most—from Cézanne and van Gogh through Matisse, Diego Rivera, and Picasso—was no longer in contention. By the 1950s the modernist architecture that the museum had dubbed the "International Style" was mainstream and had completely replaced Beaux-Arts classicism and eclecticism in the world of commercial architecture. Photography, film, architectural drawings, and models as well as industrial design and modern furniture began to be collected by other museums; the Museum of Modern Art had won its argument with the skeptics. Questions were no longer about the value of modern and contemporary art, or the validity of principles such as abstraction, but rather focused on which modern and contemporary art was most compelling and whose abstraction was most sophisticated.

In this period the difficulty of realizing the plans of deaccessioning work as it turned fifty years old began to become apparent. Though the museum continued to pursue this possibility, it became increasingly clear that it would not come to be. Thus the permanent collection of the Museum of Modern Art continued to grow. Larger collections, an ever-increasing public attendance at exhibitions, growing departments (and departmental staffs)—from the expanding library and film collections to ever-diminishing storage space for paintings and sculpture— all contributed to the need for more space, which every successful collecting

5.11. Interior of an exhibition gallery, installation view of the exhibition, "Art in Our Time: 10th Anniversary Exhibition, Painting, Sculpture, Prints." The Museum of Modern Art, New York. May 10, 1939, through September 30, 1939. Photo: Robert Damora. © Digital Image © The Museum of Modern Art/Licensed by SCALA / Art Resource.

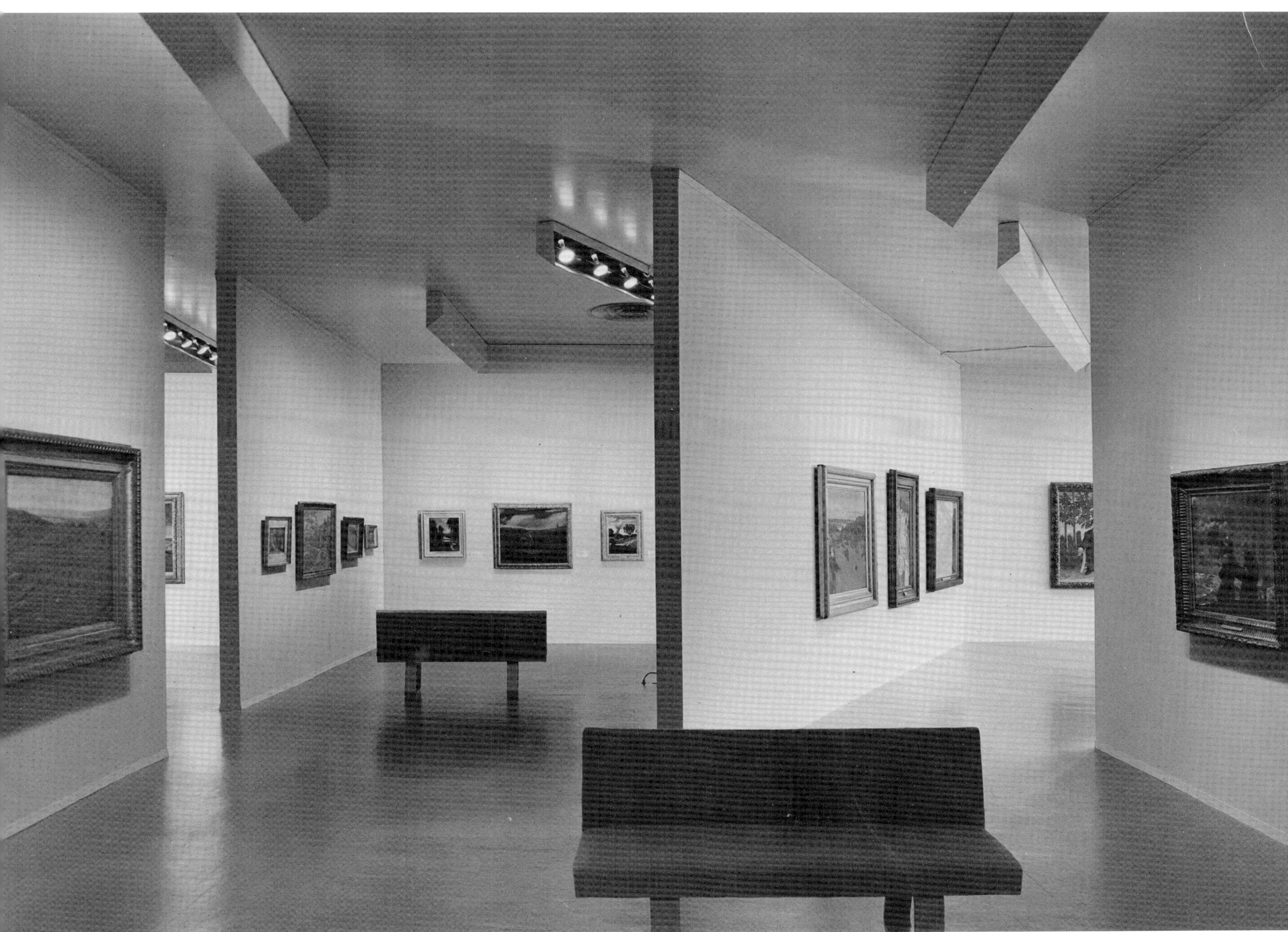

institution invariably requires. The Museum of Modern Art just arrived at this point a lot more quickly than most institutions.

All of the museum's directors and trustees would confront the same fundamental problems of physical expansion and collection development from the late 1940s to the present. These problems are well summed up in Director John B. Hightower's report of April, 1970, titled *New Directions for the Future*:

> American institutions today are being compelled to re-think their role in society and re-evaluate their responsibilities not only to themselves, but to the variety of communities they serve. It is a tumultuous process for many but one that is basic to the original purpose of the Museum of Modern Art. When the Museum was founded in 1929, it was predicated on a radical, and repeatedly courageous, departure from the 19th century concept of a museum. It devoted itself to art that was neither established nor, necessarily, recognized. It took risks no museum had taken before. Its perceptions were immediate rather than reflective. Through Alfred Barr, its first director, and later, Rene d'Harnoncourt, his successor, the Museum ranged imaginatively across a variety of concerns including urban planning, product design, film and photography—creative forms of human expression that had, for the most part, not even been acknowledged as art up to that time.
>
> [. . .] Their combined influence is apparent everywhere, perhaps most immediately noticeable in such areas as contemporary architecture, graphic design, the paintings and murals for public buildings and corporate offices. The Museum now possesses the world's finest and most comprehensive collection of Twentieth Century art. Today, the Museum is acknowledged as the preeminent institution of its kind in the world. As such, it ranks as one of the country's most timeless and invaluable national resources.
>
> To a large extent the Museum has essentially accomplished what it set out to prove forty-one years ago. So-called modern art cannot be dismissed as frivolous or undisciplined, as it once was. The collections receive attention and respect from scholars, students, international visitors, and the general public in ever-increasing numbers. The influence of the Museum of Modern Art is reflected in the major museums of America, all of which have made space and funds available for the display and purchase of contemporary works of art. It has become, in a sense, the victim of its own success. [. . .][10]

Bold though some of Hightower's statements in this quotation are, they are not hyperbolic.

The problem of being "the victim of its own success" was not unique to the 1970s, either; it was and remains the chief problem facing the museum since the end of World War II. This difficulty of trying to continue to be an institution that sets taste and influences the reception of new moments in, and movements of, the ever changing landscape of contemporary art, while maintaining the identity, perspective, and collections that established its reputation in the first place, is

5.12. Exterior view of the 21 West 53rd Street addition to the Museum of Modern Art, known as the Grace Rainey Rogers Annex, designed by Philip Johnson, 1950 (no longer extant), adjoining main building designed by Philip L. Goodwin and Edward D. Stone, 1939. Photographed 1953. © Digital Image © The Museum of Modern Art/Licensed by SCALA / Art Resource.

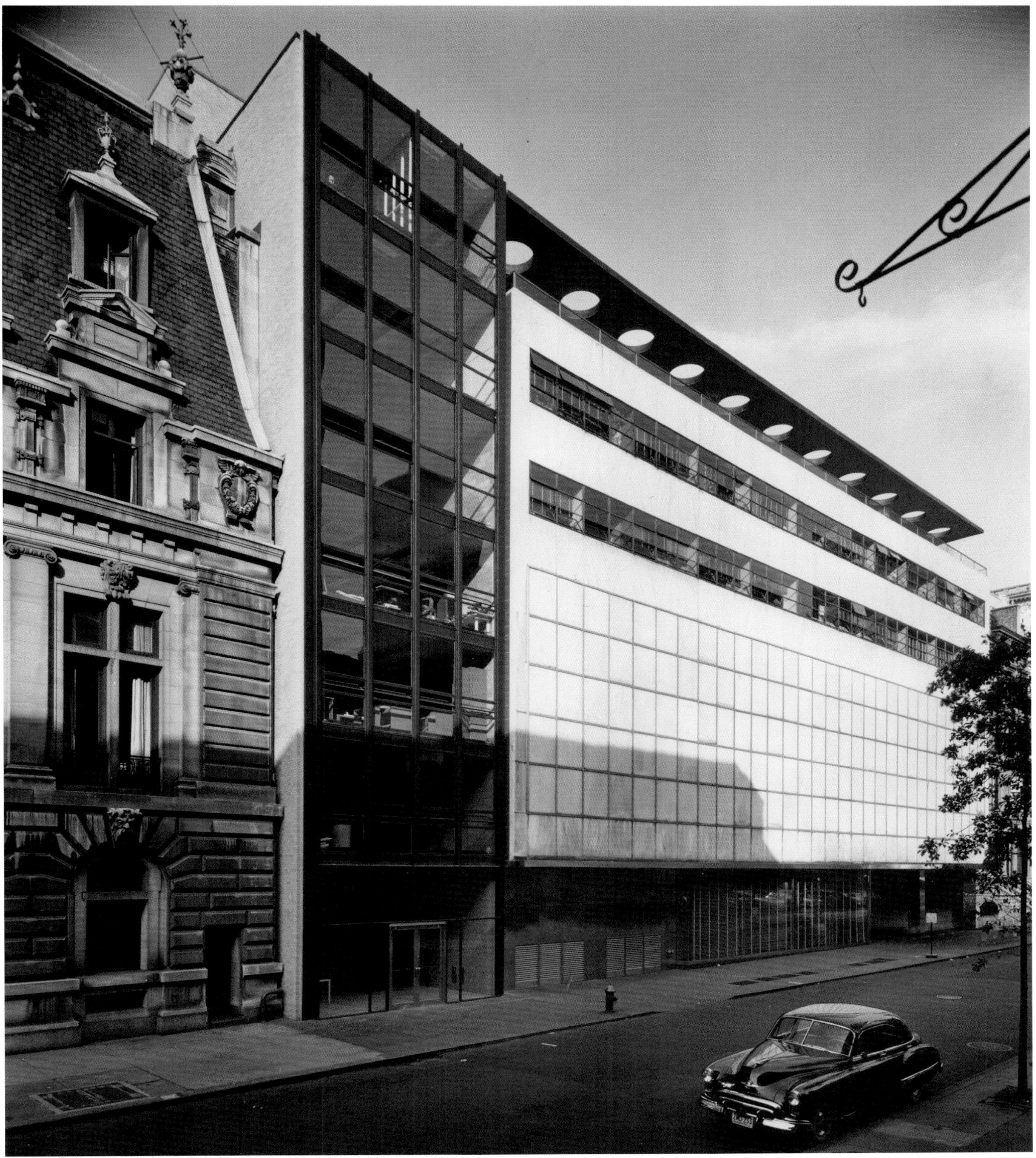

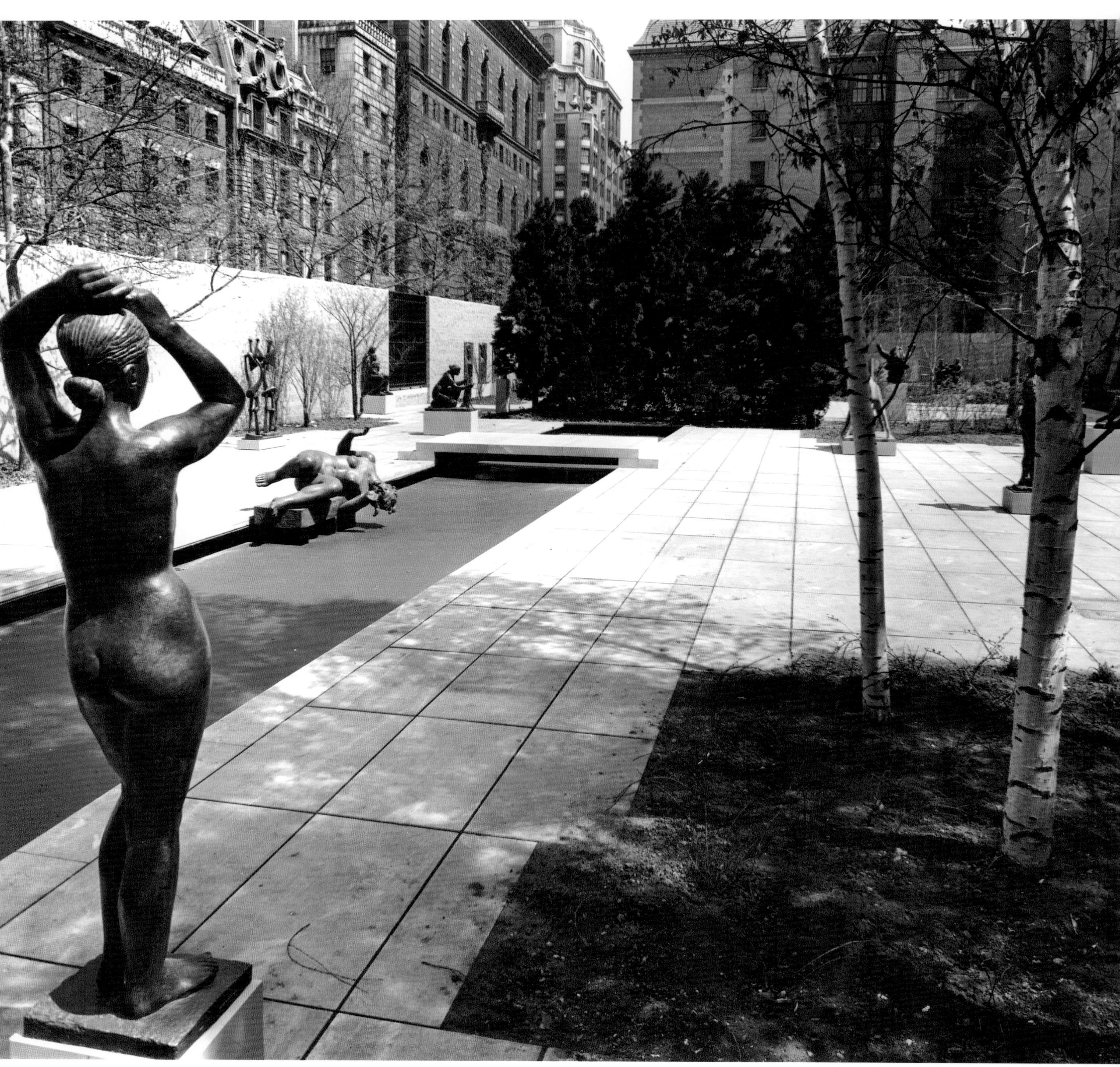

a constant tug-of-war that will always pull the Museum of Modern Art in two diametrically opposed directions: it defies the realm of the possible to accomplish both. As the "modernism" of the type of work displayed in the Armory Show of 1913 approaches its centennial, the chasm between "modern" and "contemporary" becomes ever wider—particularly now, when the art world has moved not merely beyond the "modern," but even beyond the "postmodern." In this sense, abandoning the idea articulated in 1933 of deaccessioning works when they reach fifty years in age would be the defining element in creating the chief problem that would face the Museum of Modern Art for the rest of its life. One could even argue that had the museum followed that course, the word *modern* would still be a synonym of the word *contemporary* vis-à-vis the description of art—the museum was that important in formulating the canon of "modernism."

Additions to the physical plant of the Museum of Modern Art since the completion of the Goodwin and Stone building all had to address this problem of reconciling the history of modernism—here modernist architecture (and the museum building itself as one of the movement's major monuments in New York)—with a continuance of the museum's policy to use its own building as an example of contemporary design and an ideal space for the viewing of modern and contemporary art in all media. Already by 1946, a mere seven years after the opening of the Goodwin and Stone building, the museum was working on plans to expand. A plan was drawn up by Goodwin for a major new wing extending from the west side of the sculpture garden north to 54th Street (later the site of the Whitney Museum, from 1954 to 1966, and currently the site of the Taniguchi addition to the Museum of Modern Art). This plan would be the first of many such large-scale but unexecuted projects.

The first major addition to the museum that would actually be executed was a small, narrow one just to the west of the Goodwin and Stone building (fig. 5.12). Like the majority of architectural projects undertaken by the Museum of Modern Art between 1950 and 1970, the architect of this addition was Philip Johnson, founding curator of the museum's Department of Architecture.[11] This addition would not contain any gallery space, only space for educational programs, storage, library stacks, and offices (including Johnson's own office as Curator of Architecture). This addition (on the site of the current residential tower designed by Cesar Pelli) was certainly an elegant example of the "International Modernism" that Johnson advocated back in the museum's first major architectural exhibition in 1937; however, by 1951, this type of structure and aesthetic was no longer so special in contemporary architecture.

The choice of the very talented but rarely innovative Johnson as the museum's unofficial architect of record from 1950 to 1970 is very suggestive of the tension that dominated (and continues to dominate) all of the museum's decisions between adherence to the aesthetic of high modernism, on the one hand, and a continuance of the early policy of advocating the radical and theretofore unaccepted in contemporary art and architecture. Though all of Johnson's projects at the museum were elegant and graceful (and one of them, the redesign of the Abby Aldrich Rockefeller Sculpture Garden, was truly brilliant), none was a bold new departure from the accepted

5.13. View of Abbey Aldrich Rockefeller Sculpture Garden, the Museum of Modern Art, New York, Philip Johnson, 1953. Photographed 1953 by Alexandre Georges. Photographic Archive, The Museum of Modern Art Archives, NY. © Digital Image © The Museum of Modern Art/Licensed by SCALA / Art Resource.

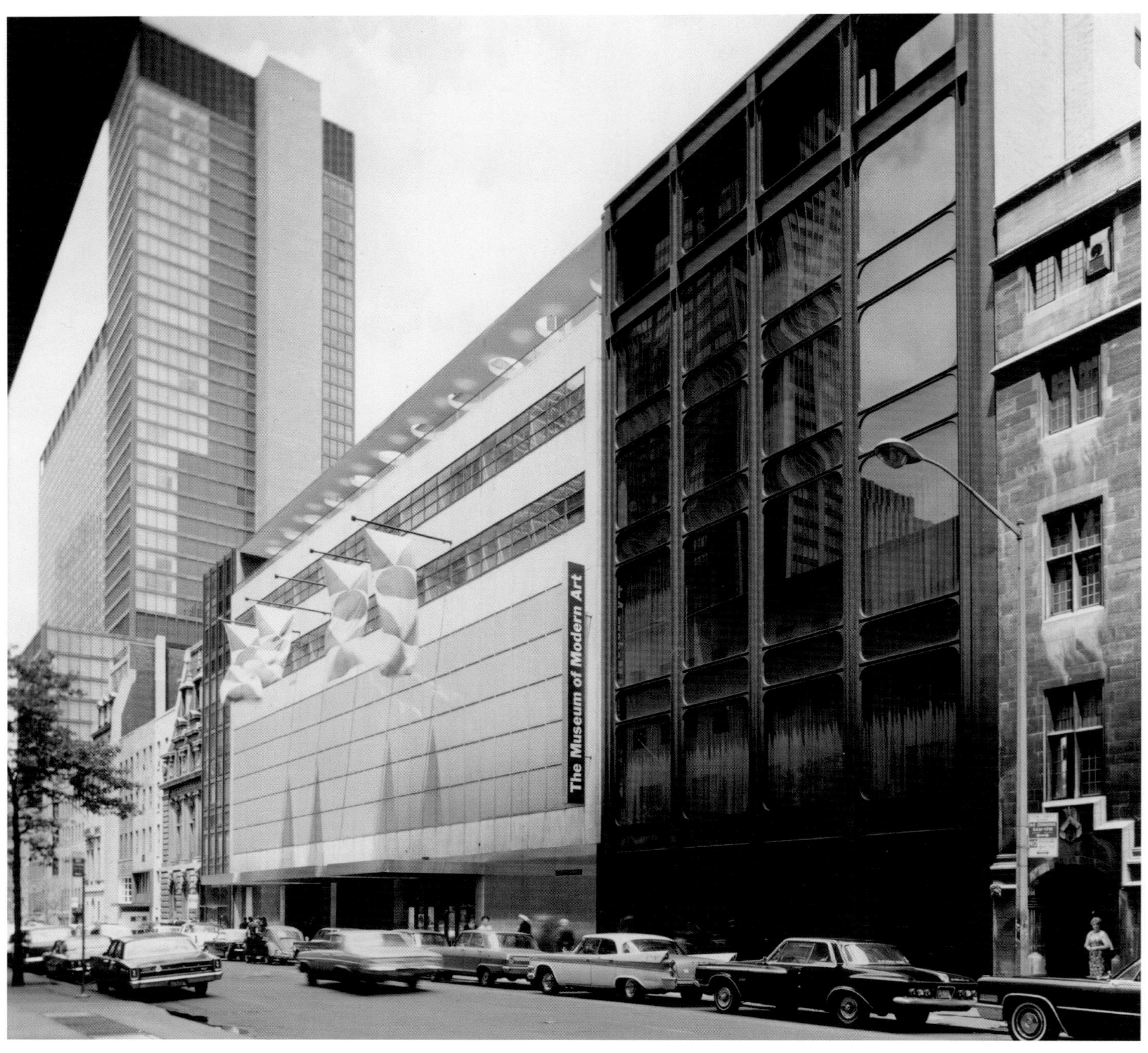

5.14.Fifty-third Street façade of East Wing of the Museum of Modern Art, New York, Philip Johnson, 1964. © Digital Image © The Museum of Modern Art/Licensed by SCALA / Art Resource.

architectural orthodoxy of its time—indeed Johnson, perhaps more than any other major protagonist of twentieth-century architecture, can be seen as a follower of trends and fashions in architecture, from the strict adherence to Mies van der Rohe's aesthetic in his own Glass House in New Canaan, Connecticut to the exaggerated postmodernism of his AT&T Building in Midtown Manhattan, with its "Chippendale" crown.

Johnson's obsession with being current contributed greatly to his success as the museum's curator of architecture and design, and his success there and as a critic and ambassador of contemporary architecture played a vital role in shaping

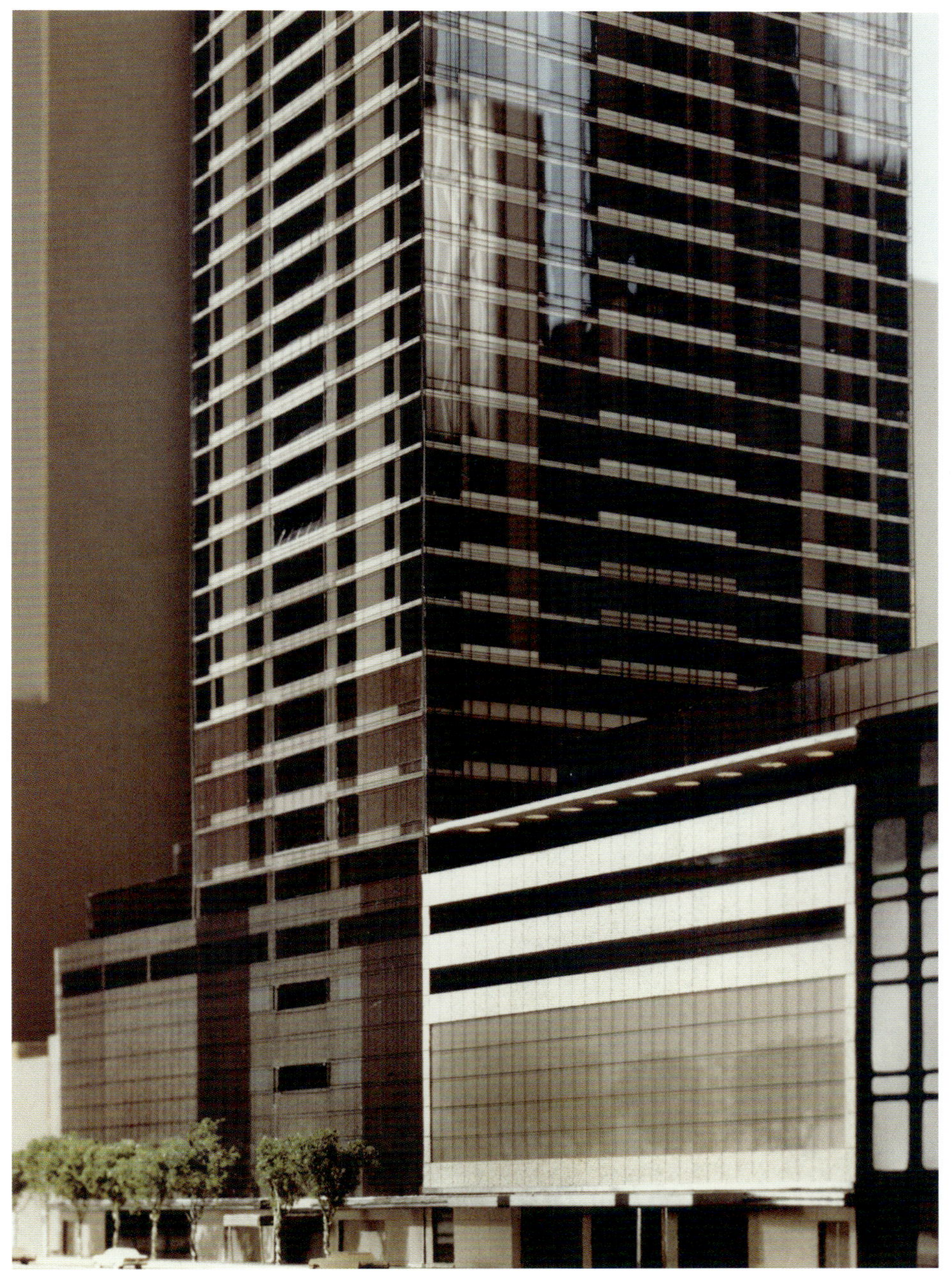

5.15. Model of The Museum of Modern Art, showing the west wing and tower designed by Cesar Pelli & Associates, 1984; center building designed by Philip L. Goodwin and Edward D. Stone, 1939; east wing, designed by Philip Johnson, 1964. Director's Office Records, records management box 1772. The Museum of Modern Art Archives, New York. © Digital Image © The Museum of Modern Art/Licensed by SCALA / Art Resource.

twentieth-century architectural history. However, a survey of the various projects he developed (both executed and unexecuted) at the Museum of Modern Art does indeed reveal how the museum retreated from its position as a pioneer of avant-garde design in its own physical plant. Where the Goodwin and Stone building can largely be seen as the bridge between the application of modernist design principles from a residential setting to a public or corporate one, most of Johnson's projects seem to echo what was going on contemporaneously in the commercial architecture of the museum's midtown neighbors.

For the sake of brevity and owing to the fact that few of these projects remain intact and have been analyzed at length elsewhere, the various Johnson additions and proposals are treated only in passing. The most significant and best preserved of Johnson's architectural contributions to the Museum of Modern Art would certainly be the Abby Aldrich Rockefeller Sculpture Garden, constructed between 1951 and 1953 (fig. 5.13). Indeed this space was, and remains, one of the most beloved quiet urban garden spaces in New York City, a true oasis, and one that the museum wisely retained with as little alteration as possible through two major expansions and redesigns of the elevations that border it. Johnson played a major role in the design of the Whitney Museum, which would be the western terminus of the Sculpture Garden,[12] designing its façade and the Museum of Modern Art's Terrace Restaurant on its ground floor (see Chapter 3, fig. 3.6). After the Whitney abandoned this building and opened its current home in the Marcel Breuer building on the Upper East Side of Manhattan, this building became part of the Museum of Modern Art (until it was demolished to make room for the Taniguchi building), containing the museum's Study Center. As early as 1959 the museum commissioned Johnson to design an East Wing; the size of this project was continually reduced from its initial, very ambitious scale, which would have stretched all the way to 54th Street. A smaller East Wing was realized, the 53rd Street façade of which still remains (fig. 5.14). The earlier scheme is a clear example of the type of "midcentury modernism" that dominated the design of cultural institutions of the time (from projects such as Lincoln Center to the Los Angeles County Museum of Art) and that is seen by many to have led to the backlash against modernism and the rise of postmodernism from the late 1960s through its moment of ascendancy in the 1980s. The reduced project, as executed, was largely a return to the Mies van der Rohe–inspired architecture that Johnson used in the 21 West 53rd Street addition earlier, though the curved elements within the steel grid are very much a product of their own time. This project contained additional gallery space as well as an expanded lobby and bookstore that were contained in a remodeled ground floor of the Goodwin and Stone building. On 53rd Street the new East Wing, along with the 21 West 53rd Street addition, formed black bookends for the much larger white façade of the original building. The new entrance and lobby were relocated to the center of the Goodwin and Stone building, and the curving canopy was replaced by a symmetrical rectangular one, ruining the most interesting design element of the façade (this entrance and lobby have thankfully since been restored to their original design).

The first major addition designed by an architect outside of the museum's inner circle (Goodwin was a trustee, Johnson a curator) would be that awarded to Cesar Pelli in 1977. This project, which was opened to the public in 1984, included an expansion of the museum and the construction of a residential tower (known as the Museum Tower) that would be owned by the museum and used to generate further revenue. Construction of this new section of the museum required the demolition of Philip Johnson's first addition, the 21 West 53rd Street building. This site, to the west of the original Goodwin and Stone façade and the property

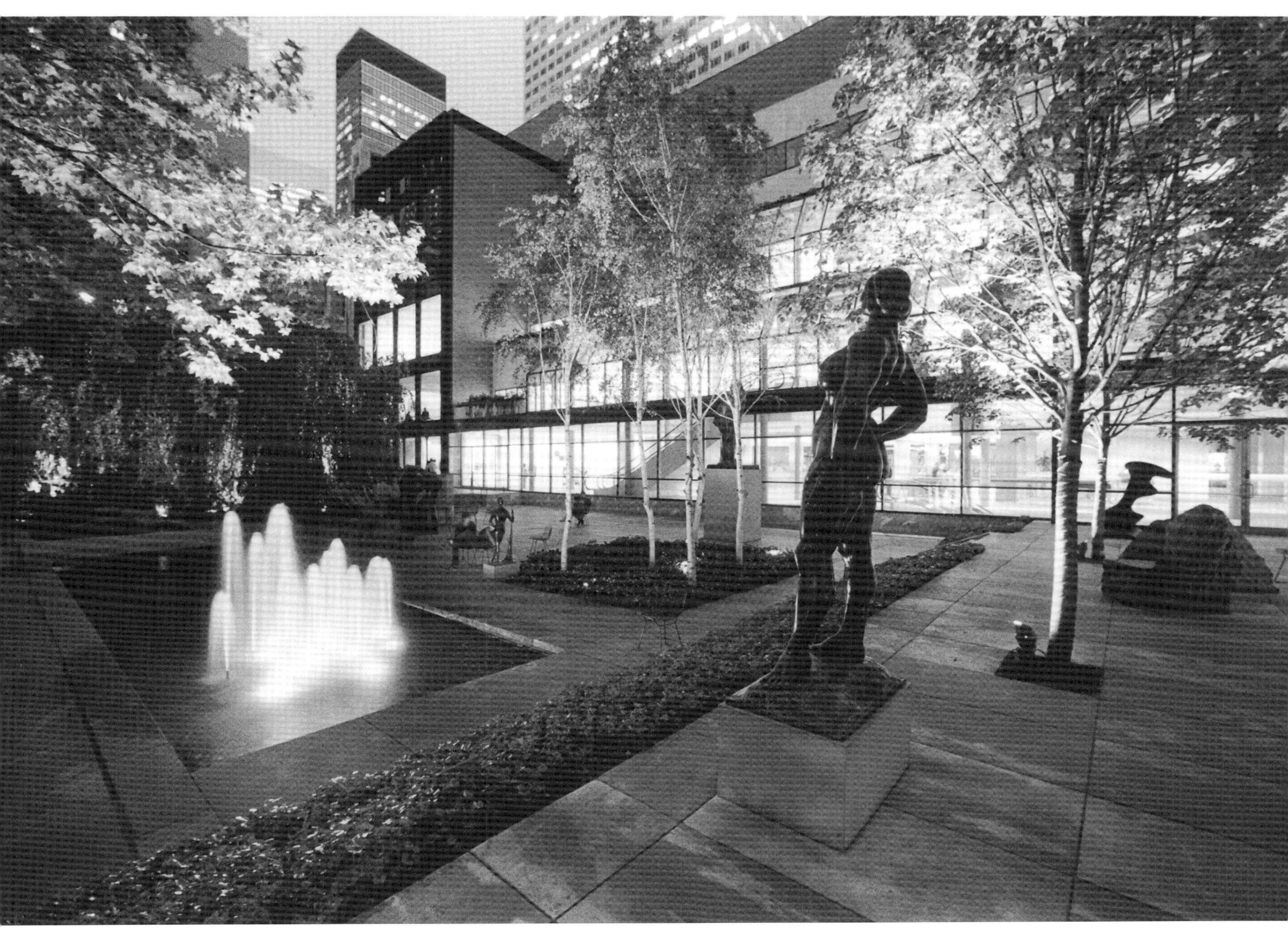

5.17. Interior of the Garden Hall,
The Museum of Modern Art, New York,
Cesar Pelli. 1984. © Digital Image
© The Museum of Modern Art/Licensed
by SCALA / Art Resource.

immediately to its west, would be used for the entrance to the new residential tower (fig. 5.15). The floors of the new tower above the lobby and contiguous with the Goodwin and Stone building and the old Whitney Museum building (the tower, like the Johnson 21 West 53rd Street building before it, linked these two separate projects) would contain space, including galleries, used by the museum and connecting with it on the upper floors of the Goodwin and Stone building.

While the greatest increase in square footage under the Pelli addition was found in the Museum Tower, the most profound change in the experience of the museum-going public was contained in the addition on the north side of the Goodwin and Stone building (figs. 5.16 and 5.17): here Pelli designed a glass and steel shed containing a new circulation system with escalators, allowing visitors to move up and down the museum in a straight line. The north wall of the original building was removed where it met the new structure. The space created by this addition was a new type of space for the Museum of Modern Art: a large, dramatic, multilevel atrium-like space, suggestive of the types of entries and grand staircases found in traditional museums such as the Great Hall at the Metropolitan Museum or the radical architectural statement of the central rotunda of the Solomon R. Guggenheim Museum. Although this addition did not directly affect the smaller scale of the galleries in the older buildings, it moved the visitor's experience away from the domestic scale that the museum had theretofore always maintained by creating a more "institutional" spatial feeling and circulation. The original Goodwin and Stone staircase was left in place (it remains to this day), but circulation was moved away from it; the new path was centralized in Pelli's addition.

It is somewhat ironic that the project that literally brought a residential component to the museum complex was the same project that began to remove the domestic scale and atmosphere from the general public's experience of the building and its display strategy. Indeed, the inclusion of residential units (invisible to the general visiting public) was an exercise in the museum's branding and revenue-raising efforts rather than an investigation of the relationship between residential and institutional architecture and design. This shift from a more domestic scale and design to a more institutional aesthetic anticipated the direction that the museum would later take with the Taniguchi project, its latest expansion.

THE TANIGUCHI BUILDING AND THE FRICTION
BETWEEN MODERN AND CONTEMPORARY ART

In 2001 the museum announced its most ambitious addition—an addition so large that it required the closing of the 53rd Street complex for three years. To accommodate this closure, the museum moved to a temporary facility in the New York City borough of Queens, across the East River from Manhattan—the only time the museum has been absent from its midtown location (fig. 5.18). This temporary

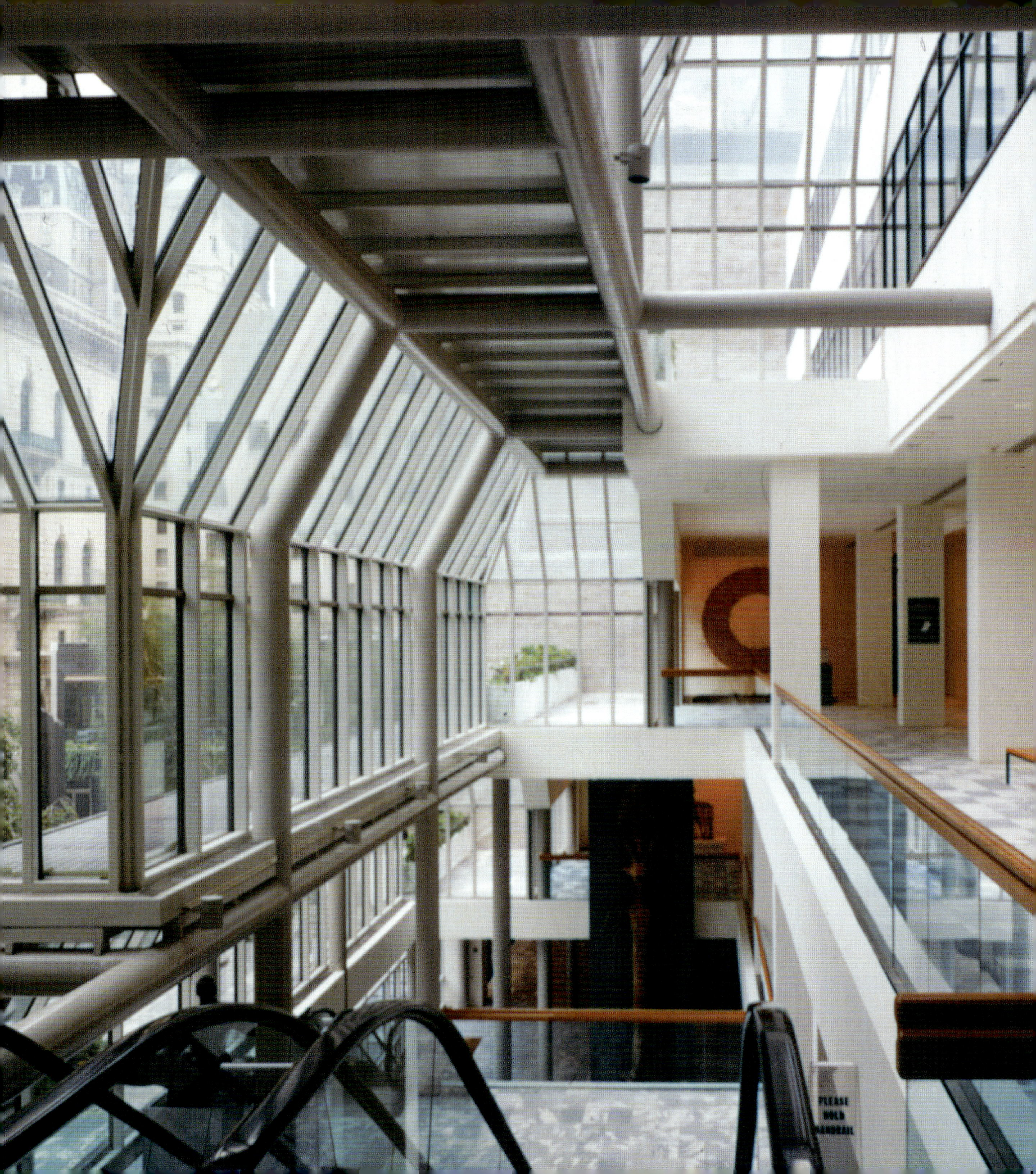
PLEASE
HOLD
HANDRAIL

facility was housed in a remodeled industrial building, formerly the Swingline Staple factory. For the major expansion of the permanent facility in Manhattan, the museum selected architect Yoshio Taniguchi as the winner of its competition. Taniguchi, an accomplished architect in his native Japan, had not at that time built in the United States. He had a substantial corpus of museum buildings already to his credit, and his style fit well into the modernist tradition that the museum continued to advance.

Vast and elegant, the new facility contained large-scale galleries for the permanent collection, temporary exhibitions and contemporary art as well as very substantial office space and larger homes for the library, archives, and study centers (see fig. 5.19). A reading room, a new design and book store, and food service facilities were also contained in the new buildings. A colossal entrance was added on 53rd Street to the west of Pelli's Museum Tower; the ground level and entrance of the Goodwin and Stone building were lovingly and accurately restored to their original, pre-Johnson state, though they are now used as the entrance to the administrative offices and not used by the general public. Johnson's East Wing entrance was repurposed as the entrance to The Modern, the museum's luxurious full-service restaurant and bar. The former Whitney Museum building was demolished and replaced with the new gallery wing (fig. 5.20). Also demolished was the Pelli steel and glass greenhouse facing the garden with its escalators. A circulation system of escalators was installed to the southwest of the new central atrium, and a new entrance fronted 54th Street. A large, open entrance hall linked the 53rd Street entrance to that opening on 54th Street. To the west of the Museum Tower, above the new galleries, a smaller tower contained the museum's offices. On the east end of the Sculpture Garden, fronting 54th Street, a new wing contained the Library, Archives, and educational facilities of the museum. A huge central atrium, reached by stair from the entrance hall, became the architectural centerpiece of the new incarnation of the Museum of Modern Art (fig. 5.21).

Much of the colossal scale of the new parts of the museum was dictated by the desire to comfortably and efficiently display the larger works that have become the norm in the minimalist and postminimalist practices of contemporary art since 1970. Most of these could not have been displayed in MoMA's older facilities because there were no loading dock facilities or galleries large enough to accommodate them; examples recently exhibited at the museum include the work of Richard Serra and Martin Puryear. This tremendous new scale was carried through the public, nonexhibition-oriented spaces as well, such as the entrance hall and the central atrium. Gone forever is the more intimate, domestic scale of the original experience that the public had when visiting, though the museum has wisely moved the galleries of the Departments of Photography and Prints and Drawings to the galleries that remain in the Goodwin and Stone building, because smaller-scaled work needs these more intimate galleries to be properly viewed.

These new, very large spaces respect the modernist aesthetic that the museum has always advocated, yet they also seem to follow a now-established tradition

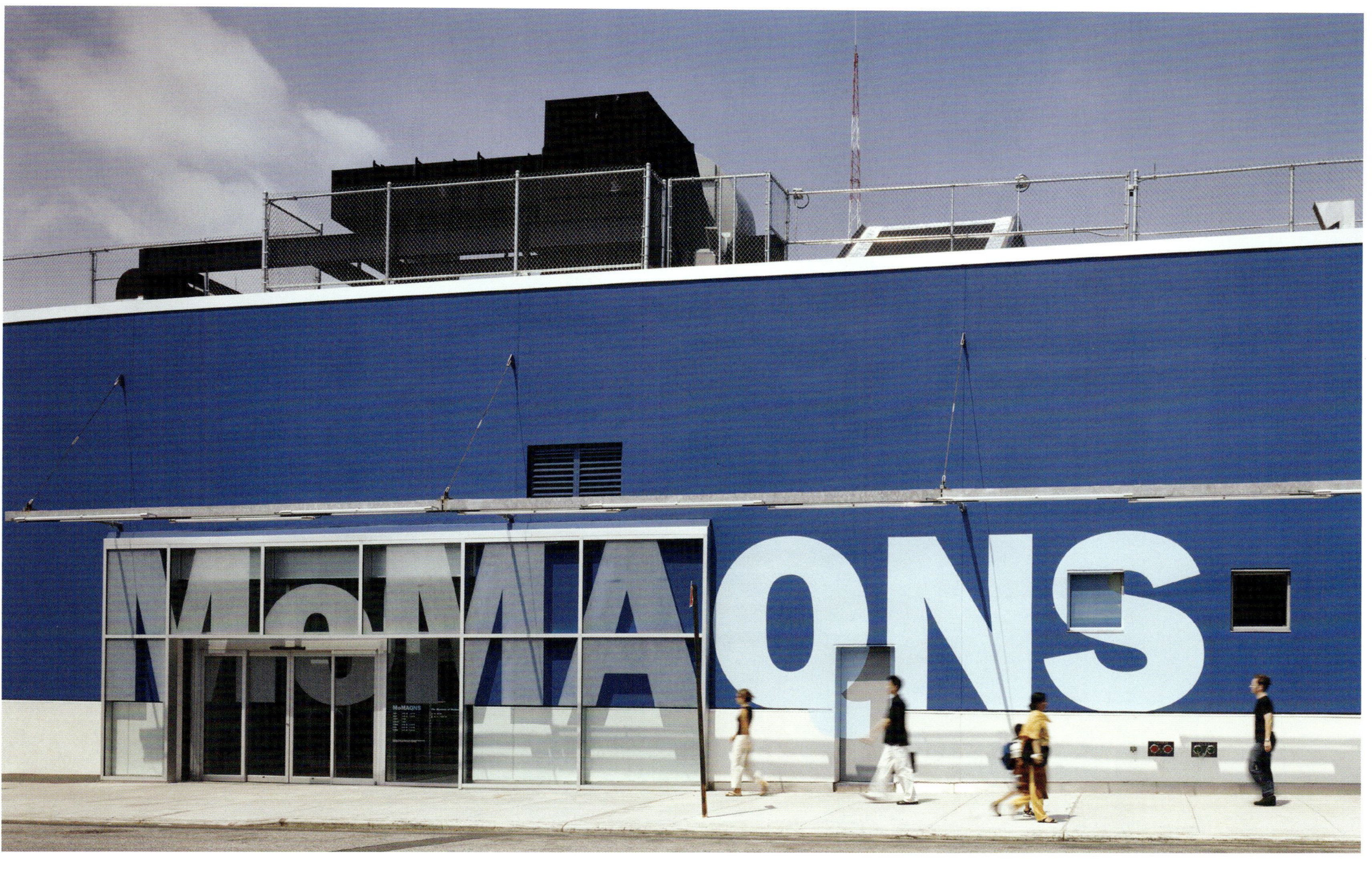

of expansive corporate spaces, recalling the wide open spaces typically found in corporate lobbies, airports, and shopping malls, rather than setting a standard that such spaces would later emulate. New functional requirements facing virtually all contemporary museum buildings clearly contributed to this fact. Museums now need large open spaces for revenue-generating events, from patrons' opening parties to corporate rentals, and the new entrance hall and atrium clearly function very well for such endeavors. However, displayed art can be lost in such vast spaces, and they can make a visitor feel small when he or she is going through them on a typical museum visit rather than as a guest at such functions. Designing such multi-use spaces has always been a challenge for museum designers—one that is rarely solved to satisfaction—though the Temple of Dendur gallery at the Metropolitan Museum of Art comes to mind as a rare success in such a multi-use space: it is a room that works well for large social gatherings while providing an excellent context for the large work (a complete Ancient Egyptian temple) that is on display within it.

5.18. Exterior view of MoMA QNS in Long Island City, Queens, New York, the temporary home of the Museum of Modern Art during the construction of the Taniguchi addition, Cooper, Robertson & Partners and Michal Maltzan Architecture, 2002. © Digital Image © The Museum of Modern Art/Licensed by SCALA / Art Resource.

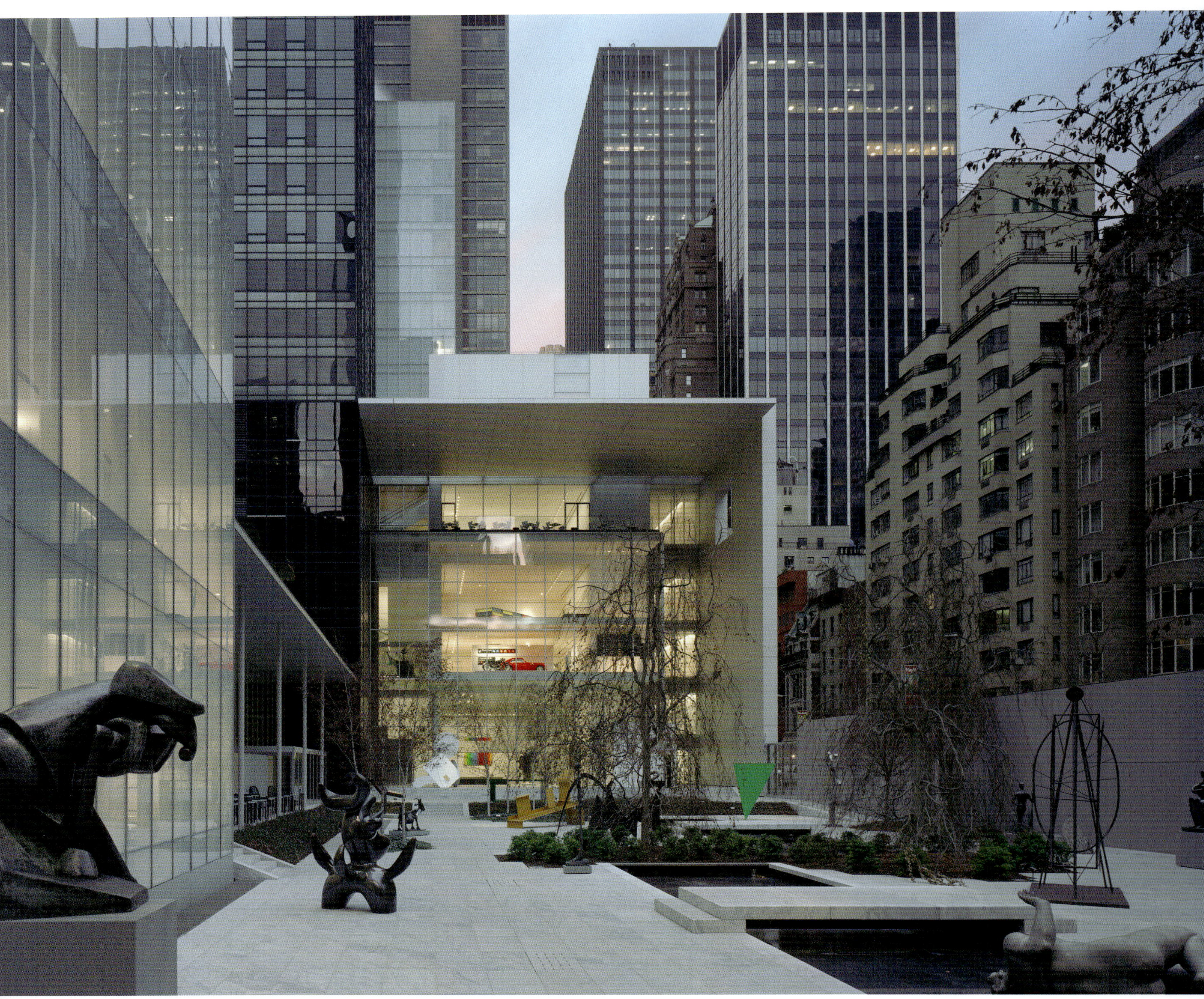

5.19. View of the Sculpture Garden
and 2004 additions to the Museum of
Modern Art, Yoshio Taniguchi, 2004.
Photograph © Timothy Hursley. © Digital Image
© The Museum of Modern Art/Licensed by
SCALA / Art Resource.

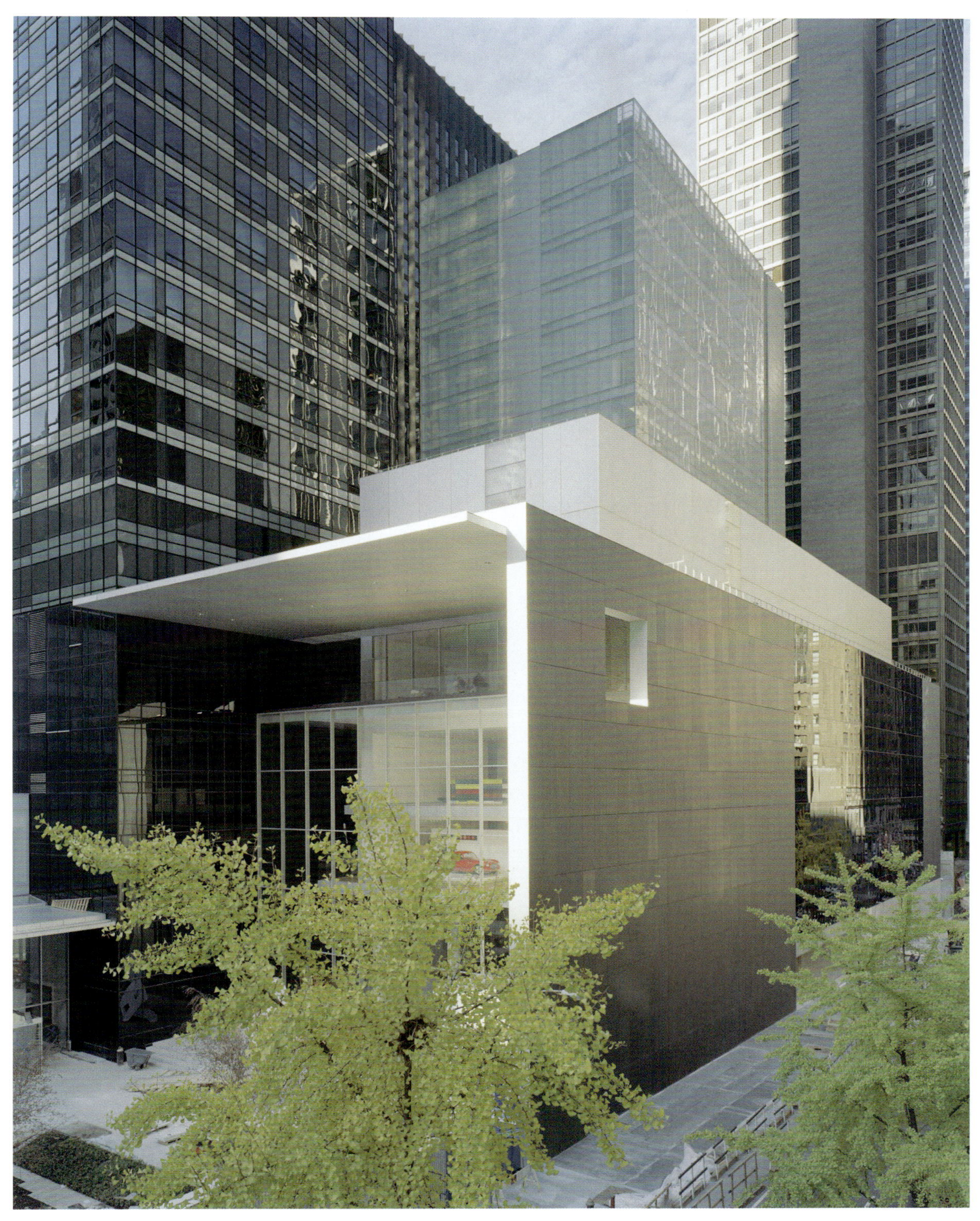

5.20. New gallery wing of the Museum of Modern Art, seen from 54th Street, Yoshio Taniguchi, 2004. Photograph © Timothy Hursley. © Digital Image © The Museum of Modern Art/Licensed by SCALA / Art Resource.

Taniguchi was given a nearly impossible task in designing the new Museum of Modern Art. Indeed, he inherited the problem that John Hightower so eloquently discussed in the document quoted above—Taniguchi had to design a new facility for an institution that had largely become a "victim of its own success." The Museum of Modern Art was founded with a goal and mission of establishing a place in the United States for the proper appreciation of modern art. In 1929 this meant the art of "modernism," from van Gogh and Cézanne to what was then truly contemporary art. This artwork was not highly prized or collected by museums in the United States (or abroad, for that matter). To successfully make its argument, the Museum of Modern Art was forced to assemble the greatest collection of the art of modernism ever assembled. Through a failure to reach agreements (which the museum sought in earnest to negotiate) with other leading art museums for a policy of deaccessioning such work as it ceased to be "contemporary," the Museum of Modern Art found itself the steward of this peerless collection that it will never again be possible to assemble.

Nonetheless, the museum sought to preserve its role as an important center for the advancement of art that is truly contemporary. As the scale and content of contemporary art is always in flux, it is probably impossible to build one museum that can provide the proper context for all of the work on display, from the late nineteenth century to the present (and leaving room for works from a future that cannot be forecast). This friction between "modern art" and "contemporary art" was, to some extent, acknowledged by the museum with its affiliation with the P.S.1 Contemporary Art Center, located in Long Island City, Queens, New York, in January of 2000 (before the construction of the Taniguchi building). P.S.1 avoids the conflict of today's contemporary becoming tomorrows mainstream art by not having a collection and serving only as an exhibition space. Unlike the art world of 1929, in the twenty-first century it is not necessary to make an argument for the importance of contemporary art; it is well accepted by the arts establishment. Nevertheless, the Museum of Modern Art continues to collect contemporary art, even if it takes fewer risks than its affiliate in Queens with what it decides to exhibit.

Taniguchi and the museum as an institution were faced with the daunting task of preserving a coherent identity for the model museum of modernism while maintaining the flexibility and freedom to collect and display an ever-broadening universe of contemporary art. That the architectural philosophy of the modernism of the 1920s exhibited in the original Goodwin and Stone building would have to be reduced to a modernist "style" in the early twenty-first century was probably inevitable. Taking a step back from the project, it is truly a credit to the vision and program of the Museum of Modern Art from its very founding that the art and architecture that it fought so hard to elevate from the contempt of the American public are now indeed the art and architecture of the establishment. Few, if any, cultural institutions can claim such success in shaping tastes and altering the course of the history of art, architecture, and the collecting practices of sister institutions, both at home and abroad.

5.21. Interior view of the the Donald B. and Catherine C. Marron Atrium, The David and Peggy Rockefeller Building, The Museum of Modern Art, New York, Winter 2005. The Museum of Modern Art Archives, New York. © Digital Image © The Museum of Modern Art/Licensed by SCALA / Art Resource.

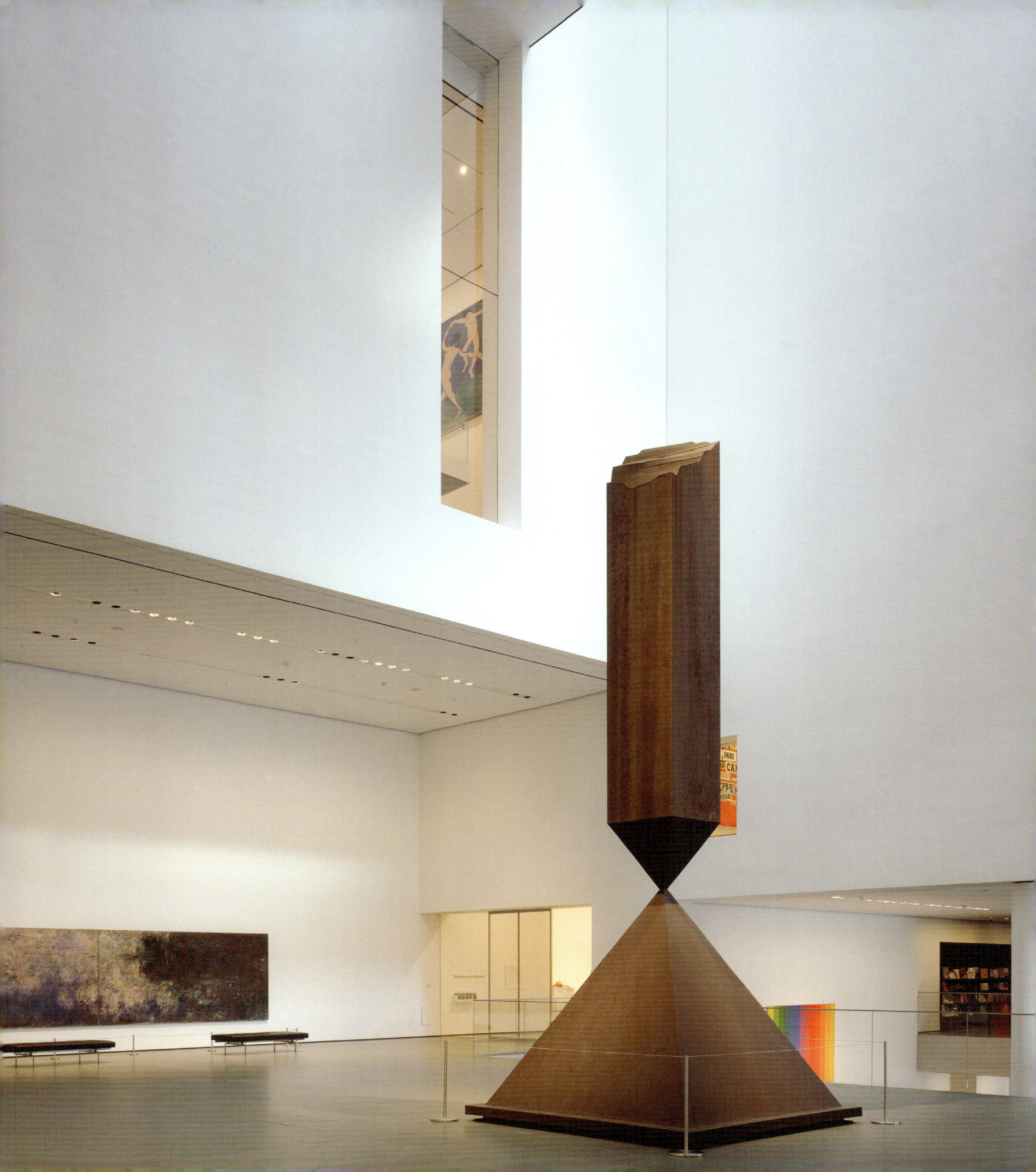

CHAPTER 6

THE ART INSTITUTE OF CHICAGO

"It was planned with great care for exhibition purposes, and we confidently believe there is no better building in existence for the exhibition of pictures and fine art objects, as regards lighting, accessibility, simplicity of arrangements and convenience of classification."

— Excerpt from *Annual Report of the Trustees for the Year Ending June 5, 1894*, 1894, p. 13, Art Institute of Chicago Archives

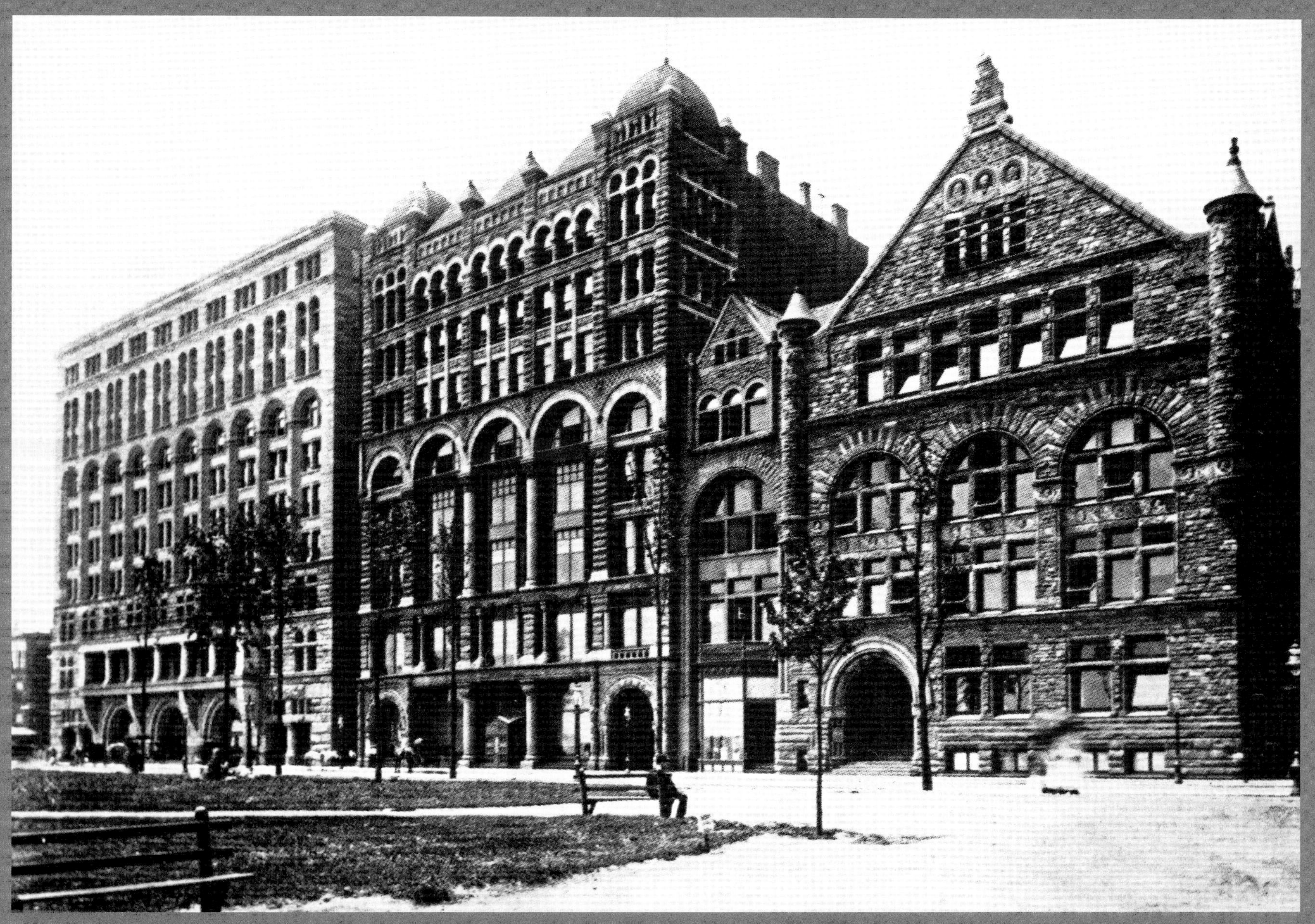

6.1. View of the second building of The Art Institute of Chicago (at right; now demolished), at the corner of Van Buren and Michigan Avenue, c. 1887, adjacent to the Studebaker (now Fine Arts) Building and the Auditorium Building, Architects: Burnham and Root, C44820, The Art Institute of Chicago. Photography © The Art Institute of Chicago.

THE ART INSTITUTE OF CHICAGO AT A GLANCE

Corporate name:	The Art Institute of Chicago
Address:	111 South Michigan Avenue, Chicago, Illinois, 60603
Opening date:	May 24, 1879, as the Chicago Academy of Fine Arts
Opening date of current location:	December 8, 1893
Architect of main building:	Shepley, Rutan & Coolidge
Architects of major additions:	Shepley, Rutan & Coolidge; Coolidge & Hodgdon; Howard Van Doren Shaw; Holabird, Root & Burgee; Shaw, Metz & Associates; Skidmore, Owings & Merrill; Hammond, Beeby & Babka; Renzo Piano
Dates of major expansions:	1898, 1901, 1903, 1910, 1916, 1924, 1925, 1927, 1939, 1958, 1962, 1976, 1988, 2009
Previous venues:	Southwest corner of State and Monroe Streets (1879–1882); corner of Van Buren and Michigan Avenue (1882–1887; on same site, new building opens November 19, 1887, occupied until opening of current venue)
Collecting scope:	Encyclopedic (Western and non-Western, all media, ancient through contemporary)
Major units:	Museum, school, Ryerson and Burnham Libraries
Amenities:	Restaurant, cafeteria, bookstore, gift shop, members' lounge, auditoriums

INTRODUCTION

The Museum of the Art Institute of Chicago is one of the great encyclopedic collections in the United States. Following the chronology of acquisitions at a museum of the resources and quality of the Art Institute of Chicago (or the Metropolitan Museum of

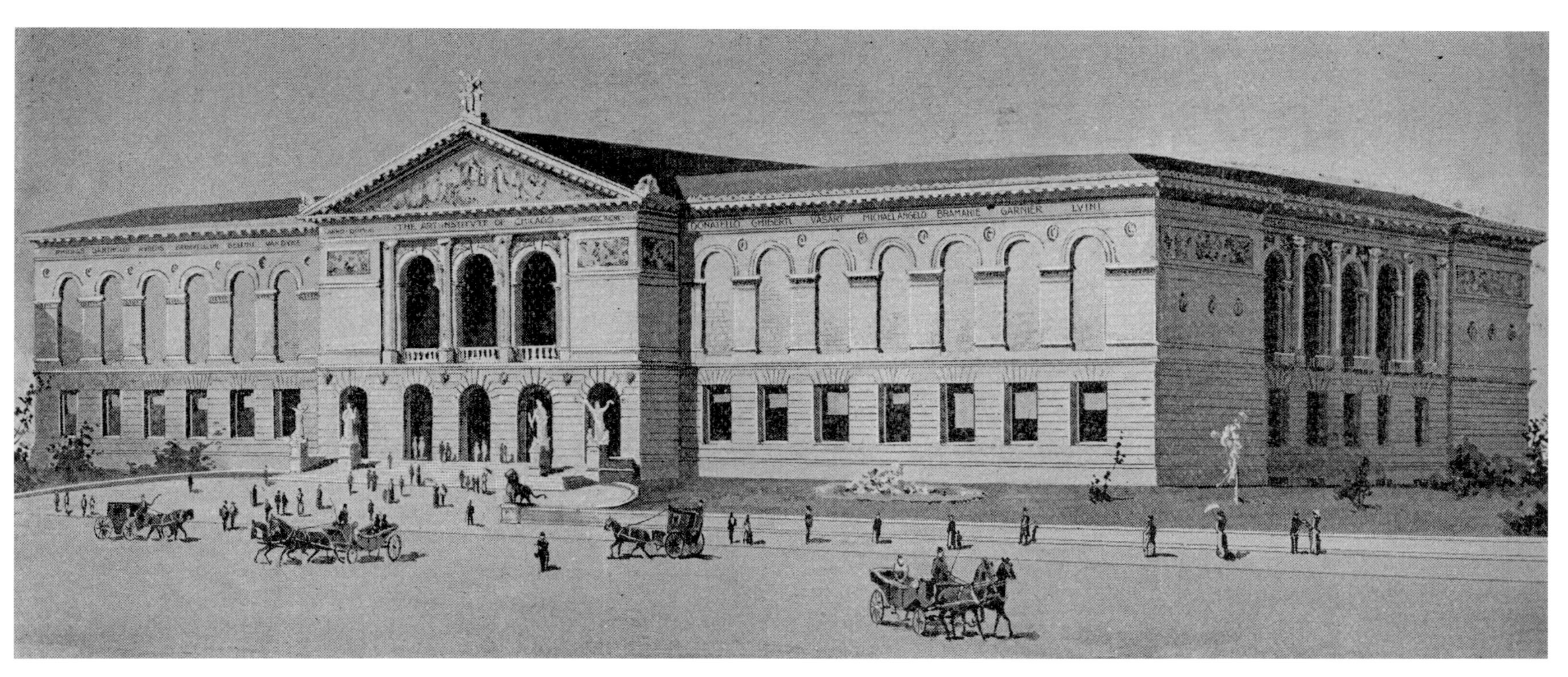

6.2. "The Art Institute. Michigan Avenue, opposite Adams Street." * The Art Insitute of Chicago : Annual Report of the Trustees, June, 1894, G31485, The Art Institute of Chicago.
Photography © The Art Institute of Chicago.

Art in New York, the National Gallery in Washington D.C., or any of the great general collections) reveals the history of taste and collecting in the United States. The works included in such collections represent our society's always changing and expanding canon of what qualifies as great art. These collections answer, as satisfactorily as possible, the age-old question of "What is art?"; further, their always-evolving inventory forces designers, museum directors, and curators to change standards of exhibition, storage, and climate control to best accommodate them.

It cannot come as a surprise that a gallery and art school founded in the middle of the nineteenth century would begin with a collection of plaster casts and prints and first expand to include genuine antiquities and Old Master paintings, all from Europe and none contemporary. Over time, and as the Museum of the Art Institute of Chicago's reach began to extend far beyond its accompanying school and play a central role in the artistic culture of Chicago, the Midwest, and the nation, its collections grew to include non-Western art, contemporary art, architecture, photography, and every other important medium, culture, and period. The Art Institute of Chicago is not merely representative of this type of encyclopedic collection; it is also one of the very finest.

The Art Institute's rich history predates its current home in a building first used as part of the World's Columbian Exhibition of 1893, but that building, designed with its future as the home of the museum in mind, is the nucleus of a large series of new wings and expansions that are also representative of the growth of such institutions with large, broad collecting scopes. The complex of buildings dating from 1893 to the present (with Renzo Piano's modern wing having opened in May 2009) provides a visual history of late-nineteenth- to early-twenty-first-century art museum design. A visit to the Art Institute of Chicago is thus not merely a walk through art history, but also a journey through the architectural history of the American art museum.

FOUNDATION, EARLY HISTORY, AND PURPOSE OF THE ART INSTITUTE OF CHICAGO

The corporate name of the Art Institute of Chicago dates to December 21, 1882; however, what would become this important museum and school was founded earlier, its formal incorporation taking place on May 24, 1879 as the Chicago Academy of Fine Arts. This academy was itself a successor to, and to some degree a resuscitation of, the Chicago Academy of Design, founded in 1866. This history is clearly explained in a "Fact Sheet on the Art Institute of Chicago" of 1962, which lays out the chronology here summarized:

- *1866*. The Chicago Academy of Design was founded, it was located on the southwest corner of State and Monroe Streets and destroyed in the Great Fire of 1871; it faced bankruptcy in the national panic of 1877.

- *1879*. The school was renamed the Chicago Academy of Fine Arts and incorporated as a non-profit, educational institution. The Board consisted of Marshall Field, Ferdinand W. Peck, Murry Nelson, George E. Adams, Charles W. Hamill. George Armour was elected President.
- *1882*. The name was changed again on December 21, 1882, and the Art Institute of Chicago was born. Property was purchased at the southwest corner of Van Buren and Michigan Avenue; architects Burnham and Root were engaged to erect a three-storey building. Galleries were formally opened on November 19, 1887.
- *1893*. On December 8, 1893, the Italian Renaissance building erected at Adams and Michigan for the World's Columbian Exposition's Congress of Religions was opened as the permanent home of the Art Institute of Chicago. Shepley, Rutan and Coolidge of Boston designed the building.[1]

The early history of what would become the Art Institute of Chicago is representative of the contemporaneous history of Chicago and the United States generally in the post–Civil War era, as there was a growing desire to show the Northeast that it did not have a monopoly on high culture. The emergence of Chicago as a center of wealth and industry and its recovery after the Great Fire of 1871 (of "Mrs. O'Leary" fame) would lead not only to such important events as the World Columbian Exposition of 1893 (for which the main building of the current venue of the Art Institute was originally constructed), but a general desire to create the institutions that being a cultural capital demanded.

The actual foundation of the original Chicago Academy of Design was relatively humble, however:

> The first effort to establish an Art school in Chicago was made in 1867 by a number of young men that were working in lithographing establishments, engraving, and sign-painting houses.
>
> They organized a class and secured a room and some plaster casts with which they could work. From time to time they hired models. This class was in existence for two years and was instrumental in organizing the Chicago Academy of Design. The object of the Academy was to conduct a school and maintain a Museum of Art. Rooms were rented in the old Crosby Opera House. At the time of the fire in 1871 both the school and important galleries of painting were in successful operating condition. [2]

The mission of the Art Institute of Chicago and its precursors was thus always twofold: it was to be a school for the education of artists and a major venue for the collection and exhibition of fine art. This study, in keeping with its subject of art museum design, concentrates on the Museum of the Art Institute of Chicago, though this special relationship with the school might present some unique issues.

Unfortunately, the paintings on exhibition at the original Academy of Design were destroyed in the Fire of 1871. The current collection of the Museum of the

Art Institute of Chicago began to be assembled in 1881, when their galleries were located at on Van Buren Street. [3] The year 1887 marked a decisive moment in the history of the Art Institute of Chicago with the construction of the first purpose-built home for the school and gallery, which had previously been housed in rented rooms. [4] This building was erected on the site of the previous building at the corner of Van Buren Street and Michigan Avenue and was designed by the firm of Burnham & Root (fig. 6.1). This four-floor Romanesque revival building housed both the school and gallery.

At its inception in 1887, the Art Institute's collection consisted mainly of plaster casts of ancient Greek and Roman sculpture and prints of Old Master paintings. Such a collection would have been typical of a gallery intended primarily for the instruction of artists, following the European academic model of the times. However, shortly thereafter, the Art Institute began collecting original works of art in earnest: in 1890 Phillip Armour and Charles Hutchinson donated a collection of Greek antiquities; also in 1890 fourteen Dutch and Flemish Old Master paintings were contributed from the collection of Prince Demidoff. In 1891 the Chicago Society of Decorative Arts voted to use their funds to purchase objects for the Art Institute's collections. Thus, by the time the board of the Art Institute decided to expand and agreed to create a permanent building (which would begin its life as the Congress for Religions at the World's Columbian Exhibition of 1893), they had already set their minds to becoming one of America's leading art collections and began to make worthy acquisitions, both through their own efforts and by appealing to the broader society of Chicago, which shared a common interest in establishing a first-rate institution in its city.

CROSSING MICHIGAN AVENUE:
THE SHEPLEY, RUTAN & COOLIDGE BUILDING

As mentioned above, the design and construction of the current home of the Art Institute of Chicago, on the lake side of Michigan Avenue, was linked to the World Columbian Exposition. *An Annual Report of the Trustees* of the Art Institute of 1891 explains this relationship:

> On February 25, 1890 it was determined by joint resolution of Congress that the World's Columbian Exposition, the World's Fair of 1892–93, commemorative of the discovery of America, should be held in Chicago. The idea appears to have suggested itself in several quarters at the same time that the holding of this fair might furnish an opportunity to secure a permanent art museum building for Chicago, since the former world's fairs in other cities and countries have each left behind them one or more memorial buildings. By common consent it has been assumed that the Art Institute would become the heir and occupant of such a building. [5]

The report later states that the "the area of land thus granted is 400 feet front by about 300 feet deep, if the Illinois Central railroad track shall remain where it now is." [6]

This new building, which would initially serve as the hall for congresses at the Exposition before being turned over to the Art Institute, was designed by the Boston architectural firm of Shepley, Rutan & Coolidge. The *Annual Report* of 1894 describes the new building:

> The new building is built of Bedford limestone, thoroughly fireproof, and may be described as in style Italian Renaissance, the details classic and of Ionic and Corinthian orders. The front is 80 feet back from Michigan avenue, the building 320 feet long, the wings 170 feet deep, with projections which make the whole depth 208 feet. The rear and centre portions are not yet built. It was planned with great care for exhibition purposes, and we confidently believe there is no better building in existence for the exhibition of pictures and fine art objects, as regards lighting, accessibility, simplicity of arrangements and convenience of classification. A view of the building and plans of the main floors accompany this report. [7]

The view and plans mentioned in the report are an exterior perspective rendering and plans of the first and second floors (figs. 6.2–6.4). The plans published in the 1894 report show that the museum had already worked out a master plan for expansion, beyond the initial program of the World's Fair building, which was basically a U-form in plan. The master plans show the eventual goal: a solid block, closing the open end of the *U* with more galleries and creating a central spine. The courts left in the center of the plan would be filled with an auditorium on the north side and a library on the south side of the new spine.

New and important acquisitions of works continued apace with the construction and opening of the museum building, ensuring that the collections of the Art Institute would be worthy of their new home. In 1893 the museum acquired the Henry Field collection of Barbizon paintings, beginning to establish the Art Institute's strength in nineteenth-century French art. In 1894 the museum accepted a donation of a large collection of Egyptian antiquities. The year 1899 saw an expansion of holdings in Barbizon and French academic paintings with the acceptance of the A. A. Munger collection, while 1900 saw the first foray of the museum into Asian art and contemporary French painting with the acquisition of the Mr. and Mrs. Samuel Nickerson collection, which included "jades, Japanese bronzes, lacquers, porcelains, and contemporary French paintings."

The master plan shown in the drawings published in the trustee's report of 1894 was fairly well followed in the next decade. The architects for the projects of this period remained Shepley, Rutan & Coolidge, the designers of the original structure. The year 1898 saw the completion of the auditorium, Fullerton Hall (fig. 6.5), with a glass dome and chandelier designed by Louis Comfort Tiffany. The auditorium was situated in the northern courtyard, as envisioned in the master plan. Also in

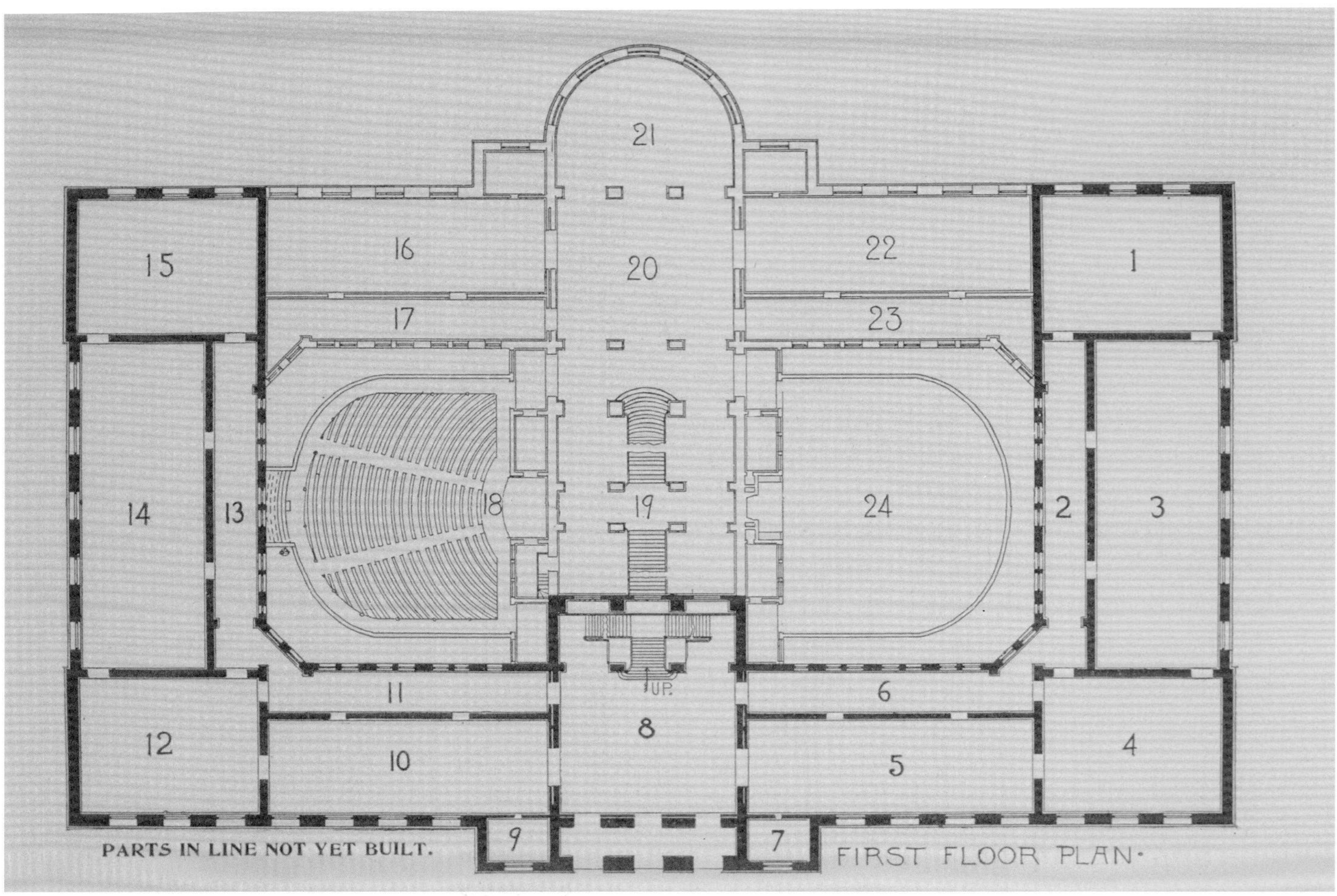

6.3. Catalogue of the 7th Annual Exhibition of Paintng and Sculpture by American Artists, Oct. 29–Dec. 17, 1894, p. 5: plan of first floor galleries, E15514, The Art Institute of Chicago. Photography © The Art Institute of Chicago.

accordance with the master plan and designed by Shepley, Rutan & Coolidge was the Ryerson Library, in the southern courtyard of the original building (fig. 6.6). The library's reading room had a horseshoe plan with tables in the center and reference stacks in the aisles. The reading room was lit by a skylight and clerestory windows. The Grand Staircase was completed later, in 1910, also following the location as outlined in the master plan (fig. 6.7). The only serious departure from the original master plan in this period of expansion was the elimination of the apse on the east side (facing the lake), which is made clear in the plan of 1905 (fig. 6.8). [8]

In 1910, in tandem with the widening of Michigan Avenue, the terrace and balustrade surrounding the museum were added (fig. 6.9). Thus, although the original building of 1893 contained only 141,000 square feet (approximately), a tiny fraction of the current area of the Art Institute, its public face to Michigan Avenue and Chicago's Loop was virtually complete by 1910 and offers a nearly identical aspect to today's visitor as it did to his or her predecessors a century ago. This identicalness is largely the result of the fact that the east side of the museum building was bound by the tracks of the Illinois Central Railroad and that

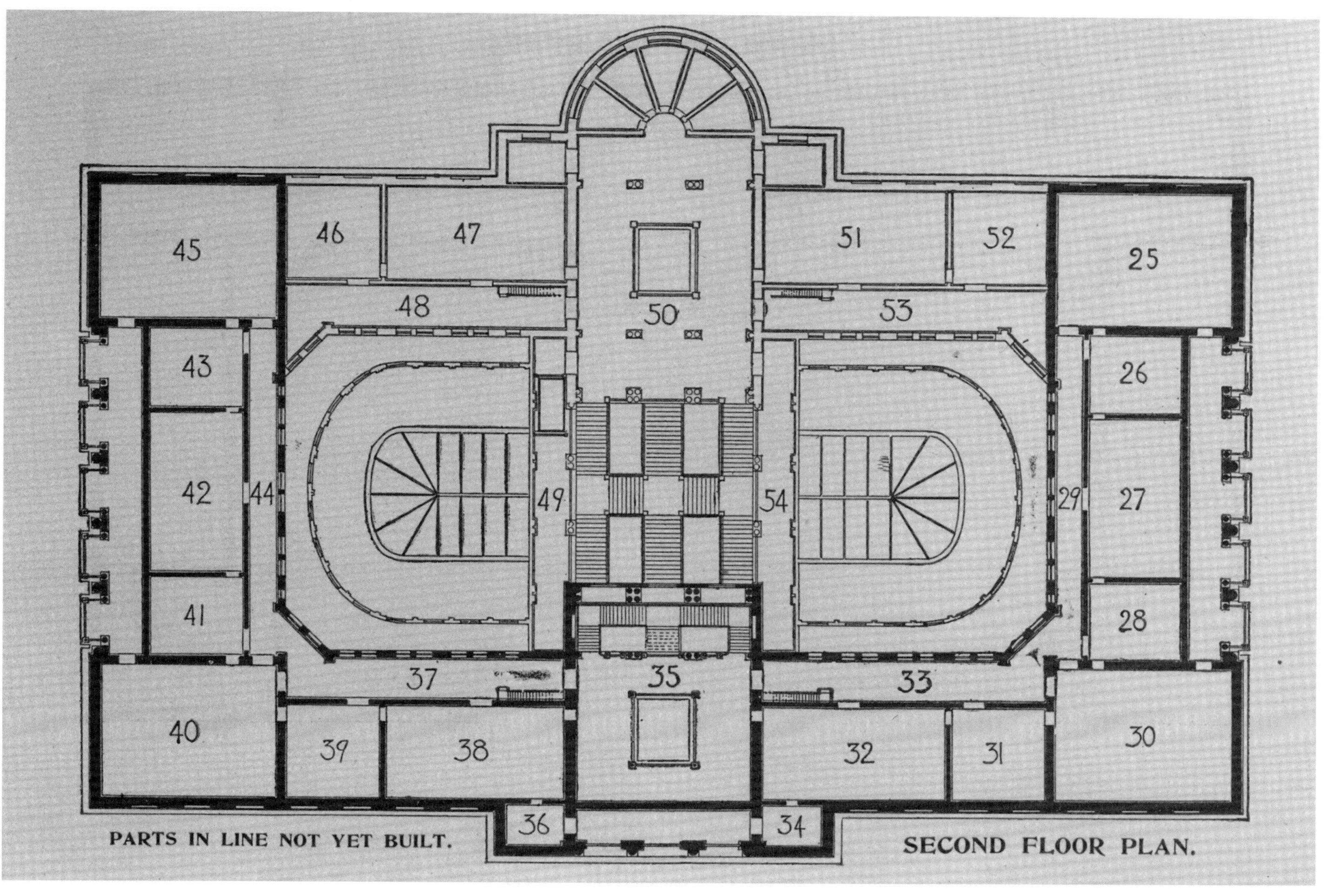

later expansion would be accomplished by creating a bridge over these tracks, behind the original building, with most subsequent additions taking place east of the tracks, on the lake side.

The Art Institute continued to evolve as a collecting institution as well as a building in the early years of the twentieth century. The year 1906 saw the acquisition of El Greco's *Assumption of the Virgin*, and in 1907 the Department of Prints and Drawings was formally established. In 1910 an organization called Friends of American Art was founded "with the purpose of donating works of American art to the museum." In 1912 a bequest by Daniel Burnham laid the foundation for the museum's Architectural Library (today the Burnham Library). Clearly Chicago's dream of having an art museum worthy of a cultural capital was being realized. The Art Institute was amassing an important collection and had completed a monumental, beautiful, yet practical home for its housing and exhibition.

An interesting sidebar concerning the place of the Art Institute of Chicago in the art world of the early twentieth century is the fact that whereas no New York

6.4. *Annual Report*, Art Institute of Chicago: 1895-1901, page 4, Second Floor Plan, E10556, The Art Institute of Chicago. Photography © The Art Institute of Chicago.

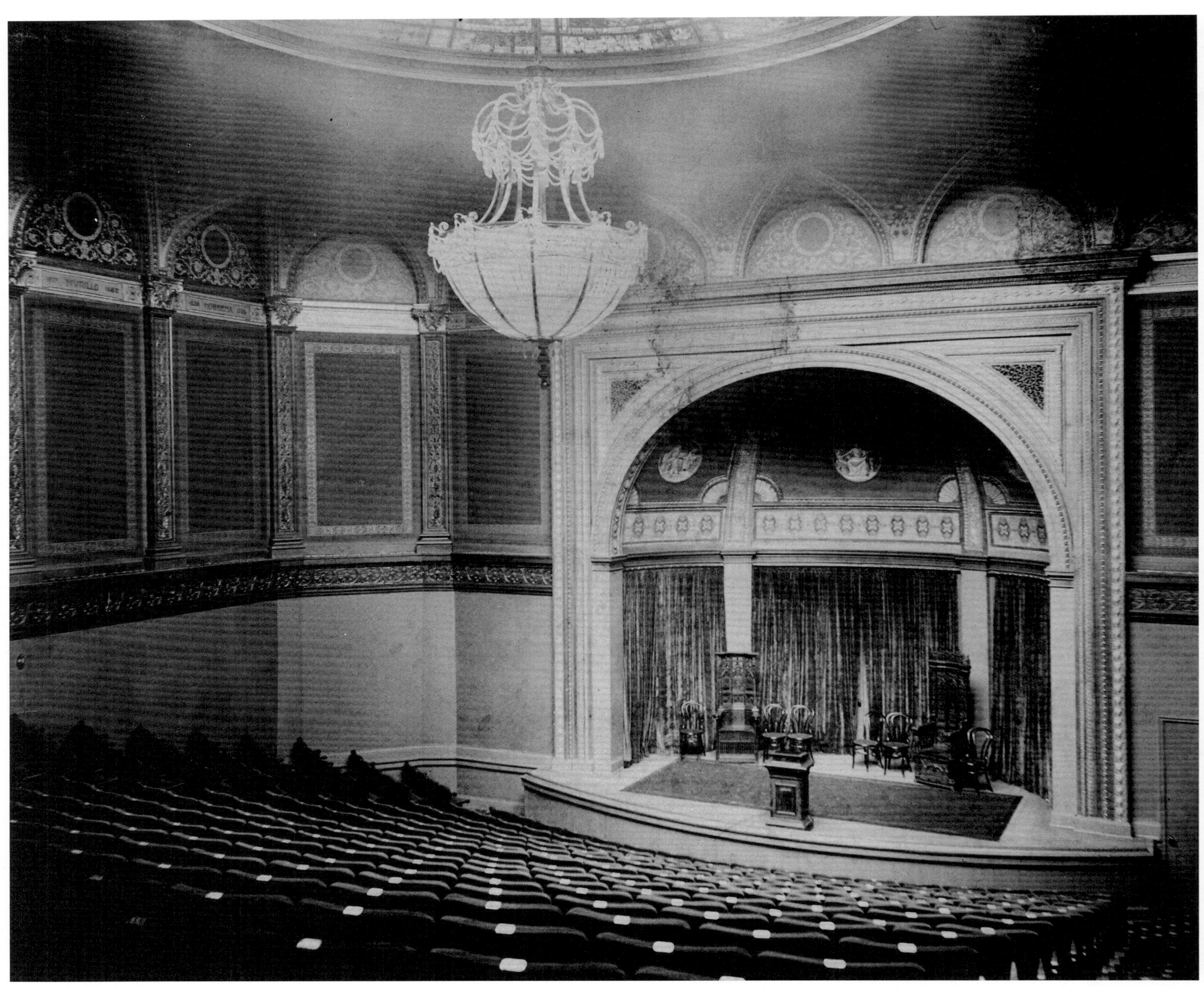

6.5. Fullerton Hall, The Art Institute of Chicago, E34021, The Art Institute of Chicago. Photography © The Art Institute of Chicago.

6.6. Sheply, Rutan amd Coolidge, 1901. Interior view of the Ryerson Library, photographed 1933, C11480, The Art Institute of Chicago. Photography © The Art Institute of Chicago

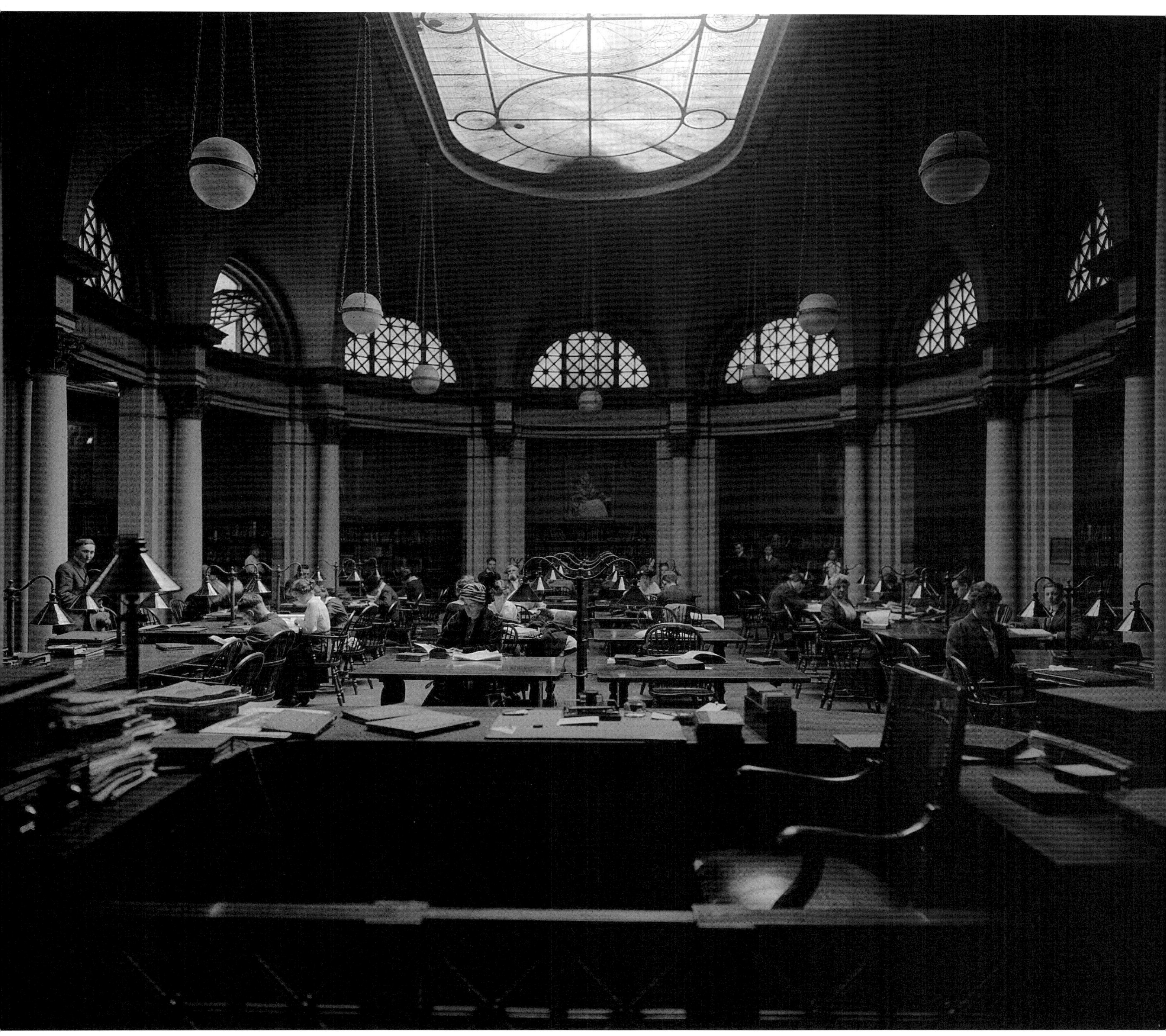

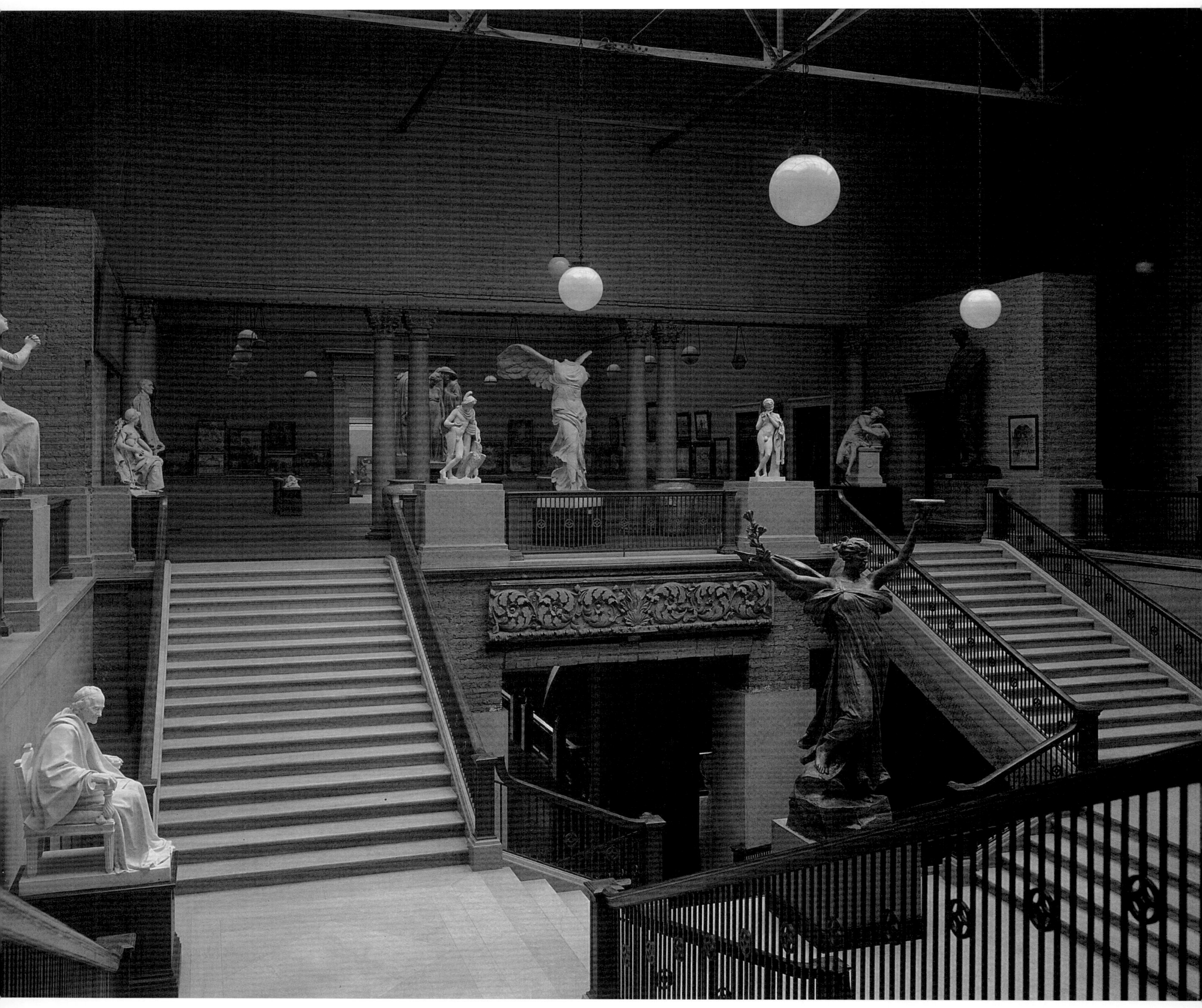

6.7. Grand Staircase, Art Institute
c.1900, C591, The Art Institute of
Chicago. Photography © The Art Institute
of Chicago

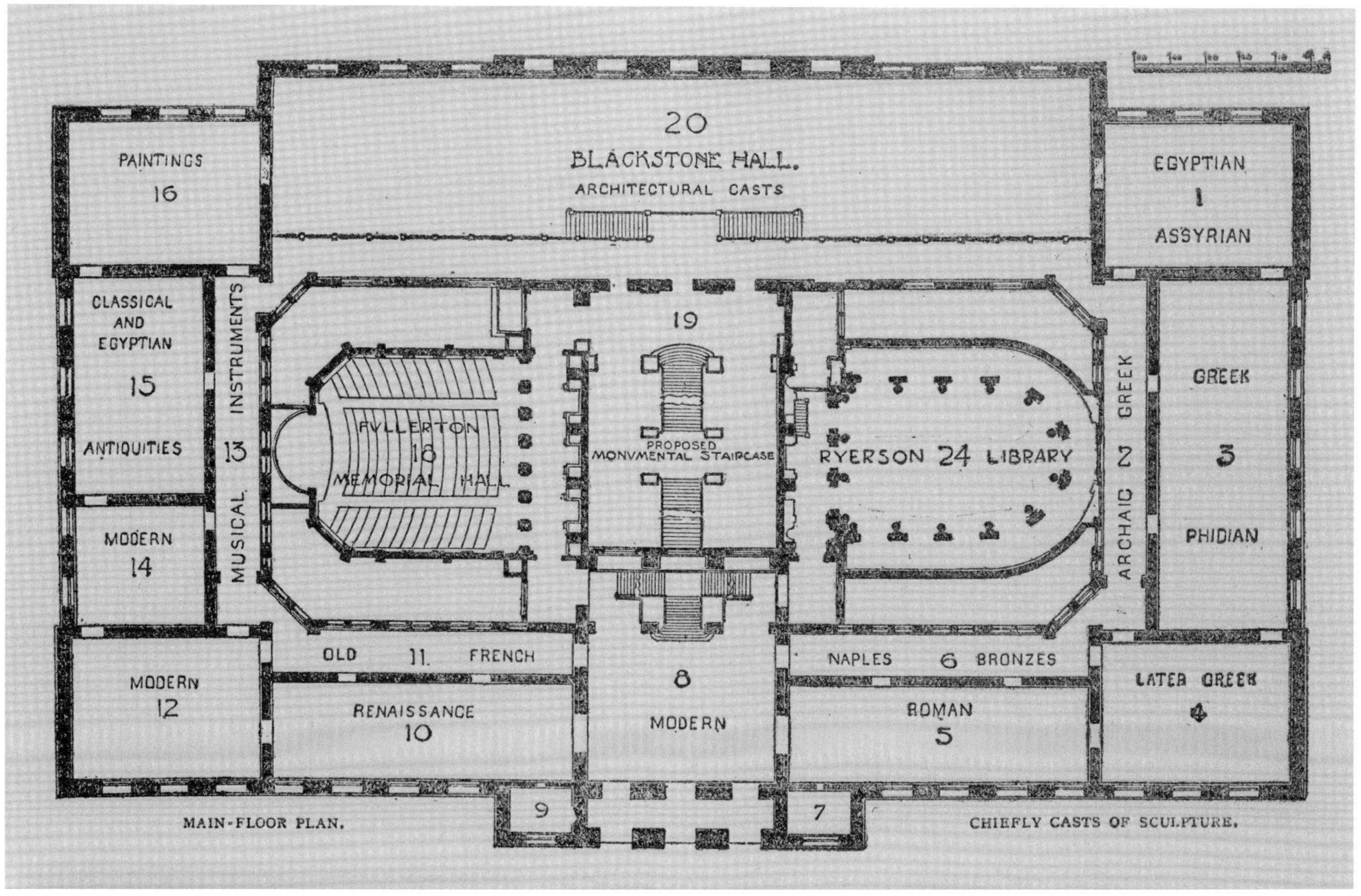

6.8. Catalogue of the 18th Annual Exhibtion of Painting and Sculpture, 1905–06, First floor of galleries of AIC, E15656, The Art Institute of Chicago. Photography © The Art Institute of Chicago.

museum was interested in serving as a venue for the now famous International Exhibition of Modern Art, or "Armory Show," of 1913, the Art Institute served as the exhibition's Midwestern venue. The Association of American Painters and Sculptors did indeed show a reduced form of this then infamous, now much lauded, exhibition from March 24 through April 16, 1913 (fig. 6.10). Though the museum was in no way committed to collecting such avant-garde art at the time, it did see display of this seminal exhibition as consistent with its mission as an educational institution and remained committed to hosting it, even after the bad reviews it received from the New York press.

CROSSING THE RAILROAD TRACKS: EXPANDING THE ART INSTITUTE

By the 1910s it was clear that the collections and programs of the Art Institute would require more space, and that expansion would require breaking the now-closed rectangular plan of the main building. Rather than adding wings to the

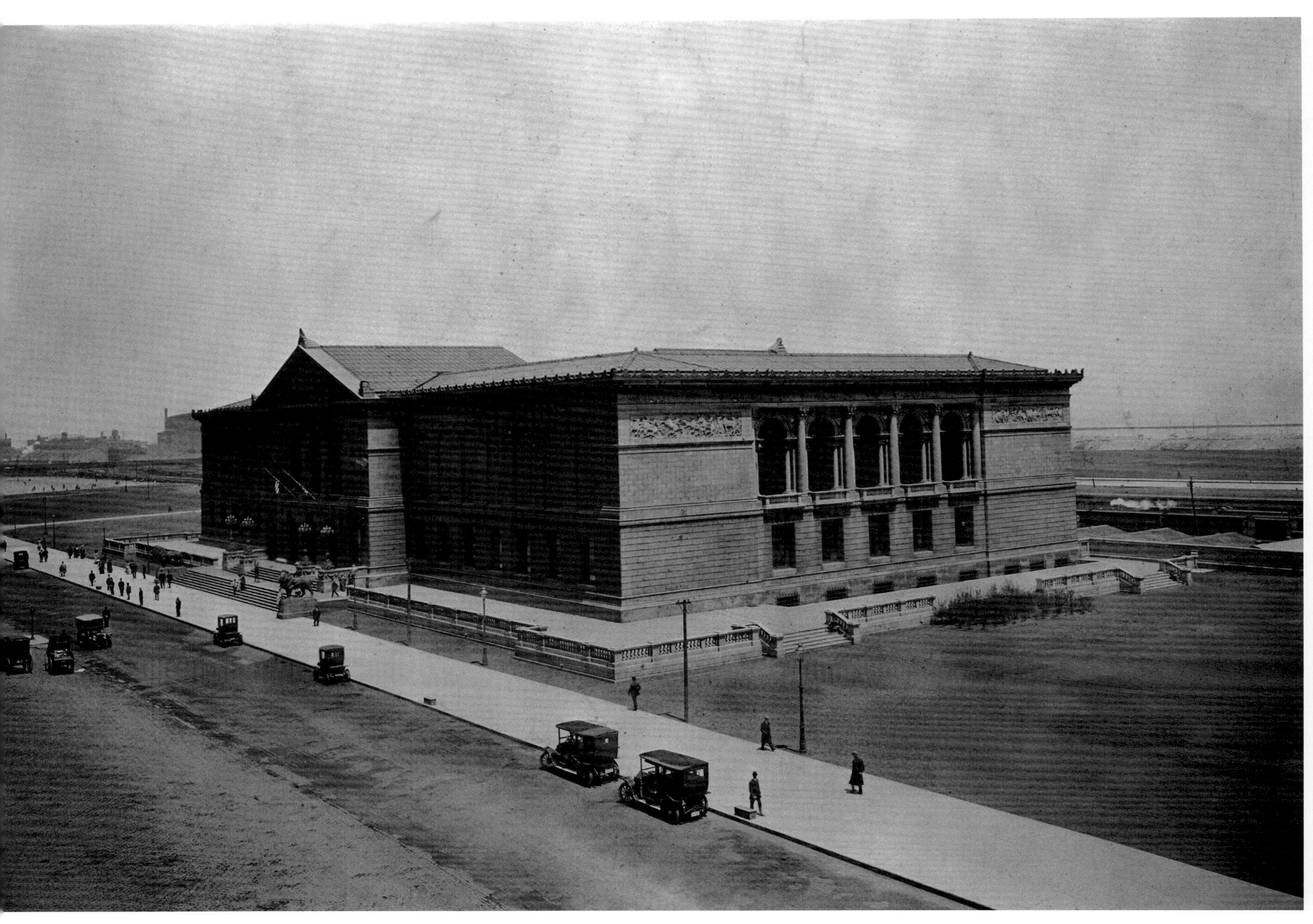

6.9. The Art Institute of Chicago, exterior, from the southwest. Electric cars on street, copy negative made from original photograph, circa 1910, C33782, The Art Institute of Chicago. Photography © The Art Institute of Chicago.

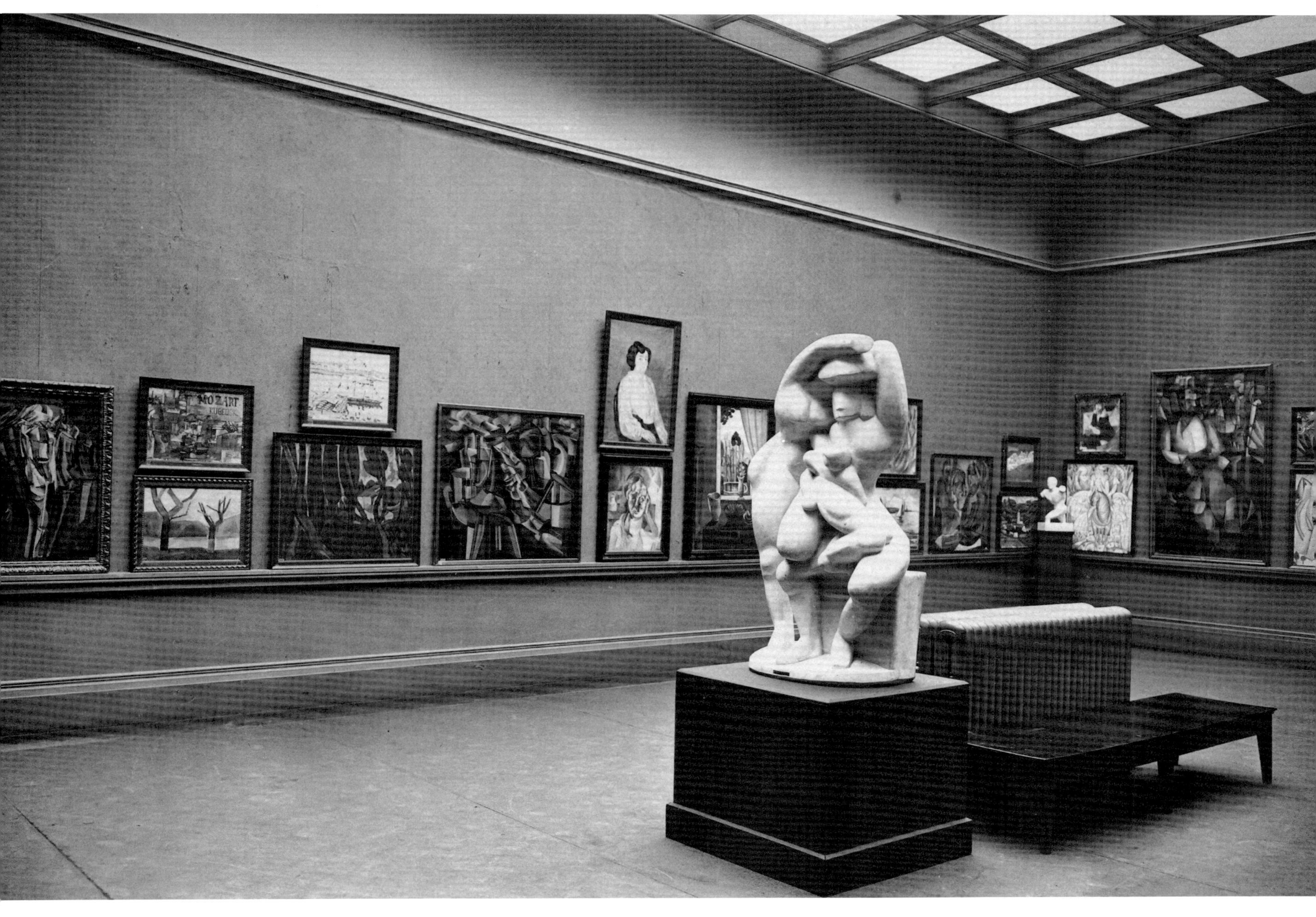

6.10. International Exhibition of Modern Art, 3/24/1913 to 4/16/1913 ("The Armory Show"). View of gallery 53, C22457, The Art Institute of Chicago.
Photography © The Art Institute of Chicago.

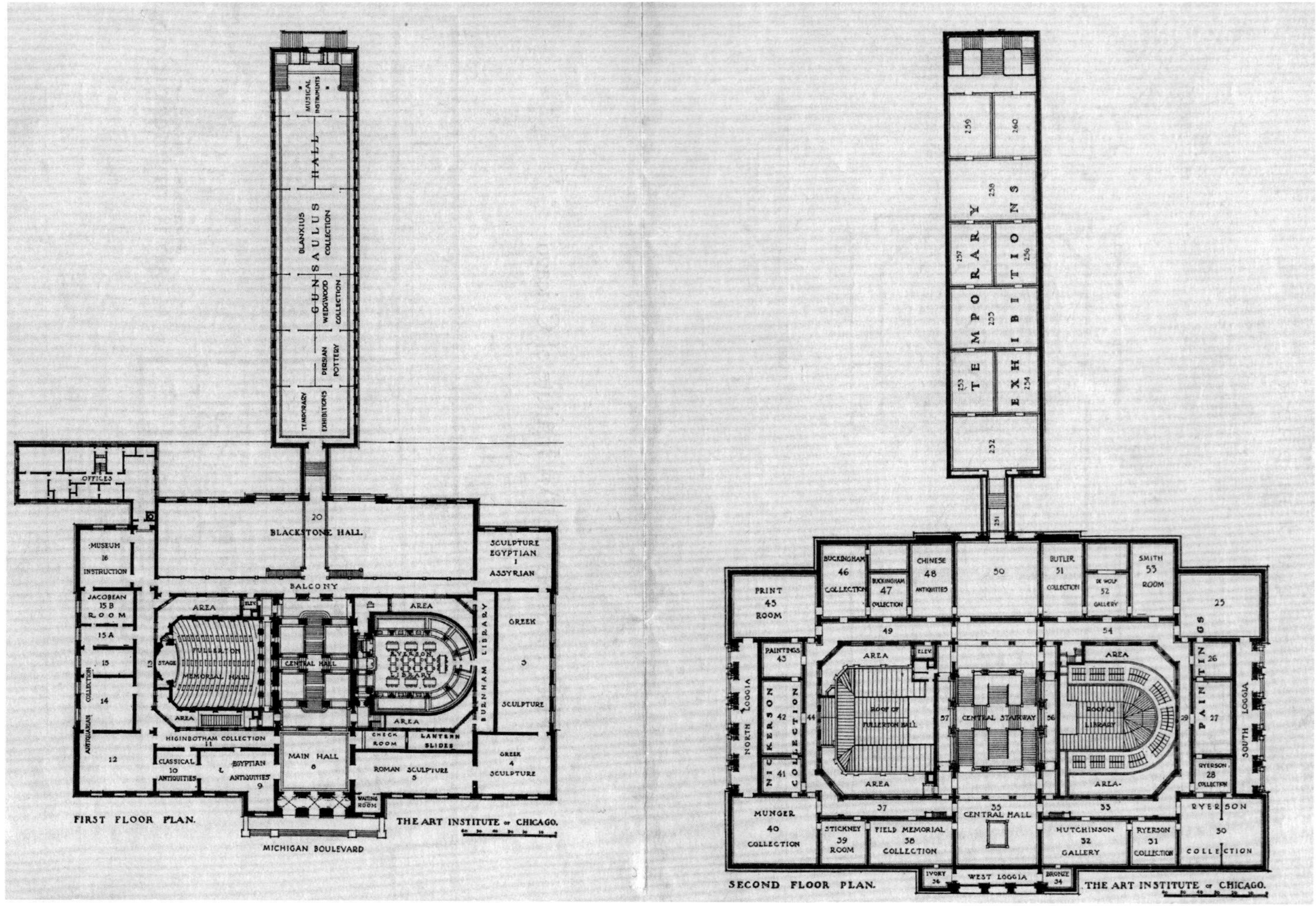

6.11. First and Second Floor Plan of the Art Institute of Chicago after the addition of Gunsaulus Hall, G31484, The Art Institute of Chicago. Photography © The Art Institute of Chicago.

north and south of the main building (following the model of many expanding museums, including the Metropolitan Museum of Art in New York), the board of the Art Institute decided to maintain the architectural integrity of the original façade and instead to expand behind the main building, eastward, toward the lake. Of course, immediately east of the existing building lay the tracks of the Illinois Central Railroad. For this reason the first major addition to the now-completed main building would, by necessity, assume the form of a bridge.

Named Gunsaulus Hall and opened in 1916, this new set of galleries was a narrow, two-story addition, continuing the central east–west spine of the main building over the tracks (figs. 6.11 and 6.12). Shepley, Rutan & Coolidge continued as the museum's architects for this project. Gunsaulus Hall was not only important for providing additional space for the museum to grow, it also solved an important problem for future expansion: it bridged the pit created by the railroad tracks and created a central point east of the tracks from which the museum could expand further. Gunsaulus Hall thus served as a linking building to all future expansions east of the tracks from the main building on Michigan Avenue.

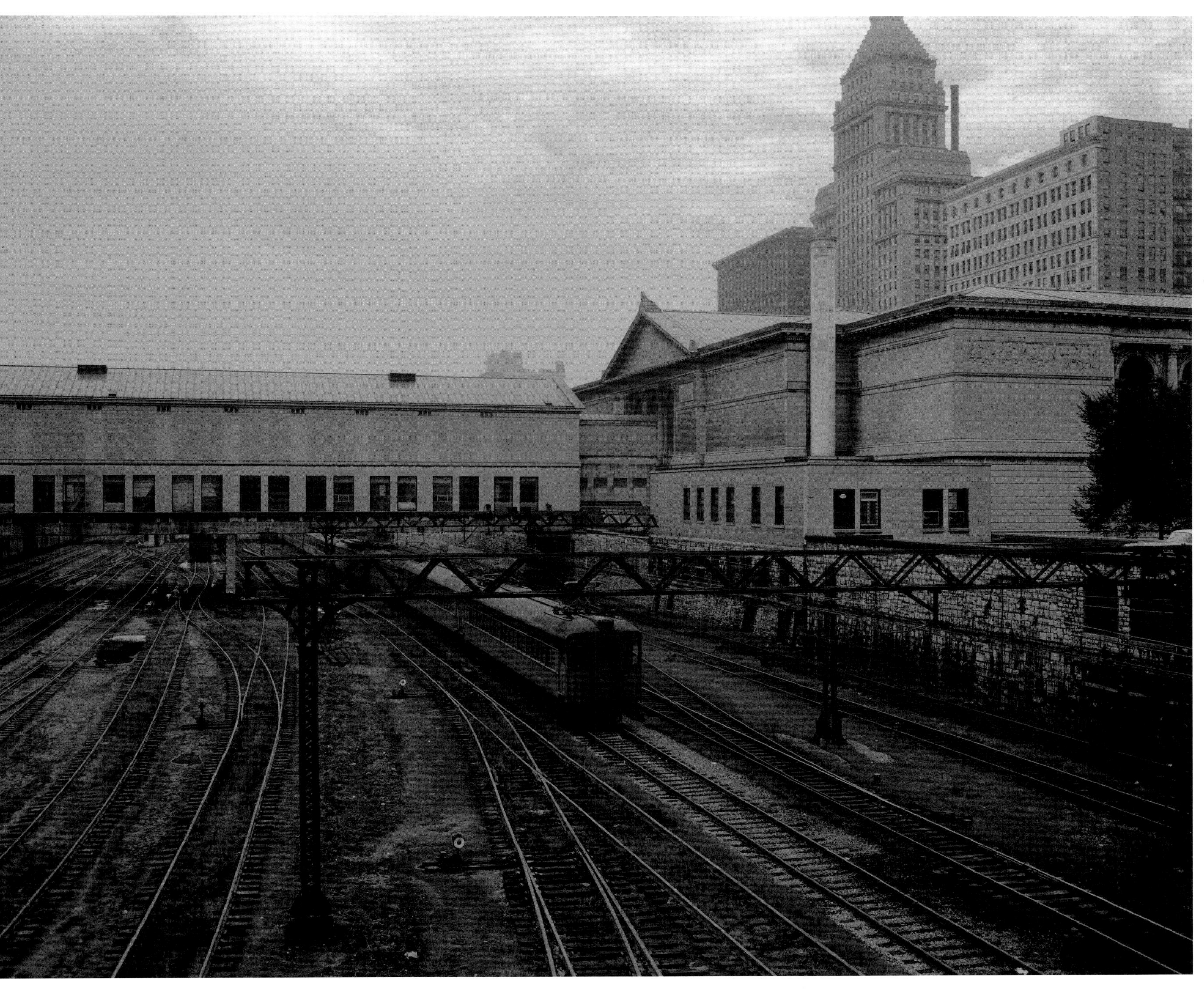

6.12. Exterior View of Gunsaulus Hall
taken from Monroe Street bridge over
train tracks, August 1954, E03925,
The Art Institute of Chicago.
Photography © The Art Institute of Chicago.

Even as the Art Institute expanded architecturally in the 1910s and 1920s, ever greater demands were made on its spaces as its collections grew dramatically in both quality and quantity. In 1921 the Department of Oriental Art was formally created, and 1922 was a particularly important year for bequests and acquisitions, with fifty-two paintings from the Potter Palmer collection bequeathed to the museum. This collection included works by Monet, Degas, and Delacroix. The same year the Kimball collection was donated to the Art Institute through the bequest of Mrs. Evaline Kimball. This collection consisted of twenty-two paintings, chiefly English, including the work of Turner, Lawrence, Reynolds, and Constable. In 1925 James Deering bequeathed the museum works by Tiepolo and Manet. Clearly, by the mid-1920s the Art Institute had established one of the premiere collections of European Old Master and nineteenth-century paintings; it had begun seriously

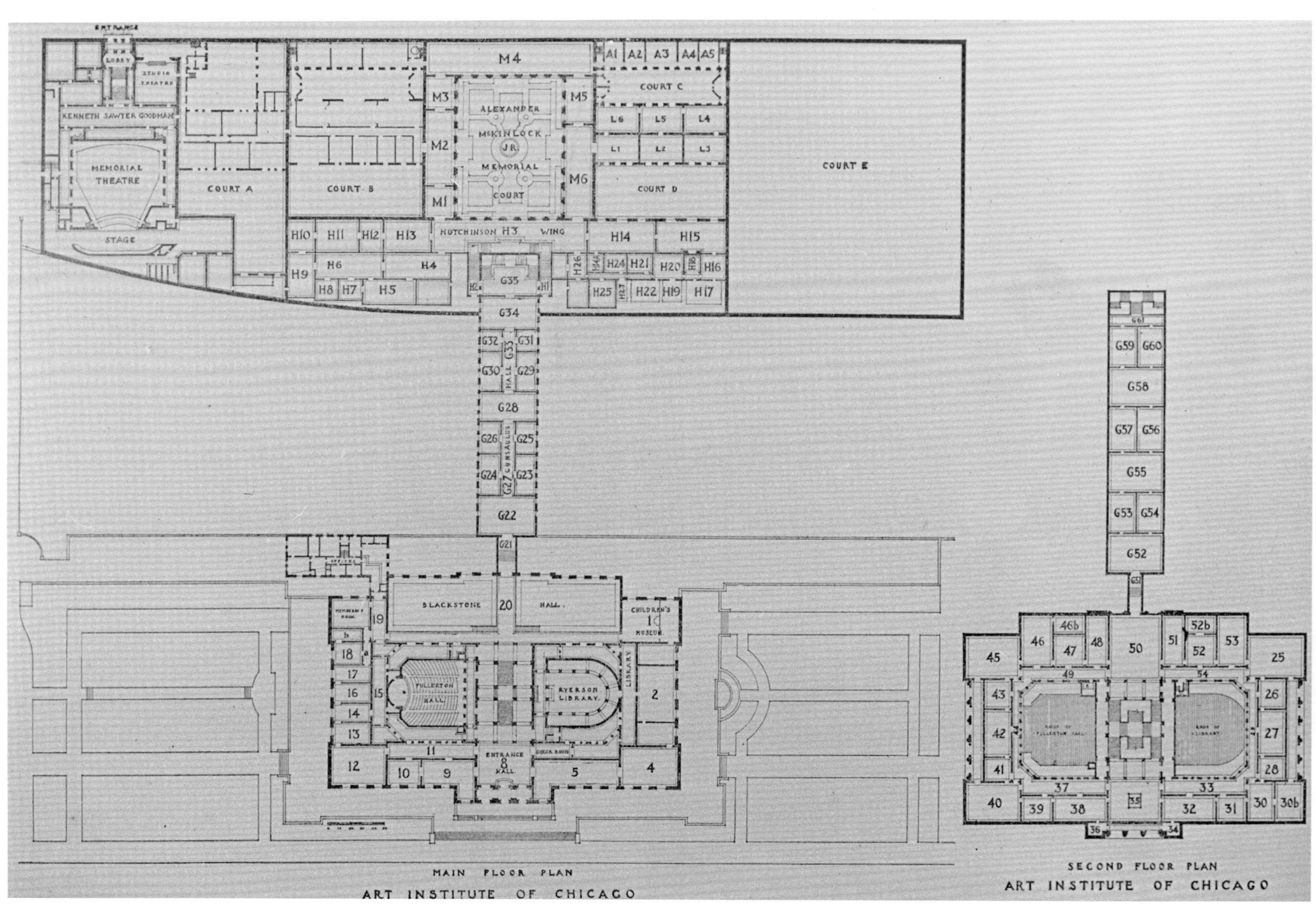

6.13. Art Institute of Chicago, plan of the first and second floors, c.1930, E15212, The Art Institute of Chicago. Photography © The Art Institute of Chicago.

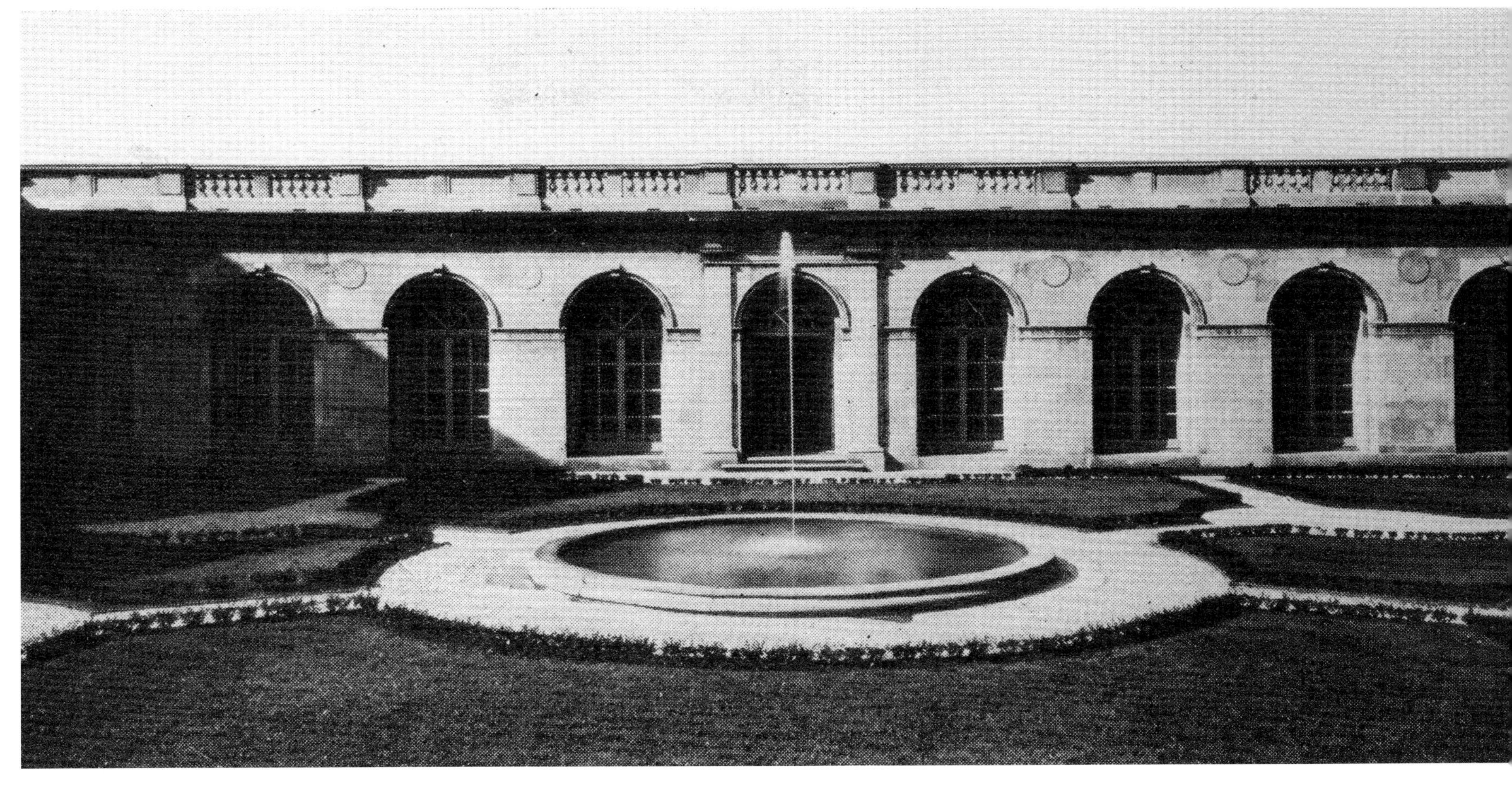

collecting Asian art and the decorative arts as well. From this point forward, the Art Institute would no longer need to prove itself to potential donors or the world of art criticism; it had joined the ranks of the elite art museums of the United States and had little competition as the leading cultural institution in the very wealthy and important city of Chicago. This status would guarantee a steady flow of bequests of the highest quality and a continuing need to make space to accommodate such treasures.

New acquisitions, new departments, and the needs of the Art Institute's school all demanded further expansion. Gunsaulus Hall became a bridge in both a literal and figurative sense with the addition of the Hutchinson Wing, east of the railroad. Though only one floor in elevation, the Hutchinson Wing was a vast expansion, containing additional galleries, space for the school and an elegantly landscaped outdoor courtyard, known as the George Alexander McKinlock, Jr. Memorial Court (figs. 6.13 and 6.14). The Hutchinson Wing was designed by architects Coolidge & Hodgdon and opened to the public in 1924. In the following years, additions were made to both the north and south of the Hutchinson Wing: the Goodman Theater,

6.14. McKinlock Court, *Bulletin of the Art Institute of Chicago*, vol. 18, no. 7 (Oct. 1924), p. 92, E15579, The Art Institute of Chicago. Photography © The Art Institute of Chicago.

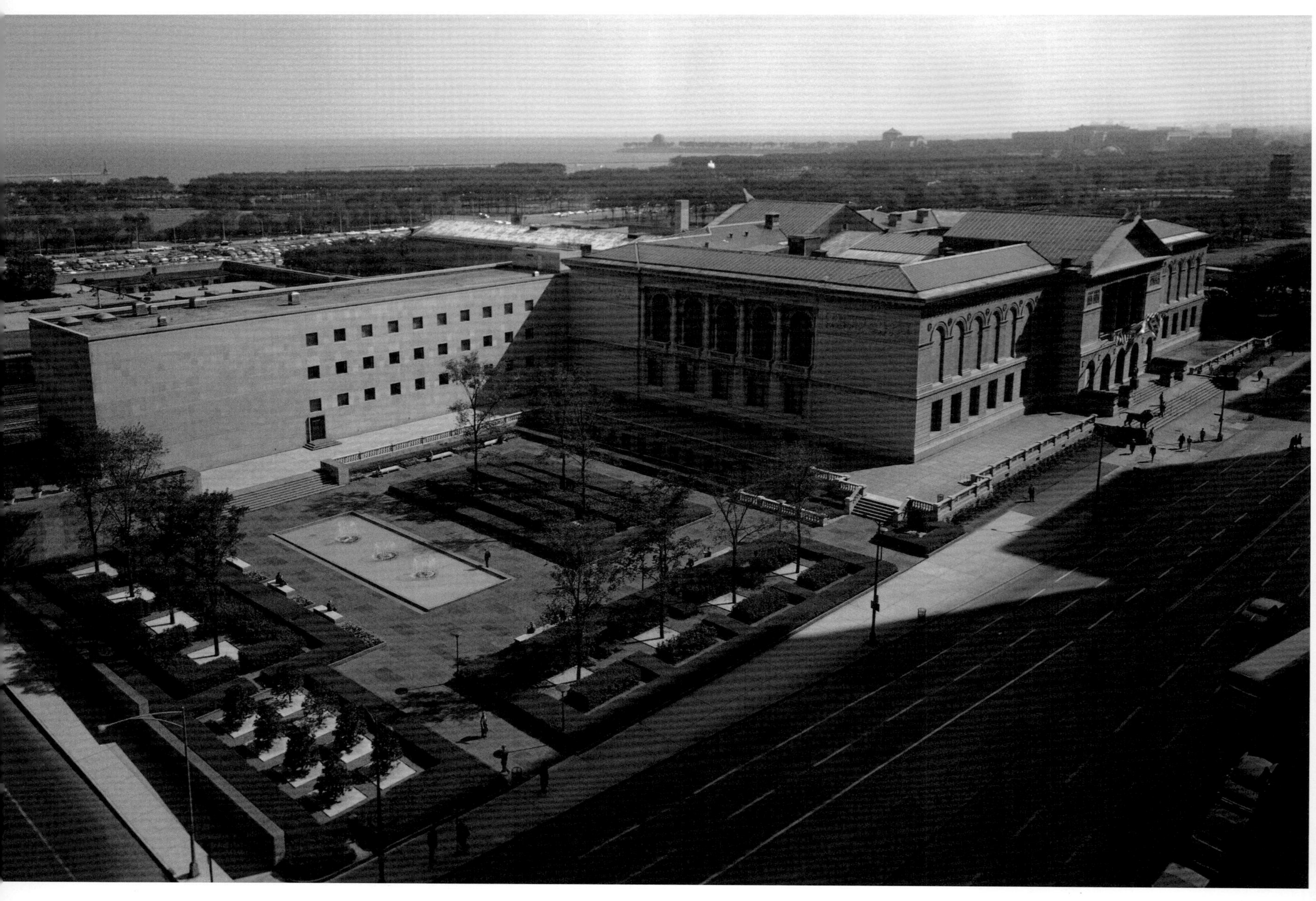

6.15. The Art Institute of Chicago from the
9th floor of the University Club, C26178,
The Art Institute of Chicago. Photography
© The Art Institute of Chicago.

6.16. Museum Exterior, Columbus Drive
Entrance, copy negative from original
photography by Hedrich-Blessing,
C46261, The Art Institute of Chicago.
Photography © The Art Institute of Chicago.

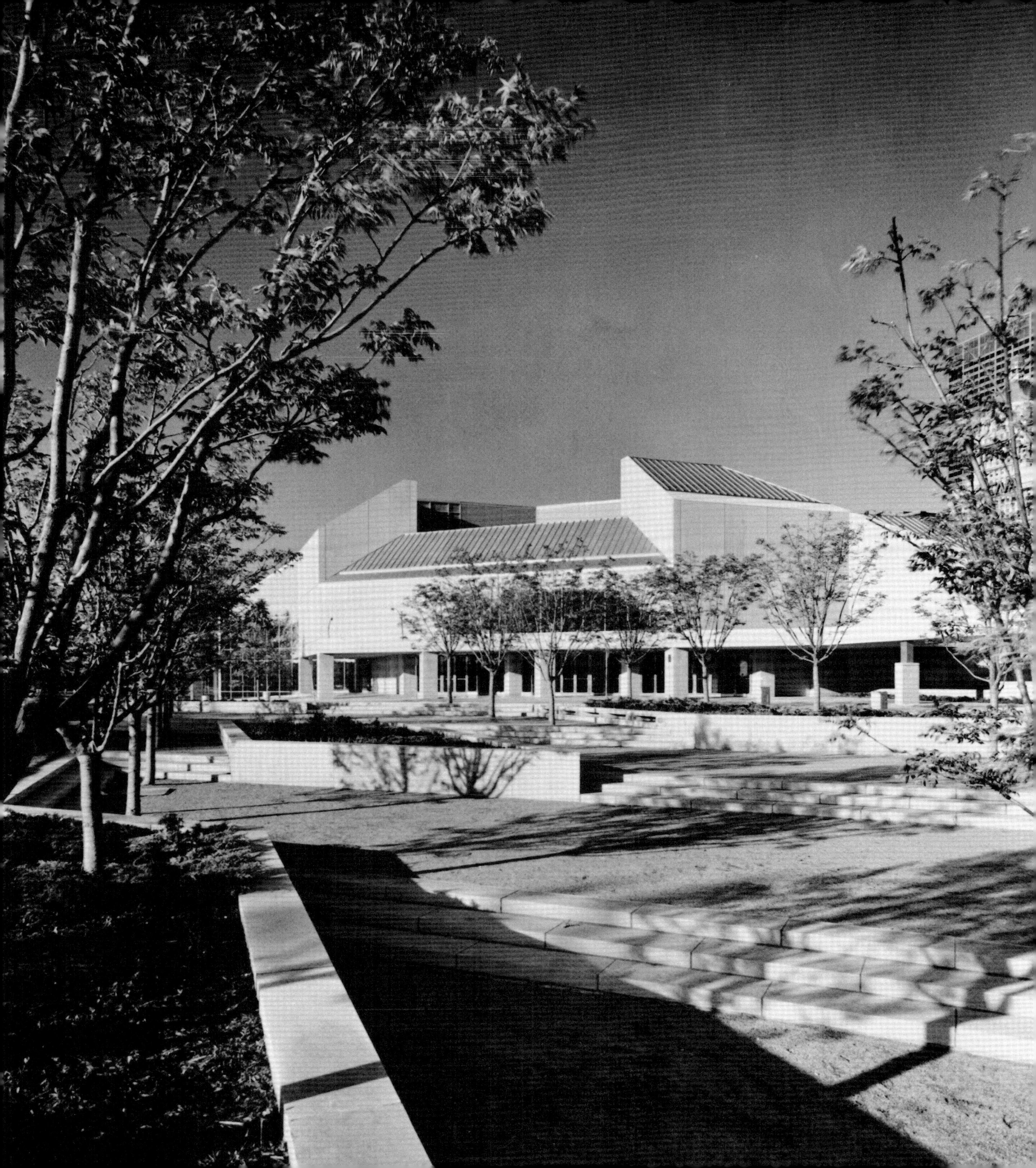

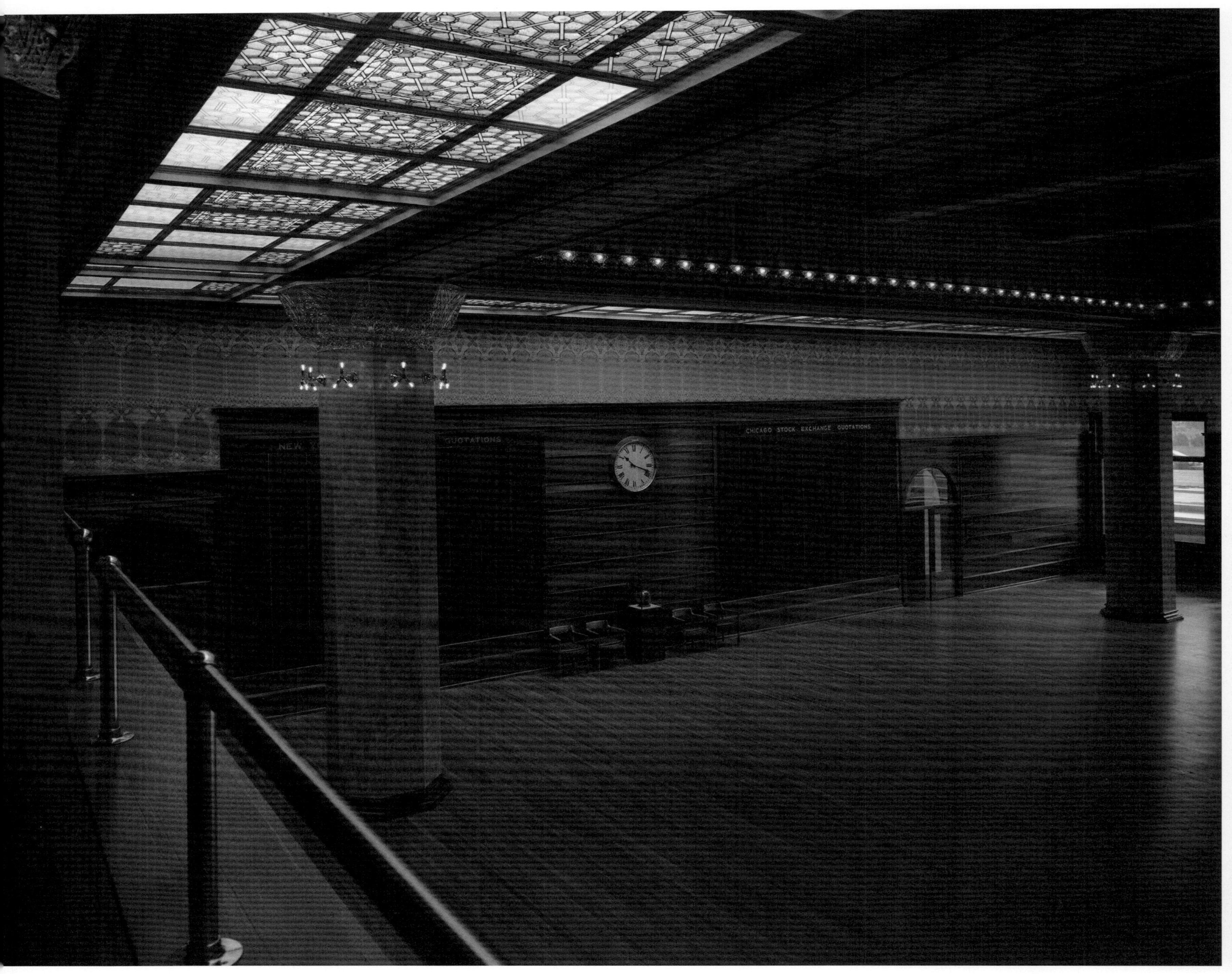

6.17. Adler & Sullivan, 1893-94. View of the reconstructed Trading Room from the Chicago Stock Exchange, 1976-77, C43902, The Art Institute of Chicago. Photography © The Art Institute of Chicago.

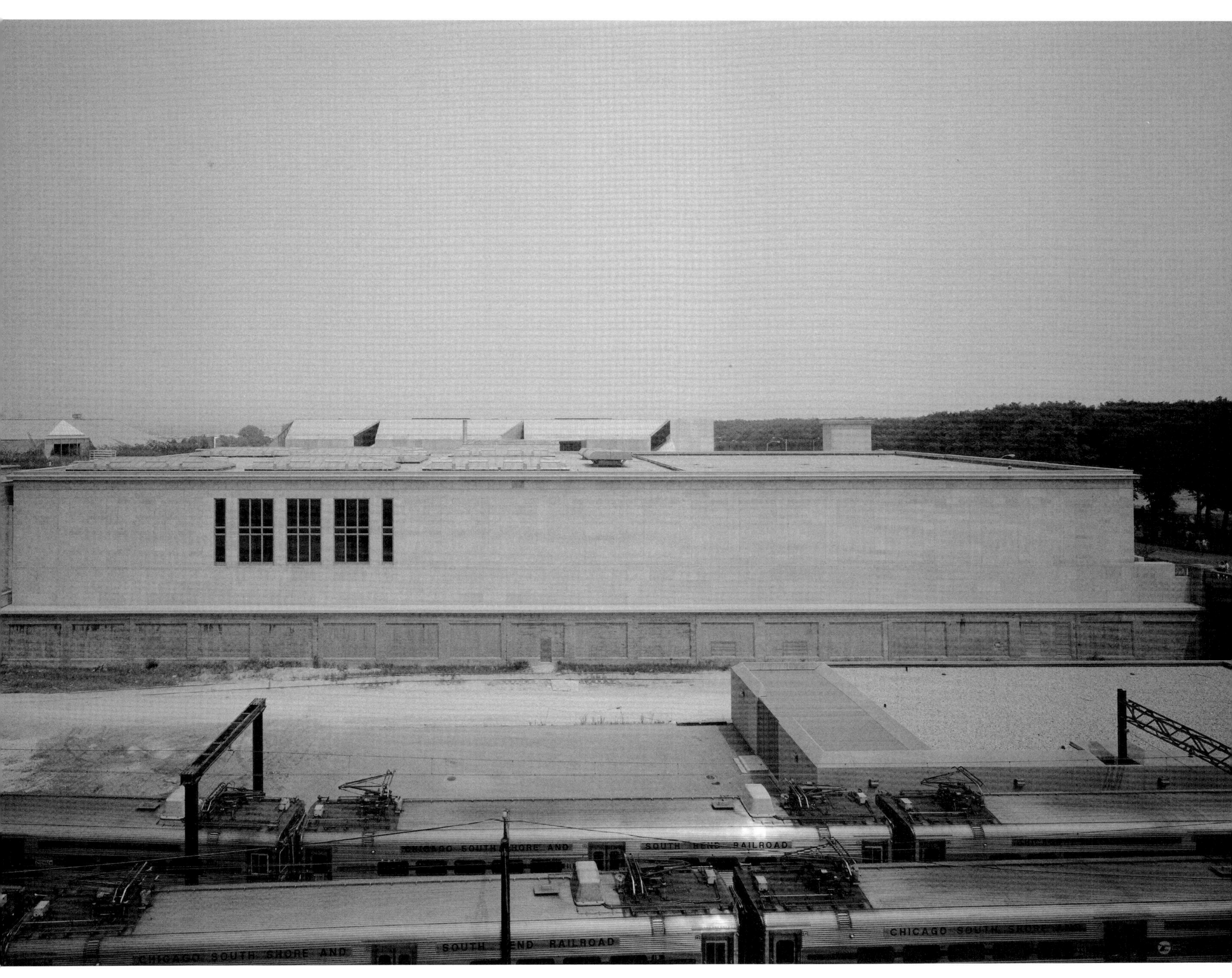

6.18. Rice Building, exterior, west façade, E16133, The Art Institute of Chicago.
Photography © The Art Institute of Chicago.

designed by Howard Van Doren Shaw, added in 1925 to the north; and the Agnes W. Allerton Wing, containing the galleries of the Department of Textiles, designed by Coolidge & Hodgdon and added in 1927 to the south. Further additions to the Goodman Theater were made in 1929 and 1938.

It seems that only a world tumult on the scale of the Second World War could stop the continuous expansion of the Art Institute of Chicago. Following the work of the late 1930s, no major new building projects were taken on until the late 1950s. In 1958 the B. F. Furguson Memorial Building was completed, just west of the railroad tracks, connecting with the main building at its northeast corner. Designed by architects Holabird, Root & Burgee, this relatively nondescript building contained the Art Institute's administrative, curatorial, education, and conservation offices as well as back-of-the-house programming such as shipping, receiving, carpentry, and paint shops (fig. 6.15). The building's chief virtue for the museum-going public was the fact that it freed up space in the existing buildings for use as galleries by relocating and centralizing the nonpublic functions of the museum. In the corresponding southeast position, west of the tracks, the Morton Wing, containing exhibition galleries and designed by Shaw, Metz & Associates, opened in 1962. Like the Furguson Building, the Morton Wing is relatively nondescript externally and is little seen, as it is set back from Michigan Avenue and intersects the main building on the east side, just west of the railroad.

From 1974 to 1976 the Art Institute embarked on a very ambitious project, pushing further to the east (fig. 6.16). Although the bulk of this project was to be the new home for the School of the Art Institute of Chicago, it would also provide a new east entrance to the museum as well as a new cafeteria, restaurant, members' lounge, and additional gallery space. This project was designed by the firm of Skidmore, Owings & Merrill and opened to the public in 1976. Much more daring architecturally than the projects undertaken by the Art Institute in the 1950s and 1960s, this eastern addition was the first truly contemporary addition to the museum, all the previous expansions being much more committed to maintaining continuity with the original Beaux-Arts building. In 1977 the Trading Room from the Chicago Stock Exchange Building (designed by Adler & Sullivan, 1893) was reconstructed adjacent to the new east wing (fig. 6.17). This project was executed by Vinci–Kenny Architects. The Stock Exchange Building itself was demolished in 1972, and its reconstruction by the Art Institute is indicative of its commitment to the architecture of Chicago, the city usually considered America's architectural capital.

If the 1970s saw the most radical departure taken from the traditional Beaux-Arts architecture of the Shepley, Rutan & Coolidge main building (now know as the Allerton Building), the 1980s would see a return to a more classically inspired architecture in the Art Institute's last completed major addition. Open to the public in 1988, the Daniel F. and Ada L. Rice Building was the largest single expansion of the museum to date, increasing usable gallery space by almost one-third (fig. 6.18). Designed by architects Hammond, Beeby & Babka, this new wing was

6.19. Visitor's Guide. First Level, G31272, The Art Institute of Chicago. Photography © The Art Institute of Chicago.

FIRST LEVEL

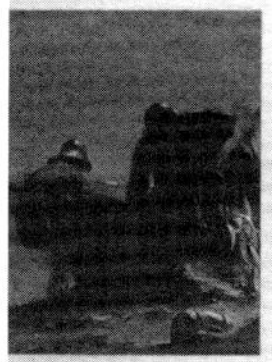

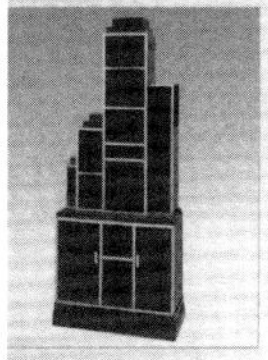

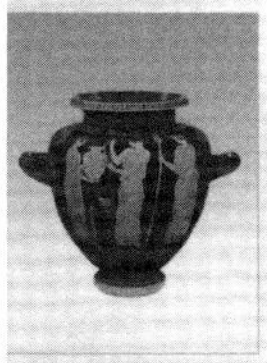

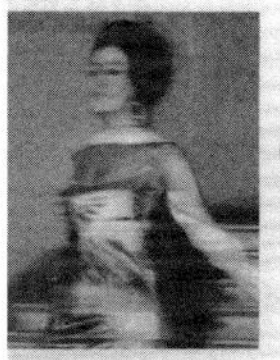

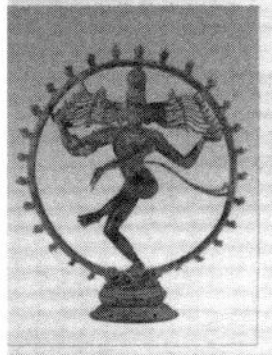

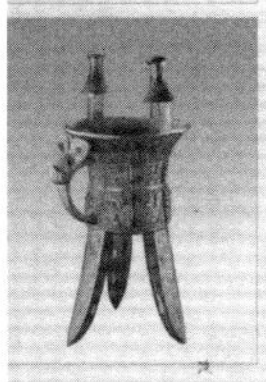

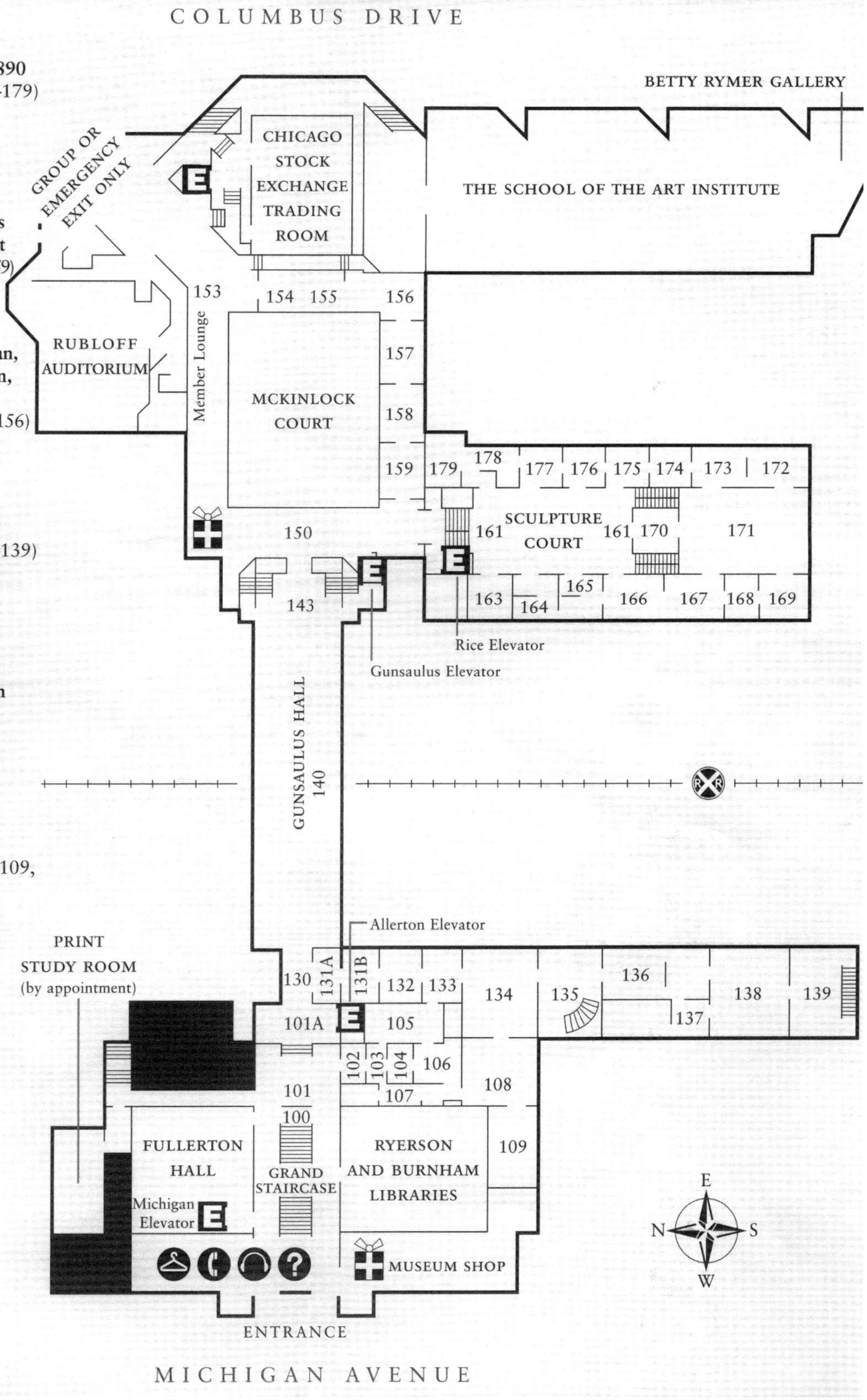

designed for special exhibitions as well as galleries for the display of American art, European decorative arts, and twentieth-century American art. Architecturally, Rice Hall is conceived of in a stripped-down classicism, very much in homage to the architecture of the original. This is particularly strongly articulated in the Roger McCormick Memorial Court, a multiheight space lit by a skylight on top of a trabeation supported by simplified Doric columns.

THE ART INSTITUTE AND THE CHALLENGES FACING AN ENCYCLOPEDIC MUSEUM

A look at the visitor floor plan of the Art Institute of Chicago from 2008 reveals just how complex and rambling the museum has become after more than a century of building growth and expansion (fig. 6.19). One of the rare virtues of the Art Institute is the fact that in spite of this very complex building history, a visit is still relatively coherent (in a way not made obvious by looking at the floor plans). A challenge that is unique to the encyclopedic museums among the types of museums covered in this book results from the reality that no period, movement, or culture can ever be ruled out of scope. Art history always moves forward, and new interests in areas of art production from past moments and cultures always continue to arise. If an encyclopedic museum is true to its mission (which the Art Institute has always been and continues to be), it must remain inclusive and collect not only new works, but entirely new categories, media, and types of art.

Although certain works may be considered less important in the present than they were in the past and therefore put into storage, representation of the major movements and cultures must be preserved in permanent installations as well as temporary exhibitions. Thus future expansion can never be ruled out; in fact, it should be assumed. Unlike the other case studies in this book, the Art Institute of Chicago is not bound by the collecting interests of a visionary founder (such as Henry Clay Frick or Dominique de Menil) or a relatively narrowly defined collecting scope (such as at the Georgia O'Keeffe Museum, The Whitney Museum of American Art, or the Museum of Modern Art). Financial limitations and the areas of interest and expertise of individual directors and curators may influence what is collected at a given time. Acquisitions made available through bequests also play a role in determining what type of art enters a museum (though bequests often involve the right of the museum to sell works for acquisitions funds without accessioning them).

Nonetheless, the encyclopedic museum is not bound to stay true to its earlier collecting policies and philosophies in the same manner as most other types of museums. To the contrary, the encyclopedic museum strives to be inclusive of the ever-expanding definition of what constitutes great art in the always-changing multicultural and polycentric world of art production. This case study, which differs

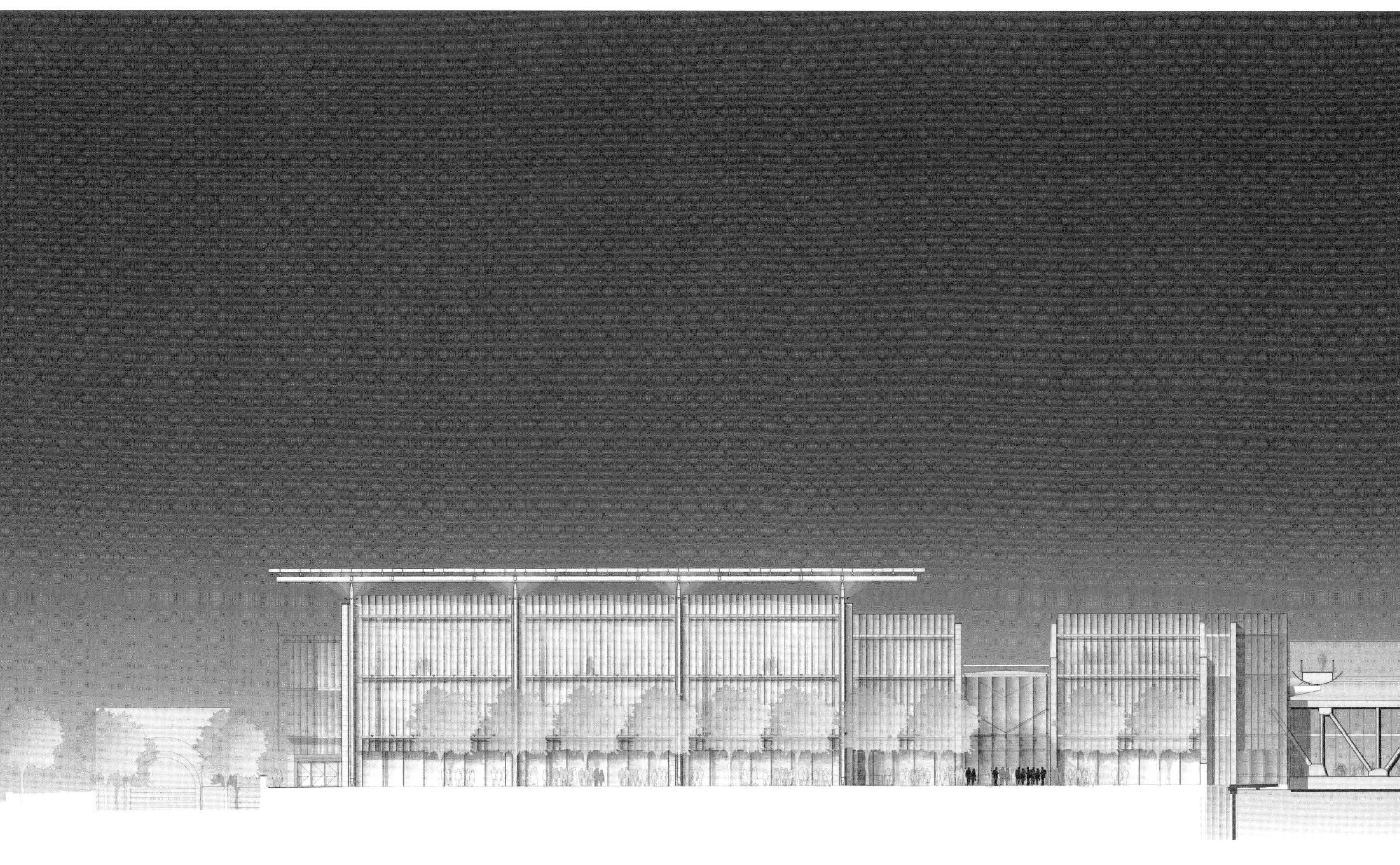

from the others in this book by being largely a chronology and catalogue of the architectural projects of the museum, is indicative of the special pressures facing this type of institution. Encyclopedic museums must always look forward and expand with the universe of what is considered to be important art.

In expanding to keep up with its always-widening mission, the museum building itself becomes a document in this living history of art. The architectural history of Chicago, specifically, and the United States and world, generally, is tracked in the building campaigns of the Art Institute of Chicago in much the same way that the work on exhibition within it traces the history of art. From the World's Fair architecture of the 1893 Allerton Building, to the midcentury modernism of the Furguson and Morton wings to the 1970s corporate modernism of the Rubloff Building, to the 1980s postmodernism of the Rice Wing, to Renzo Piano's contemporary architecture in the Modern Wing currently under construction (see

6.20. Modern Wing, North View, Rendering: Renzo Piano Building Workshop, image provided for publicity of the Modern Wing. G30630, The Art Institute of Chicago. Photography © The Art Institute of Chicago.

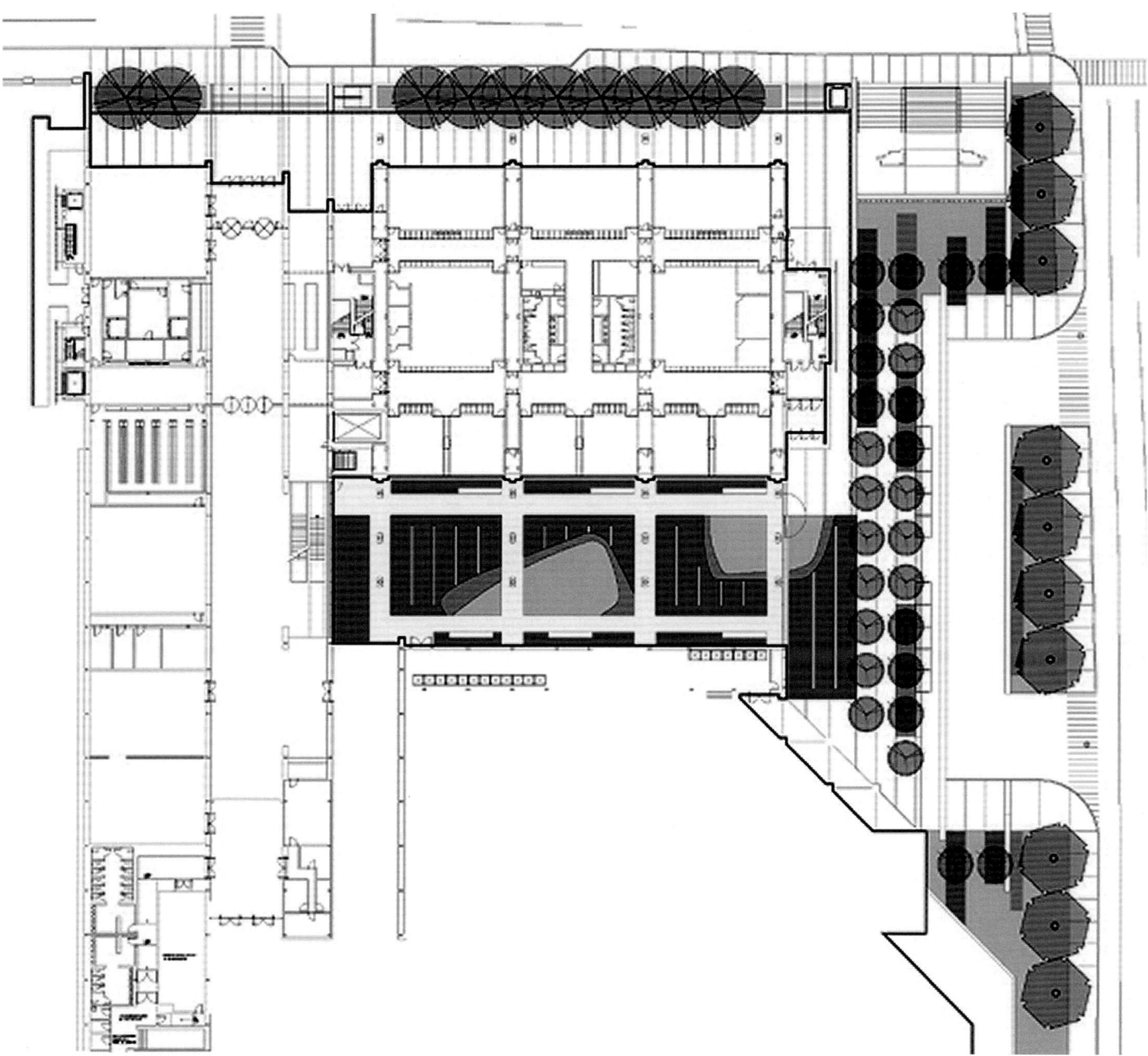

6.21. The Art Institute of Chicago, Green
Space, Renzo Piano Building Workshop
and Interactive Design Inc., May 2004,
G22009, The Art Institute of Chicago.
Photography © The Art Institute of Chicago.

below), the Art Institute of Chicago presents a concrete history of the architecture of the late-nineteenth- through early-twenty-first-century American art museum. What could be more fitting for an institution dedicated to the collection and exhibition of work from throughout the history of art?

THE ART INSTITUTE OF CHICAGO MOVING FORWARD:
RENZO PIANO'S MODERN WING

The latest building project of the Art Institute of Chicago is the new Modern Wing, which opened to the public on May 16, 2009. [9] Designed by Renzo Piano (the architect of the Menil Collection in Houston as well as the designer of the Whitney Museum's project in downtown Manhattan and many other museum projects in the United States and abroad), this new wing is the home of the Art Institute's collections of twentieth-century modern and twenty-first-century contemporary art. The new wing adds 264,000 square feet to the museum (its largest single expansion), including 65,000 square feet devoted to galleries (6.20, 6.21). The new wing has been designed in keeping with the very highest standards of sustainable design. Made of steel, glass, and limestone with green terraces and gardens, this building, situated to the north of Rubloff Building (east of the railroad tracks), makes a bold statement.

It is only natural that the Art Institute of Chicago will have a new building by one of the leading twenty-first-century contemporary museum designers to house its strong collection of modern art and its growing collection of twenty-first-century contemporary art. Following the precedent of the past expansions of the museum, the new wing is just that, a new wing, located to the northeast of the original Allerton Building on Michigan Avenue, and largely visually autonomous from it, preserving the narrative of the history of architecture from the last six generations or so that the buildings of the Art Institute present so well. This narrative illustrates not merely the history of architecture of the Art Institute of Chicago but the history of America in this period, from the World's Columbian Exposition of 1893 to the present.

CHAPTER 7

THE ROLE OF THE MUSEUM BUILDING IN THE EXPERIENCE OF THE MUSEUM VISIT

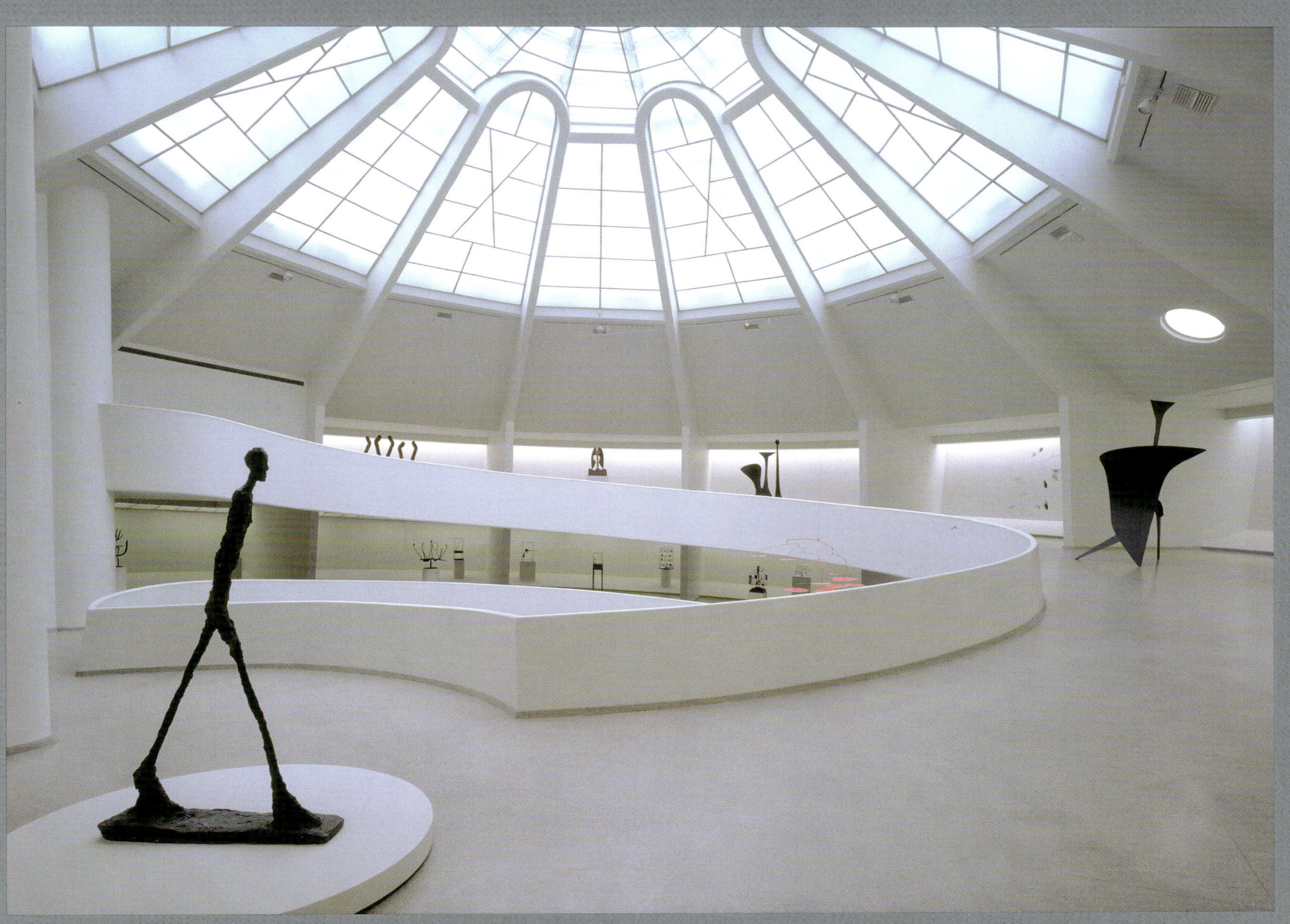

7.1. Installation view of "Picasso and the Age of Iron," Solomon R. Guggenheim Museum, New York, March 19-June 13, 1993. Photograph by David Heald. © The Solomon R. Guggenheim Foundation, New York.

7.2. Solomon R. Guggenheim Museum, New York. Photograph by David Heald. © The Solomon R. Guggenheim Foundation, New York.

The primary functions of the art museum are the collection, preservation, and exhibition of works of art. Obviously, the design of museum buildings should address these three issues first and foremost. A successful design must provide enough space for the proper storage and care of works of art, in the correct climates. Furthermore, a well-designed museum has ample gallery space, scaled appropriately for the works exhibited within it, properly lit, and allowing for comfortable circulation of visitors. Good museum architecture, however, goes far beyond these and other minimal requirements. A museum building should be designed not only in accordance with sound general principles regarding the proper care and display of art and the needs of its visitors and employees, it should also mirror the philosophies and personalities of the institution housed within it. Sometimes the architecture of the building itself helps an institution to articulate these philosophies and personalities.

Yet there is also a danger associated with the design of museum buildings. Architecture, like painting, sculpture, and the other media collected by museums, is an aesthetic pursuit, and great architecture, like important works in any medium, tends to make a statement, oftentimes a rather loud one. A great museum building, however, must not compete with or dominate the works exhibited within it. On the other hand, a museum needs a strong, distinguished architecture to create its institutional identity and to help provide the best and most memorable experience for its visitors. This tension between the vessel of the museum building and the art collections contained within it is the great challenge that faces both museum boards and designers whenever the prospect of a new building or expansion is undertaken or even considered.

Naturally, different types of institutions, with very different collecting scopes, can have different architectural solutions. Yet most museums face some similar fundamental choices concerning the relationship they would like to establish

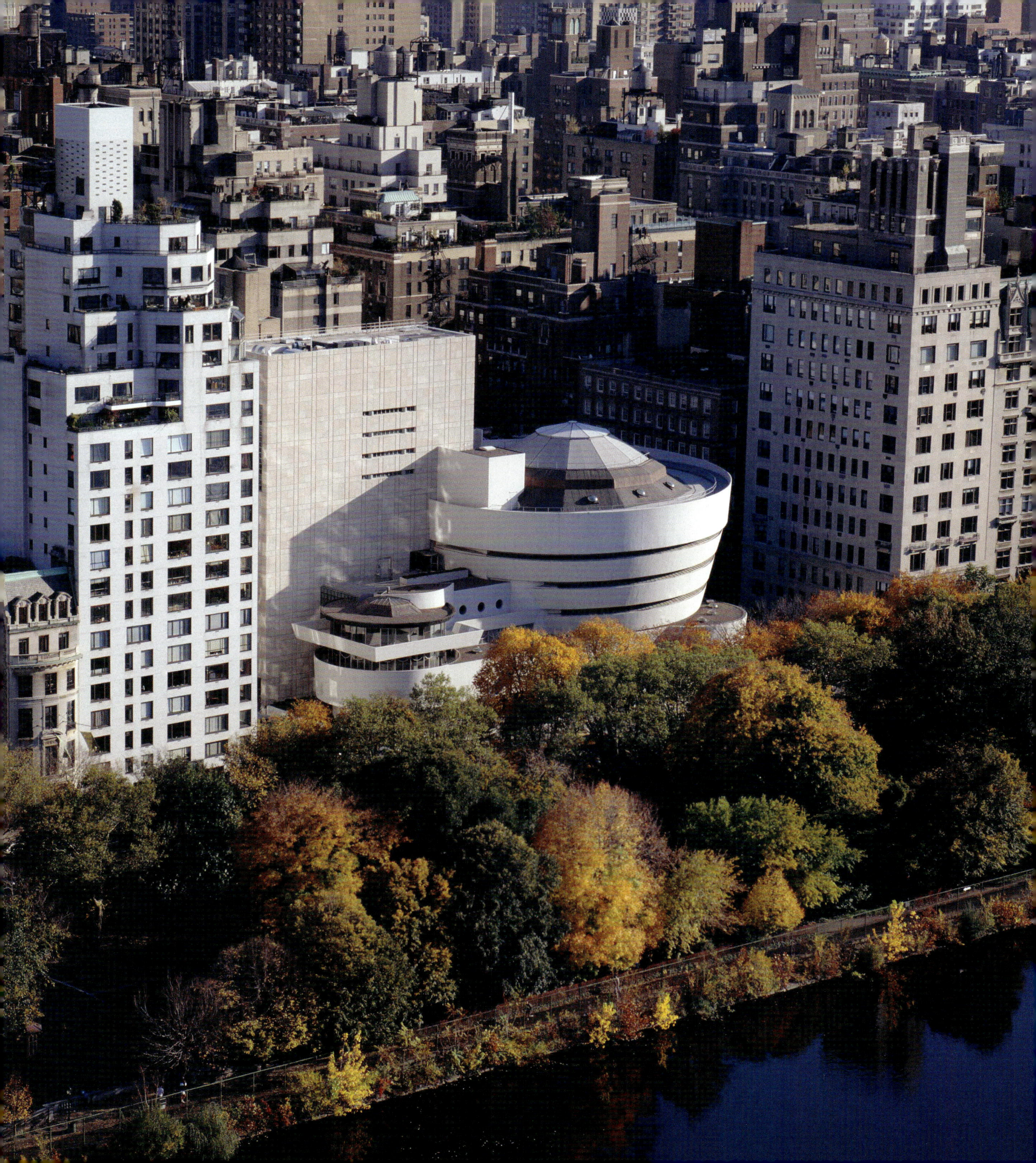

between the work on display and the building in which this exhibition takes place. Among the most important questions facing clients and architects is the question of how "visible" the architecture should be. This issue is particularly salient in relation to the building's interior—specifically, inside the actual galleries.

Most contemporary museums have large entrances and public spaces where the architecture is necessarily dominant. These spaces serve several functions: circulation of large crowds, ticketing, coat checks, as well as doubling as event spaces for both museum events and outside corporate events (a large source of revenue for many museums). The relationship between these spaces and the actual spaces reserved for the exhibition of artworks is an important one. Should strong architectural themes be visible throughout a building? Should they be restricted to certain monumental, though ancillary, spaces? Should additions to older museum buildings respect the architecture of the originals? Should they challenge them? These are just some of the many important aesthetic questions facing clients and designers when approaching the building type of a museum. Obviously, how these questions are answered depends largely on the goals and missions of the institutions asking them, as well as the individual personalities and judgments of those charged with making such decisions.

VISIBILITY OR INVISIBILITY

"Raise a lot of money for me, I'll give you good architecture. Raise even more money, I'll make the architecture disappear," architect Yoshio Taniguchi is quoted as saying in reference to his project for the 2004 expansion of the Museum of Modern Art in New York.[1] Setting aside how well he might have succeeded at designing an "invisible" museum or whether or not the museum was able to raise enough money to fully exploit Mr. Taniguchi's talents, the architect clearly acknowledges the principle that a great art museum should largely be invisible to its visitors; it should be ancillary to the work on display and should elegantly showcase the museum's collection rather than compete with it. [2]

Of course, *visibility* means different things in different types of museums. At a museum such as the Frick Collection, which seeks to preserve the feel of the home of a great collector, invisibility would signify that the visitor feels that he or she is in Mr. Henry Clay Frick's home, not in a public institution.[3] In this case, what is being hidden is not competing architecture (the Frick is one of the great residential buildings of New York City), but instead all of the necessary alterations required to turn a house from the early twentieth century into a museum that can function smoothly in the early twenty-first century, providing the proper conditions for the art on display and a comfortable and safe circulation for a visiting public.

Yet although the goal of invisibility might be shared by institutions from as far apart on the American art museum spectrum as the current edition of the Museum of Modern Art and the Frick Collection, invisibility is by no means sought by all museums. Perhaps the most radical of museum interiors, and an inspiration for many that would follow, can be found at the Solomon R. Guggenheim Museum in New York (fig. 7.1). Almost universally hailed as one of the greatest interiors (and strongest architectural statements) of the twentieth century, Frank Lloyd Wright's towering rotunda is anything but invisible. It is not merely an atrium space or entry area (though it is also both of these things); virtually all of the original gallery space opens on to this rotunda. As visitors walk up or down the ramp, they are faced with the art on display on one side and an amazingly articulated architectural void on the other. It takes a certain type of art to work well in such a space. This arrangement also puts strong limits on curatorial decisions of what can and cannot be displayed to advantage here. Large paintings that require an observer to view them from a distance or large sculpture in the round do not work well in this space. As is discussed below, the Guggenheim has addressed these problems in its later additions.

The desire for architecture to play a very visible mediating role in a visitor's experience of a museum can also be achieved through very subtle means, and the missions of some museums all but require such an approach. This approach is clearly illustrated by returning to the Museum of Modern Art, though this time in its 1939 iteration. Although sharing a "white cube" gallery aesthetic with the current edition, the original Goodwin and Stone building had a scale derived from domestic modernist architecture as well as a lobby and member penthouse recalling European avant-garde architecture. These were not intended to be seen as "neutral spaces" in the way the same types of designs might be seen today, but rather sought to establish the proper context in which to view the abstract art of modernism. This point is clearly made manifest by a comparison of an installed gallery at the Museum of Modern Art in 1939 (see fig. 5.11) and an installation photograph of modernist art hung in a traditional museum gallery, such as was found at the Armory Show when exhibited at the Art Institute of Chicago in 1913 (see fig. 6.10). In the case of the 1939 Museum of Modern Art, the gallery architecture was clearly designed to highlight the qualities of the work on display and create a proper context for its appreciation, not to compete with it.

By 1939 the Museum of Modern Art held a broad definition of art and was the first American museum to feature a Department of Architecture and Design. So to an extent, the building itself was viewed as a "museum object," as were its furniture, fixtures, and appointments. However, these more interesting touches were largely contained in the lobby, staircase, and members' lounge. Whereas they were compatible with the art in the galleries, the galleries themselves were simple white cubes. The purpose of these spaces was largely didactic: the museum sought to advance the cause of modernism, not just in painting, sculpture, photography, and film but also in architecture. Far from striving for invisibility, therefore, the museum sought to make the so-called international modernism of contemporary Europe visible in Midtown Manhattan for the first time. It is perhaps a testament

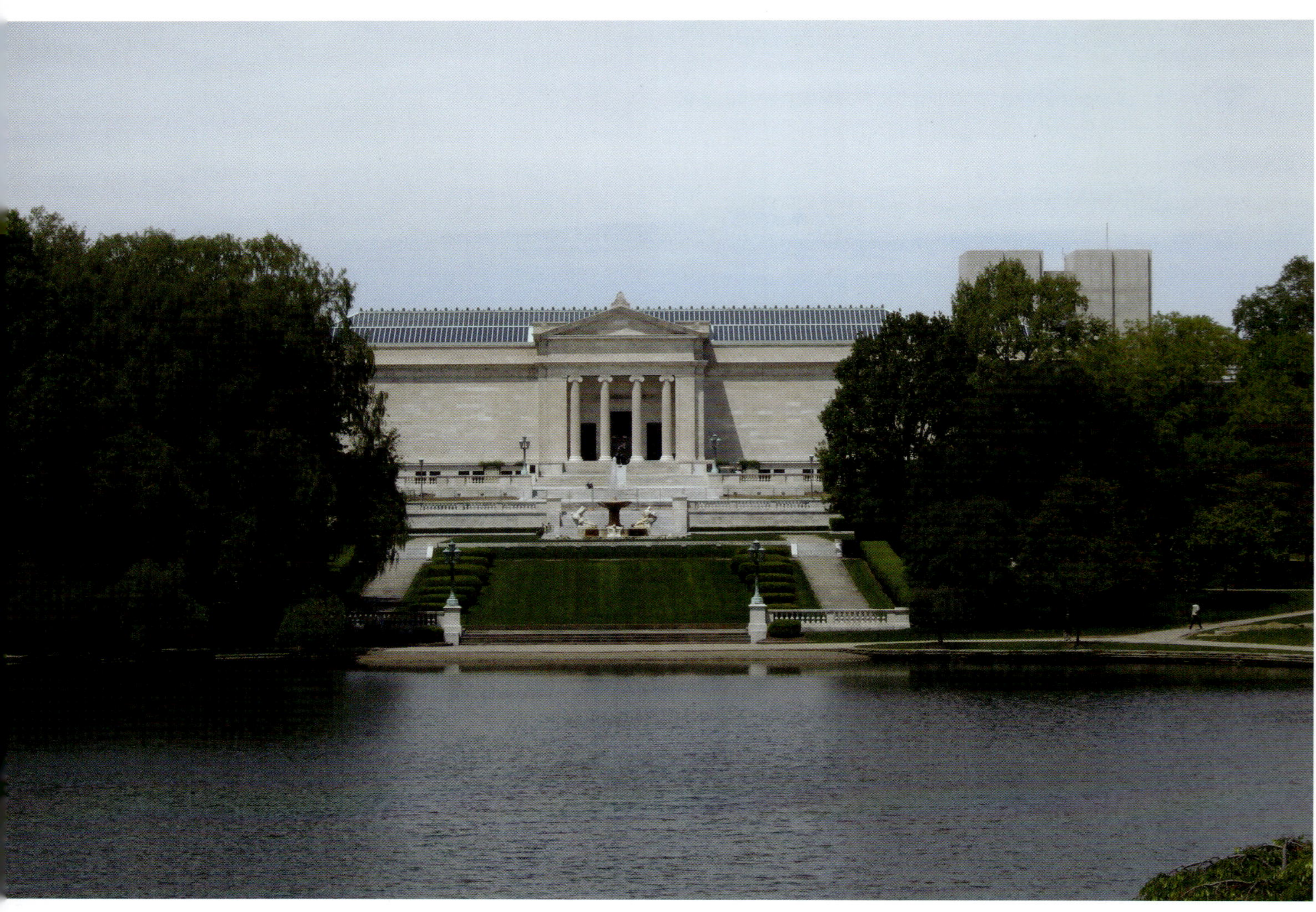

7.3. Former entrance, Cleveland Museum of Art, Hubbell and Benes, 1916. The Cleveland Museum of Art.

to the museum's successes of 1939 that in 2004 Taniguchi's modernist aesthetic at the same location could even be thought of as "invisible," though its actual scale, planning, function, and circulation owe very little to the high modernist architecture of the period between the World Wars.

RELATIONSHIPS BETWEEN BUILDING PROJECTS WITHIN A MUSEUM

Invisibility may well be a goal for which some museums strive in their buildings; however, this invisibility is obviously metaphorical, and no matter how respectfully a building is designed, it will have its own character and usually can easily be dated to within a decade or so of its construction by anyone with even a dilettante's knowledge of the history of architecture. It is not surprising that all six of the case studies analyzed in the preceding chapters of this book include expansions or

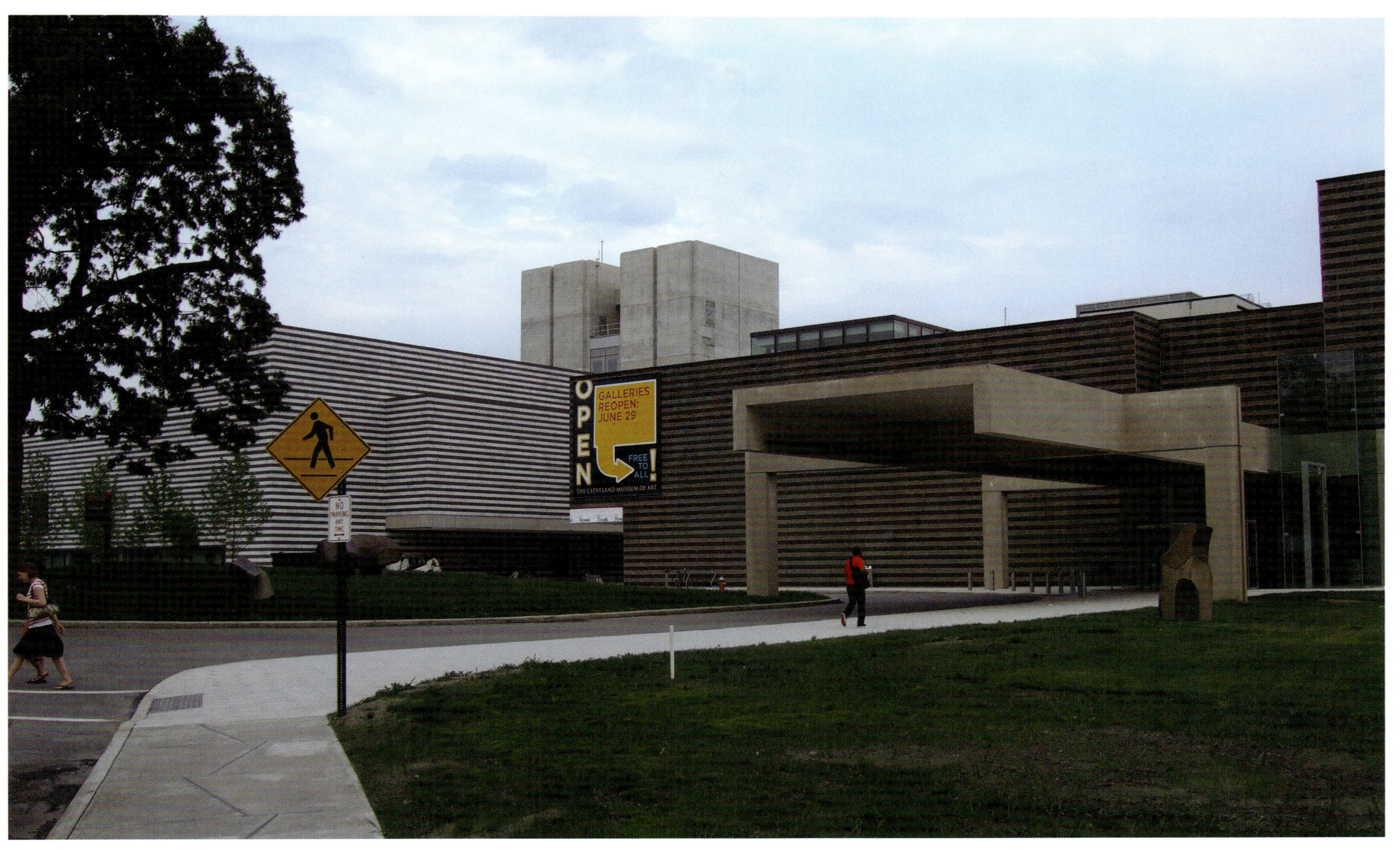

additional buildings beyond their original venue or original venue at the current location. As most museums today are already thinking of their next expansion even as they open a new wing, another important design question arises: How should additions relate to what is already built?

Naturally, this question too has no simple or universal answer. Again, both clients and architects must deeply consider the missions, traditions, and philosophies of the institutions they serve as they approach this problem. The Frick Collection, an institution that is so closely identified with its original mission and origins as a private residence, has perhaps achieved as close to a seamless integration of additions to the original fabric as possible. Few visitors to the Frick realize that the Entrance Hall, Garden Court, Oval Room, Music Room, and East Gallery were not part of the original house, nor were they designed by the same architect, or even in Henry Clay Frick's lifetime. Fewer still would imagine that the Reception Hall and the 70th Street garden date from the 1970s. Maintaining the feel and spirit of Mr. Frick's residence was deemed essential to the atmosphere the collection

7.4. Entrance to Cleveland Museum of Art, Marcel Breuer, 1971.
The Cleveland Museum of Art.

wished to maintain and to the context desired for the exhibition of the work the founder collected and the compatible works that the museum continues to acquire and exhibit. The Frick is aided by the fact that its collecting scope is limited to the types of works that Henry Clay Frick collected; no problems are created by the acquisition of more recent works on a different scale or requiring different types of lighting or climate controls. Continuity of collections and contexts allows for continuity in architectural design.

The Solomon R. Guggenheim Museum required a different kind of seamlesness in its expansion of the 1990s. Owing to the iconic status of the exterior of the museum as well as its famous interior, any alterations to the building would have to be as near to truly invisible as possible. However, due to the limitations that the helix of the rotunda placed on the amount of space available for the display of art, and the types of art that could even be displayed, the museum required more traditionally shaped, proportioned, and scaled galleries. Some art, particularly larger-scale modern and contemporary art, all but requires large white-cube galleries for proper display. In order to meet this need, architects Gwathmey Siegel & Associates built a tower on the northeast corner of the existing building (fig. 7.2). From Fifth Avenue this tower is nearly invisible; internally it is invisible from the central rotunda except where it is accessed from the ramp through doorways in the outer wall. These new galleries successfully gave the Guggenheim not only more space, but much greater curatorial freedom. However, they do interrupt the inexorable journey of moving up or down Frank Lloyd Wright's ramps, which was a major part of the spirit of the original museum. For this reason, the Guggenheim often holds separate exhibitions in the rotunda and tower galleries.

Not all museums require the architectural unity of the Frick or Guggenheim, however. In fact, some institutions benefit from a diversity of architectural scales, motifs, materiality, and designs. As discussed in Chapter 6, a plurality of buildings and wings with seemingly disparate and unrelated architecture can be a virtue at a large encyclopedic museum, as different wings can complement the different types of objects on exhibition within them. Further, the scale and proportion of galleries can more easily be adjusted to the art displayed inside: modern and contemporary painting, sculpture, and installations tend to be considerably larger than nineteenth-century and Old Master paintings. Architecture from different periods at larger encyclopedic museums itself becomes another document of the history of art. This narrative of architecture is a perfect foil and setting for the very project of the encyclopedic museum.

Accepting the principle that museum expansions do not need to be consistent with the architecture of an original building (which is the rule at museums that are not bound by the precise vision of one collector or the iconic status of a particularly important building in the history of architecture) still leaves museums and designers with some unique challenges. How does the new wing or building address and relate to the existing structures? How does the new space affect the circulation of the original? Does the new space merely provide new gallery space,

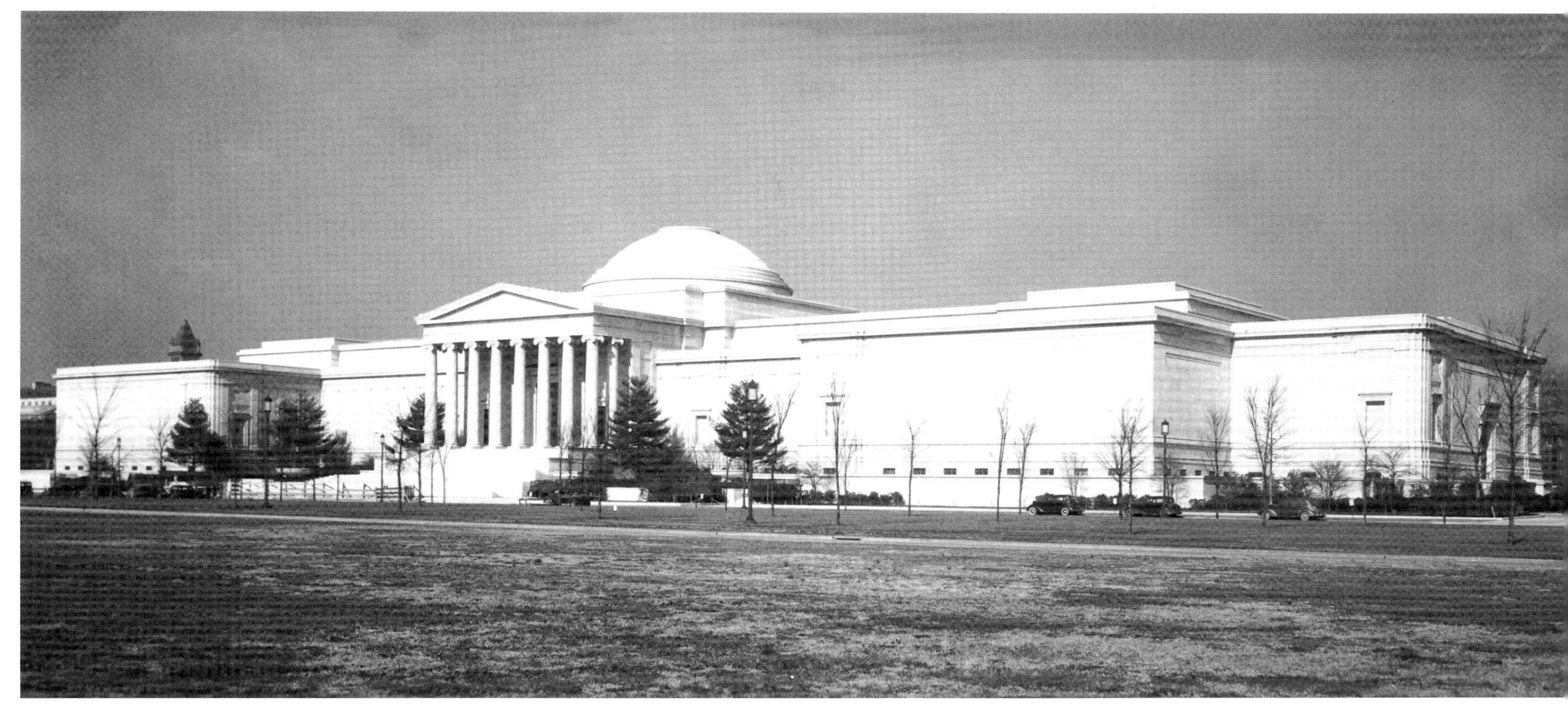

visitor amenities, and work space for employees, or does it completely transform visitors' experience of the museum? Obviously, there are different answers to these questions, and a look at the various responses of different institutions reveals the virtues and vices of some of these solutions.

The solution to these questions at the Art Institute of Chicago was to create a central spine behind the original building of 1893 from which different wings would be added (see Chapter 6 and fig. 6.19). This model preserves the primacy of the original entrance to the museum and the original building as the identity of the museum. Entering the Art Institute of Chicago from its main entrance on Michigan Avenue in 2009 is much the same experience as it would have been in 1893. Once inside, the Grand Staircase leads the visitor to the central spine of Gunsaulus Hall, from which access is given to a veritable plethora of different wings from periods ranging from the early twentieth century to the present. Each of these wings has its own character, some Beaux-Arts, others modern, postmodern, or contemporary. Each has its own scale, appropriate for the different types of work displayed within. Some of these subsequent buildings even have their own ancillary entrances, such as the Skidmore, Owings & Merrill project of the 1970s. Yet all of them seem to disappear behind the original Shepley, Ruton & Coolidge building of 1893 when the visitor approaches the museum on Michigan Avenue at Adams Street.

The Cleveland Museum of Art took a radically different course than the Art Institute of Chicago. The Cleveland Museum created a new principal entrance that completely transformed visitors' experience of the museum. As in Chicago, access to the Cleveland Museum was previously gained through a classically inspired Beaux-Arts entrance, designed by Hubbell & Benes in 1916 (fig. 7.3). However, Cleveland chose to create a new principal entrance in its subsequent, modernist expansion (fig. 7.4). The Cleveland Museum employed Marcel Breuer in 1971 (and is currently employing Rafael Viñoly for further expansion) to add a great deal of space for galleries and programming. This project succeeded in helping the museum adjust its identity and place greater emphasis on its concern with modern and contemporary art, as well as expanding amenities and educational and administrative spaces. Unfortunately, the spaces left by the former "grand entrances" are difficult to repurpose, and much of the drama of the original architecture, both from the interior and the exterior, was lost. Former entrances and the symmetrical design of the earlier, classical building can create a confusing and anticlimactic circulation for visitors.

Yet another solution to the problem of relating a major expansion to a large existing museum is that adopted by the National Gallery of Art in Washington, D.C. The strategy adopted in Washington was to build what is visually an entirely separate and autonomous building. Although I. M. Pei's East Building of 1978 (fig. 7.6) is connected to the original John Russell Pope building of 1941 (fig. 7.5), this linkage only occurs underground and is thus invisible from the National Mall. Both buildings have their own entrances and plenty of space between them, which allows each building to maintain its own identity. The contrast between the two buildings is profound, but their isolation from each other allows the differences to constitute a dialogue rather than a source of friction. This architectural contrast further telegraphs the contents of the two buildings: the Pope building contains the Old Master and nineteenth-century art, whereas the Pei building houses modern and contemporary works of art.

Not surprisingly, the solution to the issue of how visible and dominant a museum building should be differs widely from one institution to another. Likewise with the problem of whether additions should blend in or contrast with existing buildings. It is the specificity of the collections of particular museums and their unique missions that makes the art museum very nebulous as a "building type." Other building types, from hotels and retail to office buildings and banks, all tend to have the same functional requirements and differ chiefly in scale and aesthetic concerns. Art museums face all the same issues that challenge any other major building type with the addition of their responsibility to their collections, which differ from every other museum, and to their particular mission, vision, and history, which again vary from one sister institution to another. Museum boards that take on expansion and the designers they employ must be able to discern where innovation and strong architectural statements may work, and where restraint and respect for existing buildings, previous history and the collections themselves must be maintained.

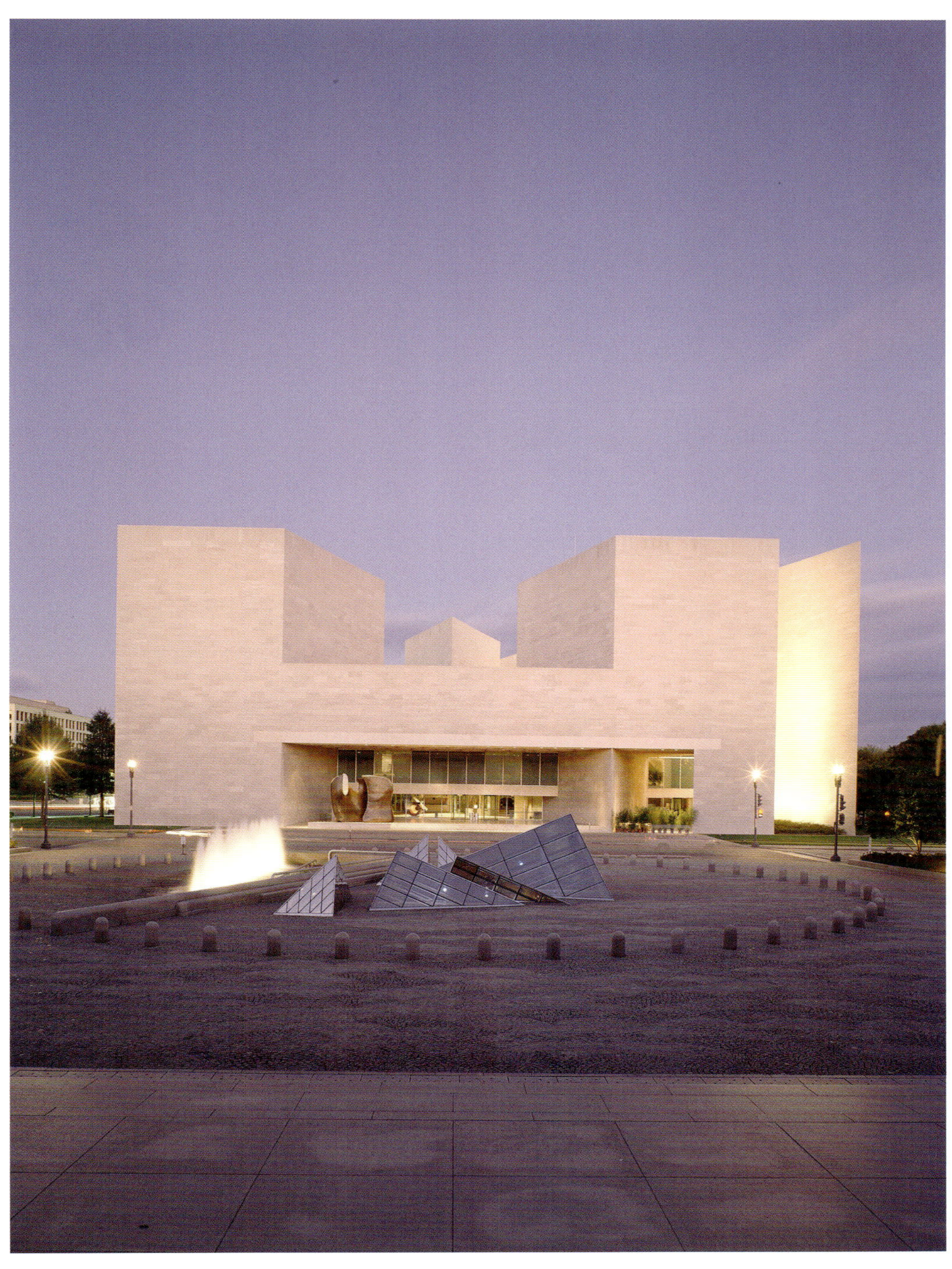

CHAPTER 8

THE ART OF THE (IM)POSSIBLE:

DESIGNING FOR CONTEMPORARY ART

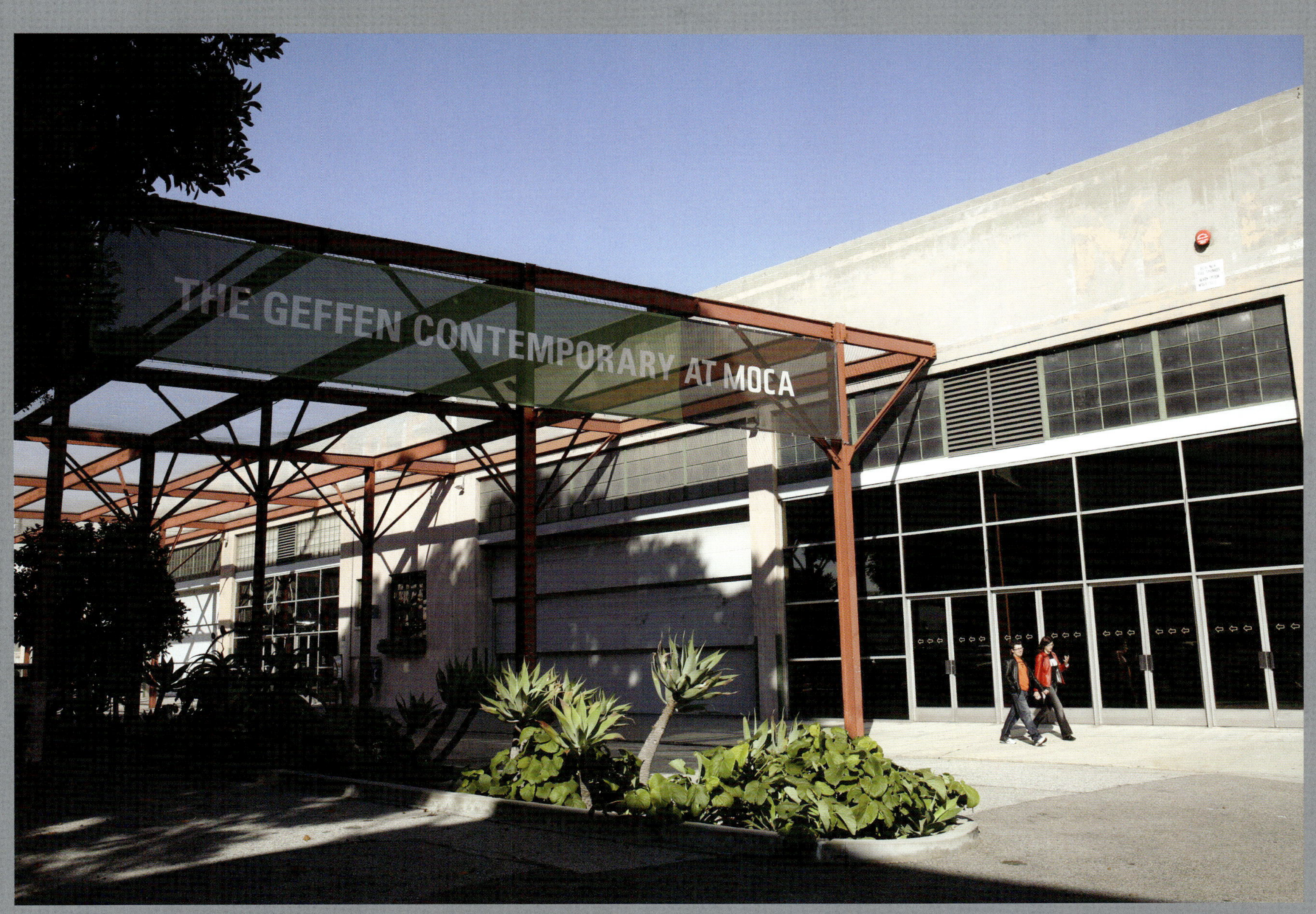

8.1. Exterior view of the "Temporary Contemporary" or Geffen Contemporary Art at MOCA, Frank Gehry, 1983.

Any museum that collects contemporary art is faced with the difficult challenge of trying to anticipate the next trends in art production. If an institution's collections are limited to the art of the past, a proper exhibition context for its holding can be established with relative ease. The correct scale, proportions, lighting, and climate of the galleries are known and finite. Not so when planning for the exhibition, collecting, and preservation of works that do not yet exist. Over the course of the twentieth and twenty-first centuries, contemporary art has grown beyond the traditional media of painting and relatively modest-sized sculpture to include all media, large installations, and even traditional techniques employed on a truly colossal scale. Galleries have become ever larger to accommodate such work. Will this trend continue or will the pendulum swing back to smaller works? No one can answer this question. Yet the growing dominance of contemporary art in our current museum culture and art world seems unlikely to change anytime soon.

THE CHALLENGE OF HOUSING CONTEMPORARY ART

In 1933 Alfred H. Barr, Jr., the founding director of the Museum of Modern Art, profoundly illustrated the unknown trajectory of contemporary art with a diagram in the shape of a torpedo inexorably moving forward into an uncertain future, with its propeller containing the art of the past that was the foundation for modernism.[1] In his initial vision for the Museum of Modern Art (the first great American museum devoted to modern art, which was, of course, the contemporary art of its time), Barr hoped to find a way to avoid having a truly "permanent" collection. He wanted to have a museum where the collection would mimic his model of a torpedo moving forward. As noted previously, he wanted a formula in place so that works could be deaccessioned or sold after fifty years to another museum, the proceeds going to the purchase of what would now be deemed the experimental contemporary art of the

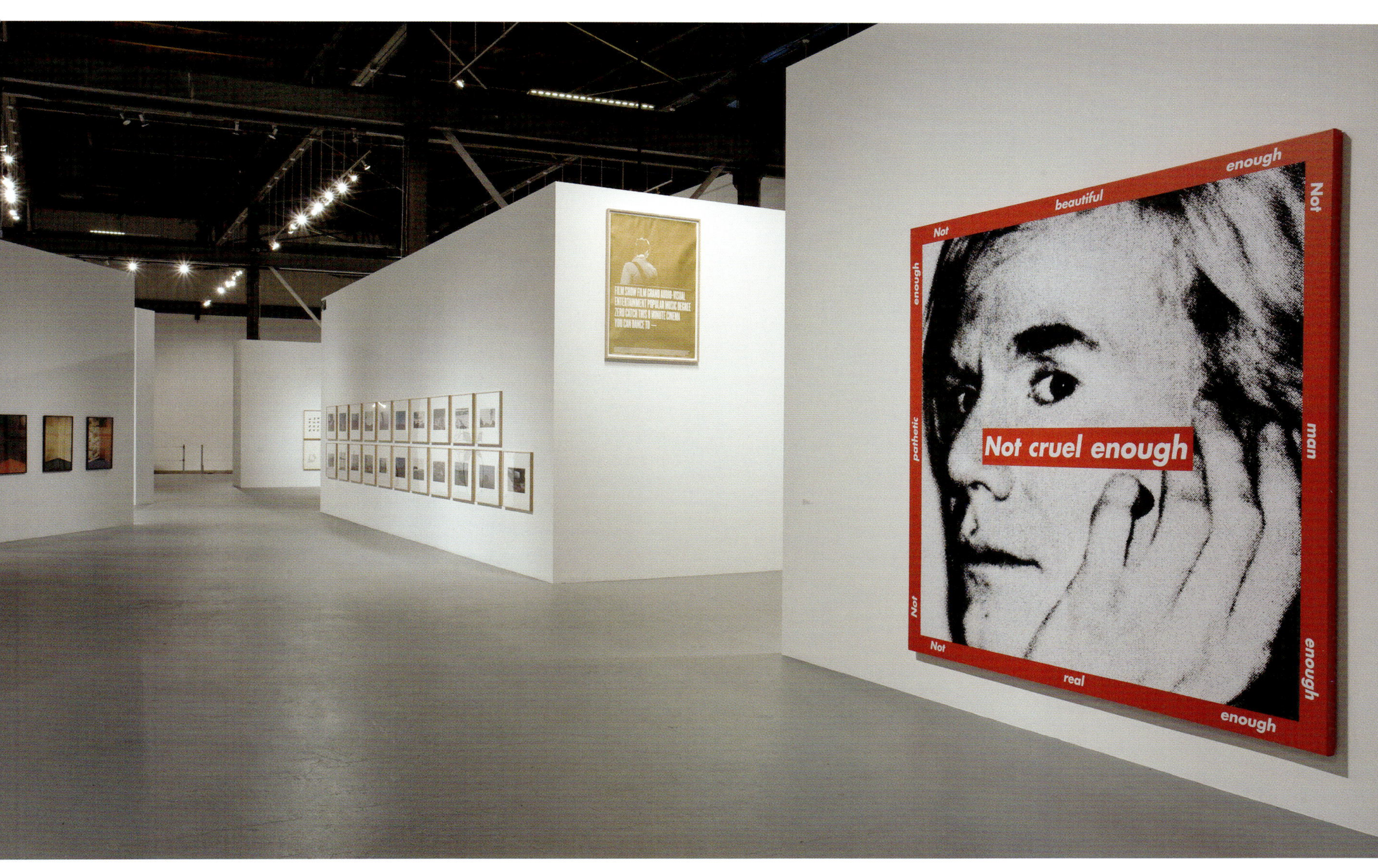

Not
beautiful
enough
Not
enough
pathetic
Not
Not cruel enough
man
Not
real
enough
enough

day. Brilliant though this conception was, it was unworkable for a number of reasons. First and foremost, other institutions were naturally reluctant to agree to acquire what the Museum of Modern Art thought would be the enduring masterpieces of contemporary art—had they been convinced of the value of such work, they would have acquired it themselves. Second, by the time many of these works reached their "retirement age," many of them had indeed become canonical and much beloved by the museum's own membership and constituency; modern masters from Cézanne to Picasso have shaped the very popular identity of the Museum of Modern Art.

When the Museum of Modern Art was founded in 1929, the words *modern* and *contemporary* were synonymous. Largely owing to the success of the collecting policy of MoMA, which was most interested in abstract European art, the term *modern* began to be associated with such artistic strategies and movements, allowing the reaction to it to be labeled *postmodern* and creating a division between the modern and the contemporary: not all contemporary art can now be considered modern, and most of the canon of modern art is no longer contemporary. Furthermore, the modern art that MoMA was designed to exhibit when its building opened in 1939 was conceived on the scale of the residential interior. Much of the contemporary art exhibited in the Museum of Modern Art today (in Taniguchi's new facility opened in 2004) is so large that no loading dock was large enough to allow for its entry into the museum, and no gallery was scaled large enough to contain it (e.g., the work of Richard Serra or Martin Puryear). The galleries that currently remain in the original Goodwin and Stone building house the departments of Photography, Prints and Drawings, and Architecture (which exhibits architectural drawings and models)—all work that is still on a relatively small scale and can be exhibited comfortably in the old galleries with their domestic proportions.

Of course, not all contemporary art is on the scale of Richard Serra's sculpture. The Menil Collection manages to house all of its work, including that of Cy Twombly and John Chamberlain, in its relatively intimately scaled galleries and pavilions. When needing a larger venue to properly exhibit its large Dan Flavin installation, it used a gutted grocery store (Richmond Hall) to house it. This approach works well within the context of the Menil's campus context, and the scale of Richmond Hall fits nicely in the Montrose neighborhood, which contains all of the Menil's buildings and the related chapels. The Menil's vision and collecting scope are not encyclopedic, however; rather, the collection is representative of a particular artistic vision and spirituality, and it is not conceived as being representative of current trends in contemporary art.

CONTEMPORARY ART IN THE ENVIRONMENT OF THE TRADITIONAL ART MUSEUM

Encyclopedic museums such as the Art Institute of Chicago and museums with open-ended collecting policies such as the Museum of Modern Art or the Whitney

Museum of American Art simply build new wings, buildings, and venues to accommodate whatever forms and sizes new art-making practices require. Older works can continue to be accommodated in their existing facilities, though it is not unusual for such institutions to use new construction as an opportunity for changing exhibiting strategies and rehanging galleries. Such expansion often leads to excellent opportunities in which the built environment is designed and constructed with specific works and types of works in mind. Special galleries for newer media such as film and video are particularly beneficial, as such work is often much better viewed in dedicated spaces.

An interesting case study indicative of some of the problems associated with building a museum dedicated to contemporary art is presented by the Los Angeles-based Museum of Contemporary Art (MOCA). In 1983 the museum established a temporary venue while it was undertaking the construction of its permanent home. This temporary facility, then called "the Temporary Contemporary" (now the Geffen Contemporary at MOCA), was a former garage for the squad cars and vehicles of the Los Angeles Police Department in the Little Tokyo neighborhood. Architect Frank Gehry was brought in to convert this space into a museum gallery. The large open plan of this facility was ideal for the display of all sorts of work on different scales and could easily be divided and redesigned with temporary partitions and architectural elements; industrial objects, automobiles, and all manner of large sculpture and installations were easily displayed (figs. 8.1, 8.2). On the completion of the museum's permanent home on Grand Avenue in Downtown Los Angeles (now known as MOCA Grand Avenue; see figs. 8.3, 8.4), it became apparent that the new facility, designed by Arata Isozaki and opened in 1986, was not capable of displaying the complete range of exhibitions that the huge, industrial space of its predecessor could easily mount. For this reason the temporary facility became a permanent satellite venue of the museum. Of course the name of this museum is subject to the same ambiguity that any museum with a permanent collection must face. Its collecting scope is defined as art since 1940 and so includes excellent representatives of such important twentieth-century art movements as abstract expressionism, pop art and op art. Although important moments in the history of art, these works are no longer "contemporary," strictly speaking, and are easily exhibited in the museum's downtown venue. The Geffen Contemporary allows for the continued exhibition of work of virtually all possible media and dimensions.

NONTRADITIONAL APPROACHES
TO THE EXHIBITION OF CONTEMPORARY ART

In recent years several institutions have endeavored to solve the conundrum of building for contemporary art through less traditional means. One of the many challenges that face all museums is achieving a correct balance between curating

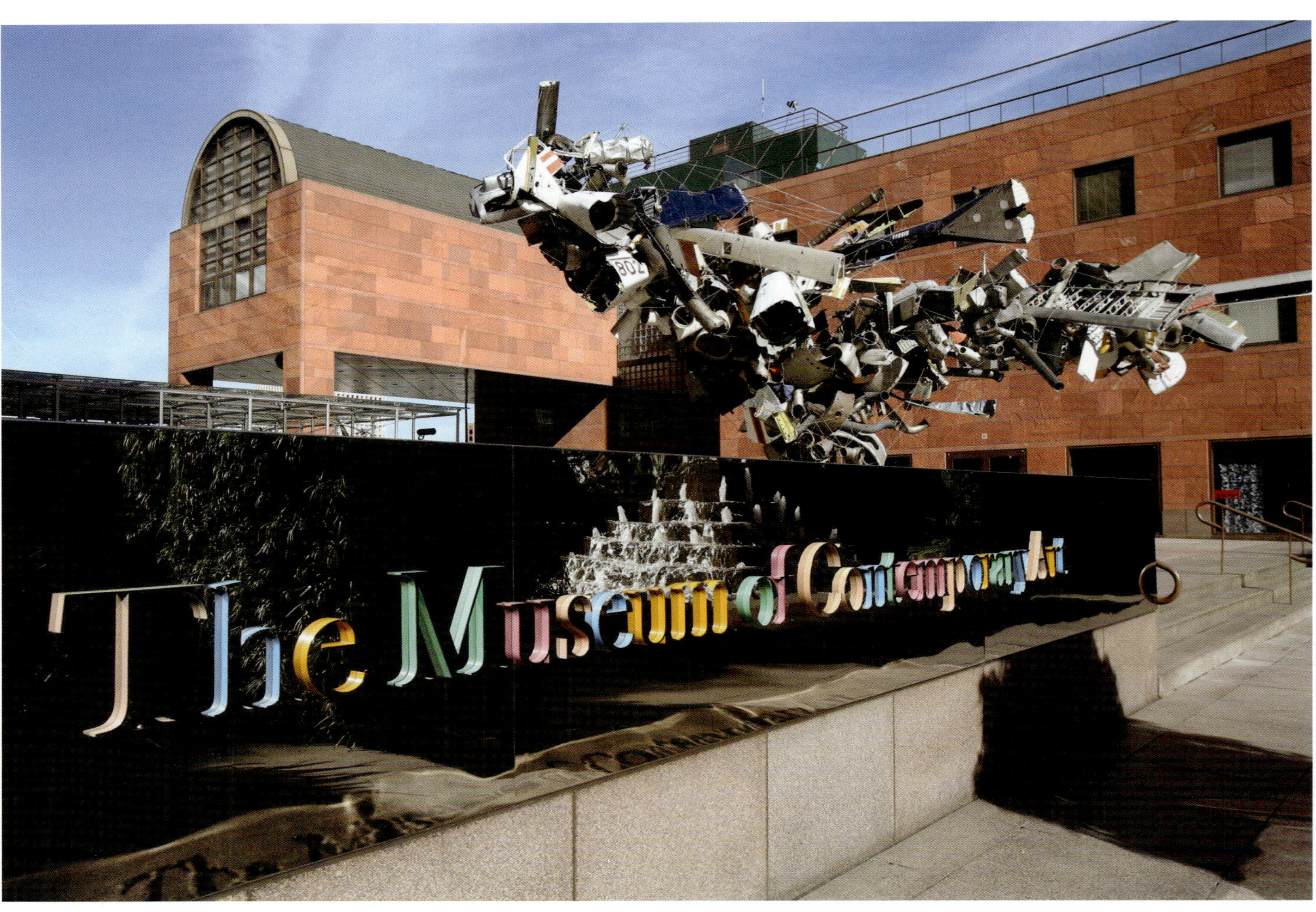

8.3. Exterior view of the MOCA Grand Avenue, Arata Isozaki, 1986.

exhibitions consisting primarily of works loaned from collectors, galleries, and other museums, and exhibiting objects from their own collections. Indeed, part of the traditional definition of an art museum, as noted, is that it is an institution that conserves, catalogs, exhibits, and makes available to scholars and the public its own permanent collections. Museums that neglect their own collections are a popular target for art critics. Some of the solutions to the problems of exhibiting contemporary art, adopted by exhibiting institutions in the twenty-first century, involve moving away from the traditional model of the museum altogether.

The New Museum of Contemporary Art in New York, for example, is truly committed to contemporary art, in its narrowest definition—that is, art made by living artists. Although named the "New Museum," this institution is not a museum in the strictest, most traditional sense of the word because it has no permanent collection; all of the works exhibited within it are loans from artists, galleries, and other institutions. In the art world such institutions are usually referred to by the German name of *Kunsthallen* or exhibition halls. Unlike the typical European *Kunsthalle,* however, the New Museum offers all of the visitor services and amenities

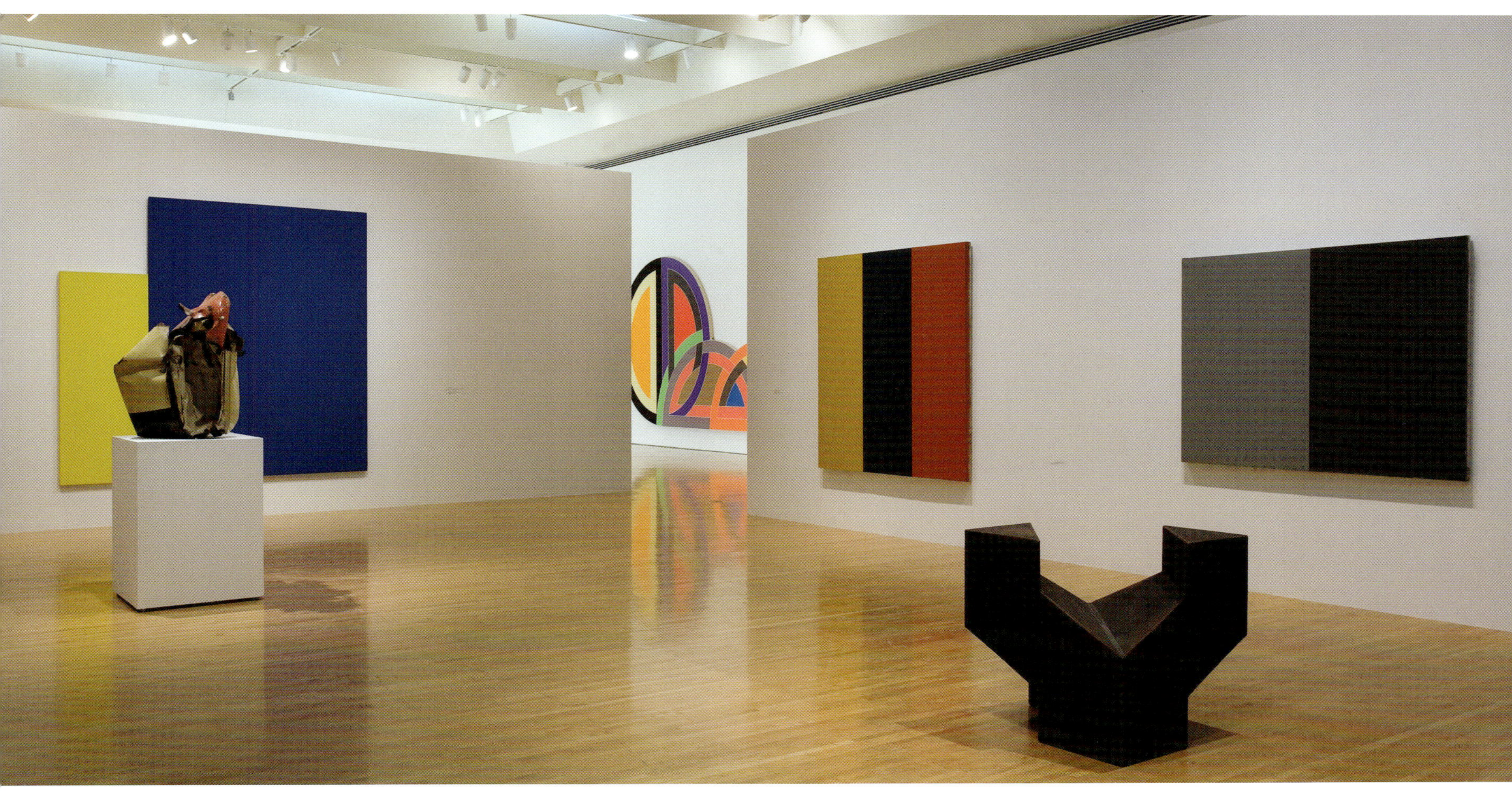

8.4. Interior view of the MOCA Grand Avenue, Arata Isozaki, 1986.

typical of a contemporary museum, including a cafe, bookstore, and auditorium. The New Museum has its own curatorial staff, publishes catalogs, and performs the types of scholarly work usually undertaken only by traditional museums (unlike the various alternative art spaces found throughout the United States and abroad). This unusual arrangement allows not only for the elimination of the semantic problem of when artwork ceases to be contemporary; it avoids completely the problems of a "permanent collection" as articulated by Alfred Barr in his "Torpedo Report."

Founded in 1977, the New Museum opened its current facility in December 2007, located on the Bowery on Manhattan's Lower East Side, a district itself in transition and becoming a home to both contemporary artists and the galleries that represent them. Designed by architects Kazuyo Sejima and Ryue Nishizawa/ SANAA of Tokyo, the New Museum is a stack of large, simple white cubes that present artists and curators with a great deal of freedom (figs. 8.5 and 8.6). In plan and organization this facility is largely an homage to Marcel Breuer's Whitney Museum, with an open ground floor containing a bookstore, a café, and a small gallery. Access to the upper galleries is through two elevators, one a freight elevator

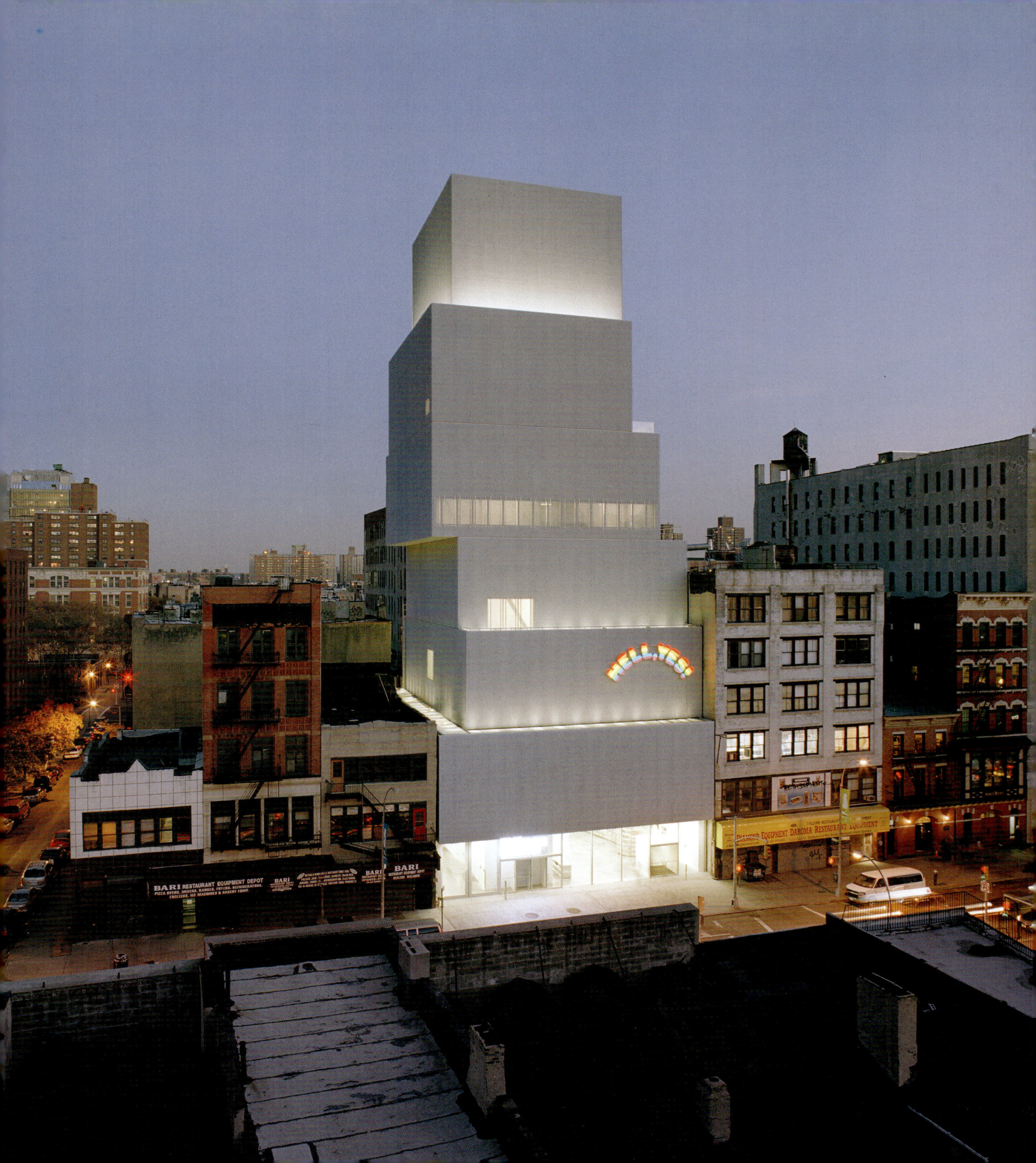
HELL, YES!
BARI RESTAURANT EQUIPMENT DEPOT
EQUIPMENT DAKOMA RESTAURANT EQUIPMENT

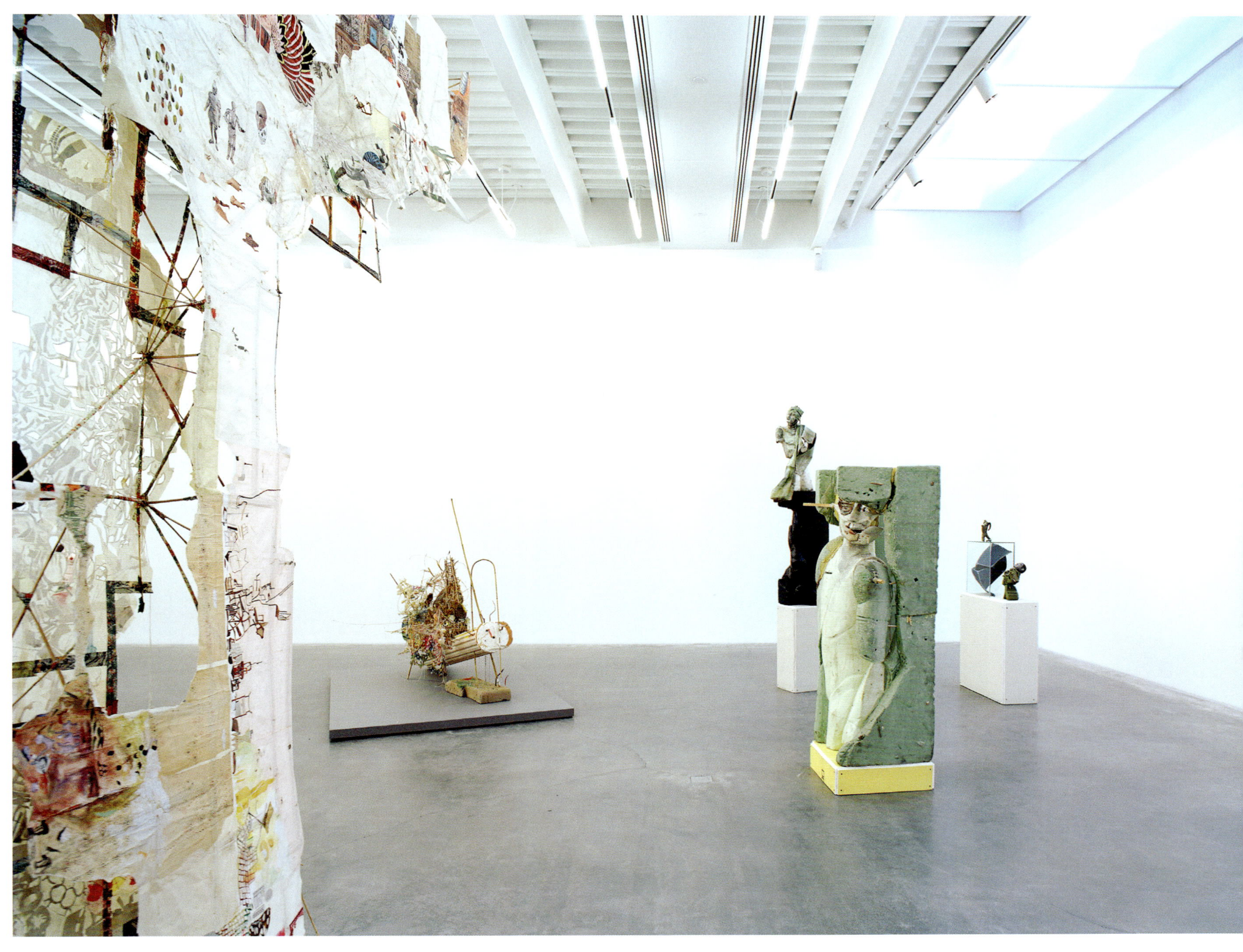

8.5. Exterior view of the New Museum, Kazuyo Sejima and Ryue Nishizawa/ SANAA, 2007. Photograph © Dean Kaufman.

8.6. Interior view of the New Museum, Kazuyo Sejima and Ryue Nishizawa/ SANAA, 2007. Photograph © Dean Kaufman.

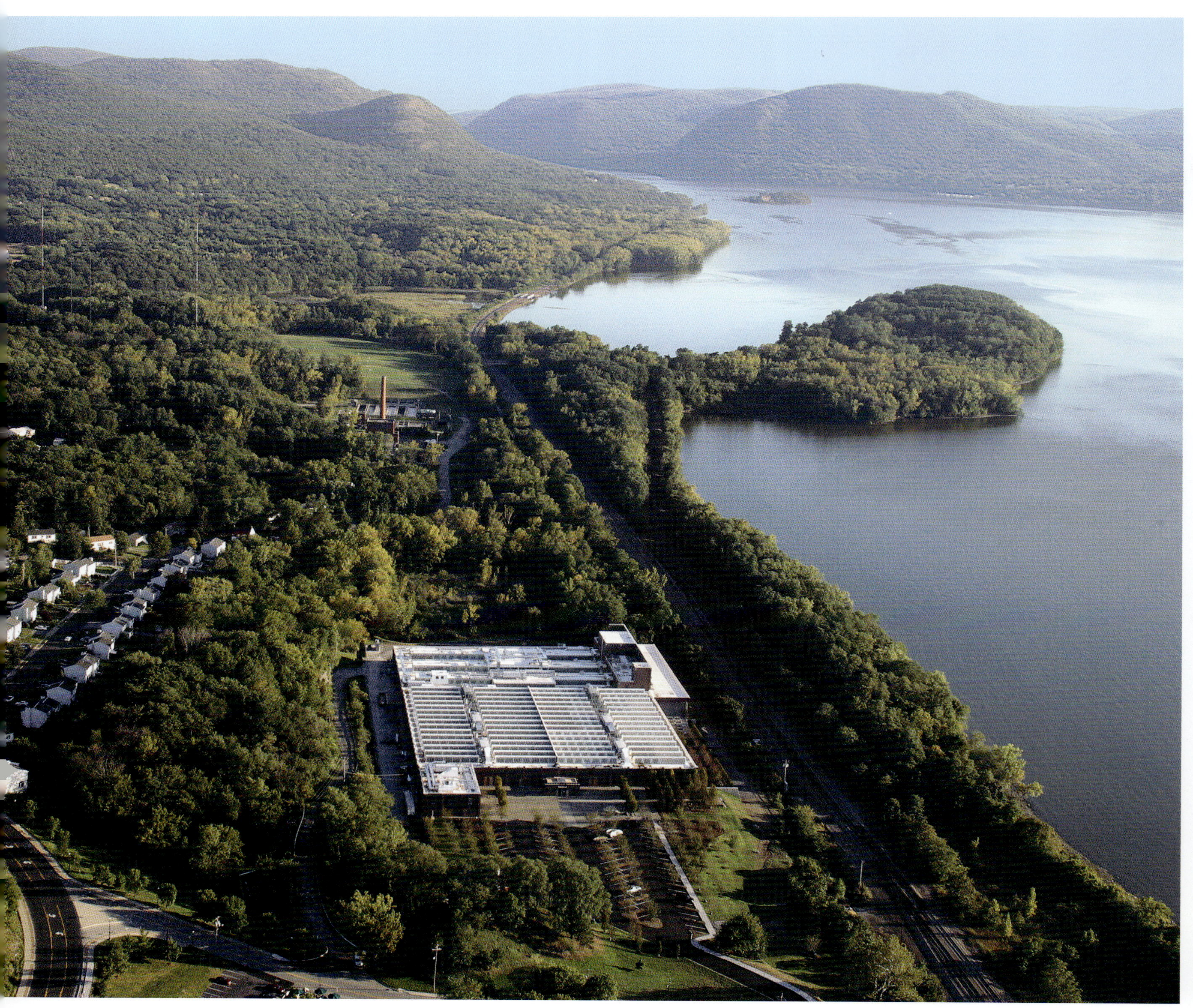

8.7. Exterior view of DIA: Beacon, Riggio Galleries, Robert Irwin and OpenOffice, 2003.

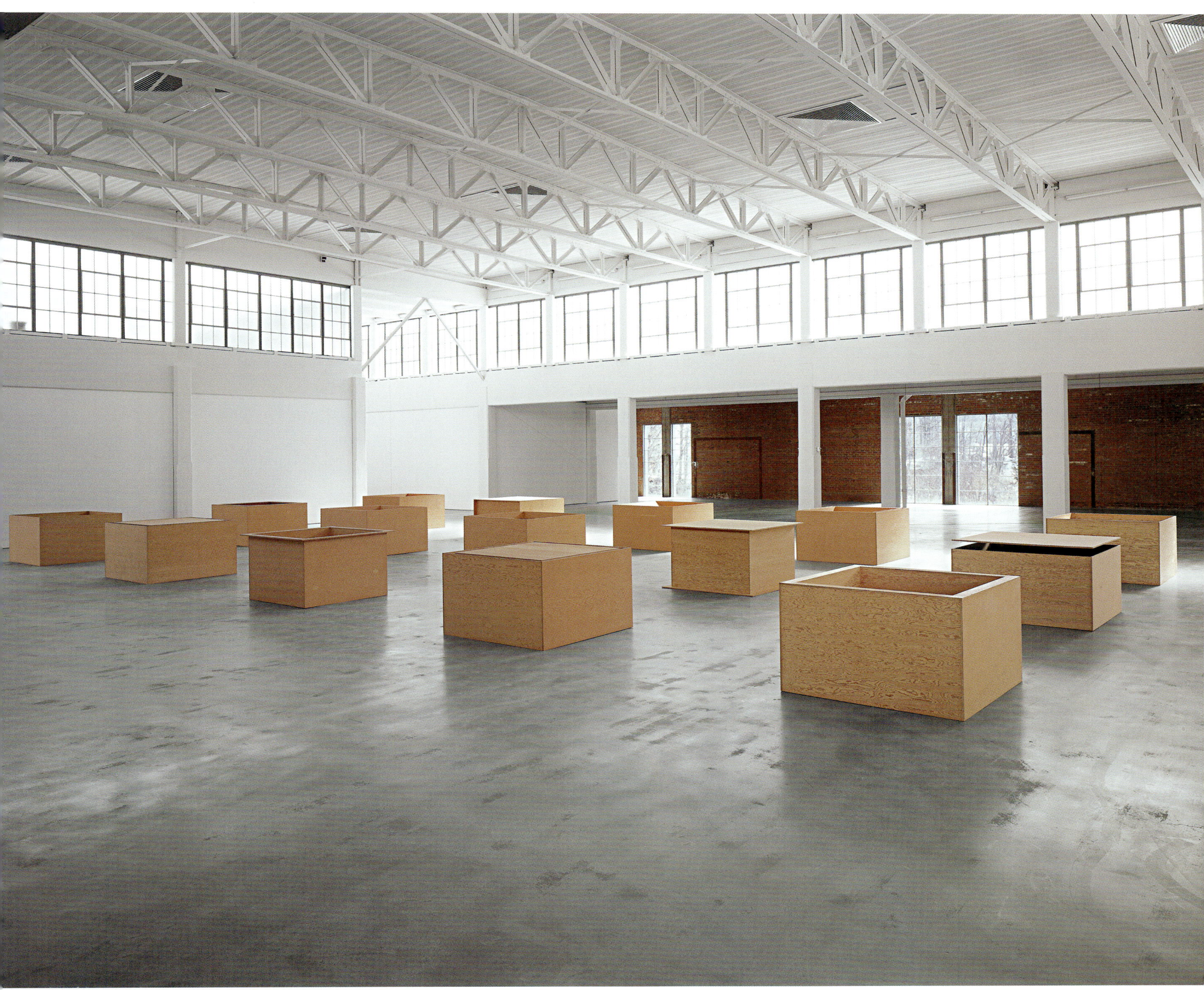

8.8. Interior view of DIA: Beacon, Riggio Galleries, Robert Irwin and OpenOffice, 2003

as at the Whitney. The galleries above are also free plans, as at the Whitney. Such large free plans for galleries permit the greatest amount of curatorial freedom possible within the overall footprint of a building, with no walls or barriers limiting the possible arrangement of works on exhibition. Such open plans also allow for the introduction of partitions and museum furniture, as needed, for a specific installation. The exterior also can be seen as a riff on Breuer's Whitney, with its stack of cubes at different levels of projection from the street.

A strategy nearly opposite that of the New Museum was pursued by the DIA Foundation with its construction of the DIA: Beacon, Riggio Galleries located in the town of Beacon in New York State's Hudson Valley. Housed in a former Nabisco packaging factory built in 1929 and designed by architect Louis N. Wirshing, Jr., DIA: Beacon contains a permanently installed collection of works acquired by collectors Philippa de Menil (daughter of John and Dominique de Menil; works from the 1960s and 1970s) and Heiner Friedrich (works from the 1970s and 1980s; see figs. 8.7 and 8.8). While the collection includes work by such artists as Andy Warhol, it is best known for its extraordinary holdings in 1970s art, emphasizing minimalist art and including works by such artists as Richard Serra, Agnes Martin, John Chamberlain, Gerhard Richter, Dan Flavin, Donald Judd, Bernd and Hilla Becher and Louise Bourgeois.

Like the New Museum, DIA: Beacon provides many of the visitor amenities found at more traditional museums, including a bookstore and café. The elements of the traditional museum that are missing at DIA are galleries devoted to loan shows and an open-ended collecting policy. DIA: Beacon also avoids the conundrum of Barr's "torpedo" by functioning as a snapshot of a moment in the history of contemporary art. Although the works on display will cease to be "contemporary" over time, the installation will continue to provide a context for the moment in art history from which they came. Even the installation of the works becomes a document of the artmaking (and curatorial) practices of the last third of the twentieth century. For this reason the design of the venue assumes particular importance, for it, like the work on exhibition, is conceived of as permanent. The former industrial space of the Nabisco factory is an ideal setting for the large-scale work on display within this museum. Many of the works themselves are on a large, industrial scale, often made of the very materials and even substance of the product of heavy industry (such as the giant steel sculptures of Richard Serra or the crushed automobiles of John Chamberlain). The natural lighting provided by the sawtooth roof of the factory works very well, and the large, free plan is essential for the display of such works. The conversion of the factory to its museum function was designed by artist Robert Irwin and architectural firm OpenOffice and opened to the public in 2003.

Obviously, DIA: Beacon, which is a permanent installation, and the New Museum, which has no collection, represent two extremes in recent architecture for contemporary art. Many other important, recent, and contemporary art venues have incorporated various elements from more traditional institutions and fused them

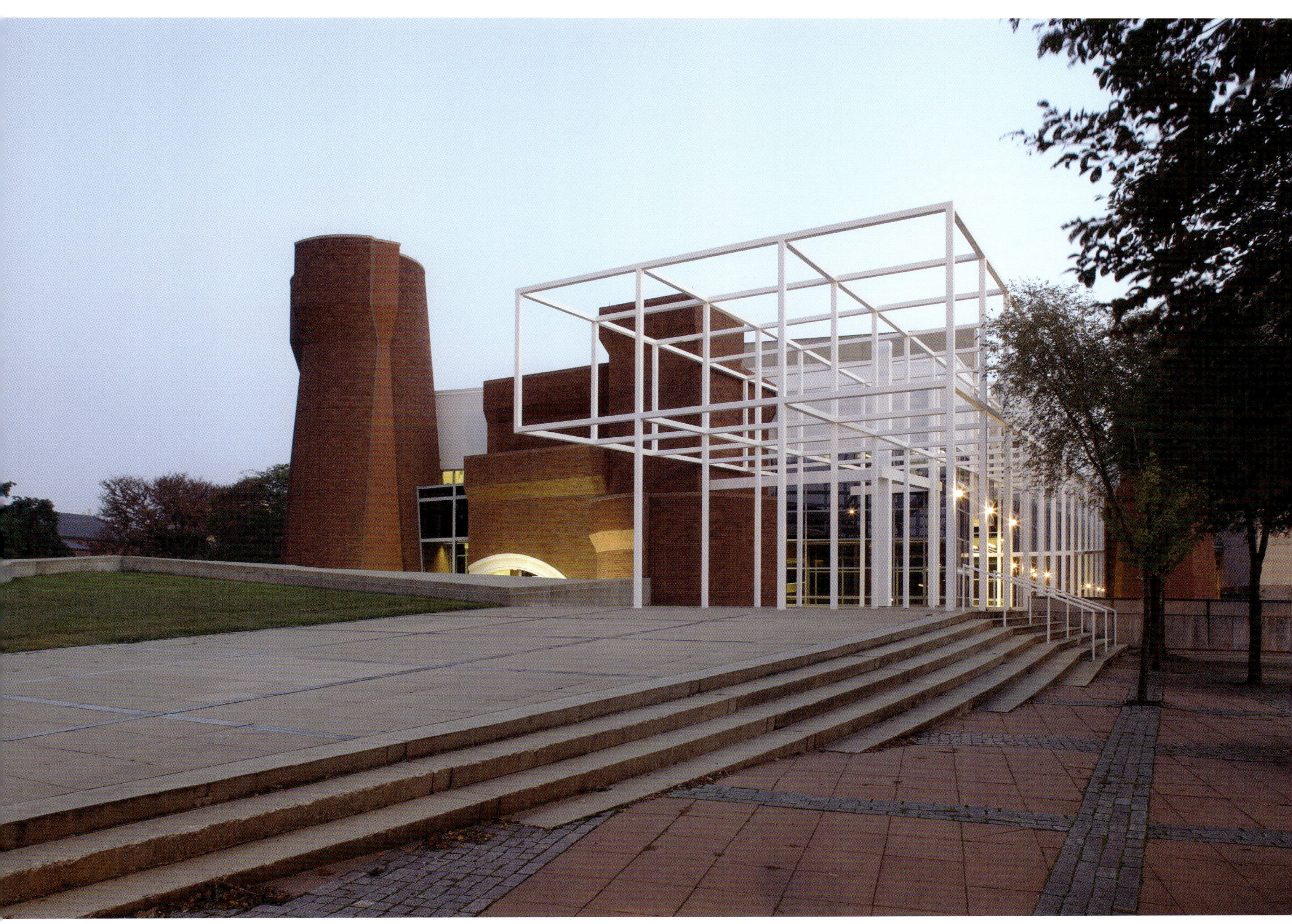

8.9 Exterior view of the Wexner Center
for the Arts, The Ohio State University,
Columbus, Ohio, Eisenman/Trott
Architects, 1989. Wexner Center for the
Arts, Columbus, Ohio.

with radical new architectural statements that are salient works in their own right. Among these the Wexner Center for the Arts, at Ohio State University in Columbus Ohio (designed by Peter Eisenman and Richard Trott and opened in 1989), stands out. The Wexner was among the first of Eisenman's large public commissions and a strong example of what he termed "deconstructivist architecture," with walls and ceilings dissolving into open grids and parts of towers recalling the nineteenth-century armory that previously stood on its site (fig. 8.9). In addition to gallery space, the Wexner has spaces for film screenings and the performing arts as well as a bookstore and cafe. Though chiefly an exhibition space, the Wexner features a permanent landscape installation by artist Maya Lin.

In 2006 the Institute of Contemporary Art/Boston (ICA/Boston) opened a new facility, designed by Diller, Scofidio & Renfro. This building followed the museum's decision to begin assembling a permanent collection in the year 2000 (the ICA/Boston had previously been a *Kunsthalle* exclusively), though exhibitions of borrowed objects are still the major emphasis of the institution. The new ICA/Boston is notable for its architecture, which directly engages its site on the Boston waterfront. Unlike many museums that tend to make entrances and atriums the centerpieces of architectural statements, the ICA/Boston's "mediatheque" (a gallery with computer stations that can be used by the public to research artists, exhibitions, and the collection) and theater are both built facing the waterfront, terminating with glass walls that directly open onto the water (fig. 8.10). Such engagement with its stunning site works well to enhance the patron's visit to the museum without distracting from the work on exhibition in the galleries. The galleries here are spacious and column free, permitting great latitude regarding what types of objects can be displayed.

Indeed, as contemporary art becomes more and more popular with the general public and ever-more-dominant and sought after in major public collections, the various challenges it presents to museum professionals, architects, and designers will become increasingly important. As the diversity revealed by this brief survey of some recent projects illustrates, there is no single approach or simple solution to the problem of designing exhibition venues for contemporary art. One hundred years ago, art museums in America tended to collect similar types of works, chiefly in the media of painting and sculpture; most of the buildings that housed these collections were symmetrically designed Beaux-Arts buildings. Today all manner of work is made and collected, in virtually every conceivable medium; it can therefore come as no surprise that the buildings that house such work no longer follow the rules and traditions of their antecedents. We live in fertile times that evoke a myriad of artistic responses; the structures built for collections of such work are part and parcel of these times. The success of an art museum building can only be assessed through consideration of how the architecture addresses the work collected or exhibited within it, how it helps to make such work accessible to museum visitors, and how it facilitates the preservation of this work. Over time, the buildings themselves become documents in the history of art.

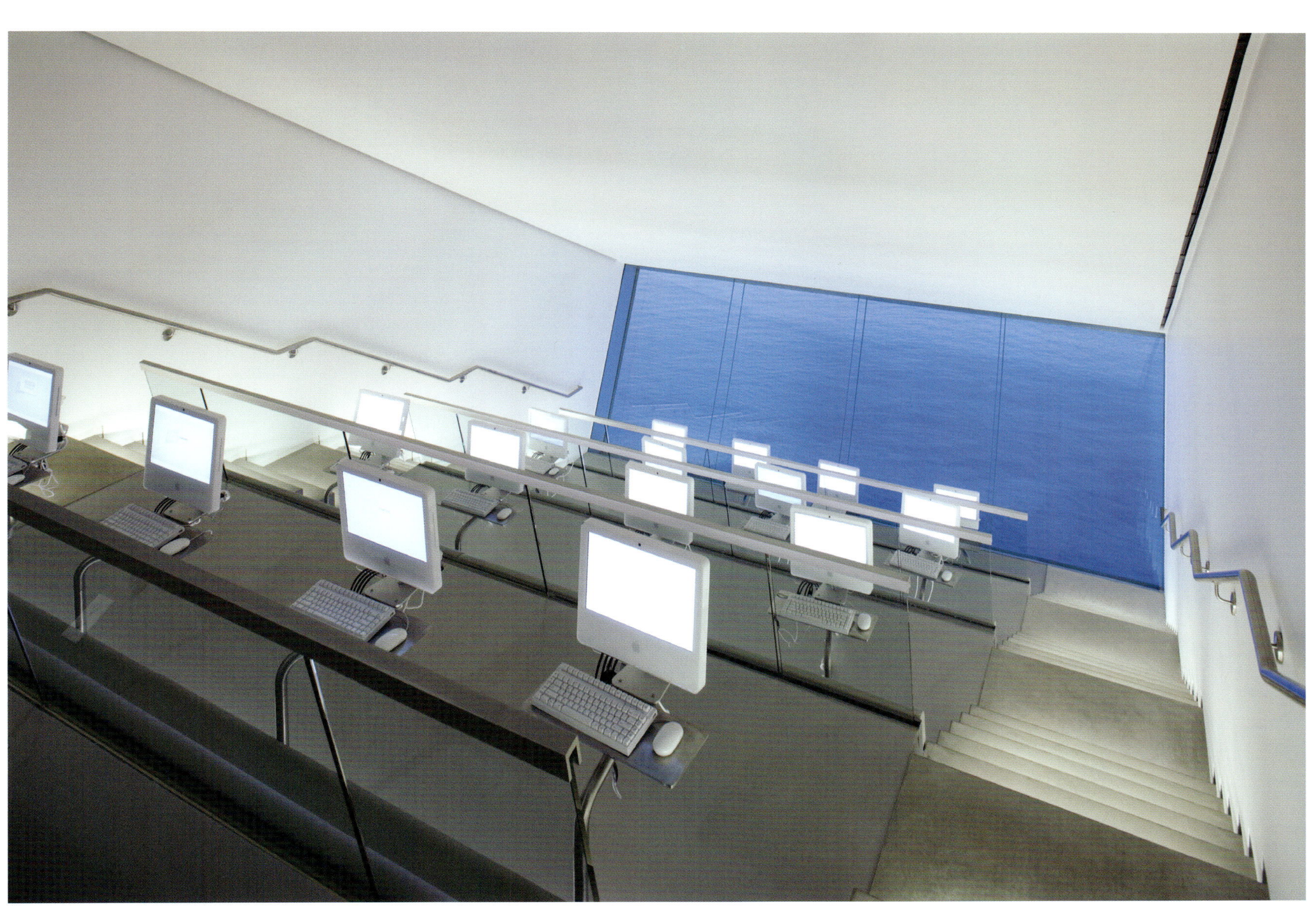

8.10 Interior view of the Poss
Family Mediatheque, The Institute of
Contemporary Art/Boston. Diller Scofidio
+ Renfro Architects. Photo: Iwan Baan.

ENDNOTES

INTRODUCTION

1 Heckscher, Morrison H. *The Metropolitan Museum of Art: An Architectural History*. New York: The Museum, 1995.

2 See "Muses" and "museum." *The Oxford Classical Dictionary,* 2nd Edition. Oxford: Oxford University Press, 1970.

3 Flavius Josephus. *The Great Roman–Jewish War*. Mineola, NY: Dover (VII.5.7, pp. 392–393), 2004.

CHAPTER 1

1 Much has been written on Henry Clay Frick as a collector and the formation of his art collection. A very complete yet concise introduction can be found in Bailey, Colin B. *Building the Frick Collection: An Introduction to the House and its Collections*. New York: The Frick Collection in association with Scala, 2006. An in-depth look at all of Frick's residences and their history as residences is available in Sanger, Martha Frick Symington. *The Henry Clay Frick Houses: Architecture, Interiors, Landscapes in the Golden Era*. New York: Monacelli Press, 2001.

2 All extracts from the will of Henry Clay Frick are from the Frick Family Papers on deposit from the Helen Clay Frick Foundation, housed at the The Frick Collection/Frick Art Reference Library Archives, New York.

3 Articles of incorporation from the Frick Family Papers on deposit from the Helen Clay Frick Foundation, housed at The Frick Collection/Frick Art Reference Library Archives, New York.

4 For a detailed history of the formation of the Frick Art Reference Library during its early years, see Knox, Katharine McCook. *The Story of the Frick Art Reference Library: The Early Years*. New York: The Library, 1979.

5 These documents survive in the Clapp Notebooks now housed in The Frick Collection/Frick Art Reference Library Archives and form the source of the documents and sketches here presented and discussed.

6 From "Provisional Status as of January 28, 1932," Clapp Notebook 1, The Frick Collection/Frick Art Reference Library Archives.

7 From "Report on the Plans for Alterations and Additions to The Frick Collection as Submitted by John Russell Pope, September 15," Clapp Notebook 1, The Frick Collection/Frick Art Reference Library Archives.

8 Her sketches are preserved in Clapp Notebook 2, The Frick Collection/Frick Art Reference Library Archives, dated February 28, 1932.

9 Press packet cover letter, from The Frick Collection Central Files, 1935, The Frick Collection/Frick Art Reference Library Archives, dated December 11, 1935.

10 Data in this table are derived from "Comparative Table of Floor Areas, Present Library and Proposed Library, November 3, 1932," The Frick Collection, Records of Organizing Director, Frederick Mortimer Clapp, Notebook 2, The Frick Collection/The Frick Art Reference Library Archives.

11 The information in this section comes from an interview the author held with Ms. Anne L. Poulet, director of The Frick Collection, on May 13, 2008.

CHAPTER 2

1 Details on the life of John and Dominique de Menil are taken largely from the obituary of John de Menil in *The Houston Post,* June 10, 1973. Author's copy courtesy of the Menil Archives, the Menil Collection, Houston, Texas, hereafter Menil Archives.

2 One hundred sixty-three exhibitions total. This figure is taken from the Exhibition History file at the Menil Archives. All exhibition information in this section is from this file.

3 For chronology and history of the conflicts surrounding the commission and construction of the Rothko Chapel, see Elliott, Clare, and Miranda Isabel Lash. 2007. *The Menil Collection. Art Spaces*. London: Scala Publishers, 2007.

4 See note 1.

5 "Museum Projections," no date [1981], Menil Archives.

6 "Menil Collection to Be Housed at New Facility in Houston, Texas," October 10, 1981, the Menil Archives.

7 "Statement," issued with press release, October 10, 1981, Menil Archives.

8 "Project Information," December 16, 1981, Menil Archives.

9 "Presentation by Renzo Piano," April 21, 2007, transcript of recording of presentation, Menil Archives.

10 Quotations of Mr. Helfenstein are taken from an interview conducted over the telephone on November 20, 2008.

11 For a transcript of Barr's early ideas regarding the collection of the Museum of Modern Art and for his diagrams outlining a narrative of the history of modern art, see Appendix B: Report on the Permanent Collection, Museum of Modern Art, 1933.

CHAPTER 3

1 Trustees' names and date of creation of trust as well as following block quotations taken from "Deed of Trust, Whitney Museum of American Art," November 27, 1935, Frances Mulhall Achilles Library, Archives, Whitney Museum of American Art, New York, hereafter Whitney Archives.

2 "Statement issued by Mr. Taylor on behalf of Mr. Osborn [William Church Osborn, president of the Metropolitan Museum] and Mrs. Miller [Flora Whitney Miller, president of the Whitney Museum] at the annual meeting of the Corporation of the Metropolitan Museum of Art, January 18, 1943," Whitney Archives.

3 "Whitney Museum Becomes Part of the Metropolitan Museum of Art," *New York Herald Tribune,* January 19, 1943; copy consulted at Whitney Archives.

4 "Notes on the Architecture of the New Whitney Wing," undated Whitney internal document, probably from 1943, Whitney Archives.

5 For further discussion of the Metropolitan Museum's expansion plans of the early 1940s and the proposed Whitney Wing, see Heckscher, Morrison H. 1995. *The Metropolitan Museum of Art: An architectural history*. New York: The Museum.

6 Letter to Mrs. G. Macculloch Miller, dated February 3, 1944, Whitney Archives.

7 Announcement, dated October 1, 1948, Whitney Archives.

8 See Chapter 5: The Museum of Modern Art; Chapter 8: The Art of the (Im)possible: Designing a Museum for Contemporary Art; and Appendix B: Report on the Permanent Collection, Museum of Modern Art, 1933.

9 Letter dated May 31, 1949 from Flora Whitney Miller (president, Whitney Museum) to Thomas W. Braden (secretary, Museum of Modern Art), Whitney Archives.

10 "Whitney Museum to Erect New Building in Garden of Museum of Modern Art," joint press release of the Museum of Modern Art and the Whitney Museum of American Art, May 31, 1949, Whitney Archives.

11 See Peter Reed, "The Space and the Frame: Philip Johnson as the Museum's Architect" in Johnson, Philip. *Philip Johnson and the Museum of Modern Art*. Studies in modern art, 6. New York: Museum of Modern Art, 1998.

12 The terms of this sale, as well as the composition of the collection being liquidated were designated in a letter dated October 11, 1949 from Flora Whitney Miller to the Museum of Modern Art concerning the coordination of the collections of the two museums, Whitney Archives.

13 Olsberg, R. Nicholas. *Breuer's Whitney: An Anniversary Exhibition, September 11–*

December 8, 1996. Collection in context. New York: Whitney Museum of American Art, 1996.

14 "Whitney Museum Announces Plans for Purchase of New Site for Enlarged Museum and Sale of Its Present Building to Modern Museum," press release dated June 17, 1963, Whitney Archives.

15 Square footage numbers extracted from undated document (c. 1961–1963), "Whitney Museum, Existing Usable Space and Estimated Requirements in New Building," Whitney Archives.

16 *A Program for the New Whitney Museum of American Art: In the Service of American Art*, 1964, Whitney Archives.

17 Quotations and chronology regarding the genesis of the Michael Graves project are from "Expansion History," Whitney internal document, dated February 7, 1990, Whitney Archives.

18 Nicolai Ouroussoff, "Whitney's Downtown Sanctuary," *The New York Times,* May 1, 2008.

19 "Mission Statement" from Long-Range Planning Committee, Statement of Policy, December 1992, Whitney Archives.

CHAPTER 4

1 "Grand Opening of the Georgia O'Keeffe Museum set for July 1997 in Santa Fe," press release of the Georgia O'Keeffe Museum, February 5, 1997, Georgia O'Keeffe Museum Research Center Institutional Archives, hereafter O'Keeffe Archives.

2 "Anne Windfohr Wed to John L. Marion," *The New York Times,* May 27, 1988.

3 From press release cited in note 1.

4 "Georgia O'Keeffe Museum Research Center: Research Opportunities in American Modernism," 2007 information brochure, O'Keeffe Archives.

5 "Georgia O'Keeffe Foundation to Transfer Assets to Georgia O'Keeffe Museum," press release dated May 31, 2005, O'Keeffe Archives.

6 Previous purpose of building from press release quoted in note 1.

7 "Research Center Facts," Georgia O'Keeffe Museum website, retrieved August 30, 2008.

8 For discussion of the Museum of Modern Art's role in developing the canon of modernism, see Chapters 5 and 8 for an exploration of the problems associated with designing for modern and contemporary art. See Chapter 2, on the Menil Collection, for a discussion of a late-twentieth-century museum that closely follows the model of the Museum of Modern Art.

9 Representative exhibitions selected from complete run of gallery brochures, O'Keeffe Archives.

10 Interview with Barbara Buhler Lynes conducted over the telephone, October 30, 2008.

CHAPTER 5

1 For further discussion of the Armory Show, see this chapter, below, and Chapter 6 for discussion of the show's subsequent exhibition at the Art Institute of Chicago.

2 Excerpt from Alfred H. Barr, Jr., "Minutes of the Junior Council of the Museum of Modern Art, Second Meeting, March 8, 1949." Junior Council Records, Museum of Modern Art Archives (hereafter MoMA Archives); published in Bee, Harriet Schoenholz, and Michelle Elligott. 2004. *Art in Our Time: A chronicle of the Museum of Modern Art.* New York: Museum of Modern Art, p. 16.

3 "The University of the State of New York Education Department Provisional Charter of the Museum of Modern Art," September 19, 1929, MoMA Archives, Reports and Pamphlets: Architectural Plans. The charter lists the founding Board of Trustees as Lizzie Bliss, Josephine B. Crane, Frank Crowninshild, Paul J. Sachs, Mary Sullivan, Abby A. Rockefeller, and A. Conger Goodyear.

4 "A Short Chronology of the Museum of Modern Art, 1929–1977," March 1977, MoMA Archives, Reports and Pamphlets, 1970s (10). All dates of construction projects, events,

and exhibitions at the Museum of Modern Art from 1929 to 1977 otherwise not credited come from this document.

5. "The Museum of Modern Art," October 1929, MoMA Archives, AHB 9a.1A.

6. *The New York Times*, September 9, 1929, from "Editorial and General Comment," MoMA Archives, AHB 9a.1C.

7. "The Film Library," *Annual Report of the Executive Director, July 1937–June 1938*, p. 63, MoMA Archives, AHB 9a. 11A.

8. "Policy of the Museum with Regard to the Status of the Permanent Collection," May 28, 1936, MoMA Archives, AHB 9a. 10C. For further discussion of the Museum of Modern Art's plan to deaccession works of art older than fifty years and to work with other institutions, see Chapter 3: The Whitney Museum of American Art; Chapter 8: The Art of the (Im)possible: Designing for Contemporary Art; and Appendix B: Report on the Permanent Collection, Museum of Modern Art, 1933.

9. For detailed discussion of the battle between Barr and the trustees regarding the architect of the new building, see Alice Goldfarb Marquis. *Alfred H. Barr, Jr.* 1989. *Missionary for the Modern*. Chicago: Contemporary Books, pp. 167–170.

10. *New Directions for the Future* by John B. Hightower, director, Museum of Modern Art, April 1970, MoMA Archives, Reports and Pamphlets 1970s (5), pp. 1–2.

11. For an in-depth treatment of Philip Johnson's architectural work at the Museum of Modern Art, see Johnson, Philip. 1998. *Philip Johnson and the Museum of Modern Art*. Studies in modern art, 6. New York: Museum of Modern Art.

12. See Chapter 3 for a discussion of the Whitney Museum and its former building adjacent to the Museum of Modern Art and more on Philip Johnson's role in its design.

CHAPTER 6

1. From "Fact Sheet on the Art Institute of Chicago," a 1962 press release from the Art Institute of Chicago, Institutional Archives of the Art Institute of Chicago, hereafter referred to as AIC Archives.

2. "General Information about the Development of Art in Chicago," by N. H. Carpenter, no date (after 1914), AIC Archives. N. H. Carpenter served as secretary, director, and business manager of the Art Institute from its foundation.

3. *Ibid.*

4. All dates from 1879 to 1992 relating to building projects and acquisitions of works of art are from "Time-Line for the Art Institute of Chicago," AIC Archives, unless otherwise stated.

5. *12th Annual Report of the Trustees,* 1891, p. 14, AIC Archives.

6. *Ibid.,* p. 19.

7. *Annual Report of the Trustees for the Year Ending June 5, 1894,* 1894, p. 13, AIC Archives.

8. For complete chronology of construction projects through 1988 at the Art Institute of Chicago, see "The Art Institute of Chicago Buildings 1879–1988: A Chronology," *Art Institute of Chicago Museum Studies,* vol. 14, no. 1. (1988), pp. 7–27.

9. Information on the Modern Wing taken from the project website, http://www.modern-wing.org, retrieved December 25, 2008.

CHAPTER 7

1. Taniguchi quotation cited in John Updike, "Invisible Cathedral," *The New Yorker,* November 15, 2004, p.

2. See Chapter 5 for discussion of the Museum of Modern Art.

3. See Chapter 1 for analysis of the Frick Collection.

CHAPTER 8

1. "Report on the Permanent Collection," 1933, MoMA Archives, AHB 9a. 7A, reproduced in Appendix B.

SELECT BIBLIOGRAPHY

Note: This book is primarily an archival study. The most important sources for research were the archives of the six museums that make up the case studies:

AT THE FRICK COLLECTION
The Frick Collection/Frick Art Reference Library Archives
  Henry Clay Frick Papers
  The Frick Family Papers on deposit from the Helen Clay Frick Foundation

AT THE MENIL COLLECTION
Menil Archives

AT THE WHITNEY MUSEUM OF AMERICAN ART
Frances Mulhall Achilles Library, Archives

AT THE GEORGIA O'KEEFFE MUSEUM
The Georgia O'Keeffe Museum Research Center Institutional Archives

AT THE MUSEUM OF MODERN ART
Museum of Modern Art Archives:
  Reports and Pamphlets
  Alfred H. Barr Papers

AT THE ART INSTITUTE OF CHICAGO
Institutional Archives, Art Institute of Chicago

The secondary source literature on this topic is quite vast. Here are listed only the books and articles that were most relevant and consulted in this project. This compilation is not meant to be exhaustive. Works not generally relevant but referenced in the text of this book are cited in the notes.

Art Institute of Chicago and Neil Harris. *Chicago's Dream, a World's Treasure: The Art Institute of Chicago, 1893–1993*. Chicago: The Institute, 1993.

Art Institute of Chicago. "The Art Institute of Chicago Buildings 1879–1988: A Chronology." *Art Institute of Chicago Museum Studies* Vol. 14, No. 1, (1988): pp. 7–27.

Art Institute of Chicago. "From the Archives: Photographs of the Art Institute of Chicago, 1893–1933". *Art Institute of Chicago Museum Studies* Vol. 19, No. 1 (1993): 5–29.

Bailey, Colin B. *Building the Frick Collection: An Introduction to the House and its Collections*. New York: Frick Collection in association with Scala, 2006.

Bee, Harriet Schoenholz, and Michelle Elligott. *Art in Our Time: A Chronicle of the Museum of Modern Art*. New York: Museum of Modern Art, 2004.

Berman, Avis. *Rebels on Eighth Street: Juliana Force and the Whitney Museum of American Art*. New York: Atheneum, 1990.

Biddle, Flora Miller. *The Whitney Women and the Museum They Made: A Memoir*. New York: Arcade, 1999.

Elliott, Clare, and Miranda Isabel Lash. *The Menil Collection*. London: Scala Publishers, 2007.

Heckscher, Morrison H. *The Metropolitan Museum of Art: An Architectural History*. New York: The Museum, 1995.

Hewitt, Mark A., and Paul LeClerc. *Carrère & Hastings Architects*. New York: Acanthus Press, 2006.

Johnson, Philip. *Philip Johnson and the Museum of Modern Art*. New York: Museum of Modern Art, 1998.

Knox, Katharine McCook. *The Story of the Frick Art Reference Library: The Early Years*. New York: The Library, 1979.

Lowry, Glenn D., and Terence Riley. *The New Museum of Modern Art*. New York: Museum of Modern Art, Department of Publications, 2005.

Lynes, Barbara Buhler, and Georgia O'Keeffe. *Georgia O'Keeffe Museum Collections*. New York: Abrams, 2007.

Lynes, Barbara Buhler, and Georgia O'Keeffe. *Georgia O'Keeffe Museum: Highlights of the Collection*. New York: Abrams, 2003.

Marquis, Alice Goldfarb. *Alfred H. Barr, Jr.: Missionary for the Modern*. Chicago: Contemporary Books, 1989.

Olsberg, R. Nicholas. *Breuer's Whitney: An Anniversary Exhibition, September 11–December 8, 1996*. New York: Whitney Museum of American Art, 1996.

Piano, Renzo, and Lia Piano. *The Menil Collection*. Genova: Fondazione Renzo Piano, 2007.

Ross, Barbara. *The Museum of Modern Art at Mid-Century: Continuity and change*. New York: Museum of Modern Art, 1995.

Sanger, Martha Frick Symington. *The Henry Clay Frick Houses: Architecture, Interiors, Landscapes in the Golden Era*. New York: Monacelli Press, 2001.

Shkapich, Kim, and Susan De Menil. *Sanctuary: The Spirit in/of Architecture*. Houston, TX: Byzantine Fresco Foundation, 2004.

Stoller, Ezra. *Whitney Museum of American Art*. New York: Princeton Architectural Press, 2000.

COMPARATIVE TABLES

TABLE 1
MUSEUM FOUNDING AND COLLECTING SCOPE

MUSEUM	FOUNDER	DATE	COLLECTING SCOPE
Frick	Henry Clay Frick	1920*	European and American fine and decorative arts
Menil	John and Dominique de Menil	1987	Twentieth century, ancient, Byzantine, African, Oceanic, and the Americas
Whitney	Gertrude Vanderbilt Whitney	1931	American Art, emphasizing modern and contemporary
O'Keeffe	John and Anne Marion	1995	Work of Georgia O'Keeffe and related works
Modern	Founding trustees**	1929	Modern and contemporary art, architecture, film
Art Institute	Group of Chicago artists	1866***	Encyclopedic

* 1920 is the date of incorporation; creation of the museum was specified in Frick's will 1915.

** Lizzie Bliss, Josephine B. Crane, Frank Crowninshild, Paul J. Sachs, Mary Sullivan, Abby A. Rockefeller, and A. Conger Goodyear.

*** As Chicago Academy of Design, 1879 as Chicago Academy of Fine Arts, and 1882 as Art Institute of Chicago

TABLE 2
DATE AND ARCHITECT FOR MAIN BUILDINGS OF CURRENT VENUES

MUSEUM	OPENED	ARCHITECT
Frick	1935	Thomas Hastings
Menil	1987	Renzo Piano
Whitney	1966	Marcel Breuer
O'Keeffe	1997	Richard Gluckman
Modern	1939	Philip Goodwin and Edward Durrell Stone
Art Institute	1893	Shepley, Rutan & Coolidge

TABLE 3
VISITOR AMENITIES

MUSEUM	BOOKSTORE*	GIFT SHOP	CAFE**	RESTAURANT	MEMBER LOUNGE
Frick		x			
Menil		x			
Whitney	x	x	x	x	
O'Keeffe	x	x		x	
Modern	x	x	x	x	
Art Institute	x	x	x	x	x

*If separate from Gift Shop.

**If separate from Restaurant.

TABLE 4
SECONDARY PROGRAM SPACES (EXCLUDING GALLERIES AND CIRCULATION SPACES)

MUSEUM	AUDITORIUM	LIBRARY	CLASSROOMS	SCREENING ROOM*
Frick	x	x		
Menil		x		
Whitney		x	x	x
O'Keeffe		x	x	x
Modern	x	x	x	
Art Institute	x	x	x	

*Smaller than auditoriums and designed primarily for showing films and video installations.

TABLE 5
DATES OF MOVES, ADDITIONS, AND MAJOR EXPANSIONS

MUSEUM	ORIGINAL VENUE	SUBSEQUENT VENUES	MAJOR ADDITIONS
Frick	1914		1935, 1977
Menil	1987		1995, 1996
Whitney	1931	1954, 1966	1996, 2012
O'Keeffe	1997		2001
Modern	1929	1932, 1939	1951, 1964, 1984, 2004
Art Institute	1879	1882, 1887, 1893	1898, 1901, 1903, 1910, 1916, 1924, 1925, 1927, 1939, 1958, 1962, 1976, 1988, 2009

REPORT ON
THE PERMANENT COLLECTION,
MUSEUM OF MODERN ART, 1933

AUTHOR'S NOTE

The following document, a report written by Alfred H. Barr, Jr., founding director of the Museum of Modern Art in 1933, is reproduced in full. This document is valuable because it clearly outlines many of the problems that still challenge museums and their design to this day. Methods of acquiring an exceptional permanent collection are explored in great depth. The problems that face all museums regarding the need for storage, gallery space for permanent collections and loan shows, and the desire to always expand, both in collections and architecturally, are clearly articulated. The difficulty of reconciling permanent collections and a commitment to contemporary art is investigated most profoundly. The original is an unpublished typescript (MoMA Archives, AHB 9a. 7A); I have corrected obvious typographical errors, but otherwise tried to preserve the format of the original.

[PAGE 1]

THE PERMANENT COLLECTION

I   IN 1929

Quotations from "A New Art Museum," published by the Trustees of the Museum of Modern Art in the summer of 1929, before the opening of the Museum's first exhibition:

"All over the world the rising tide of interest in modern movements in art has found expression not only in private collections but also in the formation of public galleries created for the specific purpose of exhibiting permanent as well as temporary collections of modern art.

"Nowhere has this tide of interest been more manifest than in New York. But New York alone among the great capitals of the world lacks a public gallery where the works of the founders and masters of the modern schools can today be seen. That the American metropolis has no such gallery is an extraordinary anomaly.

"——the public interested in modern art cannot depend upon the occasional generosity of collectors and dealers to give it more than a haphazard impression of what has developed in the last half century.

"First of all it (the Museum) would attempt to establish a very fine collection of the immediate ancestors of the modern movement; artists whose painting are still too controversial for general acceptance. This collection would be formed by [Page 2] gifts, bequests, purchase, and perhaps by semi-permanent loans.

"Other galleries of the Museum might display carefully chosen permanent collections of the most important living masters, especially those of France and the United States, though eventually there should be representative groups from England, Germany, Italy, Mexico, and other countries."

II   THE MUSEUM HAS NOT FULFILLED ONE OF ITS FUNDAMENTAL PURPOSES

The fact that the public museums of New York did not include among their permanent collections painting by the foremost masters of the past fifty years was offered in 1929 as one of the principal reasons for the founding of the Museum of Modern Art. Again and again it was pointed out that the New Yorker, unlike the citizen of Chicago, London, Berlin, Amsterdam, Moscow or Munich, could not enjoy or study the work of van Gogh, Gaugin, Seurat, Matisse, or Picasso unless he happened to know a wealthy collector, or unless a dealer happened to be exhibiting a few paintings for a few weeks. After four years the Museum, in spite of its avowed purpose, has done surprisingly little to alter this situation. Of course the first two years were considered as a period of trial. During this time temporary loan exhibitions were to indicate whether there were really sufficient interest in Modern Art [Page 3] to make a permanent institution advisable. But this policy was continued with little alteration during the third and fourth years and will be apparently during the fifth. Except during the summer months the Museum has never afforded New York a chance to see a representative collection of modern pictures—and our records show that most visitors during the summer are transients. In other words, the New Yorker can see a Sargent of a Meissonier all year round but he has to wait till hot weather sets in, or go to Chicago, before he can be sure of seeing a van Gogh, or a Matisse, or a Kandinsky.

III   THEORY AND CONTENTS OF AN IDEAL PERMANENT COLLECTION

1. The Permanent Collection may be thought of graphically as a *torpedo moving through time*, its nose the ever advancing present, its tail the ever receding past of fifty to a hundred years ago. If painting is taken as an example, the bulk of the collection, as indicated in the

following diagram, would be concentrated (at present) in the early years of the 20th Century, tapering off into the 19th. The propeller of the torpedo represents the "Background" collections.

[PAGE 3A
CONTAINS DIAGRAM I: "TORPEDO" DIAGRAM OF IDEAL PERMANENT
COLLECTION, see FIG. B.1]

[PAGE 4]

2. *The ideal permanent collection would contain the following Departments*

Department I. *Painting, Sculpture, Graphic Arts.*

    1. The 19th century ancestors of the modern movement up through
       Impressionism (one or two fine examples each)
    2. The immediate ancestors of contemporary painting:
       a. European—Cézanne, Gauguin, van Gogh, Seurat
       b. American—Homer, Ryder, Eakins
    3. Contemporary painting, European (France, Germany, England, Italy, etc.)
       American (United States, Mexico)
    4. Sculpture since Rodin
    5. Water colors, drawings and prints corresponding more or less
       to the painting collection; photographs
    6. *Supplementary "Background" collections of European and non-European
       sources and prototypes of modern painting and sculpture

*Note: These are the two small collections represented by the propeller of the torpedo.

One of these collections would be a group of fine paintings representing those phases of older European traditions which seem most significant at present: for instance, a Fayum portrait, a Byzantine panel, Romanesque miniatures, Gothic woodcuts, a Giotto school piece, a Florentine panel of the XVth century, a follower of Masaccio or Piero della Francesca, a Venetian XVIth century figure composition (Titian or Tintoretto), a Bruegel school piece, a Rubens, a Poussin, a Greco, prints by Rembrandt, Blake, Piranesi, etc. The second "Background" collection would be composed of a small group of non-European works of art, Coptic textiles, Scythian bronzes, Japanese prints, Chinese painting, African and pre-Columbian objects.

The purpose of these two supplementary collections is educational:

1) to epitomize the character, variety, and continuity of the European tradition.

2) To show what non-European traditions have influenced European and American art in the past fifty years.

3) To destroy or weaken the prejudice of the uneducated visitor against non-naturalistic kinds of art.

[PAGE 5]

Department II. *Architectural, Industrial and Commercial Arts*

    1. Architecture of the 19th and 20th centuries with special emphasis on the past
       fifteen years; models and enlarged photographs (exteriors and interiors)
    2. Furniture and utensils (design in heavy industries would be represented
       principally by photographs)
    3. Posters and advertising art, typography

Department III. *The Film Department*

    1. Negatives of masterpieces
    2. Positives
    3. Stills (photographs)

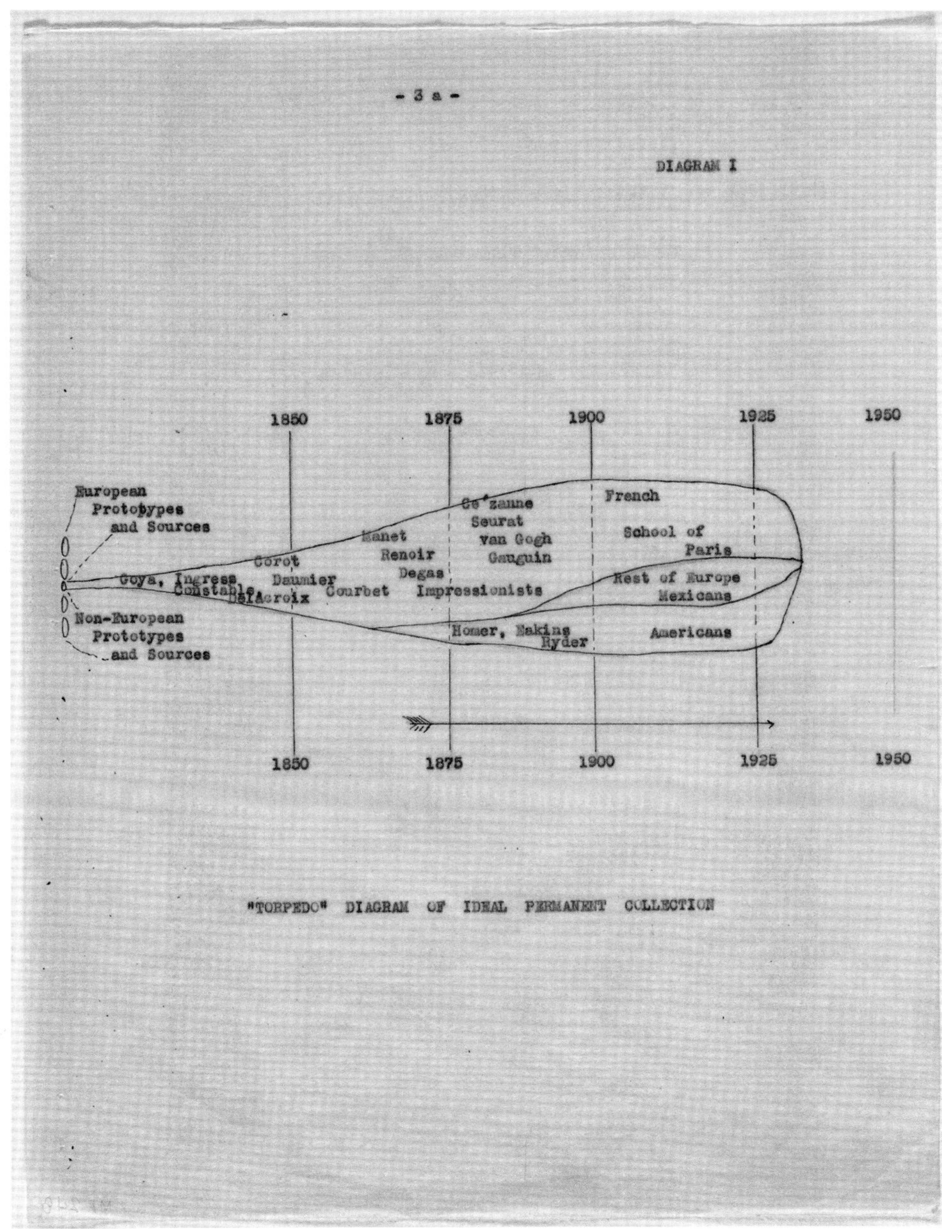

B.1. "Torpedo" Diagram of Ideal Permanent Collection. Alfred H. Barr, Jr. Papers, 9a.7A. The Museum of Modern Art Archives, New York. 1933. © Digital Image © The Museum of Modern Art/Licensed by SCALA / Art Resource.

IV PRACTICAL FORMATION OF PERMANENT COLLECTION

The formation of the Permanent Collection is modified by many factors among which three require discussion. A) Relation to other institutions. B) Acquisition. C) Exhibition and preservation of permanent collection.

A. Relation to Other Institutions. The Department of Architecture, etc., has almost no rivals in architecture proper. In industrial and commercial design the Metropolitan Museum has a small permanent collection principally of costly furniture and decorative objects of "art Nouveau" and "modernistic" design which would scarcely conflict with our Museum's permanent exhibits.

The Film Department is in too tentative a condition to require discussion at present.

The Department of Painting, Sculpture and Graphic Arts in its Permanent Collection is confronted by very complicated relations with other institutions. The *permanent collections* of seven museums and semi-public institutions should be considered. (For more general analysis of these institutions consult report "Other Institutions.)

> The Metropolitan Museum
> The Whitney Museum
> The Dale Collection
> The Brooklyn Museum
> The Société Anonyme
> The Gallery of Living Art
> The Solomon R. Guggenheim Collection

1. Of these the *last three* may be grouped together. They are of minor importance at present. Only the Gallery of Living Art is easily accessible to the public. Nevertheless if combined these three collections would form the most complete collection of experimental or advance-guard European art in America and possibly in the world. For this reason friendly relations should be cultivated by the Trustees, Advisory Committee and Staff with Miss Dreier of "The Société Anonyme," Mr. Galletin of "The Gallery of Living Art," Mr. and Mrs. Guggenheim and their advisor, the Baroness von Rebay, with a view to inducing them to give their collections to the Museum.

The Brooklyn Museum, although it owns more advanced European paintings than the Metropolitan, is practically in another city and need be seriously considered only if its permanent collections should undergo a radical change in policy.

2. *The Metropolitan Museum*

a) European Painting: Through the Havemeyer Bequest [Page 7], the collection of modern French painting up through the Impressionist generation, has now become one of the finest in the world, though still comparatively weak in works of the Neo-classic and Romantic periods. The last fifty years of French Painting have been rather casually represented from time to time by loans from the Dale, Oppenheimer, and Stephen Clark collections. It seems probable that the Dale Collection (q.v. below) will pass to the Metropolitan though not till after the deaths of the donors.

The present scope of the Metropolitan's permanent collection of European painting suggests the following policy in relation to our permanent collection. The Metropolitan's collection stops with the Impressionist generation, that is, about fifty years ago. *Fifty years <u>ago</u>* makes a convenient date for the beginning of the bulk of our collection. At present we would wish to have one or two paintings, preferably small but typical, by earlier 19th century masters such as Delacroix, Corot, Courbet, Daumier, Manet, Renoir, and Degas. Cézanne, who might form a transition between the two collections, is at present extensively represented both in the Metropolitan and the Bliss collection. *Our European collection proper would then begin* with Seurat, van Gogh, Gauguin, Toulouse-Lautrec, Rousseau, none of whose paintings is owned by the Metropolitan.

It is of great importance to come to some agreement with the Metropolitan about the dividing line of the two collections *with a view to adjusting future gifts to the two institutions. If* it comes to bargaining our Museum is in a strong position only if the collections of our Trustees are considered as potentially ours more than they are the Metropolitan's. The fifty year period [Page 8] might be taken as a starting point. Paintings approximately over fifty years old would then be under control of the Metropolitan; paintings less than fifty years old would be under ours, *irrespective of ownership*—this arbitrary age limit to be *adjusted* by a committee drawn from the Trustees and Staff of each institution. This arrangement would eliminate, temporarily at least, the problem of capital loss and gain *through change of ownership*—"capital" in this case implying the prestige as well as money value.

Four illustrations will serve:

1) In 1935 Seurat's *Port en Bessin* in the Bliss collection will be fifty years old. There will be little question about the permanent value of Seurat or the importance to the Metropolitan of owning eventually a fine group of works by this great artist. The committee will then have to decide whether it is more valuable to the public to keep the Seurat for five or ten years more in our Museum or transfer it immediately to the Metropolitan. 2) If our Museum should be given an Ingres figure composition, it would be transferred immediately to the Metropolitan, which needs such a picture badly. 3) If our Museum was given a Courbet landscape, the committee might easily permit it to remain in our gallery where two good Courbets would be valuable. The Metropolitan, which is already rich in Courbets, would not need it. 4) If the Metropolitan were to be given a Picasso it would ordinarily be transferred to our galleries, as would a Lehmbruck or a Matisse.

This arrangement might be active for a trial period of five or ten years. Then if it worked successfully the question of ownership, i.e., transfer of "capital" assets, might be considered.

b) *American Painting in the Metropolitan:*

The question of American painting is more difficult because of the apparently fixed status of the Hearn Fund which provides the Metropolitan with $10,000 a year for the purchase of contemporary American pictures. While no picture of even faintly left-wing character has been bought with the Hearn money, the center and right wing of American painting is now fairly well represented in the Metropolitan's galleries and store rooms. Before discussing our policy toward the Metropolitan's American collection, the [Page 9] Whitney Museum must be considered. Our relation to the Metropolitan Museum may, however, be visualized by amplifying the "torpedo" diagram of our <u>ideal</u> permanent collection. [Diagram II: METROPOLITAN MUSEUM AND MUSEUM OF MODERN ART: Permanent collections of European and American Painting, fig. B.2]

3. *The Whitney Museum*

The Whitney Museum's permanent collection includes a few 18th and 19th century paintings of varying quality, but these are greatly outnumbered by contemporary work. Very few pictures by academic painters are included so that the collection supplements to a large extent the Metropolitan's collection, although recent purchases from the Metropolitan's Hearn Fund have [Page 10] caused a great deal of overlapping and will apparently cause more in the future. Much of the collection was originally purchased by the Whitney Studio Club to aid promising or struggling artists. As a result it contains many mediocre works, many of which are however kept in storage. Like those of the Metropolitan, the more recent purchases by the Whitney Museum have been more distinguished than the earlier.

4. *The Problem of Our American Collection*

The Metropolitan's Hearn Fund purchases cover the right and center of contemporary American painting; the Whitney Museum covers the center and left wing. In the past the Metropolitan has spent about $10,000 a year, the Whitney some $20,000. Potentially there *ought* to be no room for a third public collection of American art. Consequently it might be held that we should withdraw from the field entirely so far as our permanent collection is concerned, devoting funds and space and study to European painting and sculpture. *Actually*, however, several arguments may be advanced against our withdrawal from the American field.

1. The general mediocrity of both the Metropolitan and Whitney collections.

2. Our location is more accessible to the out of town visitor and the New Yorker.

3. The presence of first rate contemporary foreign pictures in the same building and or even the same wall would be an advantage to as well as competition for American works.

A great many more people, especially foreigners, see the English contemporary pictures in the Tate, and German, in the Kronprinzen Palais, because of the presence in both these galleries of French pictures.

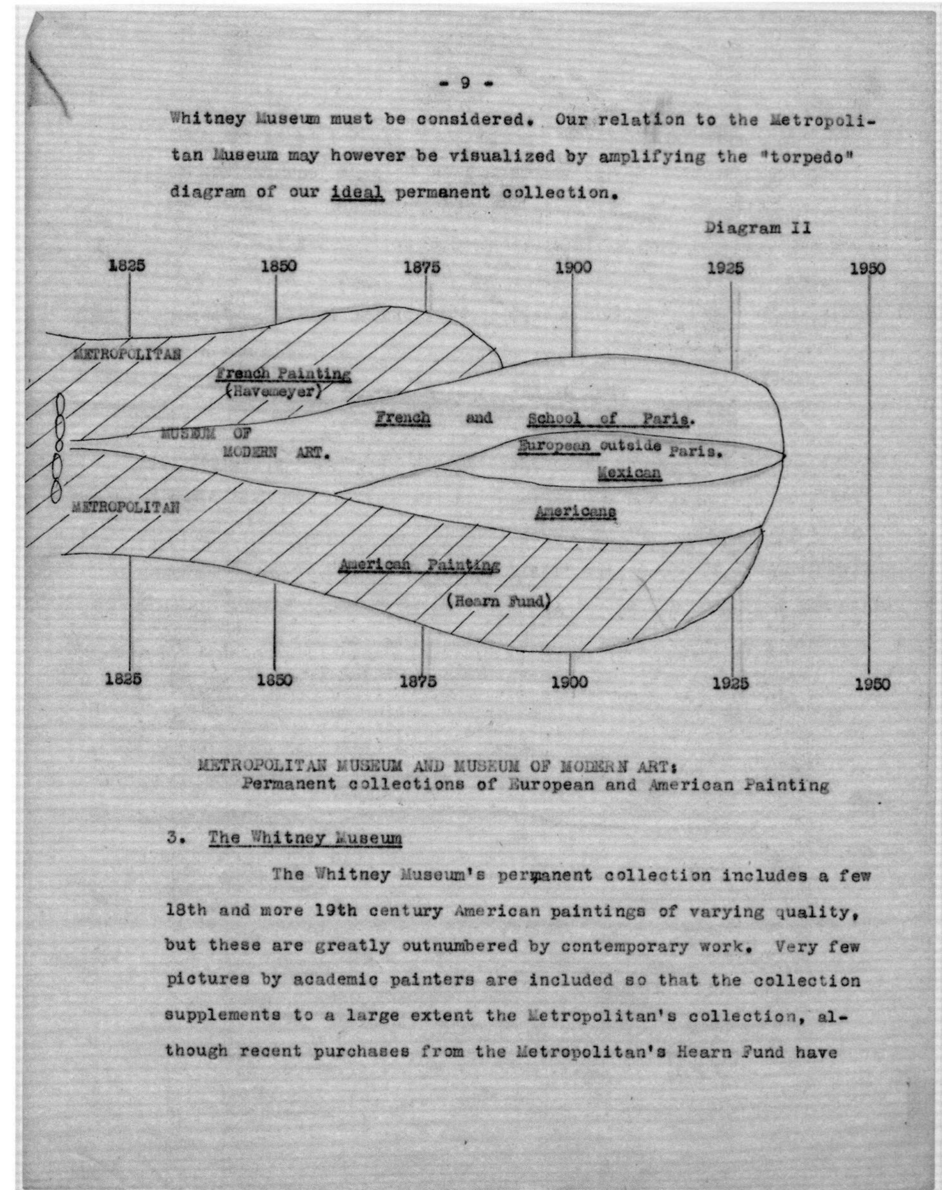

- 9 -

Whitney Museum must be considered. Our relation to the Metropolitan Museum may however be visualized by amplifying the "torpedo" diagram of our _ideal_ permanent collection.

3. The Whitney Museum

The Whitney Museum's permanent collection includes a few 18th and more 19th century American paintings of varying quality, but these are greatly outnumbered by contemporary work. Very few pictures by academic painters are included so that the collection supplements to a large extent the Metropolitan's collection, although recent purchases from the Metropolitan's Hearn Fund have

B.2. Torpedo diagram, "Metropolitan Museum and Museum of Modern Art: Permanent collections of European and American Painting," page 9 from the final third draft of the report, "Report on the 'Permanent Collection'" 1933. Alfred H. Barr, Jr. Papers, 9a.7A. The Museum of Modern Art Archives, New York. © Digital Image © The Museum of Modern Art/Licensed by SCALA / Art Resource.

4. For politico-artistic reasons it might be poor strategy to [Page 11] abandon our American permanent collection at this time of rising nationalism and raising money.

To make a permanent American collection effective there must be: a) Money for immediate purchase, or trustees willing to buy and give paintings on short notice. b) Space to hang the pictures for at least six months or a year. c) Time either for the director or some one else to scout for possible acquisitions.

The picture of three New York Museums competing with each other for contemporary American pictures should bring joy to painters and dealers, but it _would offer little evidence of intelligent cooperation_ or efficient economy among the museums themselves.

Our policy toward our permanent collection of American painting and sculpture need not be crystallized immediately. Should the Hearn Fund be put under our control or should the activity of the Whitney Museum be seriously curtailed, our policy would then be automatically clarified. In the meantime our work in American architecture, industrial and commercial art should be emphasized.

If, however, we continue to form an American collection, our acquisition policy should be at once daring and exclusive. We have at present neither space nor money nor time to form a "representative" collection. This may be left to the other two institutions.

5. *The Dale Collection*

At the moment the Dale collection is not yet opened as a semi-public gallery. It is not yet certain whether American paintings will be included with the French. The French pictures, however, will form the most important part of the collection. [Page 12]

Taken as a whole the Dale Collection of French pictures is most importantly weighted in the third quarter of the 19th century—Corot, Renoir, Courbet, Degas, Manet, that is, about the same period as the bulk of the Havermeyer collection. There are two or three fine Cézannes and van Goghs, secondary Gauguins and no (?) Seurat paintings, so that the late 19th century is not adequately represented. The 20th century school of Paris group, while it contains many fine pictures, is remarkable for its wealth of Modiglianis and large pre-Cubist Picassos. The more adventurous phases of 20th century painting in Paris are almost untouched—while younger painters represented are principally of the neo-Courbet–Corot reaction.

In short the Dale Collection, formidable as it is, is narrowly confined to Paris and even in that restricted field is incomplete in several important areas. I would be premature at the present time to formulate any policy toward the Dale collection.

6. Conclusion

The potential position of the Museum's permanent collection toward its competitors may now be indicated with some completeness by Diagram III, which retains the torpedo as its nucleus. The permanent collection, though at present negligible in size, is still central in position, for the Museum, alone among American institutions, plans a program of national and international scope in painting, sculpture and graphic arts, supported by architecture, movies, and industrial arts (which are not indicated in the diagram.)

[PAGE 12A
contains Diagram III: MUSEUM OF MODERN ART IDEAL PERMANENT COLLECTION in relation to ACTUAL PERMANENT COLLECTIONS OF OTHER NEW YORK MUSEUMS, fig. B.3.]

[PAGE 13]

B. *Acquisition of Permanent Collection*

The theory of our permanent collection of modern art, based upon a metabolic principle of continual building up and tearing down, has been explained in Section III and condensed in the "torpedo" diagram.

Building up a permanent collection should not be left to chance. Most museum collections are largely the result of accident: and they show it, though only very few people can comprehend what these same museums might have been had their formation been planned instead of haphazard.

A plan of campaign, a system of strategy is necessary. This requires the full cooperation of the Trustees and Advisory Committee and much time and thought on the part of the staff.

1. *Three Channels of Acquisition:*

Works of art are acquired (except by conquest or revolution) in three ways:
1. Purchase. 2. Gifts from the living. 3. Bequest.

1.*Purchase*; money comes from the following sources:

a) A steady income from a fund for purchasing (e.g. the Hearn Fund at the Metropolitan).

b) Occasional lump sums (Courtauld's gift to the Tate of 150,000 pounds in 1924).

c) Money raised for a specific purchase either from one or several donors (e.g. our vain attempt to raise money to purchase the Seurat *Parade* in 1930).
2. *Gifts* from the Living: These may be the accidental result of the museum's force of attraction (e.g. gifts from Mrs. Sadie May). Usually, however, they are the result of the [Page 14] generosity of people already connected to the Museum or people whose good will has been aroused, often through deliberate cultivation.
3. *Bequests*: These too may be unforeseen, but more often bequests come from Trustees, or from those whose interest in the Museum has been cultivated.

Of these three channels *acquisition by purchase is* the most valuable; first because it can be used before the death of the donor, second because the acquisition can be more or less controlled by the museum. Mr. Courtauld's gift of $700,000 to the Tate for the immediate purchase of modern French paintings is an example. Ten years have passed since 1924 but *New York public collections have not yet nearly equaled the collection of masterpieces* by Seurat, Gauguin, van Gogh, and more recent men, *bought by the Tate* with this fund, not to mention Mr. Courtauld's subsequent gifts of pictures bought by him for the Tate and with the Tate's approval.

If the gift is a work of art rather than money for purchase, it is obviously better to receive it from a living donor than a dead one. One of our Trustees eight years ago gave to the Art Institute of Chicago a collection of modern pictures worth now at least a half a million dollars. It included Seurat's greatest masterpiece and very fine works by van Gogh, Gauguin, Henri Rousseau, Matisse, Picasso, and others. Had the donor preferred to *leave* these pictures as a bequest, Chicago would have rendered the Birch-Bartlett Collection far less valuable; for it is <u>now</u> that the *great pictures of the present and the immediate past must be made easily and continually accessible* to the public. [Page 15] It is a fundamental paradox that *as time goes on the great modern pictures of today become* more important to the Metropolitan *but less important to the Museum of Modern Art.*

If for some reason owners may not feel able to give even essential works to the Museum, the *semi-permanent loan* may prove a solution to this dilemma. The Courtauld or Bartlett gifts would have been just as available to the public had they been semi-permanent loans. The semi-permanent loan, however, is decidedly weak strategically for it does not add to the prestige of the Museum, nor does it attract other gifts, nearly so much as outright gift. (The immediate value of semi-permanent loans is discussed under "The Provisional Museum Collection," at the end of this report.)

2. *Inducing Gifts to the Permanent Collection*
 1) *Emphasis upon the Permanent Collection*: Gifts may be induced indirectly by emphasis upon the permanent collection already acquired.
   a. The permanent collection *should be well shown* in the best galleries. The most important items should *always* be on view, and a good portion of the rest should be shown six months out of the year.
   b. The permanent collection *should be catalogued.*
   c. *And publicized* with the same care as the loan exhibition (of course the same volume of publicity is not to be expected).
   d. *New gifts should be treated with honor* and should be publicized and exhibited within a reasonable length of time. [Page 16]
 2) *Cultivating Donors to the Permanent Collection*
   a. *Collectors* of modern art should be interested in the permanent collection in order to persuade them to give paintings; immediately, or by bequest, or as semi-permanent loans. Gifts of paintings can sometimes be induced in the form of *memorials.*
   b. Cultivation of these collectors can be done even more effectively by *Trustees* than by the staff—especially if the Trustees themselves can give paintings or let it be known they intend to leave part of all of their collections to the Museum.
   c. Dealers, such as Duveen and Knoedler, have often made valuable gifts to

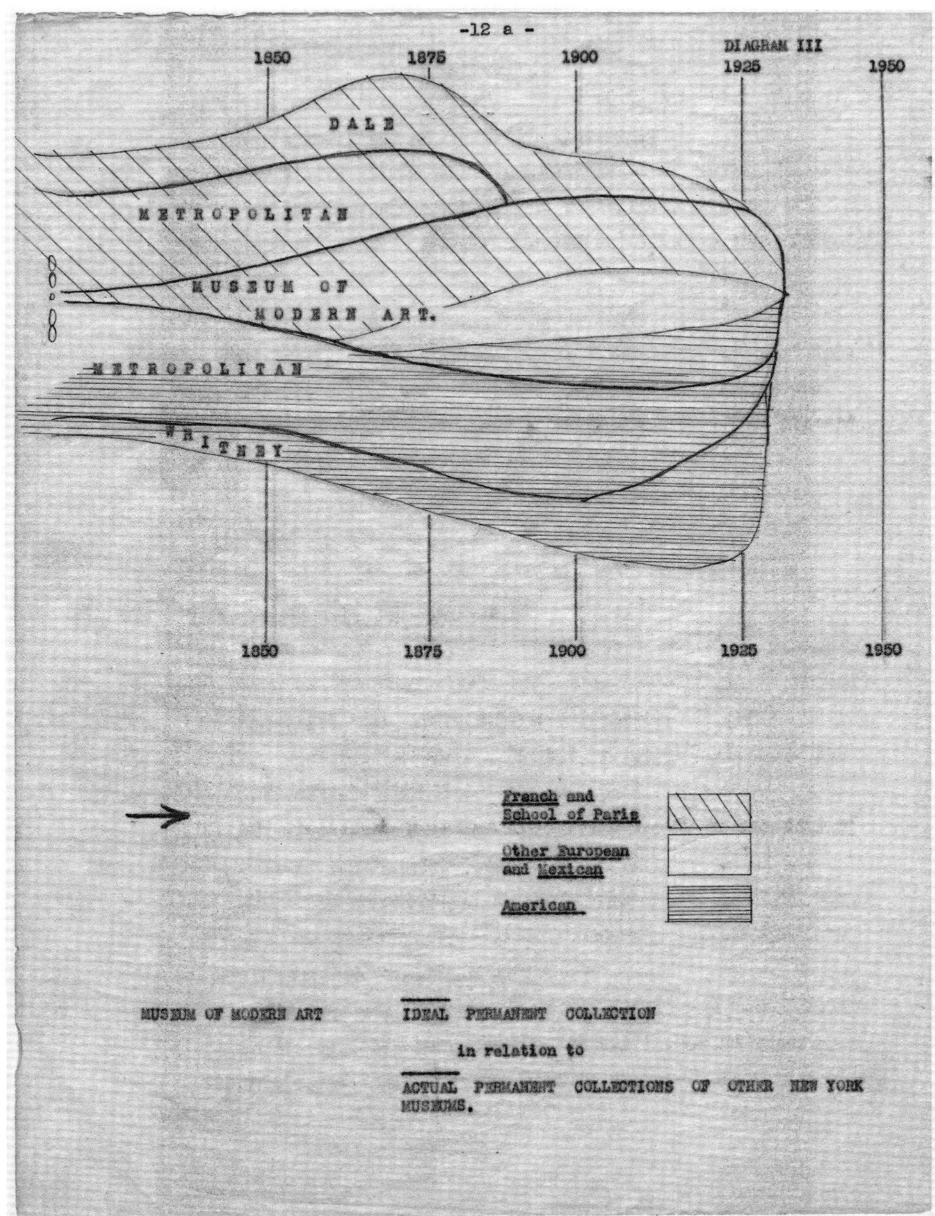

B.3. Torpedo diagram, "Ideal Permanent Collection in relation to Actual Permanent Collection of other New York Museums," page 12a from the final third draft of the report, "Report on the 'Permanent Collection'" 1933. Alfred H. Barr, Jr. Papers, 9a.7A. The Museum of Modern Art Archives, New York. © Digital Image © The Museum of Modern Art/Licensed by SCALA / Art Resource.

museums both here and abroad. Such gifts need not be refused providing no obligation is incurred.

    d. Artists also have given to Museums (Matisse to the Luxembourg). Of course, every caution must be observed in accepting gifts both from dealers and artists.

    3. *Gifts in Relation to Planning the Permanent Collection*

The plan of the permanent collection has already been sketched. This sketch might well be filled in in detail not with a view to crystallizing the collection in any way, but rather a) to avoid that haphazard growth already noted, b) to inducing gifts by indicating a want or void. *In filling in this plan with actual and potential gifts the cooperation of the Trustees is urgently needed.* An example will clarify this problem: Suppose a Trustee, Mr. X, owns a masterpiece by the great French painter, Blanc. The Trustee has always been most friendly to the Museum; from outward indications he will bequeath the picture to the Museum or may even plan to give it outright in a few years or lend it as a half yearly [Page 17] loan. In actuality, however, Mr. X may have decided in his own mind to leave the picture to the Metropolitan, or the Baltimore Museum, or to the Tate, or even to his nephews. Misled by appearances the Museum staff may neglect opportunities to fill in the gap apparently filled by Mr. X's masterpiece by Blanc, only to discover upon the reading of Mr. X's will that they have made a very bad guess. *By lack of frankness* on the part of Mr. X *or too great fastidiousness* on the part of the staff, or both, *the permanent collection will have suffered an irremediable loss.*

There are, of course, many reasons why even favorably inclined Trustees and friends would hesitate to give or bequeath pictures.

Temporary obstacles are:

a) The uncertain future of a museum as a permanent institution.

b) The lack of space for hanging.

c) The previous neglect of the permanent collection already acquired.

More general and chronic obstacles are:

d) In this post-war period of political, economic, and monetary uncertainty, good paintings are among the most dependable securities, especially those which command an international market. This fact might well prevent a collector's committing himself if he has invested heavily in works of art.

e) Potential gifts or bequests to the Museum are of course instruments of power in the Museum's affairs. The collector who committed himself would from one point of view lose some political [Page 18] power; but the loss would be offset by the power gained through having courageously and generously become an important donor.

In any case it is quite clear that the greater the degree of candor and cooperation on the part of the Trustees and their friends, the more intelligent and effective will be the development of the permanent collection. *Knowledge of the collector's intentions could of course be confined* in absolute confidence to the members of the Committee on the Permanent Collection.

4. *Acceptance of Gifts to the Permanent Collection*

a) The *terms of acceptance* of gifts to the Permanent Collection are made unconditional whenever possible.

b) *Policy of acceptance*: The following discussion may seem in part equivocal and compromising unless it be clearly realized that *the standards* of the Museum's Permanent Collection *can be expressed by what is exhibited* rather than by what is acquired. It is better to face *realistically* the fact that compromise will doubtless enter into the Museum's acceptance of gifts so long as

1. the Museum has no funds for purchase

2. the decisions are in the hands of a committee

3. large gifts of works of art usually contain desirable and undesirable items

4. there is so much difference of opinion as to the relative importance of various contemporary works of art

On the other hand the Trustees may decide to depart from the present policy in order to maintain, instead, a rigidly high standard of acquisition. Practically this may prove a boomerang for the more guesses one makes the more chances there are of being [Page 19] right ten years from now—and the mistakes of an acquisition committee will then be readily forgiven, providing they are on the side of commission and not of omission. Mediocre acquisitions can be stored, sold, given away, or circulated. But fine works not acquired are often irrevocably lost.

In accepting gifts the following factors may be considered:

1. The quality of the gift. Two levels of quality might well be considered: First, those works which seem unquestionably worthy of a place on the walls of the Museum. Second, those works which are valuable for study purposes, for loans to other museums or for inclusion in circulating exhibitions. For example, a good average Vlaminck watercolor might be refused by the Acquisition Committee because it did not seem good enough to hang permanently on the walls of the Museum. This watercolor would, however, be very useful as a unit for a circulating exhibition of modern watercolors to schools, women's clubs, and small museums.

2. The importance of the artist. Inferior works by important artists are more valuable (to the collection) than are good works by unimportant artists.

3. The importance of the donor. Under the terms of acceptance works need not be exhibited and may be disposed of at the discretion of the Museum. Nevertheless if the donor visits the Museum frequently, it may prove better in the end to refuse the gift outright.

4. The size of the gift.

5. Its appropriateness to the collection.

C. *Exhibition and Preservation of the Permanent Collection*

The present building is already inadequate for the exhibition and storage of both the Permanent Collection and Loan Exhibitions. It is not so much lack of space, though this is serious enough, but the awkward distribution of space among four floors so that there is only one large room (the second floor). While the upper floors are [Page 20] inaccessible to the public by elevator, loan exhibitions cannot be well shown on the fourth floor nor can the Permanent Collection, which should be even more accessible than the temporary shows.

Storage too will shortly become a serious problem—the basement is needed in large part for packing and storage of case and materials—the fifth, or office, floor is already congested—and the picture storage room on the third floor is full much of the time.

The Department of Architecture, Industrial and Commercial Arts will require more storage and exhibition space, especially after its large traveling exhibition, "Modern Architecture," completes its itinerary.

The Film Department does not yet exist except as a paper program (cf. report prepared by Director, June 1932). For exhibition space it will require a projection hall. Exhibitions of "stills" (photographs made during the course of production) can be held in ordinary galleries. For storage of films fireproof vaults are required by law. Both the projection hall and storage vaults could be secured through renting or by arrangement with other organizations.

A temporary solution of this congestion is offered below in Section V, "The Provisional Museum Collection."

[PAGE 21]

THE "PROVISIONAL MUSEUM COLLECTION"—
a temporary substitute of the Permanent Collection

The Permanent Collection is faced by a lack of funds, lack of space, and competition along certain lines from two or three far more richly endowed institutions. The Trustees should not be discouraged by these handicaps. An excellent *temporary solution of the problem* is at hand, providing the Museum can depend upon its friends not so much for money—but for loans of works of art.

The *Bliss Collection* and the *present Permanent Collection* together already form a nucleus which, if *supplemented by loans* from private collections, *would form a representative collection* of modern painting, sculpture, graphic arts, and architecture. These combined groups might be called, for convenience, the "Provisional Museum Collection." The "Provisional Museum Collection" would be flexible; it could be expanded or contracted to meet the exigencies of space, but it would be maintained with the plan of the future Permanent Collection in mind. As a rule it should occupy from one-third to one-half the Museum Gallery space. In any case its best units should almost always be on exhibition. Only under the most exceptional circumstances should masterpieces such as the Daumier, the Picassos, the finest Cézannes from the Bliss Collection, the large Maillol and Lehmbruck bronzes, be hidden from view. For at least two months during winter as well as throughout the summer the "Provisional Museum Collection" should be expanded to fill the whole building with a magnificent general exhibition of modern art.

INDEX

Page numbers in *italic* refer to captions.

K

Kahn, Louis, 48, 49
Kimball, Evaline, 188
Klee, Paul, 47
Kunsthallen, 218

L

Lachaise, Gaston, *160*
landmark status, 41
Library of Alexandria, xv
lighting
    Menil Collection, 51–52, 55, *56*, 61
    natural, 51–52, 55, 56, *61*, 224
Lin, Maya, 226
Louvre, xvii, xviii
Lynes, Barbara Buhler, 130–31

M

Magritte, Rene, 47
Marion, Anne and John, xviii, 118
Menil, John and Dominique de, xiii, 44.46–47,
    48, *49*
Menil, Philippa, 224
Menil Collection
    acquisitions policy, 47–48
    additions, 44, 58, 66, 235
    admission fees, 66
    aerial view, *52*
    architect selection, 50
    collection characteristics, 44, 46, 50–51,
        70–71, 234
    design goals, 48, 51–52
    elevations, *56, 57*
    entranceway, *58*
    floor plan, 54, 55
    funding, 44
    future prospects, 67–71
    gardens, 56–57
    location, 44
    museum design characteristics, 42, 51–52,
        54–58, *61–65*, 70, 216
    origins, xviii, 44–47, 48–50, 234
    programs and amenities, 234, 235
    significance of, xiii, 66–67
    storage space, 51, 52, 57–58, *66*
Metropolitan Museum of Art, xiv, xviii
design characteristics, xviii
    Museum of Modern Art and, 142, 240–41
    Temple of Dendur gallery, 165
    Whitney Museum of American Art and,
        78–86, 108
Miller, Flora Whitney, 76, 81
Miller, G. Macculloch, 72, 90
mission statements, ix–x, 109–10
Montefeltro, Federico da, xvii
Morgan Library and Museum, 37
Munger, A. A., 177
museum design, generally
    American evolution, xvii–xix
    artistic media and, xix
    case studies, xi, xii–xv. see also *specific
        institution*
    challenges, viii–ix

in classical antiquity, xv–xvi
for contemporary art exhibitions, 154–57,
    168, 214–26
current and emerging challenges, xix
European evolution, xv–xvii
as expression of museum philosophy and
    personality, 202
factors influencing, ix–xi, 204
functional demands, viii, x, 202
historical and stylistic evolution, xi, 147
historical milieu, x, xix
palatial forms, xvii
relationship to collection, 202–4, 207–8, 210
scale, 164–65, 216, 217
visibility, 37, 204–6
see also collections; future of museums and
    museum design
Museum of Contemporary Art (Los Angeles), *213,
    214,* 217, *218, 219*
Museum of Modern Art (New York), xix, 214–16
    aerial view, *134*
    architects, 134, 157–62, 234
    architectural space, 205–6
    collection characteristics and policies, 134,
        138, 140–42, 152–57, 234, 236–47
    concepts of modern and contemporary art,
        154–57, 168
    early exhibitions, 140
    educational mission, 134, 137–38, 147
    expansions and additions, 134, 157–62,
        235
    film collection, 137, 140
    galleries and artworks, *152*
    Garden Hall, *162*
    Goodwin and Stone building, 142–47, 205
    Grace Rainey Rogers Annex, *154*
    Heckscher Building, 138
    libraries, 140
    lobby, *149*
    location, *133,* 134
    Marron Atrium, *168*
    Members' Lounge penthouse, *148*
    Metropolitan Museum of Art and, 142,
        240–41
    O'Keeffe and, 126–27
    origins, xviii, 136–39, 234
    programs, units and amenities, 134, 234, 235
    sculpture garden, *95, 142,* 146, *157,* 160, *166*
    significance of, xiv, xviii, 125, 132, 134–36,
        137, 147
    Taniguchi building, 162–68
    temporary Queens location, 162–64, *165*
    theaters, *145, 146*
    Whitney Museum of American Art and,
        86–91, 92, 108, 241

N

National Gallery of Art, xiv, xviii, *209,* 210
Newman, Barnett, *47,* 48, 58, *60*
New Museum of Contemporary Art (New York),
    218–24
Nickerson, Samuel, 177
Nishizawa, Ruye, 219, *221*
Noel, Auguste, 74, *86,* 90–91
Noel & Miller, 74, 80, 90–91
Noguchi, Isamu, 82